Bristol Studies in East Asian International Relations

Series Editors: **Yongjin Zhang**, University of ...,
Shogo Suzuki, University of Manchester, UK and **Peter Kristensen**, University of Copenhagen, Denmark

---

This series publishes cutting-edge research on the changing international politics of East Asia. It covers the security dynamics, the causes of conflict and cooperation, and the ongoing transformation of the region, as well as the impact of East Asia on the wider global order.

The series contributes to theoretical debates within the field of International Relations. Topics studied in East Asia can shed fresh light on disciplinary debates while the theoretical insights can challenge and enrich the propositions of mainstream IR theories which have been derived mostly from the European experience. In welcoming theoretically informed and theoretically innovative works, this series will play an important role in developing and establishing new Asian schools of thought in International Relations theory.

Also available

The Responsibility to Provide in Southeast Asia:
Towards an Ethical Explanation

By **See Seng Tan**

Find out more at

bristoluniversitypress.co.uk/
bristol-studies-in-east-asian-international-relations

Bristol Studies in East Asian International Relations

Series Editors: **Yongjin Zhang**, University of Bristol, UK, **Shogo Suzuki**, University of Manchester, UK and **Peter Kristensen**, University of Copenhagen, Denmark

---

International advisory board

Find out more at

bristoluniversitypress.co.uk/
bristol-studies-in-east-asian-international-relations

CHINA RISEN?

Studying Chinese Global Power

Shaun Breslin

BRISTOL
UNIVERSITY
PRESS

First published in Great Britain in 2021 by

Bristol University Press
University of Bristol
1–9 Old Park Hill
Bristol
BS2 8BB
UK
t: +44 (0)117 954 5940
e: bup-info@bristol.ac.uk

Details of international sales and distribution partners are available at bristoluniversitypress.co.uk

British Library Cataloguing in Publication Data
A catalogue record for this book is available from the British Library

ISBN 978-1-5292-1580-9 hardcover
ISBN 978-1-5292-1581-6 paperback
ISBN 978-1-5292-1582-3 ePub
ISBN 978-1-5292-1583-0 ePdf

Cover design: blu inc, Bristol

Front cover image: iStock/bjdlzx
Bristol University Press uses environmentally responsible print partners.

Printed and bound in Great Britain by CMP, Poole

Contents

List of Figures

List of Abbreviations

AI	Artificial Intelligence
AIIB	Asian Infrastructure Investment Bank
APEC	Asia Pacific Economic Cooperation
ASEAN	Association of Southeast Asian Nations
BRI	Belt and Road Initiative
BRICS	Brazil, Russia, India, China, South Africa
CCP	Chinese Communist Party
CCTV	China Central Television
CDB	China Development Bank
CELAC	Community of Latin American and Caribbean States
CFIUS	Committee on Foreign Investment in the United States
CGTN	China Global Television News
CI	Confucius Institute
CIC	China Investment Corporation
COFDI	Chinese Outward Foreign Direct Investment
CS	China Solution
CSFM	Community of Shared Future for Mankind
DAC	Development Assistance Committee
ESRC	Economic and Security Review Commission (United States)
EU	European Union
Eximbank	Export-Import Bank of China
FOCAC	Forum on China–Africa Cooperation
FDI	Foreign Direct Investment
FMPRC	Foreign Ministry of the People's Republic of China
G20	Group of Twenty
GDP	Gross Domestic Product
GPDCC	Great Power Diplomacy with Chinese Characteristics

GS	Grand Strategy
IMF	International Monetary Fund
IPE	International Political Economy
IR	International Relations
LLC	Limited Liability Company
M&A	Mergers and Acquisitions
MIC2025	Made in China 2025
MOFCOM	Ministry of Commerce
NDRC	National Development and Reform Commission
NSC	National Security Commission
NTIR	New Type of International Relations
ODA	Official Development Assistance
OOF	Other Official Flows (of finance)
PRC	People's Republic of China
R&D	Research and Development
SAFE	State Administration of Foreign Exchange
SCO	Shanghai Cooperation Organisation
SDR	Special Drawing Rights
SOE	State-Owned Enterprise
UN	United Nations
WHO	World Health Organization
WTO	World Trade Organization

Acknowledgements

How long does it take to write a book? Given the argument that I make in the book that first encounters with China can influence the sort of questions that you subsequently ask, then the real answer is probably 37 years in this case. But in terms of the immediate task of putting this specific book together: sitting in front of a screen and typing everything up took about a year; if you include trying out various parts of it at workshops and conferences then it's more like five years. During this period, I benefitted greatly from a number of trips to China and am particularly grateful to the China Foreign Affairs University and the Fudan Institute for Advanced Studies in Social Sciences for providing visiting professorships in 2016 and 2018 respectively.

Special thanks go to the Leverhulme Trust for the award of a Major Research Fellowship, 'China Risen: What is Global Power (and in what ways does China have it)?' (MRF-2016–103). In addition to the financial support that made the project possible, I am also grateful for the flexibility they displayed when the coronavirus pandemic disrupted my plans for the final stages of the project in early 2020. Thanks also to Jill Pavey at Warwick University for managing the financial and administrative consequences that result from research funding success.

Thanks to this funding, when not in China, I have spent the best part of three years working from home. As those who also have done so will know – either from choice or as a result of the pandemic – this can place interesting new burdens on those who are also at home. So last but not least, thanks to Sarah for coping with me both when I've been away for long periods, and also when I haven't been; I'm not sure which is hardest, but I suspect it's the latter.

Introduction

Since at least the early 1990s, China's rise has been identified as 'a defining element in post-Cold War international politics' (Shambaugh, 1996, 180), and questions have been asked about what China's leaders might do to try to change the world once they had the power to do so. We are a now at a point when we no longer just need to use the future tense. To be sure, we can still speculate about the future. But we now also have real-world examples to analyse and evaluate. Identifying a defining moment when China made some sort of transition to global power status with the ability to push for change is not an exact science. The identification of China as a global power began to become relatively common in the mid-2000s, but really became a well-established 'common sense' position in the years following the global financial crisis.[1] China might not have been seen as the predominant global power in all issue areas, but by as early as 2012, surveys showed that China was already popularly thought of as the world's leading economic power among respondents in North America and Europe (Pew Research Center, 2013). And all of this was just as Xi Jinping was taking power, and before he had begun to signal a new direction for China, with both the desire and ability to take a new global role.

While a few have gone to the next step and endowed China with superpower status,[2] there is no need to see China in this way or as closely catching the US (though many do) for it to be thought of as a global power. And being *a* global power is certainly not the same thing as being *the* single global power or the predominant one. Nor does it mean that China's rise is over. It could continue to rise even further either as a result of what it does, or as relative power capabilities shift as others decline. Or it might suffer a decline or even a crash as a result of indigenous or endogenous shocks, or a reconfiguration of global power structures and alliances. Many historic great powers have subsequently become far less great and far less powerful, and past trajectories are certainly no guarantee of future ones. Even so, talking about China as a rising power is out of odds with how it is widely regarded and treated, and it is probably time to use the language of China risen.

So what does it mean and how does it inform what is studied in this book? Political slogans and sloganizing are part and parcel of daily life in China. Numerical mantras are particularly favoured; the 'Three Represents', the 'Four Comprehensives' and the 'Eight Honours and Shames' are just three of the many examples of Chinese politics by numbers. These three examples were personally associated with the political programmes of Jiang Zemin, Xi Jinping and Hu Jintao respectively, designed to distil down their agendas, objectives and priorities into simple and memorable constituent elements. So, in the spirit of establishing personal agendas in this way, the aims and objectives of this book can be explained by first announcing and then unpacking the 'Three Intents', the 'Four Extents', and the 'Eight Arguments'.

The three intents

What is global power (and in what ways does China have it)?

This book has been constructed to do three main things. The first and most basic objective is to disaggregate different potential sources of Chinese global power, to assess how they have changed over time, and to consider how effective each could be in attaining a variety of Chinese objectives. This is done by discussing the evolution of Chinese strategies and agendas for global change in Chapter 3, and then outlining Chinese power resources in key arenas; economics in Chapter 4, the power of attraction (soft power) in Chapter 5, and China's normative power and global governance reform aspirations in Chapter 6. This is not an attempt to find one single discrete source of Chinese power. Rather, it is an attempt to identify the relative significance of different power resources, accepting that this significance can differ over time and from place to place.

It is also built on the understanding that how others respond to China is rarely, if ever, a consequence of any one single type of power resource. Rather, it is typically the consequence of the way that different elements interact. After introducing the concept of soft power, Nye (2009) subsequently added the concept of 'Smart Power' to the International Relations (IR) lexicon, to indicate that the soft on its own was rarely enough to bring about change in others. What worked was the right combination of both soft and harder power resources. Calling it 'smart' implies the deliberate deployment of different Chinese power resources in a conscious and thought out manner. Or if not the result of deliberate strategy, the different resources should be mutually reinforcing and combine to lead in a common direction. On occasions, this is indeed the case with Chinese international interactions, with the appeal of China as a new type of international financial actor enhanced by the actual financial resources that are disbursed. But on other occasions, different dimensions of what is being said and done go down different tracks. The example of the mixed messages deployed as part of Chinese medical and crisis diplomacy during the COVID-19 pandemic (as discussed in Chapter 5) is particularly apposite here. At other times, different dimensions do pull in the same direction, but not necessarily the one that serves Chinese interests. European responses to Chinese strategic signalling and changing overseas investment patterns discussed in Chapter 1 are a good example here. As these outcomes are only occasionally the result of intelligent design, it seems appropriate to turn down the opportunity of deploying an overarching Smart Power perspective, while recognizing that it has something to say about how soft and harder power resources combine to produce effects.

The power to do what?

Such an assessment requires asking a couple of prior questions. What exactly does it mean to be (or have) global power, and what is this power used to do? China's global power status is often asserted rather than specifically defined or quantified. A lack of clarity and shared understanding creates a number of problems in trying to understand what different people mean. That said, a widespread common sense acceptance of China's global power status and capabilities provides a simple indication that whatever the threshold for being a global power is, China has already crossed it. There might be disagreement over at what point this acceptance becomes widespread enough to count as a consensus that matters. Perhaps it is when such an understanding of global power becomes a source of power in itself by resulting in an action or response that would otherwise have not come about. For perception to result in power, then others need to make decisions and act (or indeed, to decide not to act) based on their assessment of what your interests are and how you will react (Clarke, 2011). This understanding of the importance of how perceptions and pre-assumptions shape policy is at the heart of much that follows in this book.

Another definition of being a global power is that national interests and objectives have a global impact. Using this understanding, James Kynge (2009: 6) argues that China had it from around 2003–4, when growing Chinese demand for a whole range of goods and resources had implications for pretty much every part of the world. Shambaugh (2013: 8) has questioned if this is really a form of power at all, as being a global *actor* is not the same as having the ability and intent to influence and change others. Students of power in IR in general, though, have argued that power can indeed include unintentional consequences of action (Baldwin, 2002). Both positions have merit. Responses to China's rise are influenced by a whole range of factors. Some of them are the result of deliberate Chinese policy designed to have transnational effects, and some of them are the external consequences of domestic change; change that has global outcomes that result from the sheer size of China and the speed of transformation in so many issue areas. After all, a world changed is still a changed world no matter if changed by design or not. But developing effective policy responses becomes much more difficult if intent is assumed when it isn't there, and assumed evidence of state intent is in reality evidence of Chinese international actors trying to attain other types of ends.

It is important then – but far from easy – to try to identify what is the result of the deliberate use of economic statecraft, what is a byproduct of it (at times unintentionally so) and what is the result of independent action. This allows us to interrogate the extent to which China's international interactions are the consequence of a Grand Strategy (GS) organized and delivered by the state. At the same time, though, it is also important to remember that perceptions (and policies) are not just a consequence of material interactions, but can also shape the way that those interactions are parsed and understood; hence the importance of the third intent that we will turn to shortly.

Structural power

A further understanding of what global power is, and what it is for, is captured by Susan Strange's (1998) understanding of structural power. Here the focus is not on the distribution of power within the existing order, or even on the ability to get others to change their behaviour or choices. Rather, it focuses on the ability to change the very nature of the global order itself and change those global structures that all others have to operate within. This can include the creation of institutions of global governance, as 'the international organisation is above all a tool of national government, an instrument for the pursuit of national interests by other means' (Strange, 1996: xiv). This has clear salience in the Chinese case through the construction of new structures designed to govern relations with different states (or groups of states), and/or to provide global public goods. The Asian Infrastructure Investment Bank (AIIB) is a very clear example of such institutional innovation, but we can also include the range of different bodies that have been set up to act as means of facilitating interaction with different groups of states. We can add to this agenda attempts to shape debates and policy within existing institutions of global and regional governance, efforts to change the formal distribution of power and informal mechanisms of influence within some of them, and a strong preference for some bodies as 'legitimate' sites of global interactions and governance over others (Guo Jiping, 2019).

Beyond organizational reform and design, structural power refers to changing the norms that underpin the way that states interact with each other, and the whole way in which the global economy is organized. And while not using the specific concept of structural power, it is this understanding of what global power can be used to achieve that is at the heart of most analyses of Chinese global power. As one of the most authoritative students of power in international politics puts it:

> As China rises, it will inevitably seek to convert its growing material resources and economic success into influence over other states and international affairs more generally. It will also seek to revise the rules of international politics and alter existing regimes to suit its interests. Every great power in history has sought to wield such influence. There is no reason to expect that China will be different. (Lake, 2017: 357)

It makes sense, then, to go beyond the simple aim of identifying different power resources in different issue areas in the first intent. As such, the second intent refers to providing an assessment of whether China – or more correctly, China's leaders – can exercise structural power defined in this way. This requires not only looking at the extent of China's desire and ability to do so, but also the response of other global actors to what they think the ambitions of the newly risen global power really are.

Studying China's rise

The third and very much related intent is to understand how assessments of Chinese global power and the consequences of Chinese rise are formed, and how and why these understandings change. Here there is a particular focus on the way that attitudes and policy responses shifted quite considerably in parts of the world in the 2010s, even before the COVID-19 pandemic. Again, the analysis in Chapters 3 to 6 plays an important role here too, as it was the changes in the nature of interactions in these areas that resulted in shifting perceptions. This included a rather significant modification of the way that China's leaders communicated their intent and objectives to different audiences, as well as changes in specific types of exchanges and contacts. The more that Chinese power resources have grown, and the more that the leadership has been prepared to outline what they want to do with this power, then the more suspicion and concern about Chinese intentions has grown too.

But it goes further than this too. The questions we ask about China and some of the basic assumptions that inform different theoretical and conceptual starting points can shape the way that events and information are understood. Indeed, it can and does influence what sort of actions are considered to constitute evidence in the first place, let alone how it is subsequently interpreted and presented to others. As such, Chapter 1 establishes the ways in which different conceptual frameworks are constructed and used to try to predict China's future fortunes and/or behaviour. This includes considering how different theoretical preferences lead in diverse directions, the consequences of asking questions about China's domestic political economy as opposed to questions about China's global impact, the potential significance of the location of the observer, and how and when they first encountered China.

For some readers, Chapter 2 will be unnecessary. It focuses on how studying domestic debates and political economy dynamics in China helps us to understand the nature of bounded autonomy and bounded pluralism; where and when actors are free to present their own ideas and pursue their own agendas, and the way that the state can shape and limit these freedoms. This then in turn helps us recognize which actions and consequences can and should be seen as resulting from deliberate state intent, which shouldn't, and which are difficult to fully deconstruct and so should be treated with caution. This is not an original position by any stretch of the imagination, and many students of Chinese politics, economics and society will be very familiar with the arguments being made. Yet many analyses of China's international impact do indeed assume a unitary Chinese interest pursing a coherent and coordinated state strategy, and either downplay, ignore, or overtly reject the insights of those with more domestic focuses. So, while I too think that this chapter should be unnecessary, and its arguments simply taken for granted, they clearly aren't (taken for granted) in much of the literature and so it isn't (unnecessary).

The four extents

The evolution of any research project is shaped by constraining factors. In this case there are four main factors that influenced what is covered, and perhaps more important, what isn't. The first of these is the researcher. The argument will be made in Chapter 1 that the location and experience of the observer matters in helping shape their views and perceptions. As such, it stands to reason that this applies to this study as well. Even the very argument that location matters is, by definition, influenced by the location of the person making the argument. As such, it is only right to acknowledge that the location of this observer shapes the nature of this project too.

This book is written by a European scholar based in a UK university, who has spent a considerable amount of his professional career working on collaborative European Union (EU) funded projects, and at least as much time in China working on projects with Chinese scholars. One possible effect is that the plurality of interests and ideas within Chinese debates is given a relatively high status in this study because of familiarity with a number of the actors in those debates. Another, as will soon become clear, is that the focus of analysis is tilted to how 'the West' — to use the terminology that is typically used in China — has responded to China, with a particular emphasis on European and UK examples. The sources consulted and cited also reflect this. For example, the first instinct is to go to UK media sources when news breaks rather than US ones. This is nothing to do with any idea of a hierarchy of importance. It is simply a reflection of experience, access and expertise. It does have consequences though. The nature of the US–China relationship probably looks rather different when viewed from the outside than from within (an issue we will return to shortly). Things presumably look even more different when viewed from Africa, Latin America, Central Asia and other developing areas too. And both sets of differences could be important determinants of however the world will be organized as the consequences of the COVID-19 pandemic play out.

Studying moving targets: China under Xi Jinping

The second 'extent' relates to time. Choosing the pandemic as an end point for this study was relatively easy. As will be argued in a little more detail later in this Introduction, the collateral effects of the pandemic (beyond fighting the virus itself) were to exacerbate existing problems and accelerate existing trends. So, in one respect, it shouldn't be thought of as a turning point as much as a crystallization of challenges that had been building for a few years. That said, the extent of the dislocations and the speed of the accelerations mean that identifying 2020 as an era changing year is apposite. The extent and nature of China's international economic relations were affected by what happened both at home and in partner countries, and China's self-identity as a responsible and trustworthy global actor was seriously questioned. While it will be many years before we know the long-term consequences of all of this, we can have a good guess that the future won't be a mirror of the past.

Identifying a clear starting point was somewhat more problematic. Chinese analysts tend to refer to what they call the International Financial Crisis (rather than global)[3] as a key turning point after when the US was no longer able to 'rule the world' without challenge (Yu Zhengliang, 2012: 95). But the perceived decline of existing powers goes further back than this. The US led interventionist strategy in the Middle East was the first sign of if not an end to American supremacy, then at least the beginning of a transition from a unipolar global order to something else (Feng, 2012). This created the idea of a 'period of strategic opportunity' for China to do more to attain its objectives – an idea that became more popular as other global power shifts played into China's hands (Xu, 2014). Xi Jinping's rise to leadership is also often cited as marking the start of a new era. Yet China's international economic interactions had already gone through more than one change of pattern before 2012. And as Chapter 3 will show, the shift towards a more proactive articulation of Chinese interests and an agenda for forms of global change also preceded Xi's assumption of power.

So in trying to understand power and policy under Xi, it is not helpful to focus *only* on the Xi era itself. This places too much emphasis on the decisions of one person, and underplays the significance of longer-term trends: both trends within Chinese thinking and policy and also in the thinking and policy of pre-existing global powers. All that being said, things certainly moved into a new gear under him, not least because of his personal identification with a range of foreign policy initiatives and ideas. Xi has signalled Chinese intent to domestic and foreign audiences in different ways too. He has also changed the structures of security policy making to concentrate more power in bodies that he controls. This consolidation and concentration of pre-existing thinking and trends under Xi has also resulted in a transition from a dissatisfaction with the global order and a desire for it to be changed, to a firmer commitment that China is willing and able to take the lead in bringing about this change. China might have been a tentative great power actor and reformer under Hu, but it has become a self-identified and clearly articulated one under Xi. And as Yan Xuetong (2019: 26–7) puts it, 'while the previous leaders from Deng Xiaoping onward set greater store by wealth' things changed under Xi because 'the new Chinese leader had faith in power'.

The trick is trying to get the best possible balance between focusing primarily on changes in the Xi era, while also showing how these changes relate to what came before. The analysis in each chapter is built on an understanding that Xi as an individual leader really has changed things, and in some areas very significantly. It is also built on the belief that his ideas and strategies did not emerge ex nihilo in 2012. The extent of the study, though, could always be extended – particularly backwards in time. To a degree, then, the extent of the temporal basis of the study has been traded for the extent of the issue area coverage. And as we shall see shortly, even this is far from total.

Is it always too early to tell?

Time and timeliness are important in another way as well. There have been a number of times over the years when things that were previously taken for granted suddenly and unexpectedly no longer could be. With the benefit of hindsight, it might be obvious why communist party rule came to end in the Soviet Union and Eastern Europe. Or if not obvious, then understandable. But it certainly did not look inevitable even in the summer of 1989. The same could be said about the global financial crisis. In very different dimensions and to different degrees, both impacted on Chinese politics and China's global role, and the full extent of their consequences for China took many years to play out. Indeed, in the case of the Chinese response to the global crisis, the long-term implications of the debt-driven response were still not clear even as the coronavirus began to spread and generate a new multidimensional public health *and* economic crisis over a decade later.

It is rather facile to say that things can and do change very quickly. But it is facile and true. Many of the certainties or likelihoods that seemed to exist when Xi Jinping succeeded Hu Jintao in 2012–13 were no longer certain or likely at all by the end of his first term as leader. The institutionalized nature of power transition that had evolved in the post-Mao era is one example. The relative significance of state and market in the Chinese economy, and also the overall direction and ultimate endpoint of economic change, might be others. And so too is the extent to which China's leaders are prepared to not just accept but actively seek forms of global leadership, and to challenge some of the norms and principles that have underpinned the global order.

Neither can we have any confidence that any of today's apparent certainties will be certain tomorrow. As such, we should be careful in rushing to reach immediate conclusions and make immediate judgements. The China Investment Corporation (CIC) did not turn out to be the type of global financial actor that some feared it would become when it was launched in 2007. Neither has the impact of the AIIB on the global financial order been as destabilizing or even revolutionary as was predicted at the time (Koike, 2015). Or at least, not yet. We saw a rush to pass judgement on the consequences of the plan to fund and/or construct infrastructure projects across large parts of the world via the Belt and Road Initiative (BRI), only for a number of initial conclusions to be questioned as various proposed projects hit problems or were rejected by host governments, and enthusiasm for getting involved in the initiative waned in China itself. What looked in the first instance as a warm embrace of China's project didn't take long to look like a rather short-lived honeymoon instead. Then again, what subsequently looked at the time like a pushback might instead look like teething problems when viewed with the benefit of future hindsight.

It is also far too early to know what the Community of Shared Future for Mankind (CSFM) or the New Type of International Relations (NTIR) really mean in practice, let alone what a world guided by these principles might ultimately look like. And while it has probably always been too early to tell, the sheer number of new initiatives and the number of new concepts and aspirations that have been promoted under Xi mean that any predictions need to be treated with even more caution than normal. And that's before we add on the even greater global uncertainty generated by the COVID-19 pandemic.

Quite simply, China's continued rise to ever greater global power cannot be taken for granted. Even before the coronavirus outbreak raised questions over the long-term prospects for Chinese (and global) growth, many economic analysts were questioning whether China had the right fundamentals in place. Lardy (2019), for example, pointed to the renewed emphasis on the state vis-à-vis the market under Xi Jinping as an example of a policy choice that had actually reduced China's chances of continuing to succeed. A number of researchers have argued that the way that the leadership supposedly 'successfully' responded to past financial difficulties has in fact contributed to greater financial fragility in the long term. They conclude that fundamentally reforming the financial system remains the key to securing China's long-term prospects (Collier, 2017), with some arguing that financial turmoil and/or crisis is still the most likely scenario.[4] Others are unconvinced that China's leaders will be able to deal with the numerous domestic challenges that they face, and will be domestically preoccupied rather than asserting real global leadership for years to come.[5]

There also remains a strong(ish) school of thought that rather than being well on the way to global superpower status, China is instead heading for a comprehensive crash caused by corruption, environmental destruction and an unsustainable growth model.[6] From this perspective, while the economic impacts of the COVID-19 outbreak were significant challenges in themselves, the way that the virus first took hold and spread was taken as evidence of deeper seated structural shortcomings that would result in different types of crises recurring in the future. These inherent governance failings in the system are also understood to be aggravated by the growth of US–China tensions, which will accelerate economic decline and make it harder to paper over systemic failings by delivering economic progress. And here again, China's coronavirus response (and the response to that response in the US) was seen as accelerating and aggravating these pre-existing tensions in the world's most important bilateral relationship (Pei, 2020).

This is not just a case of outsiders finding negative things to focus on. A number of Chinese analysts of China's domestic political economy have also highlighted the weaknesses and vulnerabilities that could derail China in the future (Lynch, 2015). Moreover, China's leaders themselves have clearly and repeatedly enunciated their concern that radical change is needed for the whole system to survive and prosper. And not just the economic system. If you step back from the vision that Xi is trying to promote of China's global power emerging from its domestic self-confidence – an issue we will return to in Chapter 6 – much of what he has done since 2012 reflects a lack of confidence that the status quo ante could continue to deliver economically and socially, and keep the Chinese Communist Party (CCP) in power. As explained in a little more detail in Chapter 2, the way that power structures were reconfigured during his first term as a leader – including the abolition of term limits for the President – suggest a man who was acting to redress weaknesses rather than building on strengths.

These different assumptions about the efficacy and malleability of the CCP leadership (and thus the sustainability of the current system) form a crucial part of the discussion of how we study and understand China in Chapter 1. They are briefly raised here simply to show that while the dominant 'common sense' understanding is that China already has become a real global power that is here to stay, this is not accepted by all. What is said about the future should be constrained by reflecting on what has happened to inevitable futures in the past; futures that at times have turned out to not be quite so inexorable and preordained with the benefit of hindsight.

Researching what is not there

While the extent of new initiatives under Xi leads to multiple uncertainties, it is also very useful for a study such as this. It has provided a rich source of official documents and academic analyses of the supposed new thinking on IR and global order that provides an important research resource. Chapter 3 takes advantage of this by trying to identify a logical conceptual flow that translates aspiration into actions designed to achieve grand goals. Chapter 6 uses it too to ask if there is now a clearly articulated vision of what an alternative Chinese influenced (or even led) world order might look like (with the answer a qualified 'yes').

However, it also creates a number of challenges too, and the third extent refers to the way that domestic debates and discourses can be used to inform understanding of the real extent of opinions and ideas within China. This is because the wider political environment in China under Xi has had a profound effect on the nature of debate and discussion (Yin, 2019). This is not to say that all debate has been squashed. There remains a relatively vocal set of critics who are concerned that China's real power and ability to push for change has been exaggerated, and that there is a real risk of 'overstretch' as China tries to do too much internationally that it doesn't have the capacity or resources to pull off (Kelly, 2017a; 2017b). For this set of thinkers, China has 'neither the will nor the strategy to become a global leader' as it is still rather poor in relative per capita terms, has considerable domestic economic challenges to overcome, and lacks the knowledge and understanding of political dynamics in many parts of the world to be able to help develop effective solutions to global problems (Wang Wen, 2019). There is also concern that the more open China is in asserting its desire to lead or change the world, the more other powers (and particularly the United States) will alter their views of and policies towards China to prevent this leadership from happening. It's fair to say that the announcement of the imposition of new tariffs on a range of Chinese exports to the US in 2018 fed in to that concern, and generated something of a popular backlash too against those who were perceived to have overstated the extent of Chinese power (particularly vis-à-vis the United States).

Nevertheless, it is also fair to say that the political and academic environment in contemporary China means that the pluralism of debates over the nature of the world order and China's place within it have become less plural in recent years. There has been an expansion of certain themes and arguments, and a reduction in the force of alternatives to dilute them. This is no small part results from what Minzner (2019) refers to as a process of 'ideological rectification of higher education' to ensure 'political conformity' with the party's thinking and objectives. This includes tilting research funding to encourage the study (and often repetition) of official thinking. It is also likely to encourage self-imposed caution. The way in which Chinese thinking and objectives have been disseminated overseas by not just Chinese officials but also by those Chinese research institutions that have close relationships with the state only serves to increase the idea of a single Chinese voice.

If a research project decides to focus on Chinese discourses and debates, as this one does in a number of places, how far can we take what is written as reflective of the overall debate when certain positions have become much easier to articulate than others? Or how do we know that these are actually firmly held positions rather than expedient ones given the current nature of the political system; positions that might prove to be much less firmly held if the political climate changes? More than one Chinese analyst has warned against taking all of what is written too seriously. And spending time with Chinese academics discussing what China is doing and will do in the future can give an impression that is at odds with both the way that official China is presenting itself to the world, and quite a lot of what is written too. This in turn raises the question of how to report and factor in those opinions and outlooks that are communicated personally and in informal settings. And how to study what isn't being written. Perhaps the best that can be done is to report the debates with these caveats firmly in place, and accept that they are a product of the contemporary environment. As such, they probably say more about the nature of the political system than they do about the full range of opinions of Chinese thinkers.

Components of power

The fourth constraining factor takes us back to the first of the 'three intents' and relates to the types of power resources that are analysed, and the way that they are assessed. It is not original to try and disaggregate power sources and resources. From the early 1960s, David Singer's 'Correlates of War' project attempted to explain why wars sometimes happened, but not always. This entailed finding quantitative ways of assessing and comparing state power (and limitations on that power) across a range of issue areas.[7] The result was the 'Composite Index of National Capability' which calculates national power based on a state's share of six countable and material factors.[8] While not sharing the specific focus on war, a similar interest in finding measurable ways of evaluating power has influenced Chinese scholarship too, with the concept of *zonghe guoli* (Comprehensive National Power) becoming the most well-known and cited (Hu and Men, 2002). This project identified eight broad categories of 'National Strategic Resources': Economic, Human Capital, Natural, Capital, Knowledge and Technology, Government, Military, and International. Each of these is then broken down into sub-elements to produce a total of 23 measurable indicators. For example, international resources are broken down into exports and services, imports and services, royalty and license fees receipts, and royalty and license fees payments, and each state's share of the world total. On the basis of their calculations, Hu Angang and Men Honghua (2002) calculated that China was already the No. 2 global power in 2002, but that its power capabilities (and relative power) varied significantly across different issue areas.[9]

While this surprised many at the time, it was not that out of kilter with the Composite Index results, which had China surpassing the US and taking the global first place in the early 2000s. It did, however, differ rather markedly from Brooks and Wohlforth's (2015/16) calculations over a decade later that China was still considerably behind the US in terms of technological power, and even further behind in military power. Building on Beckley (2011/12), they argued that other calculations overstated the extent of Chinese economic and technological power as they failed to fully evaluate the significance of foreign technology and imported goods in Chinese exports. High Chinese export figures, then, actually partially reflected the power of other economies rather than China's, while high Chinese Gross Domestic Product (GDP) growth hid the consequential damage to the environment which would weaken China in the long run. Thus, the gap was not only much larger than even other proponents of continued US dominance calculated, but also destined to persist for the foreseeable future.

All of these approaches (and other similar varieties) are built around an attempt to find measurable indices and calculable conclusions using quantitative methods. This makes it possible to do a couple of things that a book like this one cannot do. It allows for a consideration of a much broader range of individual potential power resources (down to the very micro level in some cases), and results in clear and comparable results. Instead, the conclusions of this study have to rest on the study of more broadly defined issue areas, and are stated with less conviction and absoluteness.

Others have started from qualitative approaches and tried to disaggregate differential sources of power. This was at the heart of Lampton's (2008) distinction between what he called 'might, money and minds' in *The Three Faces of Chinese Power*. It was also an implicit underpinning of Shambaugh's (2013) categorization of China as a 'partial power' in a study that also highlighted the differences between having a global reach or impact, and having 'power'. Johnston's (2019) identification of how China views different types of international 'orders' deals as much with evaluations of perceptions of the utility of these orders to China as it does with evaluations of Chinese power within them; constitutive, military, political development, social development, international trade, international finance, international environmental and informational. But in the process, it also provides an important contribution to this 'fragmented power in a fragmented order' type of approach.

Building on these previous works, this book starts from the tripartite division of military, economic, and ideational sources of power, and then immediately begins to modify them. The single biggest modification, and the single biggest of the 'four extents', is not to look at the military at all. This is a rather big hole in a book on Chinese power; particularly as what China does in terms of deploying its military capabilities can make the many statements by China's leaders of its inherently peaceful nature ring rather hollow. It might also look like more than simply 'modifying' its predecessors. However, the intention is not to deny the importance of military power by reducing the three faces to two. On the contrary, it is so important that it deserves greater attention than it can be given here.

As will be argued in the following chapter, it is becoming increasingly difficult to keep up with what is going on in China, and what is said about what is going on in China. This is partly because of increased access to internal Chinese sources, and also because more people have more things to say. And that's without also trying to follow the theoretical literature that helps us understand what is being done and said. While a key problem of studying China when I started doing so in the early 1980s was getting hold of information and decent analyses, the problem today is keeping on top of the mountain of data that is available, and the even bigger mountain of scholarship, reports and opinions. And once you have them, the next task is working out what is informative and what is not. There is a need to take a holistic view, but it is extremely difficult to do so. As a result, and because I have a very superficial understanding of Chinese military affairs, rather than do a bad job of what others do, it seems better to leave the analysis in this area to those who do it very well. The exception is where military or military related intentions are signalled by China's leaders to external audiences; for example, through Defence White Papers or outlining non-negotiable core interests. Here, though, although the issue might be military and security related, the focus is on the way the message is being articulated and disseminated and is thus considered to constitute a sort of ideational power, rather than a military one per se.

Disaggregating power

While it might not be possible to do a quantitative study of the same number of factors that qualitative studies assess, it is relatively easy to break down the remaining broad issue areas into smaller ones, and then decide which to focus on. For example, under the broad heading of economic power, we can distinguish between productive power, market power, financial power and technological or innovative power. We can then subdivide these into smaller more discrete units. To take financial power, for example, and think about the different consequences of renminbi (RMB) internationalization, Chinese holdings of various forms of dollar denominated debt, and the growth of Chinese outward investment. While accepting that all of these are important components of both China's still evolving global role, and also perceptions of that role, there will be a specific focus in this study on Chinese financial flows in the form of aid-type financing and Foreign Direct Investment (FDI). This gives the best chance of addressing the questions of Chinese (Grand) strategies that are raised in Chapter 3, and considering if China is using economic resources to bring about structural change to the global order.

When it comes to ideational power, we might be able to distinguish between the way that China builds and projects its preferred understanding of itself (how it will act as a great power now and in the future), the promotion of normative and theoretical alternatives to the status quo, and the attraction of China's model and/or successes. The first two here focus on what China does, and the third on how others perceive what China has done. This allows us to ask how much of what is often studied as Chinese 'soft power' is really soft at all, rather than a somewhat 'harder' state project designed to bring about a shift in the distribution of global power resources. It also allows us to try and identify both differential Chinese strategies, and differential external responses. By distinguishing between the projection (which the Chinese state can try to control) and the reception (which it can't), we are reminded that while material power is something that is generated from within, ideational power depends on external perceptions and understandings.

The eight arguments

A number of core arguments can be inferred from the discussion of the Three Intents and Four Extents above. For the sake of clarity, though, it is worth restating them explicitly here alongside the other central positions that either informed this study from the outset or emerged as it was being written.

A conceptual framework: area studies, (I)PE and the politics of perceptions

First, while the aim of Chapter 1 on studying China is mainly to explain why different positions emerge, it would be strange if it did not result in a preferred mode of analysis. That preference is in part that studying the domestic political economy allows us to understand who is doing what for which reasons that casts doubt on some of the assumptions of Chinese actorness and intentions. A domestic focus also suggests that there will be much to keep the Chinese government busy for many years as they try to change the basis of legitimacy from performance defined as generating growth to something else. And studying Chinese discussions and debates about the nature of global order and China's place in it helps us understand why Chinese positions and policies have changed, and what the range of options for future policies and objectives might be.

However, this emphasis on the importance of the domestic is not enough in itself. Understanding the structure of the global political economy and the nature of transnational economic interactions sheds light on the agency of different types of actors. It also raises questions about the ease (and prudence) of assigning power in the global economy to individual states (or states alone). In addition, this study starts from the assumption that the way that evidence of Chinese intentions is sought, understood and used is often a consequence of pre-existing perceptions of what China is and wants. The importance of trust – and the lack of it – is particularly important and is considered in detail in Chapter 2. In short, a combination of three different approaches/research traditions/research focuses can help overcome some of the problems of trying to understand the consequences of China's rise.

What is political, what is International Relations?

Second, when it comes to studying China, the realm of what is considered to be political and a potential strategic state tool is much broader and all-encompassing than is the case with the study of many other countries. There are very good reasons for this. The only relatively recently started, ongoing, and uneven process of removing state control over economic activity means the hand of the state has been far from an invisible one; relatively recent for people of certain ages at least. We have been able to follow as news (or again, some of us have) the way that Chinese actors have been given permission to do the things that private and market actors have long been doing independently elsewhere. For example, we can see the direct state action – and see the consequence of that action – in ways that aren't possible when it comes to investment originating in much of the rest of the world. As shown in Chapter 4, in many cases not only do economic actors still rely on permissions, but previous freedoms can also be closed down. The nature of the Chinese political economy as discussed in Chapter 2 also often blurs the dividing lines between state and market incentives and policy drivers. And then we return to trust, and the suspicion of many of those who don't trust China that anything that is done by Chinese international actors is designed to pursue grand strategic objectives.

What this means is that certain subject areas that would not immediately leap out as being central to IR questions and concerns in the study of other countries are considered to be so in the Chinese case. So rather than leave the study of why Chinese firms invest overseas to the many very good scholars of business and management, it has become a core IR issue. Indeed, for a number of observers, it is the key to understanding the economic tools deployed to attain grand political objectives (Norris, 2016). Instead of asking what drives individual firms to invest where they do, the question is often why does the Chinese state direct or encourage Chinese firms to invest where they do? Even helping the search for simple commercial objectives – what Brautigam and Tang (2012: 800) call 'state guidance or direction with a commercial rationale' – is typically seen as being *more* political in the Chinese case than elsewhere. Many governments do lots of things to support producers, including those that have also been enthusiastic promoters of neoliberalism. Maybe all of them do. They develop industrial zones with subsidized start-up costs and infrastructure advantages, support research and development (R&D) and training, provide market intelligence and export promotion mechanisms, negotiate trade agreements and much more. All of these are designed to help companies make profits and gain commercial advantages over competitors, and can result in political tensions if the resulting playing field is considered to be too uneven by others. And as both the response to the global financial crisis and the COVID-19 pandemic show, governments of very different complexions have been prepared to step in and take direct state control of failing enterprises and to pay wages of employees in the private sector in times of crises.

If China is different, then one difference might be the extent of support that is provided relative to what happens elsewhere, particularly in 'normal' non-crisis times. Another more important difference is concern with what this support is meant to achieve. The suspicion (which takes us back to trust once more) is that there are ulterior motives that go beyond the attempt to support commercial actors, and are to do with Chinese national power. Profit and other commercial gains are seen as a means to another end rather than ends in themselves. The goal is seen as building China's comprehensive national power to give it structural power in a competitive global order to potentially change the very basic nature of that order itself.

Moreover, it is not just in economic exchanges that the political is seen or assumed. The role of the state in facilitating, shaping, and at times directly controlling a whole range of other non-diplomatic international interactions are important too. Film and entertainment, cultural exchanges, tourism, and education are four pertinent examples that will all be discussed in Chapter 5. Indeed, the extent of state involvement in these areas is one reason why various Chinese initiatives have not only failed to change minds in a number of recipient audiences, but at times have been counterproductive and hardened pre-existing negative perceptions.

States and markets

This leads us directly to the third argument, that the best way of thinking about how different interests create actual economic interactions is of 'bounded autonomy' within the overarching framework established by the centre. Changes that will be discussed in Chapters 2 and 3 have gone some way to resolving the fragmentation of foreign policy decision making interests and power that had become ever more apparent in previous decades (Lampton, 2015). But while coordination and leadership might be stronger than before, it is far from total and comprehensive. Indeed, it was never the intention to micromanage everything. The state establishes the parameters of what can be done with certain objectives in mind, and more so than is the case with 'normal' macroeconomic policy making in other types of economies. The state also contains strong levers (both economic and political) to direct and incentivize individual actors to behave in certain ways. And again, stronger levers than is the case in more (neo)liberal economies. Moreover, the state can and does intervene to change the parameters of the permissible (or preferred) if individual actions are deemed to harm the bigger national interest. And behind this state action is a party that is primarily concerned with ensuring that it retains its monopoly on political power.

Yet within this overarching framework, and as long as the parameters of the permissible are not pushed too far, individual actors have the ability to not only pursue their own interests, but also to utilize centrally promoted grand initiatives to further these interests. This includes not just private non-state actors, but different levels and parts of the state system too. So diverse interests and objectives can flourish, with the pursuit of profit and commercial gain being something that is important both at the micro level (company profits) and also the state level (building a strong and powerful China). Moreover, sometimes, an overall national goal can mean very different things on the ground in different parts of the country because of huge variations in local conditions. What is done by one local government in the name of supporting the national project can be very different from what others do under the same banner. In effect, the central state establishes grand but also often loosely defined objectives, and then leaves it to others to attain them. At times, the overarching goals are so broad that they allow these other actors to pursue their own interests along the way.

Announced strategies – even major ones like the BRI – are often a bit short on actual content and are given life as a range of different actors attempt to define the initiative in ways that benefit their own specific interests.

For example, while the state might liberalize the outward investment regime to help secure energy and raw material supplies to support long-term development plans, local and private actors can and do use this new freedom to pursue narrower commercial interests. And as long as these do not get in the way of attaining the bigger state objective, then this is deemed to be legitimate. Or, as another example, the BRI has created opportunities for different actors and interests to go overseas that weren't otherwise either possible or economically viable. In response, many have moved to associate their own specific projects and objectives with the BRI in order to utilize these new opportunities in pursuit of their own micro-derived interests that often differ from each other (Jones and Zeng, 2019; Ye Min, 2019). The state has created new boundaries of new action, and then others try and extend the definition of these boundaries in ways that benefit themselves. And given the leadership's desire to see the BRI succeed, this has largely been tolerated. But there should be no doubt that the state retains the ability to restrict this action and redraw the boundaries if circumstances change.

Dissatisfied China: building an autonomous developmental space

The fourth argument is that the overarching primary objective is still found in the domestic rather than global. It is about creating what we might call an autonomous governance and development space. This does not refer to a geographical space, though in terms of having its own conceptions of core interests accepted by others, it does entail the establishment of a shared understanding of the parameters of Chinese sovereignty. Rather, it refers to the CCP's ability to do what it wants within this policy space unconstrained by any higher level of authority or external pressure or criticism. To pursue the domestic economic strategies that it thinks serves its interests, to maintain a political system that works best for the party, to organize and govern the internet to support the party's ambitions and so on. Or as Rolland (2020: 5) puts it, 'Beijing's vision for a new international order is an outward extension of what the party wants to secure (its perpetual rule and unchallenged power) and what it rejects as existential threats (democratic ideals and universal values)'.

This entails neutralizing the ability of outsiders to constrain its freedom of action, including by rejecting the idea of a universally salient and applicable set of norms. Many Chinese scholars will disagree. Yan Xuetong (2019: 10), for example, argues that all humans in all cultures have the 'same foundations underlying universally accepted codes of conduct'. It is the way that these shared basic universal principles have been interpreted and promoted in the West to serve specific purposes that is the problem, rather than the idea of universalism per se. This example from Yan Shuhan (2018: 20) takes us away from Yan's academic analysis to a more campaigning language, but sums up the basic argument that is not hard to find in other Chinese academic papers and policy statements:

> We are resolutely opposed to 'universal values'. This is because the 'universal values' spoken by Western countries, especially the United States, are really only their values which are promoted as values that are universally applicable to all countries in the world. They also require that all countries implement them. If some countries say 'no' to this, they attack and vilify these countries, and some even use this as an excuse to intervene in these countries. We resolutely oppose such 'universal values', but we do not deny or oppose the common values of human existence.

The contention is that there are a common set of values or standards (common values of human existence), but what these mean in practice should be defined by each state according to their own histories, cultures, experiences and power capacities. For example, all can agree that it is important to protect human rights. But which human rights should be privileged and prioritized depends on individual circumstances. The emphasis on political and individual rights might be appropriate for advanced rich Western industrialized democracies, but that doesn't mean it is right for everybody. But how much do different national interpretations have to have in common for them to comprise two different strands of a single norm, rather than representing two different and contending normative positions? Whatever we call it, the overarching goal is to prevent pre-existing dominant powers using their understanding of universalist norms to serve their interests at the expense of China's.

This approach tends to assume that there is a single entity that can be called 'the West'. It refers to a group of countries which are democratic, influenced by the European tradition of philosophy and state building, and underpinned by a preference for (free) markets and individual (human) rights as the basis of society. When the term 'the West' is used in this book, it reflects this type of aggregation and reflects the way that this broad set of countries is perceived within China and referred to in Chinese discourses, despite the many differences that the individual states have with each other.

Dissatisfied China: changing the world

In addition to this primarily defensive stance in promoting normative diversity – perhaps we can even call it normative anarchy – there has been a shift under Xi with China now more prepared to offer Chinese alternatives to the status quo in a number of issue areas. And the fifth argument is that China's leaders are now more confident than at any other time in the post-Mao era to not just articulate their desire for change, but to also take the lead in searching for global governance reform. This is not a particularly remarkable or insightful suggestion as it is something that China's leaders have themselves said on a number of occasions (as shown in the Appendix). This includes the promotion of 'Chinese wisdom' as the source of future alternative reformed governance structures (Xi, 2015c; 2016b). Arguably more important, they have also shown their capacity to promote change through the concrete use of financial and other resources to establish new institutions and create new patterns of international investment and trade. The BRI can be seen as an example both of a new initiative and, through the way that it has been promoted, a signal to the wider global community of future intent as well.

China's own stated ambition repeated time and again is to 'democratize' the existing structures of global governance. Indeed, increasingly pushing for reform is identified not as an ambition but a 'duty' that China owes the world – or the rest of the unfairly disadvantaged developing world at least (Yeophantong, 2013). Exercising this duty, and achieving this objective, requires proactive Chinese strategies and partnerships with other like-minded dissatisfied states to reform institutions of global governance to ensure that they reflect the changing balance of authority between existing (Western) powers and emerging and developing states. Chinese alternatives can be found in specific issue areas (most notably human rights). There is also now a greater appetite for arguing that there is something special about China's development experience that make it something that others should learn from. By and large, the main utility of the Model (if it is one) is still in showing what others can do if they too choose to ignore neoliberal prescriptions and develop their own models based on what works best for them; for others too to develop their own autonomous governance and development spaces. Even so, that some are making the case that China has 'transcended Western development theories and underdeveloped political economy, and has provided new options for the modernization of the late-developing countries' (Sun and Li, 2017: 10) is clearly important.

Here, we can identify evolving phases of thinking that will be discussed in detail in Chapter 6. It starts by first establishing the idea of Chinese exceptionalism; the idea that China is so fundamentally different from the rest of the world that it can only be understood by studying China's own unique history and unique ways of thinking (Zhang Feng, 2013; Ho, 2014). The next stage is to then establish that all countries are exceptional and each must be viewed through its own lenses and not through 'supposed' universal ones (Rolland, 2020: 17–18). The final stage – and this is where we have moved to under Xi – is to argue that while all countries might be unique and exceptional, there is something exceptionally exceptional about Chinese exceptionalism that make its thinking and experiences relevant for others as well. This takes place alongside the promotion of a form of Occidentalism, whereby essentialized Chinese world views and positions are promoted as representing the exact opposite of essentialized Western ones. Not surprisingly, it's the Chinese ones that are presented as being morally and practically superior. It is no longer a case of Chinese norms being for China only. They are now norms and principles for the world as well.

Whose/which world order?

So is China now clearly emerging as a threat to the existing order and the status quo? Or as is typically claimed, a reformist supporter of it? Or even as Wang Huiyao, President of the Center for China and Globalization, puts it, the 'defender, facilitator and active advocator of the liberal international order' with the US under President Trump the main challenge to it (Xinhua 2019a)? In the numerous speeches and articles published around the 70th Anniversary of the founding of the People's Republic of China (PRC) in 2019, the significance of party leadership in providing every success that China had achieved was not surprisingly the main message. After that, though (as shown in the Appendix), China's contributions to world peace and prosperity and as a protector of the existing international order probably came second in the list of main messages signalled to both domestic and international audiences.

The answer in large part lies on what you consider that order to be. China's commitment is not to a liberal global order, and certainly not a US led international liberal order (whatever that might be). The order that it is committed to protecting (and reforming) is one built on sovereignty, plurality, diversity and equality. It is one that China's leaders claim is based on the sovereignty principles that underpinned the original United Nations (UN) Charter, and which have long been enshrined by China in the form of the Five Principles of Peaceful Co-Existence (Xi, 2015c; 2017e). It is an order that should be built around strengthening those organizations of global governance that cannot be easily dominated by the US. There is also a desire to increase the scope and authority of organizations that China has been a key actor in establishing, like the Shanghai Cooperation Organisation (SCO) and cooperation between Brazil, Russia, India, China and South Africa (the BRICS) (Xi, 2018e). In specific issue areas, the stress on sovereignty suggests that governance should not be provided at the global level at all, and that each individual country should instead work out what works best for itself. What this means is that China's global governance reform agenda in some functional areas (like cybersecurity) is to ensure that there is no higher level of authority above the state level at all. In others (such as the environment), the key is voluntary acceptance of rules, goals and standards rather than their enforcement.

With all of this in mind, the rather common attempt to try to dichotomize between conceptions of China as either a status quo or a revisionist power is not particularly helpful. On one level, even where there is an agenda for reform, the aim is to do it through what a major Fudan University report on global governance called an 'incremental improvement strategy' (*zengliang gaijin zhanlue*) (Chen and Su, 2014), and to avoid creating global instability (Wang Qishan, 2019). After all, there are parts of the existing order that have served Chinese interests rather well over the years. On another level, the extent of Chinese commitment to the status quo depends on which parts of the status quo ante we are talking about. Parts of it are seen as being beneficial to China and therefore something that can and should be supported and strengthened. Other parts are seen as needing reform. And there are things that are not seen as being in line with Chinese thinking, interests and objectives where there is a greater desire to provide a more fundamental challenge.

Zhao Suisheng's (2018) idea of China as a 'revisionist stakeholder' might sound like a contradiction in terms, but it is one that aptly sums up the different strands in Chinese thinking and ambition. The intention is to do different things in different policy domains based on how the existing structures in each area serve Chinese interests (or not), the extent of Chinese power resources and capabilities, and the extent of potential followership from others in support of Chinese objectives (Johnston, 2019). We might suggest that in dominant Chinese conceptions, there are different types of ordering arrangements *beneath* the overarching sovereignty ordering principle. So instead of searching for a once and for all China challenge to the existing order and a single power transition from the current system to something else, it instead makes more sense to focus on transitions within the existing order and the contestation and negotiation within different parts of the existing order that this engenders (Goh, 2013).

Leadership and followership

This understanding contains within it the sixth argument. The intention might be to do things differently in different issue areas, but that doesn't mean that this will necessarily happen. And wanting to change the world and being increasingly willing to push for change is not the same thing as being able to do it. The basic point here is that followership (or the lack of it) matters. As noted a number of years ago before the rise of China and the other BRICS was being seriously studied:

> a leader-centered approach seriously distorts how we understand the nature of leadership in international politics. Focusing on the traits, interests, and capabilities of leaders and would-be challengers may tell us a great deal about which states are bound to be the most powerful in the international system at a particular historical conjuncture. But that approach tells us little about leadership, because it tells us little about the dynamics of followership – in other words, what drives followers to follow. (Cooper et al, 1991: 395)

And the inclination to follow often appears to be dependent on whether the leading power incorporates elements of the potential follower's interests and positions into its own agenda (Schirm, 2010). So, to fully understand how China's rise might ultimately affect the world, either at the global level or in terms of individual issue areas or bilateral relations, then it is important to also study what potential followers think and want, and what they think about what China thinks and wants.

Followership and opposition

The seventh argument is quite simply and uncontroversially that in the Xi era, while China might indeed have gained followership from some, concern about the consequences of China's rise has increased quite significantly in places where it was previously viewed with less apprehension. This is most clearly evident in Australasia and parts of Europe, but others are rethinking their overall stance on China too. This is partly a result of the material changes in the nature of the economic relationship with China. However, it is also in part a result of how China's future intent has been signalled to external audiences, and China's actual diplomatic behaviour. In this respect, the vigour with which the Belt and Road was promoted by China's leaders, particularly from around 2015–17, might turn out to be a strategic mistake. In combination with other big picture strategic thinking like the push to promote indigenous innovation and achieve global leadership in some key technologies – as encapsulated by the Made in China 2025 strategy (MIC2025) – it helped reinvigorate the idea of a 'China Threat' that so much of China's previous international political marketing and nation branding was designed to assuage. In some parts of the world, the way that a state directed soft power strategy has been implemented has also focused more attention on the state that does the messaging than the specifics of any message itself.

As will be shown throughout the following chapters, the COVID-19 pandemic played a role too. It resulted in questions about China's role in supply chains (discussed in detail in Chapter 4), and criticisms of the way that the Chinese authorities tried to control the narrative of China's role and responsibilities (discussed in Chapter 5). More generally, it simply fed into a general feeling that China was not to be trusted, coinciding with ongoing economic tensions with a number of states (both trade and investment ones), concerns about the detention of foreign researchers in China, and the introduction of a new National Security Law in Hong Kong. Indeed, it's hard to believe that the international response to the extension and deepening of control over Hong Kong would have been any different with or without the pandemic; the individual national responses were founded in very real and widely held concerns about what was being done.

As such, and at the risk of falling foul of my own warning that it is always too early to tell, the pandemic is best seen as an accelerant rather than a fundamental turning point. Within China itself, it made ongoing economic transitions even more difficult than they already were. It also resulted in a ramping up of official attempts to control the narrative of China's global role. From the outside, those who already did not trust China found even more things to disbelieve, and those who thought the Chinese political system was either inherently flawed or challenging or malevolent (or all three) found evidence to support their theories. In addition, as a McKinsey report argued, it also 'fast forwarded' pre-existing international economic trends by building on concerns that had already been heightened by increased Sino-US tensions:

> The US–China trade dispute raised risks and uncertainties, and about 30 to 50 percent of companies surveyed by various institutions in 2019 indicated that they were considering adjusting their supply chain strategies by seeking alternative sources or relocating production to other geographies. COVID-19 has intensified the debate, with several governments calling for companies in critical sectors to relocate their operations back to their home countries and announcing financial support packages to facilitate this. (Leung et al, 2020: 3)

In the US, the international politics of the pandemic also collided with the domestic politics of the 2020 presidential election campaign to further intensify the focus on China as a strategic challenge.

Followership, opposition and polarity

Add the differential Chinese approach to the global order with differential responses by different countries, and this has important consequences for the way that we think about power transitions and the nature of polarity (or the lack of it). A few observers have already identified a 'return to bipolarity' (Maher 2018; Tunsjø, 2018) as a result of both Chinese ambitions for change and a narrowing of the gap in power capabilities between the still predominant US and an ever more powerful China. Others suggest that if we aren't there yet, then the bipolarizing trends evident since the global financial crisis mean we could be there very soon (Yan, 2019). Certainly, the importance of the Sino-US relationship for both sides (and for the world) cannot be over-estimated, and the language deployed by each side towards each other very much sounds like the language of bipolarity at times. Examples include during the trade war, and the various accusations of who was to blame for the origins and spread of the coronavirus. In 2020, the Trump Administration published a strategy document on China outlining a 'competitive approach' designed to repel Chinese challenges to the economy, security and 'our values' that could certainly be read as a roadmap towards a bipolar future (White House, 2020). But is an increasingly polarized bilateral US–China relationship the same thing as bipolarity per se? The eighth and final argument is that it is not. Notwithstanding the hardening of positions on China outlined in the seventh argument, the future global order is unlikely to be one of clearly defined and shared single positions that split the world in two.

There is more to polarity than just the relationship between the poles/dominant powers. For it to be truly polar, we would need to see a coalescence of groups of states around each of the poles rather than just bilateral great power competition. And there are some signs of this. As will be argued in Chapters 3 and 6, Chinese strategy for global change explicitly differentiates between different types and groups of states based on how far they are seen as being amenable to accommodating or supporting Chinese objectives. The Occidentalist project also defines China positively against the negative West. There is a very explicit attempt to create dichotomies, and dichotomy is at the heart of bipolarity. The flip side of this occidental coin is, as we have just seen (and will see again in Chapter 1), that positions on China changed in much of the non-US West in the 2010s. The direction of travel is towards ever-greater suspicion and concern. When Josep Borrell, the EU's most senior foreign affairs representative, argues that the time is coming for Europe to 'choose sides' and be 'more robust' when it comes to China, then that sounds very much like dichotomization too (Wintour, 2020).

And yet, the idea of bipolarity still doesn't seem to fit the ongoing transformation of power and alliances at the global level. Choosing sides means choosing a position on China. This is a position that you might share with others. But it doesn't automatically follow that you will be fully allied with those others on all things related to China at all times as a result. And as the international politics of the pandemic revealed quite clearly, there is no inevitable zero-sum game when it comes to international support for the US and China. The decline in support for US leadership (and indeed, the provision of it) did not simply and automatically lead to a transfer of allegiances, support and leadership to China instead. Instead, it proved quite possible to be critical of both Beijing and Washington at the same time, and to see faults in what both were doing (and indeed, to be critical of what other governments were doing or not doing at the same time too). Or even to echo Mercutio's dying condemnation of both sides of the familial based bipolar cleavage in *Romeo and Juliet*.

Despite some convergence, there has been no single approach to China even among states that share broadly similar world views and political structures (indeed, there has not been a single response *within* individual states either). We have already seen a number of Western liberal economies supporting new Chinese initiatives in the provision of global economic goods (through joining the AIIB for example), despite hostility to them from the US. Yet many of those same Western liberal actors have rejected Chinese attempts to establish its position as the basis for discussions on cybersecurity and take diametrically opposed positions to China on most human rights issues (Sceats, 2015). Conversely, at the highest possible level of generalization, it is fair to suggest that China is more likely to be viewed in a positive light in those places that share China's distrust of Western liberal democracies than in those Western states themselves. That said, not everybody in the developing world sees China in a wholly positive light, and the alternative to China as wholly negative. Even those who share Chinese dissatisfaction with the existing order do so with different degrees of enthusiasm, and end up on opposite sides of policy cleavages on other issue areas (Liu Ming, 2016). This includes the other members of the BRICS. Initial responses to the COVID-19 pandemic suggested that many developing countries were looking to China for help and leadership that the US and Europe were not providing. However, reports of discrimination against African residents of Guangzhou in April 2020 qualified this response. Rather than presage a new China–Africa partnership, there were instead (or alongside it) sprouts of new tensions as officials from Togo, Nigeria, South Africa, Kenya, Ghana and the African Union made various forms of official complaints (Marks, 2020).

If it isn't bipolarity, what about multipolarity? This is in fact the most typical explanation of what the world is becoming in Chinese analyses of global order. This might in part reflect the differential tactics deployed to deal with different parts of the world and differential Chinese capacity in different issue areas that are discussed in more detail in Chapter 3; multipolarity as strategy and goal rather than an observation of the current reality. But it also has resonance with the way that power is becoming distributed as relative power capabilities continue to shift. However, while the multi in multipolarity helpfully points to an increasing number of actors with the ability to shape the world, the notion of polarity remains problematic. It still carries with it the same connotations of states cohering around one or other pole of attraction and, by the very definition, being repelled by the alternative. This is an analytical and linguistic hangover from the Cold War when states came together and more or less stuck together across issue areas. Of course, not all states chose a side, occasionally one would defect from their polar alliance, and relationships had different levels of comprehensiveness. But the very different economic structures in the two different poles combined with the threat of war meant that you would not be attracted to one pole for military security issues and the other for economic relations.

Perhaps it is time to move away from trying to reuse concepts and terms designed to explain a previous era and come up with new ones instead. Ones that can capture the complexities of a world with some bipolar characteristics that lacks the bloc or camp-type relationships of the previous bipolar era. We see increasingly sharp divisions when it comes to questions relating to fundamental values. There does seem to be something akin to a form of polarity here in the form of a set of countries that increasingly share a rejection of what they think China is promoting, even if they don't always agree on what the alternative should look like. And on the other side a number of countries share China's broad critique of the status quo ante, but also do not necessarily have a shared vision of what they think the alternative should look like either. While reliance on China as an economic partner is also being increasingly questioned, pragmatic practicalities and necessities mean that a sudden change to polar type economic relations remains unlikely.

While the Cold War forced states into an exclusive relationship with their polar partner, the current global order encourages promiscuity.[10] It is entirely possible to have strong economic relations with as many countries as you want, and see China as a crucial future economic partner while at the same time viewing the US as the most important security partner. Or to agree with China's critique of power in international financial institutions but fundamentally disagree with Chinese positions on redefining human rights. These are not poles in the sense that to be attracted to one means you are repulsed by others, but different sites or nodes of authority in the global order, with the constellation of power and the constitution of alliances varying depending on the issue (Womack, 2016).

If we think in terms of what this might mean in concrete terms, despite the call for Europe to make a choice, for a number of Western states China might be thought of as simultaneously being: a potential partner in terms of environmental governance; a reform inclined but not revolutionary stakeholder of the existing system of economic governance; a challenger when it comes to issues like the international human rights regime (and also how we conceive of and practice international development); a potential governance competitor promoting non-liberal norms and principles in governance domains such as cybersecurity and Artificial Intelligence (AI); and a potential threat in terms of the ownership and development of key technologies and economic sectors. Indeed, such a differential approach was enshrined in a new EU strategy paper on relations with China in 2019:

> China is, simultaneously, in different policy areas, a cooperation partner with whom the EU has closely aligned objectives, a negotiating partner with whom the EU needs to find a balance of interests, an economic competitor in the pursuit of technological leadership, and a systemic rival promoting alternative models of governance. (European Commission, 2019: 1)

And all of these different potential sets of relationships co-exist while China is also a major economic trade and investment partner as well.

These different faces of Chinese power – to borrow again from Lampton (2008) – are even more stark in other parts of the world. For example, for a number of states in Southeast Asia, China is both the most important economic partner and also the single biggest potential security threat at the same time. It is a massive exaggeration to say that for a number of its neighbours, China occupies the roles that both Germany (biggest regional economic partner) and Russia (biggest security threat) play in Europe at the same time. But it is an exaggeration that highlights the problem that many regional elites face in responding to the very uneven consequences of China's rise. The search for parsimony and clarity is entirely understandable. But if the real world is messy and complex, then trying to impose clarity using concepts developed to describe previous eras isn't always wholly helpful.

Intents, arguments and extents

This might of course turn out to be a temporary state of affairs. The whole point of encouraging repatriating or relocating production is to reduce reliance and dependence on China. Though it's hard to see how this could become total, it could significantly impact on the distribution of global economic power. And in the wake of the pandemic, decoupling from China for security reasons was actively touted as a policy recommendation beyond the US (Rogers et al, 2020). Chapter 4 outlines some of the potential economic scenarios resulting from the pandemic, and while some of these could increase China's potential for economic leadership, others point in the opposite direction. Moreover, leaders change, and not just in China. When they do, policies, strategies and objectives can change too. The step back from global leadership in the US might not last forever, and neither might the more assertive tone of those who speak on behalf of the Chinese state in a particular way. Certainly, in the past, the way messages from China have been disseminated have changed if they are thought to be damaging China's image, and thus the ability to get what China's leaders want. So we are back to the second extent, and the caveat that it is too early to tell. Indeed, we have reached the point where the 'three intents' and 'eight arguments', when qualified by the limitations detailed in the 'four extents', provide the basis for what follows in the rest of this study.

Studying China's Rise

Emphasizing the need to focus on how we study China might sound like an invitation to walk down an already well-trodden path. After all, IR debates on China's rise (and there are many of them) have devoted considerable time and space to discussions of the relative merits of realist assertions that China simply cannot rise peacefully (Mearscheimer, 2006; Allison, 2017), and liberal expectations that this rise can indeed be accommodated by the existing liberal global order (Ikenberry, 2008). Of course, dig a little deeper and it's not hard to find exceptions, as a range of different theoretical positions have been deployed to try and analyse and understand China, and predict what China's rise means for the future of the world. Nevertheless, if you step back and take a panoramic view of the writings on China's rise as a whole, then the continued dominance of these two major theoretical contenders is rather conspicuous.

There are good reasons for this. These two theoretical positions are not only the most often used in IR scholarship, but have also been the most influential in terms of debating policy options (particularly in the US). Even so, many have found their dominance rather unsatisfying. So unsatisfying, in fact, that some have questioned their efficacy for understanding China at all. Rather than truly being universal international theories, so the argument goes, they are instead culturally and historically specific with realism in particular – but not just realism – built on a study of a European history that has nothing to do with China's or Asia's experiences (Hui, 2004). As they are 'inductively derived from the European experience of the past four centuries, during which Europe was the locus and generator of war, innovation, and wealth' (Kang, 2003: 57), why should we expect them to have explanatory power when applied to a very different part of the world with very different experiences of statehood and conflict? Even IR theories that have been developed in opposition to the mainstream tend to do so by building on European history and overwhelmingly were developed by Western theorists (Acharya and Buzan, 2007).

Although this and the following chapter share a degree of the dissatisfaction with mainstream theories that has inspired the search for a Chinese school, they have more modest ambitions than those engaged in new theory building. Chapter 2 will focus on what the study of domestic politics and political economy can tell us about China's global role and future ambitions. It contains a particular emphasis on diverse voices and actors, and how what is often used as evidence of intent can be a consequence of something else altogether. The primary aim of this chapter is simply to outline how and why different types of scholarship result in very different conclusions about the nature of China's rise. Here the focus is on searching for explanations that go beyond the usual emphasis in the existing IR literature between different theoretical starting points. Where you are writing from (and who you are writing for) also seems to play a role in shaping the way that China's rise is studied. This seems to be particularly (but not only) significant if the aim is to try and influence a policy audience rather than just an academic one. The starting point of the researcher's first encounter with China might also have an influence, as different research questions have tended to emerge as the dominant 'theme of the time' in different eras. Of course, research agendas can and do evolve, but first perceptions and first questions might have at least some lasting influence on some researchers.

The importance of the basic research question suggests that the distinctions between different IR theoretical positions of whatever complexion might be less important than the distinction between those asking questions about China's global impact, and those who instead focus on questions relating to domestic political, economic, and societal change. This can be shown by establishing an admittedly extremely rough typology of four different ways in which China is studied to show how the divergent focuses of each generate different research agendas that are built on different methods and theories, and utilize different evidential resources. Given these variations, it is really not surprising that these separate endeavours end up in dissimilar places. Nor does it *necessarily* matter. It would be a rather narrow academia if we all did the same thing. However, the argument here is that it really does matter when it comes to the study of China and its rise; and perhaps matters more than it does for the study of other parts of the world. It matters because what China might or will become in the future remains very much a live topic of debate. And the different futures that these approaches can generate are so diverse that they can be all but impossible to reconcile in any meaningful way. As one long-term and highly respected student of Chinese politics asked rhetorically in a private communication after witnessing two simultaneous debates on a professional discussion forum, was he alone in wondering how China could be destined for imminent global dominance and domestic financial collapse at the same time?[1]

Global power is partly innate and internally derived, emerging, for example, from the domestic build-up of military or economic resources. But power is also partly externally granted and bestowed from the outside, as others adjust their behaviour and ambitions based on calculations of power transitions. How we think of Chinese power, then, becomes an important component of that power itself if it results in real-world policies that either facilitate or attempt to block the attainment of (perceived) Chinese interests. Such calculations require establishing reliable understandings (and indices) of relative power capabilities. Hence the attempt to construct such methods noted in the Introduction. However, even if you can establish reliable statistics to start from, calculations are further complicated by less tangible and unquantifiable assumptions of future trends and intent; predictions of the likely future development of both the power resources themselves, and how they might be used to achieve what ends.

What all this suggests, then, is the importance of combining material and more cognitive based approaches to studying China. Of course, the study of international political economy (IPE) has long had a tradition of incorporating the significance of ideas to form varieties of 'constructivist IPE'. In general, these tend to focus on explaining why certain sets of ideas about the economy come to dominate in certain settings, or on how the promotion of a set of ideas underpins certain economic structures and power relations. Most often this has been applied to the acceptance, promotion and persistence of neoliberalism, and how perceptions and ideas shape the policy choices facing decision makers (Hay and Rosamond, 2002). However, the focus in this chapter is somewhat different and draws on how thinking about security and peace can be relevant for political economy, and the key issue of trust. Or more often, the lack of trust.

The politics of futurology

Trust in International Relations

Trust is at the heart of much of what is written in IR. As Rathbun (2009: 346) suggests, 'This is because many of the core differences between major theorists of international relations stem from often implicit assumptions about how states and statesmen respond to what social psychologists call "social uncertainty", a lack of knowledge about others' intentions'. A basic trust in the nature of humanity is (or should) be central to liberal thinking. Asking the right questions relating to the trustworthiness of others and their commitment to the existing order (or not) is part of the basic assumptions of one of the defining texts of realism over the likelihood of conflict (Morgenthau, 1973).[2] And Wendt's (1992) argument that the capability and intention of friends is assessed very differently from that of enemies is also a fundamental starting point of much scholarship. This is why games about cooperation and collaboration – for example, the stag hunt/stags and hares – have persisted as one of the starting points for teaching politics and IR. And whatever the theoretical preference, a defining element of the study of trust is that it entails projecting the future; predictions that can go terribly wrong if trust is assumed that turns out to be misplaced.

The primary concerns in the trust literature are how to assess the consequences of ceding control of one's interests to others (Hoffman, 2002), and how best to calculate the consequences of taking a risk by factoring in how other key actors might respond and behave (Wheeler, 2018). A third strand of scholarship, much influenced by Cold War studies, is the consequences for the international order of deep-seated and long-lasting mutual distrust between key global actors (Kydd, 2005). While not suggesting that we are in a new Cold War, this emphasis on mistrust is an appropriate starting point when it comes to looking at China. In this study, though, the attention moves away from security to political economy. Here, the focus is on how conceptions of friends, enemies, trust (and future projections) provide a basis for understanding how China's long-term objectives and intentions are received, perceived and parsed by others.

If China was not thought of as a likely challenger to the status quo, for example, then the growth of Chinese investment wouldn't be viewed with so much interest and concern (Tingley et al, 2015), and taken as evidence of this pre-assumed challenge. The way that an increase in Chinese investment is perceived is not just shaped by the nature of that investment itself, but filtered through a broader understanding of the nature of the China 'threat' to the recipient country or the global order more generally (Zeng and Li, 2019).

Indeed, as will be shown in Chapter 4 in the discussion of FDI, while the increase of Chinese Outward Foreign Direct Investment (COFDI) has indeed been dramatic and had significant impacts on a number of countries, the stock of COFDI in many Western economies is much lower than the way that it is spoken about often suggests. Mistrust is the starting point of a number of perspectives of China, and neither past Chinese behaviour that points to China's accommodation with the existing order, nor the reassurance offered by Chinese leaders of their pacific intent, is sufficient to provide the basis for trust building. As Rathbun (2017: 691) argues (though not in specific relation to China) 'power, not past action, is how states gauge intentions and judge credibility'. Moreover, trust in China's future behaviour actually declined as the argument that China's socialization into the existing order had failed to come about gained more supporters in the years after the global financial crisis (Yang Xiangfeng, 2017). As a result, Zakaria (2020: 52) argues that something akin to a bipartisan position emerged in Washington that China represents 'a vital threat' to the US, and that this results in 'an almost instinctive hostility' to all that China says and does. As we shall see in Chapter 2, this lack of trust goes both ways and perceptions *from* China (rather than just perceptions *of* China) also play a significant role in shaping the way that China's rise evolves.

Studies of trust in security studies are inextricably linked to understandings of the importance of the 'strategic signalling' of intentions, and how these signals are received by their targets – once again, with security and the threat of war the main concern. Here there is a crossover with notions of the credibility and capacity to do what is being signalled that is also at the heart of deterrence theories (Jervis, 1982/83). Once more moving from security to political economy, we can take these basic ideas and apply them to the way that the Chinese leadership has signalled its capability to emerge as a new type of economic actor, and whether these signals are deemed to be credible. For those who fundamentally lack trust in China's future intentions and perceive China as a future (if not present) danger – either to an individual nation or the existing global order more generally – such 'enemy images' of China shape the way that signals are perceived (Jervis, 1970; Wheeler, 2018). Those that fit into the enemy image are seen as credible and sometimes even inevitable, while those that don't fit the image are ignored or discounted.

(Mis)Trust in the future

One of the reasons perceptions are particularly important is that when China is being debated, the focus is still often on the future; what China might become rather than what it already is. There is nothing intrinsically wrong with such futurology at all. On the contrary, successful foresight is better than subsequently ruing that in hindsight you would have done things differently. Trying to predict what might happen and planning for different scenarios are clearly important tasks for all policy makers, and simply waiting to see what happens before acting is not a wise course of action.

That said, a future focus is not problem free. At the most basic level, if the debate is about the future, then conclusions are impossible to prove. David Kang (2003) has pointed out that even when evidence is presented to show that China has in fact most often showed an acceptance of the existing global order rather than a challenge to it, it is impossible to convince those who argue that things will be different when China really does have the power to push for change in the future. As Pan Chengxin (2012) argues, for any paradigm to be effective for its believer, it needs to have ways of discounting evidence that points to alternative explanations or predictions. Moreover, from a certain theoretical viewpoint, China's recent past is less important in thinking about the future than what happened in other parts of the world in more distant pasts; what Kirshner (2010: 59) calls 'a realist cliché to appeal to Thucydides' and the history of previous great power rivalries.

Futurology becomes even more problematic when one vision becomes dominant and contending narratives are ignored, thus resulting in preparations for a very limited number of scenarios rather than all reasonable outcomes. Or alternatively, as Irvine (2016) who has conducted the most extensive and rigorous analysis of different studies of China's futures notes, when predictions polarize around conflicting extremes, leaving little room for more nuanced intermediary positions. In 2006, Kenneth Lieberthal (2006) warned against making too many assumptions about China's future arguing that 'no major country in the world has the breadth of feasible trajectories that China has over the coming fifteen years'. Although times have changed since then, and some trajectories look more likely than others, the basic message that different futures are possible remains salient. So why, then, do certain views come to dominate debates at different times in different places?

Location, perspective and interest

Can where you are writing from be a determining factor? The instinctive response is to say no, and to point to the wide varieties of approaches and conclusions that can be found in any single country where China is studied. Different types of engagement with China can also generate different responses from within the same part of the world. For example, Peyrouse (2016) points to the co-existence of 'Sinophilia and Sinophobia' in Central Asia where there is simultaneously a desire to gain the economic benefits that China offers and also a fear of China's geopolitical clout and intentions. Within individual countries, the impact that China has can vary massively between economic sectors. At the same time as some in Ghana, Zambia and elsewhere were welcoming Chinese aid and debt forgiveness, others in the same countries were complaining about labour abuses in Chinese owned enterprises or losing their jobs through competition from China (Spring, 2009). There are even differences within a single economic sector depending on where you fit into the production and supply chain.

So it is with considerable trepidation that I suggest location can matter when it comes to explaining why certain views come to have more purchase in popular perceptions and policy debates at certain times. Fortunately, though, others agree. The 'National Narratives and the Rise of China' project run jointly by Chatham House and the Konrad-Adenauer-Stiftung starts from the assumption that while there might not be a single story and understanding of China within any individual country, there are nevertheless significant cross country differences that impact on scholarship and policy making:

> In the decades ahead, the single most significant game-changer for the future of the global system is the rise of China. But the US, Europe and Canada do not understand the implications of China's rise in the same way which has implications, not only for the future international system, but also for the future of the West, and especially, for the transatlantic relationship.[3]

This is partly because different analytical approaches dominate in different parts of the world. The above noted dichotomy between realism and liberalism in explaining (the consequences of) China's rise, for example, is more evident in some academes than others. It is also because the implications of a changing China are differentially felt across the globe. The significance of China is understandably more real and obvious in East Asia and China's other neighbourhoods than it is elsewhere. Here, the growth of the Chinese economy has long had a profound impact on both the structure of the regional political economy, and on the developmental trajectories of individual regional states. Moreover, it is here that China is also a potential security challenge as well as a key economic actor for a number of states and territories.

The idea of a China threat in general – not just a military one – has largely been much less pronounced in Europe than in large parts of Asia and in the US. To be sure there have been times when specific threats have been identified in specific areas (such as European steel industries). But by and large the economic potential that China was thought to provide – and was expected to provide in greater scales in the future – was the dominant narrative. And in the wake of the financial crisis, the prospect of attracting Chinese finance became ever more urgent and attractive too. Or, this *was* the general view. As we shall see later, from around the mid-2010s the argument that China's rise was creating an increasing number of challenges and potential long-term problems for Europe began to gain increasing support.

This historical position results from three factors. First, quite simply, Europe is not a security actor in Asia in the way that the US is. Any regional military conflict in the region would clearly have an indirect impact on Europe – in the disruption of global trade for example – but would not likely involve direct military confrontation. The same cannot be said with certainty for the US. Second, if China is a challenge to the current global order, then it is the US position as the predominant global power that is most clearly and most directly at risk. Clearly, the EU and European states are important stakeholders in the liberal global order, but that is not the same as being the predominant power facing (or looking for) potential challengers.

This is very much related to the third issue; the acceptance that there is only so much that Europeans can do to change the evolution of China's futures. To be sure, there may be ways that Europeans can encourage change in specific policy areas. But as the former UK Foreign Secretary Jeremy Hunt argued in 2019, 'I think that very few countries have any leverage at all when it comes to what happens inside China'. Hunt also argued that 'talking too loudly and too publicly about our human rights concerns just means that we lose access to senior people in the Chinese government' and thus are unable to exert any influence at all.[4] These twin positions have resulted in complaints from human rights groups that they are simply an excuse for not doing anything politically in order to make economic gains. This might be true. But a recognition of the limits of European power and influence does play at least some role in thinking about what *can* be done, rather than what *should* be done.

Given the impact of location on this specific observer, it is very much as an outsider that I suggest that the idea of a China threat has been more evident and longstanding in the US than in other parts of the West. It might also be the case that the world looks more bipolar from some locations than others. There also seems to be a much stronger feeling that a change in US policy towards China could make a difference too: a difference to the nature of the challenge from China, to the challenge to the global order, and maybe to the nature of Chinese politics itself. And the desire to try and influence a policy audience helps explain the intensity, volume and extremity of certain types of writing on China and its futures. It might also help explain Irvine's (2016) observation of the tendency to polarize. In order to get a voice heard in a crowded market for opinions, there can be a tendency to go to extremes to make a point that counters the opposite position. Suggesting that some US based work on China is intended to influence a policy audience to change track on China is not the result of forensic investigation. Many writers are very clear that they are trying to 'inform a US policy on Asia capable of responding to dynamic change' (Keller and Rawski, 2007: 4). It is also notable that many of the more extreme warnings about the consequences of China's rise are published by Regnery, which explicitly asserts that its books 'take pride in exposing the liberal bias that so often pervades the "mainstream" media'.[5] These works are in many ways *about* China, but *for* Washington.

Beyond the West, and at a rather massive level of generalization, the idea that China is viewed more positively in the developing world probably does have an element of truth. For example, while there are clearly dangers in aggregating Africa together into a single entity with a single response to China, there is more willingness to embrace China's national image promotion on the continent than in the West (Madrid-Morales, 2017). A shared dissatisfaction with the distribution of power in global institutions and the dominance of Western great powers also points to a convergence of world views and a common purpose that goes back longer than the recent growth of Chinese investment (Taylor, 2006). That China and developing countries share a common history of (anti)colonization is also something that is deliberately promoted as the basis of a special relationship (Alden and Alves, 2008).

Changing China, changing perceptions

The specific economic relationship that China has with any individual country can play an important role in shaping dominant narratives. For example, studies of the early impact of Chinese investment in Africa found that the extent to which China was depicted as a challenge or opportunity largely depended on the existing political economy of the partner country. On a very simple level, developing countries gained from trading with China if they were not in direct competition with Chinese actors – for example if they produced and exported things that China imported. But countries with existing strong export industries in the same sectors as China faced considerable challenges (Kaplinsky et al, 2007).

The growth of Chinese investment into other developing economies not only resulted in a rethinking of China in those recipient countries, but in other parts of the world as well. As will be discussed in more detail in Chapter 4, it began to change dominant views in Europe over the consequences of China's economic rise (Men and Barton, 2011). But it is the growth of investment into the developed world itself that has done more to generate a rethink. In Australia, longstanding concern over immigration from China gave way to a new era of concern built on fears of economic dependence as Chinese demand for Australian raw materials boomed. This in turn also quickly expanded into an arguably more significant alarm about Chinese interference in Australian politics (Goodman, 2017; Fitzgerald, 2018). China's security interests in the South Pacific also play a role in shaping attitudes towards China – not least in an era when the security commitment of the US in the region could not be taken for granted. Brady (2019) points to similar trends and issues in changing New Zealand perspectives of China. In Europe (and in Germany in particular), a significant and rapid increase in Chinese purchases of high-profile high-tech companies also generated a concomitant increase in concerns over Chinese objectives and strategies. The lack of reciprocal access to the Chinese market, and the prospect of the BRI altering economic and political geographies in eastern and central Europe also played a role (Wübbeke et al, 2016). Here too, what started as a primarily economic issue developed into a discussion about Chinese political influence now and in the future (Benner et al, 2018).

The suggestion in the Introduction was that the COVID-19 pandemic concentrated existing thinking and accelerated existing trends. It the long run, it is likely that it will be used as evidence to promote questioning or negative opinions by those who already held them rather than fundamentally changing minds. But that is important in itself; in particular, when it is combined with the argument that previous understandings have been proved wrong and previous policies have not worked. At the end of March 2020 in the UK, for example, Damian Green (2020) who was effectively deputy premier in the second half of 2017, argued that once the crisis was over, the UK would have to rethink its position on China: 'Essentially, for the past ten years, British policy has proceeded on the assumption that the economic gain from linking our economy closely with the Chinese was worth the obvious risks ... It was not a dishonourable bargain to try to make, but it has not worked.'

The following week the Foreign Affairs Select Committee, a parliamentary body charged with holding the UK government to account on foreign policy issues,[6] published a report condemning the 'disinformation' provided by the Chinese state including 'deliberate misleading of the WHO and scientists in other countries' (FAC, 2020). Writing in an individual capacity in the *Mail on Sunday*, the committee chairman, Conservative MP Tom Tugendhat (2020), went even further and posed a rather provocative question both to the readership and his own party leadership:

> Now, more than ever, Britain needs to consider its relationship with China, our hunger for its goods and investment. Do we want to import China's authoritarian value system as well as its products? Or should we work with other free nations and reduce our growing dependence on this dictatorship?

As the UK had not seen the same type of debate over China that had emerged in in other parts of the Western world, the pandemic provided a useful context for those who were already concerned about China (and concerned about the UK's policy towards China) to air those concerns in a new way. But perceptions were changing in any case, and there had been a growing tendency before the pandemic to not just voice concern about China, but also on the essence and nature of the UK's China policy. Even without the pandemic, it is extremely likely that the UK government would have responded in exactly the same way that it did to the implementation of the new National Security Law in Hong Kong in the summer of 2020. And it is also extremely likely that the Chinese government would have responded to this response in exactly the same way too.

Shaping perceptions: first encounters and changing questions

From area studies to beyond

Maintaining the self-awareness that the analysis in this book logically needs to be turned back on itself, if the argument that how one first encountered China might have a residual impact on research, it is only fair to say something about my own first encounters. My first trip to China was in 1984 to spend a year at Beijing Normal University as part of the first cohort of students on a brand-new four-year degree in Politics and East Asian Studies offered in the department of Politics at Newcastle University under the tutelage of David Goodman. This was a period when studying China was still a very niche operation overwhelmingly carried out in area studies departments and centres in a relatively small number of universities. Interest in studying China was largely driven by language, culture, history and philosophy, with development studies one of the more important sub-fields of enquiry. In Europe more broadly, Brødsgaard (2007, 35) argues that 'contemporary political, social and economic studies' were not even seen as constituting 'proper' China studies, but something else instead, with social science-based China studies only really beginning to become institutionally established (rather than just done by scattered individuals) in the mid-1980s and into the 1990s. Outside these area studies centres, while there were individual China scholars in various departments, there was in general a separation of the study of China from the discipline of IR. There was also rather limited external interest in academic studies of China from user communities with Japan seen as the potential next (economic) superpower and the major economic opportunity for graduates. Indeed, it's probably fair to say that Japanese studies was dominant in Asian area studies at that time.

If we jump forward three decades, then the way that this has changed might begin to tell us something about the different questions that are being asked and the different ways in which China is being studied. There is now massive external interest in China from a range of different non-academic communities (which is in part met by the growth of China research in think tanks) and an overall significant increase in studying China. However, how this ever more interesting China is studied has changed considerably. There has been something of a decline in the popularity of all area studies programmes (and not just Asian area studies), but there has been a big increase in the provision of Chinese language training. This is in no small part a result of Chinese now being offered alongside a range of disciplinary majors in joint honours programmes, or simply as an optional module in degrees that otherwise have nothing to do with China at all (including in some places that used to have specialist China or Asia centres).

Language, culture and history are still big drivers of interest in studying China, but now politics, IR and broadly defined economics and business studies are also very significant. Beyond language studies, there has also been an expansion of China related offerings in disciplinary departments (either whole modules or sections of them) and a growth of students studying China related issues at master's level. Again, many of these are now in generic disciplinary degrees rather than Asia or China specific ones. And as the rise of China has become arguably the single biggest IR topic of our time, there is considerable interest from scholars who have spent their previous careers focusing on non-China related issues. While the scale and timing of this evolution in scholarship differs from place to place, in general we can identify similar expansions of more disciplinary informed China scholarship outside the area studies tradition in most places where China is studied (Walder, 2004; Guo Sujian, 2013). As Pieke (2013) argues in his study of China studies in the Netherlands, China has become 'mainstreamed' into disciplinary scholarship.

The end of the 'China Hand'?

One final comparison between scholarship then and now is the difference in what can be done (and how easily). The number of online web resources provided by the Chinese government (often in multiple languages) stands in stark contrast to the written forms of information that were available in the 1980s. The China National Knowledge Infrastructure (which has been liberally utilized in preparing this manuscript) provides the sort of access in minutes to Chinese academic writings that would have taken years to get hold of before. Interaction with Chinese scholars is commonplace and relatively easy to arrange, and many of them have become regular publishers in English language journals and valued participants in international conferences and workshops.

In many ways, then, life is much easier. But in one way it is not. While the research problem was once finding access to information and interpretations, it is now how to cope with the mountain of information that is not just available, but often actively sent to inboxes (whether you have asked for it or not). Moreover, work on China has branched out far from the traditional and usual journals and book publishers of China related research into disciplinary based outlets. To be sure, good scholarship on China was always published in disciplinary journals. But the scope defined both in the number of articles published and also the number of disciplines that focus on China has increased massively since 1984. In truth, it was probably never really possible to keep totally on top of what was going on in China. But it certainly isn't today. Staying up to date with Chinese domestic politics alone is probably now all but impossible, let alone trying to be equally aware of Chinese international interactions. And all of this is before trying to separate out what is research, what is less well-informed opinion, and what is the re-statement of government preferences.

Add all of this together, and it creates a rather significant obstacle to realizing the assertion that it is important to try and link the international and the domestic in the study of China. Indeed, as argued in the Introduction, even if the focus is limited to the international alone, the parameters of what is considered to be part of China's global strategic action is now so broad that it is hard to stay up to date and informed. Maybe ironically, while the increased complexity and all-round impact of China across a range of issue areas means that the demand for 'China Hands' increases, that very same complexity and impact (and sources of information on it) points to the end of the 'China Hand', and the rise of the specialist instead.

Different phases, different questions

This transformation from 1984 shows how different questions have been asked about China as China changes. More important, the dominant question of the time, and who is trying to answer it also changed, resulting in the rise and fall of the relative importance of certain types of scholarship in general debates. Some voices become louder and/or more listened to, and others become harder to hear and/or side-lined. In the mid-1980s, for students of Chinese politics, the main focus was probably on trying to understand how different constellations of power were forming and reforming around a number of key questions.[7] Arguably most importantly were 'highly contentious policy disputes, such as those over the tolerable limits of free-market activity and private accumulation of wealth, the severity of the problem of "spiritual pollution" posed by the influx of Western ideas and influences, and the proper boundaries of free expression' (Baum, 1996: 5). Underpinning much of this interest was the question – and often real doubt – of whether these marketizing reforms were consistent with a commitment to socialism and one-party rule by a communist party. And this in turn was part of a wider interest in whether it was possible for the CCP to fundamentally shift the basis of its legitimacy from its revolutionary past to something new, and how it could justify now embracing some things that it used to be implacably opposed to.

Typically, the study of Chinese politics and economic reform was a separate endeavour from research on China's international relations. China was an important global actor in the 1980s, but using Shambaugh's (2013) distinction, it wasn't considered to be a global power. To be sure, it had held a formal and privileged position of global power since assuming the China seat on the UN Security Council in 1971. However, the main focus of interest was China's role as a willing pawn in power balancing between the superpowers, with few studies going beyond 'strategic triangle' interpretations in the mid to late 1980s.[8] Crucially, IR was rather narrowly defined with the focus very much on diplomatic relations between China and other states, carried out by foreign ministries and heads of states. Or put another way, the politics of international economic interactions was not yet high on research agendas (in the way that it already was with the study of many of China's regional neighbours).

The distinction between internal and external studies and between diplomacy and international economics began to blur through the way that China's leaders incrementally inserted China into the capitalist global economy. In addition to the above noted concern with spiritual pollution within China, the linkage between economic reform and international relations took on greater importance. While China was not given anywhere near the same 'free ride' into the global political economy that the US granted its earlier Asian Cold War allies (Cumings, 1987), China benefitted from primarily leaning towards the US, but with the chances of mending fences with the Soviet Union never fully taken off the agenda (Mori, 1988) ensuring that its support could not be taken for granted. Until 1989 and Tiananmen, perceptions of China in the US as a common enemy of the USSR helped provide a 'favourable international environment' for China's (re)engagement with the capitalist global economy (Pearson, 1999: 174).

While China's military modernization of course played a role in turning heads, it was the growth of the Chinese economy and in particular the growth of China's international economic interactions that were the key. Pretty much everything to do with China in the post-Mao era can be assessed as being remarkable. I suggest that the shift from the relative unimportance and almost total neglect of international economic exchanges to their centrality in the study of China's global role really does deserve that adjective. It's not just that the scope of these exchanges increased, or the speed at which they grew that are remarkable (though they are). It's that before about 1984, beyond a rather small cohort of specialists,[9] IPE type questions weren't being asked at all in general scholarship on China.

At the time, 1989 seemed to change everything. For a generation, the first contact they had with China was the extensive media coverage of the demonstrations in Tiananmen Square, with questions relating to human rights emerging as a major theme of the time. This was a theme that was to subsequently inform debates over the nature of China's economic rise (and the West's role in that rise) for many years. The subsequent collapse of communist party rule in regimes further west also reinvigorated older questions relating to legitimacy and regime stability. Trying to explain how and why the CCP survives when others fell still remains an important strand of scholarship on China today (Fewsmith and Nathan, 2018). In hindsight, though, the end of the Cold War was the more significant turning point, given that the international isolation of China that looked likely in the summer of 1989 turned out to be rather shallow and short lived. With the need to balance the Soviet Union no longer an issue, there was no need for the West to play the 'China Card' and accommodate China's wishes for geostrategic reasons (Sullivan, 1992). This created a space for attention to turn to whether the West might be able to shape China's evolution, both domestically and as an international actor. The resulting focus on human rights, though, was both mitigated and complicated by China's emergence as a global economic actor.

The 1990s became a decade in which theoretical questions about how best to try and manage China's rise came to the fore as headline debates over whether to engage or contain China were built on liberal and realist assumptions about the consequences of each. The desire to change China's political/human rights regime continued to be important, with questions raised over the morality of dealing with an ever more globally economically engaged China, thus allowing it to grow in ways that might consolidate regime legitimacy and single party rule. Notably, though, global order questions also began to be asked more frequently too, with the focus on what an unchanged China might mean for the global order, and the efficacy of different approaches in trying to manage the nature of China's rise for others (as well as for China). Equally notable, the focus of futurology shifted too. Rather than (just) asking questions about China's future, attention now began to turn to the consequent implications for the rest of the world, and particularly the nature of US global domination. Only four years after Tiananmen, Overholt (1993) was identifying China as a rising economic superpower, while Friedberg (1993–94: 13) was predicting that China would 'probably' become the world's biggest economy in 2010 leading to 'troubling' implications for Asian regional security.

The relative weight of voice of theoretically driven and world order questions increased as both the nature of the order itself changed, and the nature of China's global economic profile transformed. Much Chinese scholarship points to the global financial crisis as the key turning point. In truth, Ramo's (2004b) identification of a Beijing Consensus preceded the global crisis, and the study of power transition and the study of China had already become intimate bedfellows before 2008. That said, the crisis didn't exactly undermine the idea of a power shift, nor the idea that the way that the Chinese economy had been organized might provide a better option for other developing states than neoliberal prescriptions. Even John Williamson (2010), the original architect of the concept of the 'Washington Consensus', argued that a key consequence of the crisis had been to delegitimize neoliberalism and to strengthen the appeal of strong state alternatives such as China's. Henceforth, questions relating to China's impact, while still retaining a future focus, were increasingly predicated on the assumption that China was already a major global power (albeit one still on an upward trajectory). What any China-influenced alternative world would or could look like was typically left undefined (Christensen, 2015: 56), with the emphasis often on the desire to overthrow rather than on what would come next. Nevertheless, despite its fuzziness, the concept of a fundamental China challenge to the way the world was organized and governed became an important meme within the China risen narrative, with some pointing to its inevitability in an undefined but not too distant future (Jacques, 2009).

Studying China's rise: different types of scholarship

The point of this discussion is not to provide a comprehensive overview of China's evolution since the early 1980s – that would take more than one book to do. Rather, its significance is twofold. The first is to ask the question – no more than that – if the way that an individual or a generation first becomes interested in China shapes the way that they subsequently think about it. For example, does studying China in the early years of the post-Mao transition establish uncertainties about the compatibility of economic, social and political regimes that persist even as China becomes a global power? The success of the attempt to recreate the entire basis of CCP rule was not taken for granted in those years, and very nearly came unstuck in 1989 after a series of smaller protests and demonstrations in the preceding years. Perhaps living through and studying this period gives a greater awareness of domestic dynamics and a greater focus on the potential fragility of regime legitimacy than those who encountered China later on.

Does studying different dynamics of China's global expansion as they happen have an impact too – studying the growth of Chinese trade and overseas financial flows in 'real time' for example? Instinctively, and without any evidence whatsoever, only ever knowing China as a major economy and major global power must have an impact on the way you view the country, and the sort of questions you want to ask about it. And also on the sort of benchmarks that are used to judge a country or a regime or a leadership against. For example, economic performance might become a greater indicator of success as previous assumptions about political systems and economic effectiveness are challenged. Though not everybody would agree, Yan Xuetong (2019: 130) suggests that '[w]hen it comes to economics, global millennials are much more likely than older generations to express positive opinions about the Chinese communist government and its ability to rapidly improve living standards when compared to Western governments'. Second, and more important, the point is to show how different agendas require looking for different sorts of evidence, and can result in very different assumptions about where we are going in the future. And while the focus in much of the literature has understandably been on competing theoretical (and resulting policy) preferences, the distinction between domestic facing and internationally facing types of scholarship are arguably even more significant. Asking questions *about* China can generate a very different outlook than asking questions about the *impact* of China.

Trying to establish distinct and separate types of scholarship is fraught with difficulties, as it creates artificial boundaries and can only present a caricature of diverse and plural endeavours within each category. Perhaps it helps to think of a spectrum of approaches that contains four broad types of research, with individual researchers often operating in more than one of them. To be sure, this is still rather imprecise and rough. Moreover, these four really should be expanded to include different types of disciplinary studies. For example, those political science and economic studies that use models and are built on expectations of certain types of rational behaviour start from rather different assumptions and generate rather different types of conclusions than the other types of scholarship being discussed here. Students of law, anthropology, sociology and so on would also have their own discipline specific favoured methods and approaches. But the point is not to be precise, but rather simply to try and find a very blunt device to explain why what at first sight might appear to be research on the same thing (or country) actually often isn't. Hence the reason that different research findings talk past each other, are hard or impossible to reconcile, or simply exist in isolation from one another talking to different communities.

At one end of this spectrum are those who are most influenced by Sinology and primarily seek to understand China. For these scholars, a deep knowledge of China's past is crucial, as are language skills to enable the researcher to study Chinese produced knowledge and culture in their original forms. We might then move to the study of domestic dynamics – politics, economics, society, law and so on. As with more area studies type studies, the main intentions here are also to ask questions about China, with the goal understanding where China is going. Here, knowledge of the past is important for contextualization and comparative purposes, as too is the study of domestic Chinese language debates (both academic and policy ones). A third group could be those who focus on Chinese foreign policy making. They too seek evidence and information from domestic debates, and try and identify the key power configurations and unpick the influence of different interest groups in setting broadly defined foreign policy goals. For those who think that strategic cultures are important in shaping policy, studying Chinese history and Chinese experiences is also deemed to be important. And once more, the aim here is to ask questions about China, even though these questions have salience beyond China's borders too.

This changes when we move from primarily China-facing scholarship to those more interested with the international consequences of China's rise. A fourth and very large category is those whose main interest is to understand how China's (future) international behaviour will impact on the world. Within this grouping, there are scholars who look to China's own past to explain its (and therefore the world's) future.

This forms part of the rethinking of the universality of the theoretical foundations of IR briefly noted earlier. The more usual approach, though, is to start from one of the mainstream IR theoretical positions and to apply the resulting assumptions to the Chinese case. Not only are these theoretical starting points more important than a knowledge of China and its past, but so too are knowledge of the non-Chinese historical examples that these theories were built from. For example, understanding previous cases of global power transitions can be deemed to be the starting point for predicting how and why a rising China will act and the inevitable consequences of this action.

There is a considerable risk that sweeping generalizations oversimplify things to the extent that their conclusions become pointless. Or that they overlook so many exceptions to the overgeneralized rule that they become useless. Or both. So, it is extremely dangerous to risk doing both and suggest that those who work on Chinese domestic politics, economics, and political economy are more likely to see real obstacles to Chinese power continuing to grow than their IR colleagues. Those who study Chinese foreign policy and policy making from the inside out and are more embedded in 'Chinese studies' are also likely to be aware of the broader domestic context of China's rise, and recognize the possibility of a domestic slowdown and political uncertainties. Conversely, those are most interested in the implications of China's rise for the global order are *most likely* to be less interested in internal dynamics and thus less aware of potential challenges to current trends continuing. Or simply more likely not to concern themselves with the domestic foundations of China's rise (or otherwise) at all.

For proponents of the realist tradition, there is no requirement to study domestic politics and economics. To be sure this might be the most parsimonious characterization of the realist endeavour possible, but some realists would argue that the job of an IR scholar is to study the interplay of politics *between* states, leaving the study of politics *within* states for others to consider. By contrast, one of the building blocks of the liberal alternative to studying the basis of IR should be to try and identify which domestic interests most influence the creation of national interests and objectives. However, many liberal analyses of China and the global order start their liberal analysis at the international level, focusing on processes of assimilation and socialization. What they do less often is be liberal at the domestic level as well. Rather than study a two-level game, they instead choose to concentrate on a one-level international game.

This suggests that a simple and single national interest and objective is more often assumed in the study of China than is the case when other countries are the subject of analysis. This can result in evidence being found for pre-assumed conclusions that doesn't necessarily prove the pre-assumed point at all. For example, if certain assumptions are made about who speaks and acts for China and the coherence and unity of China as a global actor, then what is said and done by a very wide range of actors can be taken as evidence of a single coherent state strategy. Often mistakenly so in my view. This is why, as noted in the Introduction, a very wide set of activities end up as being not just political, but falling within the study of China's IR.

Imagining Chinese power

This discussion shows that different concerns come to the fore in different eras that change the nature of scholarship, the sort of questions that are being asked, and the evidence that is needed to affirm hypotheses and expectations. It's not that these 'new' questions weren't asked before or simply replace previous ones. Very good research is still taking place on exactly those same issues that were occupying scholars of China as a transitional power in the 1980s. In fact, it is not really to do with academic research at all. Rather it is about certain agendas and research questions tending to capture the popular attention at different times (and also to different extents in different places). They can also capture the policy community attention too. Though at times it might be that policy preferences shape debates rather than vice versa. They become the 'theme of the time' that can generate common sense truths that are believed irrespective of whether there is evidence to support them or not, and other voices can find it hard to penetrate the noise that is being generated by proponents of the common sense.

These themes of the time are widely viewed in China as externally derived and driven discourses that have been deliberately established to shed doubt on Chinese intentions. This is why there has been such an emphasis in China on trying to establish alternative Chinese narratives of China's rise, as will be discussed in Chapters 5 and 6. There is no denying that the idea of a dangerous and threatening China has been and remains a strong school of thought. Nor that it has had a considerable impact on policy in a number of places. Conceptions of a China threat (and the need to counter it) were becoming more widespread and louder even before the appointment of one of the authors of *Death by China* as the Director of President

Trump's National Trade Council (Navarro and Autry, 2011). However, the argument here is that imagining a China-influenced future has not been totally negative for China and at times has actually been empowering.

The thinking goes something like this. China is a difficult country to do business in because of the nature of the Chinese state, and the state's residual control over key economic entry points. As the Chinese state tends to identify companies with the countries where they are based, it is important that a national government retains good political relations with China if these companies are to do well. With the emergence of China as a major source of investment finance, potential government influenced (if not always wholly controlled) financial flows now goes in both directions. Given a competitive international environment, if your country doesn't do it, then others might build a (competitive) good political relationship with China, and consequentially gain the entry and access and finance that will be denied to you. Finally, and crucially for this argument, it is deemed important to establish a good position not just because of the tangible opportunities that China presents at any given time, but also because of the even greater opportunities that will reveal themselves in the future. China's perceived future, then, provides a form of deterrence against interfering in what China believes to be its 'core interests',[10] and has empowered China. Or put another way, the power that China is projected to possess in the future has at times resulted in it being treated as if it already had that power.

In conversations with colleagues in China, this argument was described by one very highly respected scholar as being 'facile'. China's power now was clear and manifest, so why worry about the future? This is a fair point. But there is evidence to suggest that the future remains an important component of policy making. This is partly because of the way that the nature of China's economic significance has changed, and also partly because of the way that China's leaders have signalled intent for the future. For example, the perceived future was pivotal in the adoption of a new UK policy towards China in 2015 – the establishment of what was called a new 'Golden Age' of UK–China relations. Future Chinese investment was seen as crucial in allowing for investment in energy and infrastructure projects at the same time as the UK government was pursuing an austerity programme to cut national debt. The need to improve relations with China was thought to have become particularly urgent as a result of the downturn in relations after the then Prime Minister David Cameron met with the Dalai Lama in 2012 (and the growth of Germany–China ties in the same period). It is actually not that easy to find clear evidence of political issues resulting in significant and directly caused changes in economic flows, but that was the perception. The moves towards RMB internationalization and the possibility of stock market cooperation also increased the urgency of establishing a relationship that could make the City of London the key European partner in facilitating China's financial future. The resulting 'strategic shift' (Gracie, 2015) towards China overseen by the then Chancellor of the Exchequer, George Osborne, saw human rights at best occupy a very distant secondary place behind promoting commercial relations in the Golden Era. And it is notable that it was the minister in charge of finance rather than the Foreign Secretary or the Prime Minister who was the lead actor. Indeed, the emphasis on 'money, money, money' was so striking that the then editor of *The Spectator*, a magazine that typically supports Osborne's Conservative Party, argued that Osborne was 'attempting the world record for the longest kowtow in diplomatic history', and suggested that Xi Jinping must 'marvel at just how cheaply the British can be bought' (Nelson, 2015).

To be clear, China was already very much an important economic partner for the UK. The here and now was an important part of decision making. But it's also clear that the future was too. This was made very evident in an article written by Osborne with his adviser (and originator of the BRICS acronym), Jim O'Neill, in 2015. The article's title in many ways sums it all up – 'It's in Britain's interests to bond with China now: the future prosperity of this country depends on us strengthening our relationship with the world's next superpower':

> Take yourself forward, for a moment, and imagine it is the year 2030. Children born today are preparing for exams and starting to think about their future careers. China is now the world's largest economy. Mandarin is taught in schools right across the world. And a new Silk Road for international trade, made up of roads, high-speed railway lines, bridges and airport hubs, stretches from Shanghai and Beijing through Xinjiang to Kazakhstan, Pakistan and Afghanistan before making its way to western Europe and to Britain. This isn't a fantasy. It is the 2030 that most economic forecasters now predict. (Osborne and O'Neill, 2015)

While recognizing that China faced considerable challenges ahead in making a transition to a new growth and development model, even the risks of this were discounted and turned into positives:

> Even as China's growth slows, it will continue to be a powerhouse for the global economy. As China pushes ahead with its own reform programme, with increased consumption and a demand for services, there will be many new opportunities for the UK. Opportunities for UK manufacturing, infrastructure, retail and financial services. There will also be opportunities to attract new firms to the UK. (Osborne and O'Neil, 2015)

Shaping perceptions: strategic signalling and trust

The Belt and Road Initiative as strategic signalling

In this case, Osborne was responding to not just his understanding (and perhaps hope) of what a future world order might look like, but also the way that the BRI had been promoted by the Chinese leadership, and on their behalf by a range of government agencies, think tanks and even individual academics. And while the Belt and Road is very much a concrete and material project, the Osborne example also shows that it serves a strategic signalling purpose too. It is an example of how material resources on their own are a key source of power, but so too is the way in which the state establishes an understanding in others of how it plans to use this material power in the future (Callahan, 2016).

Everything that has happened between China and BRI countries could have been done without anybody ever having mentioned the words Belt and Road in the same sentence. To be sure, the initiative has resulted in a number of measures that are designed to support the attainment of the vision; specific financial pots of money, consular support for investors, risk mitigation initiatives, education programmes to increase knowledge of BRI countries and so on. But all of these could have been offered in different ways through various targeted actions to support projects in individual countries or regions in the way that the growth of COFDI has been encouraged more generally (as shown in Chapter 4). In fact, a number of the more important (or maybe higher profile) elements of the BRI (and initiatives to support them) were already in place before it came into existence. The agreement establishing the China Pakistan Economic Corridor was signed before Xi announced the BRI, with the high-profile Gwadar

Port project preceding the Belt and Road by a decade (Blanchard, 2019: 84). While Duisburg's resurgence as the world's biggest inland port has been credited to the BRI (Oltermann, 2018), trains started to arrive from China in 2011 with the first experimental direct train to Hamburg arriving three years earlier (Pomfret, 2019).

Furthermore, the more the BRI expanded to cover an ever-greater number of participant states, the more it looked like an increasingly vague catch-all term that covered much of what Chinese actors were already doing overseas. The way that projects are reported also make it very difficult to work out what is 'normal' contact and what is BRI specific and driven. As more actors try to brand their activity as part of the BRI to take advantage of any extra benefits that might be going around, the harder it comes to work out what would have happened without the BRI. To be clear, the things that are happening along the Belt and Road really are important. The question is why bother with the BRI at all? Not why do it (in terms of what are the reasons for wanting to do the actual projects themselves), but why package, disseminate and promote it in the way that it has been? And why the apparent desire from Xi Jinping to have other countries' leaders endorse it?

The answer might be simply that Xi wanted to identify himself and his tenure in power with a grand global project. It might also be an attempt to gain the international status (Deng, 2008) and respect (Shambaugh, 2015) that many in China think it deserves and is largely lacking from the international community. It is also the case that when Chinese leaders speak on the international stage, they are also speaking to a domestic audience (Ni, 2012), in this case showing that the party has restored China to its proper and rightful place as a global power (Scobell, 2012), and gained the respect of other global powers in the process (Edney, 2015). But it is also about signalling China's great power status, and the intention to use China's material resources in certain ways to generate certain results in the future.

This interpretation has been challenged by Chinese scholars who argue that the BRI is being viewed through 'China threat' lenses, rather than through the dispassionate study of the actual intention of Xi and others. As one of the key arguments in this book is that pre-existing perceptions shape the way signals are received, then it is hard to totally disagree with this. Yet it is hard to believe that Xi and his advisers didn't know that making speeches at Davos and elsewhere and inviting participants from across the world to Belt and Road Forums would be taken by external observers as a signal of future intent. Or that the teams of think tanks and research institutions that have given presentations around the world wouldn't help reinforce the idea of the BRI as a new GS for a great power (Fallon, 2015). To be sure, even under Xi the Chinese state does not control all that is done, and a closer examination of what actually happens under the BRI shows a somewhat more fragmented and uncoordinated set of activities (Jones and Zeng, 2019). Nevertheless, the way that it has been presented to the world certainly makes it look as if it is what a former Austrian Defence Minister called 'a political marketing concept for world dominance' (Fasslabend, 2015).

So the BRI has become the political economy equivalent of establishing the 'strategic clarity' about intentions that is seen as so important in creating a real and credible military deterrence in the security realm (Jervis, 1982–83). Moreover, as it is an actual project that consumes considerable amounts of money, it is also the economic equivalent of 'sunk cost' signalling of security studies, where actual and expensive military projects are deployed to show the extent of the commitment to the policy being signalled (Fearon, 1997). The BRI has thus become a credible signal of Chinese ambitions to become the financial future for other countries – a key source of investment and other forms of finance in a post global crisis world that desperately needs this Chinese money. It is a narrative that is established by Xi Jinping's personal association with its origins and his continuing endorsement of its expansion.

It is also a narrative that has been accepted and repeated outside of China. While it is not in the power of the signaller to control its reception, they can do things to make them more acceptable. As Weissmann (2019, 239) argues, they can try and influence 'narrative acceptance' by economically rewarding those who buy into Chinese understandings. Though as he also points out, neither coerced nor pragmatic acceptance is the same as truly buying the story being sold. More important, proponents of the importance of signalling and narratives place an emphasis on establishing a credible future story by establishing a thread that links this future to the present and back into the past (Miskimmon et al, 2013). In the case of the BRI, the idea of a concerted Chinese push to act in the future in certain ways is deemed highly credible in part because of what China has already done with its material resources. The speed of growth of COFDI gave weight to the idea of an investment led global strategy. In addition, in the shape of the AIIB, there was clear evidence that if China was not happy with the distribution of power in global institutions, or the speed of change within them (or both), then it was prepared to use its financial resources to build alternatives instead (Wang Yu, 2018).

Messages, perceptions and trust

The same credibility is not so evident when it comes to other messages that Xi Jinping has tried to signal to international audiences. At the same time as he was promoting the BRI, Xi was also signalling China's commitment to an open global economy to the rest of the world at a time when other countries were turning inwards and pursing populist and nationalist agendas resulting in 'reverse globalization' (*ni quanqiuhua*) (Cao and Xu, 2018). At his speech at Davos in 2017, for example, Xi (2017a) asserted that China had a 'wide open' door to the global economy and promised that 'China will continue to contribute to global development … We will open our arms to the people of other countries and welcome them aboard the express train of China's development.' The following year he used variations of the word 'open' (opening, openness, etc) 51 times in his speech at the Bo'ao Forum for Asia (which in itself that year was on the theme of 'An Open and Innovative Asia for a World of Greater Prosperity') with China's commitment to openness contrasted with alternatives promoted by unnamed others that favoured 'isolation' and 'retrogression' (Xi 2018a). Foreign Minister Wang Yi (2018c) described the China Import Expo in Shanghai in November 2018 as 'no less than a pioneering undertaking in the history of global trade'. Old Globalization might have come from the West, but it was the same West that was now turning its back on openness with the new globalization initiated by China (Song, 2017: 11). When a new Foreign Investment Law was announced in March 2019, it was hailed as ushering in a new era of fair competition for all in a concerted media campaign. And presumably partly as a result of various forms of pushback against the BRI, Xi (2019a) spent almost as much time in his speech at the second BRI summit in 2019 on China's commitment to opening itself to the world as he did on how the Belt and Road would evolve in the future.

In contrast to the credibility of the BRI signalling, the free and open Chinese economy signal was met with considerable scepticism. While the evidence of previous Chinese action supported the message of the former, it contradicted the message of the latter. In exactly the same week that Xi was pronouncing Chinese openness at Davos, the US Chamber of Commerce in China produced a report pointing to considerable obstacles to doing business in China, 'unhealthy trends' that had made things worse rather than better, and a growing feeling that US firms were 'feeling less welcome than before' (Amcham China, 2017). China's failure to be treated as a market economy in the World Trade Organization (WTO) after 15 years of membership in 2016 (which most in China assumed would be automatic) was an indication of the relatively widely held belief in other countries that 'the State continues to pull all the necessary strings to ensure that the market does not dictate economic outcomes' (Miranda, 2018: 66). Moreover, other contemporaneous Chinese policies pointed in directions other that openness. Key among these other signals was the MIC2025 initiative, and the consequences that this might have for either the promotion and protection of domestic Chinese producers, or for technological and property rights transfers from foreign producers (or both).

Where pre-assumed positions on China are very strong, and trust in Chinese intentions is absent, there is little or nothing that can be done to shift them short of a change in the nature of one-party rule itself. Those Chinese actions and words that support the pre-existing assumption are accepted as evidence of why these assumptions are right, and those that don't are explained away or ignored. In the process, those actions that are taken as supportive evidence of the prior belief are seen as the consequences of the intent of the people at the top of the political system pursuing a unitary Chinese interest. As such, the focus in Chapter 2 now turns to question whether these assumptions are correct, or whether they represent what Zhang Falin (2017) calls a 'holism failure' that misses the range of different ideas, opinions, actors and interests that generate an increasingly large and diverse number of Chinese international interactions.

Interest, Actors and Intent: Studying the Global by Understanding the Domestic

The primary aim of Chapter 1 was to understand how different ways of studying China lead to different conclusions and predictions. It would be rather disingenuous, though, to pretend that it was a totally neutral analysis, and this chapter starts from the assumption that a full and sophisticated understanding of China's rise 'requires us to capture some of the key complex and simultaneous interactions between the global and domestic levels in the study of China's external relations' (Foot, 2013: 1). In short, the argument here is that studying the domestic can tell us things that question a number of the assumptions of those studies that focus more on the international/global level.

This rather simple statement immediately generates two important responses. The first is that it is indeed rather simple. Students of Chinese domestic politics will certainly find it an unremarkable and underwhelming re-statement of the very obvious. However, the reason that it needs to be made is that what is obvious to one scholarly community is frequently absent in scholarship that emerges from other intellectual endeavours. As Hameiri and Lee (2015) have argued, much IR scholarship on China still starts from the assumption of a single Chinese national interest and sees Chinese action as the result of state control to attain state goals. Furthermore, as suggested in Chapter 1, the neglect of domestic diversity in generating transnational activity seems to be more pronounced in the study of China than it is with the study of other states. Here the nature of the Chinese political system makes it easier to assume a conformity of interest than, for example, in liberal democracies where ideational and policy competition is much easier to observe, and frequently leads to changes in ruling parties and policies.

The second is the use of the word 'bounded' to qualify both plurality and diversity. The aim of this chapter is to show that there is more to what Chinese want and do inside and outside China's borders than just the goals of the central leadership in Beijing. Indeed, even at the apex of the power structure within central ministries and party agencies, it is not too hard to find different interests being articulated and different policy preferences being proposed. But this is not a revisionist exercise designed to provide a radical interpretation of a decentred China with a hollow or powerless central elite. Far from it. What central leaders want, do, and say not only remains hugely important, but has become even more important under Xi Jinping than it was under some of his predecessors. So it's all about balance. About trying to work out what exactly the overarching strategy is (what the leadership wants and how it thinks it can achieve its objectives), how different voices either feed into or reflect these central choices, and what room exists within the overarching strategic framework for others to try and get what they want as well.

The first part of this chapter shows how studying China from the inside out can generate conclusions and observations that challenge some of the assumptions of 'outside in' approaches that assume a more unified and coherent national project. This includes studying the importance of Chinese debates about China's place in the world, which, despite a less free environment under Xi, still reveals different interests and understandings and different voices of China. It also includes simply outlining the increasing number of actors involved in Chinese international interactions in the post-Cold War era. The emphasis in both sub-sections is on the location of interest and authority within China, feeding into the discussion of whether Chinese international interactions can be considered to constitute a form of coherent GS in Chapter 3.

The chapter has a specific focus on assumptions about the nature of China's political economy. Here the intention is to show the dialectical relationship between top-down planning and design, and bottom-up initiative and freedom of action. If we focus too much on the state, we can overlook not only the different levels and layers of agents involved in the development and implementation of policy, but also the importance of relatively autonomous actors pursuing commercial objectives. But if we focus too much at the individual firm level, then it's easy to underplay the significance of the state project in funding, facilitating and supporting commercial objectives, and providing an enabling diplomatic environment for overseas projects.

What is this China that thinks and wants?

Party, state and market

This book primarily uses the vocabulary of state and markets to make a distinction between top-down control and organization in pursuit of overall and overarching goals, and what is done by economic actors to attain individual and/or private commercial objectives. However, it is a language that creates a number of issues when it comes to studying China's political economy. As we shall see, for example, there is a need to disaggregate the state itself in the Chinese case (and in many other cases as well). More important, there is the argument that it is wrong to focus on state interests, and that the Party should be the referent point instead. It is an opinion that has considerable merit. In keeping with Leninist guiding principles, it is always the Party that should set the agenda in any policy realm, and the state is the vehicle that works out best how to deliver the Party's goals. Despite theoretically and constitutionally being separate from the party, the simultaneous theoretical and constitutional subjugation of the state to party leadership has been reinforced by an extensive system of supervision, and the domination of the state by party members; party members who might be structurally responsible to higher state officials in their work, but who are also simultaneously responsible to party superiors too.

Despite all the changes that have taken place since the CCP assumed power in 1949, one basic existential objective has remained consistent. To keep the party in power. Xi's way of dealing with the perceived challenges to party rule has been to strengthen and consolidate control: the party's control over society and his control of the party. At other times, the same goal has resulted in the partial loosening of party control over the state and a greater separation of powers. Crucially, though, this was never an agenda to undermine the Party's overall control, but rather to strengthen it by creating new foundations for its continued dominance. The aim was to construct the idea of a listening, legally bound, predictable, professional, effective and (partially) transparent one-party rule. Just with the loosening of control over the economy discussed later in this chapter, political loosening was seen as a means of strengthening. Moreover, as we have seen under Xi, the party retained the ability to reverse the situation if and when the need arose, and restore greater direct party control.

So, there is no disagreement here with the argument that it is the Party and its interests that are the ultimate driving force of state policy.

Indeed, both the importance of the continuing search for new sources of legitimacy and the ability to reverse freedoms that have previously been extended underpin much of what follows here and in following chapters. All this being said, the state does remain the key delivery actor (and mechanism of delivery) in many policy domains. The language of states and markets is also most often used in comparative analyses of political economies, perhaps reflecting the influence of Susan Strange on a range of scholars (including this one). As a result, but with a little hesitation, it is used in this book as an appropriate shorthand way of referring to different dynamics and drivers of China's international economic relations, and the different type of actors pursuing them, despite the overarching importance of party goals and objectives.

Leader-centric approaches to studying China's rise

Given the importance of the Party, and the importance of leaders in the Party, it is not surprising that leader-centric approaches have long been deployed to explain the dynamics of Chinese politics. Of course, it is not just in China that specific political epochs or eras are associated with individual leaders; often leaders whose interests and objectives diverge considerably from their predecessors. But there are clearly constraints on the freedom of individual leaders to impose their will in democracies that do not exist in one-party states. And different types of relationships between states and the markets mean that leaders in more authoritarian polities have a number of tools at their disposal to direct economic change that their counterparts in democracies don't always have.

Successive leaders have sought to make their own specific ideological contributions and to leave their own personal ideological stamp on history. Mao Zedong, Deng Xiaoping and Xi Jinping might be the three leaders who are personally named and identified as originators of the CCP's guide to action in the party constitution, but they sit in the party constitution alongside the Theory of Three Represents and the Scientific Outlook on Development introduced by Jiang Zemin and Hu Jintao respectively (CCP, 2017: 1). Implicit and often explicit in the promotion of these ideological modifications is the idea that these leaders have the capacity to change the fundamental nature of Chinese communism, and through this, the fundamental nature of China itself. The introduction of new ideas is usually supported by high-profile campaigns to promote them, and to associate the leader with the idea. The promotion of Hu's emphasis on harmonious development and building a harmonious world is a good example here of a concept that became close to being ubiquitous in China, and was actively promoted overseas through two White Papers for an international audience (State Council, 2005; 2011a). The cyclical timing of Five Year Plans, five yearly Party Congresses and National People's Congresses (NPC) provides opportunities for leaders to present themselves and their ideas. So too do the periodic massive celebrations of National Day anniversaries in Tiananmen Square. Annual government work reports at NPC sessions and party plenums might be slightly less high profile, but are still important showcases for leaders to present themselves in preferred ways.

On the international scene, Chinese leaders have also gone to great lengths to use major international meetings to announce new initiatives and to give an impression of being in control of a concerted and coherent state effort. This was the case before Xi's assumption of power (Alden and Hughes, 2009), but it's fair to say that he has made more use of them than most. This includes taking overseas trips, hosting international leaders' reciprocal visits, speaking on global stages like the UN or the World Economic Forum, and attending the now rather frequent summits of regional groupings in which China participates.

Clearly Xi (and other Chinese leaders) are important and have considerable power to guide, influence, and even at times to directly control. It's just that there is more to China than leaders alone, and assuming a single Chinese interest and identity can lead to assumptions about actions and intent that need further scrutiny. The first area of scrutiny is to question whether White Papers and official speeches are authentic articulations of real and genuinely held Chinese positions, or instead simply an attempt to persuade a sceptical audience of what China wants (d'Hooghe, 2005).

A second is to point to the insights that can be gained from studying domestic Chinese debates over the nature of the global order, China's place within it, and what China can, should or might do in the future to increase its profile and power. While ultimate strategic decisions are in the hands of the political elite, studying what others are arguing and promoting does give us an idea of the direction that these elite decisions might take in the future (Xu Jin, 2016; Feng and He, 2019; Sørensen, 2019). It also highlights key areas of consensus in China over China's national identity and characteristics – for example, over China's reactive and defensive nature – that helps explain why many international issues are perceived rather differently inside China than outside. However, it is also an endeavour that has to be handled with care.

Who speaks for China? Bounded plurality

There is a relatively longstanding acceptance that below the national leadership, there are numerous different voices calling for China to try and do different things for different reasons. Of course, there are topics relating to questions of Chinese sovereignty where a single view dominates, and challenging it remains taboo and off limits. The number of taboo issues has also increased under Xi. Probably the best known and widely discussed example is the ending of debates over the potential of moving towards a new form of constitutionalism (Creemers, 2015).

So we have what we might call a bounded pluralism, with the boundaries of what can be discussed moving over time. The force of different voices also shifts. Once more, this is not something that is new to the Xi era, with Shambaugh (2011: 20) pointing to how Chinese advocates of the 'equivalent of the Liberal Institutionalism school in the West' (which he terms the 'Globalism' school) lost ground in the years after the global financial crisis before Xi came to power. But also, once more, it is a trend that has intensified under Xi. Nevertheless, this does not mean that differences have simply disappeared. For example, a Merics report found that attempts to limit the scope of legitimate debate on the internet had reduced the extent of online plurality. But it also found that it was still relatively easy to find voices that criticized government policy from different directions; from both those who wanted China to do even more even sooner, and those with a more negative assessment of abandoning the previous emphasis on keeping a low profile (Shi-Kupfer and Ohlberg, 2017).

Weight, evidence and opinion shopping

Even though the analysis in this book has been informed by the location of its author, nobody will think that it represents an official view of a national interest. However, it is often the case that what Chinese writers say is indeed taken as an expression of either the country as a whole, or of an official Chinese position, or both. Given the plurality of debate (even in the Xi era), as Feng and He (2019) note, it is simply impossible for all of these to reflect the official view at the same time. Yet that doesn't stop these conflicting positions being imbued with a form of authoritativeness and being used as evidence of what China wants by different external analysts. Or put another way, it is rather easy to go opinion shopping to look for the evidence that proves the pre-existing point.

As Swaine (2012: 1) argues, this points to the need for care in discriminating between different levels of authoritativeness when considering what is said and proposed by different people in different places. While this has long been important, it has become even more so with the expansion of access to Chinese voices. The China National Knowledge Infrastructure makes it possible to search across a massive range of Chinese language material in seconds. Add to this all that is said on the internet and it becomes relatively easy to find evidence of state intent if you want to even if in reality it is simply an individual opinion.

Inserting interests and populating concepts

When new concepts come to China, it can take time before a consensus appears on what they actually mean. Or even how they should be expressed. As late as 2008, for example, soft power was still being translated in a range of different ways by Chinese scholars, each with different nuances (Cho and Jeong, 2008: 455), until *ruanshili* gradually emerged as the agreed best translation. More important, there was intense debate over what soft power actually meant in the Chinese context (rather than just debate over the extent to which China had it or might get it in the future). Glaser and Murphy (2009) argue that these debates had a significant influence on the way that soft power came to be thought of by Jiang Zemin, and the state promotion of (historical) culture as China's biggest soft power resource (rather than contemporary politics). This in turn, they argue, fed into official thinking on the efficacy of maintaining a low profile and the turn towards a more proactive Chinese international stance. To be sure, the debate over the meaning of soft power for China and how it might be used took place in a setting where the leadership's already articulated interest in the concept provided a facilitating environment. Even so, it is a decent example of how open and varied academic discussions influenced the formation of state policy.[1]

But even when the concept emerges from within China itself, and is pronounced by top leaders (or they associate themselves with it), there is still room for debate over what it actually means (Lams, 2018; Rolland, 2020). This has not so much persisted under Xi as become ever more prevalent, not least due to his announcement of rather ill-defined concepts and goals that are short on actual content and act more as a rallying slogan or millenarian aspiration. Many of them are built around the notion of a new beginning and a 'new era' – a term that he used 36 times in his presentation to the 19th Party Congress in

2017 (Xi, 2017e). The China Dream is one example of a 'very elusive and difficult to pin down' 'potentially all-encompassing term that invites multiple interpretations' (Bislev, 2015: 586). While it is depicted as being new thinking, it is also explained as being old at the same time. The China Dream represents the continuation of previous leaders' visions for a modern rich harmonious and powerful China distilled into a new single and simply articulated aspiration by Xi (Wang Zheng, 2014). In fact, in Xi's original conviction that 'the great rejuvenation of the Chinese nation is the greatest Chinese dream of the Chinese nation in modern times', he went back to the continuous struggle to restore Chinese greatness after defeat in the Opium Wars in 1840 (Xi, 2012).

In many respects it is an incredibly powerful concept, pointing towards China's national rejuvenation and re-emergence as a rich and powerful great power at the top table of global politics with a happy and satisfied domestic population. In its announcement and promotion, it provides a 'framing' mechanism designed to legitimate one-party rule (Bondes and Heep, 2013) by showing how the party – and in particular, this specific version of the party under Xi – will deliver China into a bright new future. But it increasingly became used as 'a somewhat ambiguous metanarrative into which one can insert any positive developments while neglecting others' (Mahoney, 2014: 27). Anything that is positive and shows China in a good light becomes part of the China Dream, while anything that isn't is conveniently ignored.

Given the scope of the China Dream, it is not surprising that it is difficult to find a single agreed and shared definition. But even what might look like more precise concepts find themselves subject to redefinition and interpretation either through a lack of clarity, or the desire to benefit from inclusion, or both. For example the concept of 'core interests' (*hexin liyi*) has been credited with establishing strategic 'bottom line thinking' (*dixian siwei*) (Yang Jiemian, 2014); those interests that China is simply not prepared to negotiate or discuss with external powers. But, although a Chinese White Paper identified these core interests as 'state sovereignty, national security, territorial integrity and national reunification, China's political system established by the Constitution and overall social stability, and the basic safeguards for ensuring sustainable economic and social development' (State Council, 2011a), this still left ample room for debating what these categories meant in detail. Because policies were being devised to support core interest issue areas, this acted as a spur for interested actors to argue that their own specific area of interest should count as a core interest (Zeng Jinghan et al, 2015).

The BRI has also changed considerably since its original inception. This is partly because more countries have been added to either the belt or the road, thus broadening its geographic scope. It has also changed as domestic actors in China have tried to include themselves and their interests within the initiative and to gain access to resources put in place to support it. Indeed, the existence of the BRI itself, rather than just a land-based Silk Road, has been explained as a consequence of provinces further east pushing to get the same preferential treatment that was being offered to western provinces and autonomous regions; a process that some observers think was a mistake that inevitably leads to limited resources being spread too thinly (Kratz, 2015: 10). Pauls and Gottwald (2018) argue that such refinement and evolution of policy is a natural consequence of the democratic centralist mode of policy making and implementation, whereby the centre sets policy and then subsequently revises it in response to input from other interests from within the system. But there is also evidence of various actors taking it upon themselves to infer 'BRIness' to their own interest (Jones and Zeng, 2019), and to utilize the opportunities offered by it to pursue local economic objectives that have nothing to do with any grander geostrategic goals (Li Mingjiang, 2019). Whatever the case, we can argue that through official, semi-official and unofficial processes, the definition of what Chinese core interests are, and the definition of what the BRI is and covers, have both become stretched. In the process, they have both lost an element of their originally intended strategic clarity.

A Chinese common sense?

Despite this emphasis on diversity, there are some common positions that have become more or less the basis of 'common sense' thinking about China's place in the world in Chinese debates. All common senses have heretics, and this is the case with Chinese common senses too. But two broad positions represent consensuses of sorts in Chinese debates, with another issue area leaning towards becoming a consensus, but not quite there yet.

The first is that there has never been a better time for China to try to push to attain its interests, and that China is 'closer to the centre of the world stage than ever before'.[2] As already noted, the idea that China had a moment of strategic opportunity to make strategic gains had been around for a decade before Xi Jinping came to power. Even so, the notion that China was now closer to getting back to where it should be was given a new impetus by Xi's above-mentioned speech on national rejuvenation in 2012. In the same year, ongoing debates over China's status were pushed in a certain direction by Xi's assertion that China needed to seek a new type of great power relations on his visit to the US. This was an argument that contained a pretty clear indication that he thought that China should now be counted among those great powers that needed a new type of relationship.

It is worth reminding ourselves that when Xi came to power, there was no strong agreement in China over China's global role and identity at all, with rejections of great power status as common as assertions of it. Now, all that remains to be resolved is how great a great power China has become, and what relative power capabilities might look like in the future. If all you ever read about China came from the *Global Times*, then you might think that a consensus about China as at least on a par with the United States already existed. This is reflected elsewhere too with 'an enhanced sense of self, ambition and confidence' resulting in assertions that China's economic and technological power had surpassed the US' at some point in the second half of the 2010s (Zhang Biao, 2019: 135).[3] Hu Angang became one of the louder proponents of this view arguing that by 2013, 'China had surpassed the United States to become the world's largest comprehensive national power' (Hu et al, 2015: 26). Bandurski (2018) argues that this was largely the result of 'a culture of inflated praise' for Xi Jinping in the media, and at a popular level, China's almost superpower status did become a common sense in around 2018. And as China emerged from the COVID-19 lockdown, it was not hard to find rather triumphalist voices comparing China's successes at home and support for others overseas with higher death tolls and a retreat from internationalism in the US and other Western states.

Dig a little deeper, though, and the idea of China having already surpassed the US is largely discounted. The dominant position is that the power gap is closing and will likely continue to narrow (Zhao Minghao, 2019). The extent of interest among Chinese scholars in the Thucydides Trap is predicated on the prior idea that China will reach parity with the US in the not too distant future. However, the reason that this does not quite count as a consensus just yet is that there also remains a relatively large school of thought that China's power has been exaggerated. As a result, Chinese foreign policy runs the risk of overstretching capabilities and capacities because its leaders have believed their own hype (Pu and Wang, 2018). China's great power status is still also frequently accompanied by the assertion that it is still at the same time a developing country 'with a long way to go before it becomes a developed one' (Qiu, 2019). So if we cut through the great power signalling that comes from China's leaders and is repeated in the media, if there is a consensus, it is that China really is a great power, but not as great and powerful as the headlines suggest. Or maybe not as great and powerful as other great powers (which means the US). There is a shared recognition of being a great power, but disagreement over what that actually means in terms of having and using great 'powerness'.

Reformism, defensiveness and trust

If the debate over the extent of Chinese great powerness revolves around capabilities, another key debate focuses on ambitions and drivers. There is a pretty firm conviction in China that outsiders either deliberately or mistakenly often misrepresent Chinese ambitions. Here the dominant position that forms the second consensus is that whatever China's power capabilities may be, China is and always will be defensive. Yes, it might be more confident in asserting its core interests (though many would argue not assertive enough in enforcing its claims in the South China Sea), and in searching for global governance reform. But, so the argument goes, it is doing so from a defensive and reactive position. The following quote from Nathan (2016: 184) is rather long, but as it pretty much sums up the overwhelmingly predominant Chinese perspective, is worth replicating in full here:

> far from being a menacing giant ... China is a vulnerable giant whose foreign policy at this point is essentially defensive. It is defending its territorial claims, defending its sea lanes of communication (or rather, seeking to build up the capability to defend them), defending its access to the global economy and seeking to weaken what it sees as an American encirclement that seeks to interfere in China's political stability, maintain its territorial division and constrain its ability to defend its own interests.

From this perspective, major projects like the BRI are not the threat to the existing way of doing things that they are sometimes portrayed to be (outside China), but rather a defensive response to an international order populated by states that are not always keen to facilitate China's further rise. It is an attempt 'to prevent a balancing coalition, either soft or hard, from emerging in the Indo-Pacific region' (Zhen and Paul, 2020: 10), and to construct a space for China to operate in as an international economic actor in the face of US hostility (Wang Yong, 2016). And if Chinese Foreign Ministry (FMPRC) personnel did come across very forcefully in their defence of China (and criticisms of others) during the COVID-19 pandemic, it was because they were forced to fight back against 'China bashing' and a concerted 'smear campaign' when instead it should have gained thanks 'both for successfully controlling the epidemic in China and for providing so much assistance to the outside world despite the limited aid it had received during its crisis' (Ma Guochan, 2020).

So entrenched is what Scobell (2003) calls a 'Cult of Defence', that even China-initiated military conflict has been explained and justified in pre-emptive defensive terms. It is also, Scobell claims, deeply embedded and believed by Chinese analysts and policy makers, and this chimes with my own interactions with Chinese scholars and policy researchers too. It is easy to dismiss such views as hiding true intentions or simply following official policy. But I don't think that this is true. As such, ignoring or discounting them makes it virtually impossible to understand the cognitive framework that Chinese thinkers are operating within, and the resulting parameters that this framework creates for thinking on regional security policy.

Just as a lack of trust influences some external perceptions of China's rise, so a lack of Chinese trust in other international actors has influenced the evolution of Chinese thinking and policy too. The argument that the West – which is often just shorthand for the US – will do whatever it can to retain its power and prevent China (and others) from rising to challenge it has many adherents in China. Just as Chinese action is parsed by some external observers as evidence of malign global intent, so US action is often seen in China as equally malign and designed to prevent China's rise. The result is a tendency towards what Lieberthal and Wang (2013) call 'strategic mistrust', where each views the others actions as negative and challenging and develops counter measures in response. These counter measures might themselves be viewed as aggressive and proactive rather than defensive and reactive leading to even more distrust. And as Lieberthal and Wang also note, the more the power gap between the two diminishes, the more strategic distrust is likely to increase.

Lind and Press (2018) investigate the way that the rise of Chinese energy related State-Owned Enterprises' (SOEs) resource seeking investments have been portrayed as an aggressive threat to the status quo ante liberal global energy market. They conclude that Chinese activity is not unusual because other countries acted in similar mercantilist ways in the past to guarantee their own energy security – and many of them (including, they argue, the US) still do. Nor is it hostile and aggressive, but instead driven by very real concerns over dependence on imported energy supplies that could easily be disrupted by unfriendly powers if they want to harm Chinese interests. It is an example of what looks like a defensive strategy born out of perceived weakness from within China being taken as worrying sign of intent by an untrustworthy and powerful China by others.

Disaggregating China

Notwithstanding the significance of the top leadership in generating frameworks, concepts and preferred common senses, there is not a single interest, or even a single understanding of what some of these concepts and common senses actually mean. There is more diversity than might appear at first sight, not least because of the way that the political climate can elevate certain positions and mask the extent of buy-in to others. The same is true when it comes to international actors. Studying the intentions of the central leadership remains essential if we are to try to understand what has been done and what might be done in the future. But it is not enough in itself, and can result in significant misunderstandings of who is doing what for which reasons. It can also lead to the consequence of action being taken as evidence of intent.

There is a need, then, to make a distinction between the international consequences of what happens in China and the intent to do something as part of a targeted strategy. The sheer size and scale of China, combined with the speed of transition, often means that domestic change has international and even truly global consequences. But building on Shambaugh's (2013: 8) importance of maintaining a distinction between being a global actor and a global power noted in the Introduction, we also need to maintain a distinction between global *impact* and global *intent*.

Disaggregating the state

Scholars have long argued that globalization leads to a shift in the distribution of authority within states. For example, a focus on the need to respond to pressures that emerge from the global economy and/or to participate successfully in it leads to economic agencies of the state becoming more powerful than the traditional foreign ministry organs of international relations (Sassen, 1999). This is not only true in the Chinese case, but arguably exaggeratedly so given the only relatively recent move away from international contacts being dominated by diplomacy-type relationships to other domains too. Even though economic reform began in the late 1970s, inward investment and trade only grew significantly in and after 1992, and outward investment only really became noteworthy in 2002 (and even then, much less important than it would become later). Admittedly, referring to the 1990s as being recent might be a consequence of age, but the scope and extent of Chinese international interactions since then has certainly been markedly different from what happened during the first four decades of the PRC.

It is not surprising, then, that the FMPRC has not got the same level of authority that it once had within the central decision making hierarchy. The nature of what the state is and what it does has changed and so a rather old-fashioned focus on 'traditional diplomatic practices, focused on interactions between foreign ministries, are insufficient to inform policies towards China' (Hameiri and Jones, 2015: 91). In addition to the resulting increased role for economic agencies, functional ministries and organizations have various degrees of shared authority for international affairs in their issue area; for example, the Ministry of Environmental Protection in international climate change discussions (Lai and Kang, 2014). Mertha (2009: 1012) further points to the influence of 'an increasing number of non-traditional – and increasingly non-state – policy entrepreneurs' in shaping outcomes, resulting in 'the pluralization of the policy process'. The formal foreign affairs bureaucracy is widely thought of as being relatively weak, and lacking methods of coordinating and communicating with the other key agencies dealing with international affairs like the military and key economic ministries (Christensen, 2012: 25–6).

Even at the higher levels of the authoritarian state bureaucracy, there can be considerable disagreement over specific policy areas, with different agencies having different international agendas. As Wang Jisi (2011: 79) put it:

> Almost all institutions in the central leadership and local governments are involved in foreign relations to varying degrees, and it is virtually impossible for them to see China's national interest the same way or to speak with one voice. These differences confuse outsiders as well as the Chinese people.

The conflict between the Ministry of Commerce (MOFCOM) and the People's Bank of China over currency reform and RMB internationalization is a particularly pertinent example here (Freeman and

Yuan, 2011). Indeed, Yao (2015: 172) not only points to conflict between these two in developing external strategies, but suggests that they actually try and harm and discredit each other in a race for supremacy. Those who have studied the way that Chinese aid policy is implemented in recipient countries also highlight rivalry between different ministries (FMPRC, Ministry of Finance and MOFCOM) being further complicated by the role and interest of key financial agencies; the China Development Bank (CDB), the Export-Import Bank of China (Eximbank), and the State Administration of Foreign Exchange (SAFE) (Corkin, 2011; Varrall, 2016; Zhang and Smith, 2017).

In the South China Sea, the International Crisis Group (2012) described an almost anarchic situation with a range of different actors – including different Chinese coast guards – pursuing different policies. Here, one of the complicating factors was the role of the Hainan Provincial Government, and one of the characteristics of Chinese international interactions in the reform era has been the growing significance of sub-national international actors (Chen Zhimin, 2005). This is particularly the case when it comes to cross-border flows – and not just of money and goods – for the ten Chinese provinces/regions that have land borders with 14 different countries (Li and Lee, 2014; Wong, 2018). As we shall see, investment from companies below the central level has become an increasingly important source of COFDI, even to places far away from provincial borders. As Li Mingjiang (2019: 274) argues, 'existing studies of Chinese power, including economic power, almost exclusively focused on the national government and elite decision makers at the central level' and so miss the importance of the individual and aggregated aims and strategies of China's many local governments.

Without asking him directly, it is impossible to know if any personal motivations led Xi Jinping to try to concentrate so much power in his own hands. It is reasonable to suggest that even if they did, one more pragmatic impetus was a fundamental lack of faith in the ability of what had become a fragmented policy process to deliver the things he wanted it to deliver (Lampton, 2015). The specifics of changes under Xi are dealt with in following chapters, with those directly related to international relations discussed in Chapter 3. Here, it will have to suffice to say that considerable steps have been taken to increase Xi's control over the party, and the party's control over the state and society.

The has been considerable focus on the process of recentralization and control under Xi. This is not only understandable, but also very necessary. Greater control, though, does not mean total control. That would simply be impossible. Indeed, Jaros and Tan

(2020: 84) argue that provincial authorities have actually been strengthened under Xi because the attainment of the various 'increasingly ambitious development initiatives' of the central leadership are largely 'delegated to provincial governments' to deliver. In particular, the resources that have been made available to support these initiatives combined with 'considerable latitude for interpreting central goals' has created new opportunities for them to creatively pursue their own priorities and agendas under the banner of resolutely following and implementing the policy of the central leadership. Utilizing the opportunities provided by Xi's association with the BRI is just one example of how top-down centralized control can result in increased resources becoming available for the pursuit of local objectives.

Moreover, as argued in the Introduction, what is considered to be political and strategic in the Chinese case covers much of what is thought of as being driven by non-state actors elsewhere. For Yao Yang (2015: 162), assuming that these economic exchanges 'are well coordinated and part of a grand plan for an ultimate aim' is a mistake, and ignores the way in which Chinese policy is not just established at the top, but also responds to bottom-up imperatives:

> Economic decisions have been deeply decentralized; as a result, the Chinese society has become as diverse as any other developing countries. The political system, on the other hand, has become much more flexible to accommodate these changes. Government policies no longer reflect the exclusive views of a few top leaders, but are often the results of the domestic politics that is bound to produce compromises among different stakeholders. This is not only true for China's domestic policies, but also true for China's external policies, especially economic policies.

State and/or market?

It's fair to say that no clear consensus exists over where the balance of authority lies in China's political economy: in the hands of private actors and market forces, or in the hands of the state. While these debates had been ongoing for decades, the way in which the Chinese state coordinated a response to the impact of the global financial crisis threw a new light on China's experiences and structures. The 'China Model' seemed able to do things that more neoliberal models could not. And do them in a way that the International Monetary Fund

(IMF) – hardly a stronghold of strong state capitalism – called 'quick, determined, and effective' (IMF, 2010: 4). As a result, a common sense of sorts did emerge that the state was in control. For example, Deng et al (2011: 41) argued that 'China remains fundamentally a command and control economy, despite its seemingly rapid embrace of markets. Compared with most developed economies and most other emerging economies, the Chinese economy remains subject to remarkably sweeping direct control by the central government.' While the language of 'command and control' might be an extreme interpretation of the nature of state control, the idea that the China Model or Beijing Consensus represented a successful strong state alternative to neoliberalism became something of a 'theme of the time' in and around 2011. Yet not everybody agreed. In 2014 for example, Nicholas Lardy (2014: 59) argued that China could not be considered state capitalist in any meaningful way, as '[t]he private sector is now the major driver of China's economic growth, employment, and exports and in recent years has even begun to contribute to the increase in China's outbound foreign direct investment'. Moreover, he even discounted the common argument that the response to the crisis had resulted in what was widely termed *guo jin min tui* (the advance of the state and the retreat of the private) arguing that the private sector remained the major driver of growth.

But things change. For Huang Yasheng (2011), while China might have become more statist in the post-crisis years, this stood in contrast to an earlier model of development that was based more on liberalization, marketization and the emergence of the private sector. It was this early period, he argues, that laid the roots for China's rapid growth and overall economic success, and not the subsequent return of a degree of state power. By 2019, Lardy was echoing this view, arguing that under Xi the support for the state sector that he couldn't find five years earlier was now very evident indeed (and in his view threatened the long-term success of the economy; Lardy, 2019).

Chapter 1 pointed to a tendency for debates over China to dichotomize to extremes, not least in an attempt to be heard and influence a policy audience. Discussions of China's political economy provide fertile ground for such dichotomization, as proponents of either free markets or more statist forms try to use China to prove their points. Yet if we dig a little deeper into the substance of the various arguments, there is actually more room to reconcile apparently contradictory positions than might appear at first sight. For example, the term 'state capitalism' that Lardy is objecting to is in itself a rather contested one. We have moved a long way from old understandings of State Capitalism as the almost total domination of economic activity in the Soviet Union. Today, the term refers to more nuanced understandings of a variety of ways in which states interact with markets to direct and guide economic activity, including fostering private sector development and interaction with the capitalist global economy (Nolke, 2014).

Perhaps the concept of *dirigisme* is more apposite – a system where the state dominates strategic economic sectors, uses its ability to control a substantial proportion of investment capital to support state priority areas, and operates through indicative (rather than mandatory) economic planning. Or maybe it's easier still to not try to find a label at all. Instead, we can simply try to identify the ways in which the Chinese state tries to govern the market and create a form of state-coordinated and guided capitalism that creates 'a unique duality … that combines top-down state-led development with bottom-up entrepreneurial private capital accumulation' (McNally, 2012: 744). One where the state sets overall plans and objectives, and then a wide range of different actors experiment with different ways of achieving those aims that can result in very different patterns of state-market relationships across the country (Heilmann, 2009).

Deng Xiaoping was not particularly bothered about labels either. In 1992 when he was promoting the reinvigoration of liberalizing reforms, he argued that:

> The fundamental difference between socialism and capitalism does not lie in the question of whether the planning mechanism or the market mechanism plays a larger role. [The] planned economy does not equal socialism, because planning also exists in capitalism; neither does [the] market economy equal capitalism, because the market also exists in socialism. Both planning and market are just economic means. (Woo, 1999: 46)

It is easy to dismiss this as sophistry and an attempt to justify why a communist party was promoting liberalization and quasi-capitalist practices. And this would indeed seem to be part of the intention. However, the last sentence had resonance in 1992 and continues to do so today. If planning and markets are just means, then means to what ends? The answer is those defined by the top leadership.

Economic activity might be undertaken by a range of actors including private ones responding to market signals. But it is a market that is designed and shaped by a state that retains significant levers to push and direct economic actors to support its own overarching goals. It sets the parameters within which economic interactions take place, how they take place, and who can undertake them. If the private sector and the market can do things that help to meet these objectives – and do things that the state sector can't do or better than the state sector does – then that's fine. Private actors can go about pursuing their own individual goals because these individual objectives are not in conflict with higher state ones, and/or are seen as a means to attaining them. Over the years since 1978, this has largely entailed first tolerating then facilitating an ever-greater role for the market and for non-state actors. Not a single smooth transition and certainly not an inevitable transition to a full and free market economy. But as statist as China might look under Xi in comparison to free market Western economies, it certainly looks massively more liberal than it was in 1984.

This has included integrating into the global economy in ways that resulted in parts of the Chinese economy looking like the most neoliberal of economies when it came to the protection and support of Chinese workers producing goods for foreign multinational companies. In the process, both Chinese and overseas private actors have had ample opportunity to seek profits and develop personal fortunes, with Chinese workers often looking like tools in the production of surplus for others, rather than the recipients and beneficiaries of China's rejuvenation that they are supposed to be (Lin, 2013). Achieving economic growth was the primary and overarching central state goal (almost irrespective of the quality of that growth at times), and with export industries making significant contributions to GDP, they were not only tolerated but actively supported and boosted through preferential state policies.

Market freedom and market failure

This freedom for the market, though, and the relative loosening of central state control, remains contingent on the market doing the things that it is meant to do. And here the overall long-term trend towards liberalization and marketization has always been conditioned by two key anxieties that are either at the heart of Chinese policy making, or very close to it. The first relates to the potential costs of changing the economic structure. The argument that the Chinese growth mode needed to be changed to make it sustainable had become widely accepted in China in the years preceding the global financial crisis. Early moves to make this shift, however, were quickly abandoned when the crisis hit, and replaced by a massive expansion of bank credit and government stimulus to prevent a sharp dip in growth and a sharp increase in unemployment. This might be an extreme example, but it is an indication of the way that a concern with the consequences of shifting the structure of the Chinese economy often results in caution in moving forwards, and sometimes a reversal of policy. The potential growth of unemployment, particularly if concentrated in certain industries and geographic areas, is a particularly important area of concern. So here the tension is between what might be best in the long term, and what is deemed politically expedient and possible in the short term.

The second is a rather fundamental conflict between wanting to use market forces and capitalist methods to promote growth, while at the same time not wanting to lose control of what those market forces are doing.[4] One manifestation of this is that while the Chinese Commercial Bank Law mandates the banks to consider commercial criteria before extending loans, Article 34 specifically also mandates them to 'conduct their business of lending in accordance with the needs of the national economic and social development and under the guidance of the industrial policies of the State' (Szamosszegi and Kyle, 2011: 51). The banks should be both market actors and agents of state policy at the same time.

In essence, the market on its own cannot do all that the leadership wants. If left to itself, it will distribute resources in ways that the leadership thinks could damage politically important sections of society, and thus potentially undermine the attainment of party and state goals. Moreover, the threshold of market failure in China is relatively low – particularly when compared to more liberal economies – and the state's preparedness and ability to step in is relatively high. In short, the market isn't trusted to do everything that the state wants to happen in the economy and to achieve the state's grander overarching objectives. And its freedom of action is subject to it serving these larger goals.

Pricing provides a good example. One of Lardy's (2014) core claims that China should be considered a market economy was that market forces set almost all prices. And this remains the case. After initial incremental moves away from a state-controlled pricing system, the 1997 Price Law made the official move to a supply and demand dominated system (Wu Qianlan, 2013: 94). Further liberalization occurred as China joined the WTO in 2001, and where state pricing still existed, greater flexibility was brought in ensure that prices were closer to market ones than before. These residual state-set prices were also changed more frequently in response to changes in what the real market price would be, preventing the re-emergence of large gaps between state and market prices that had previously been the case for a range of commodities (Lardy, 2014: 15).

That said, the ability to control prices under certain circumstances was retained in the 1997 law. This included state pricing for goods and commodities deemed to 'have a vital bearing on the development of the national economy and the well-being of the people', scarce resources, those under 'natural monopoly, and 'important' public utilities and public welfare services' (MOFCOM, 1997). This has meant that the state has retained control of pricing over key commodities that feed into virtually every other sphere of economic activity; in energy and fuel industries and in transport and communications. Moreover, it can use this control strategically when it sees fit to meet centrally defined national objectives. For example, in April 2015 it reduced power prices (and taxes) to support loss-making iron ore and aluminium producers to help offset the impact of declining market prices for the commodities (Sanderson, 2015). In addition, minimum procurement prices remain for important products like grain, and the state is prepared to step in to buy (and store) agricultural commodities to maintain high prices for producers. Conversely, other prices have been brought back under control and lowered to bring down inflation.

Pricing is just one way in which the state can shape the market that all economic actors (and not just private ones) operate within. It is also an example of where liberalizing reforms are at times suspended or put into reverse if unintended consequences arise. There are other examples too. In Chapter 4 we will see how reforms allowed more Chinese actors to invest in different sectors overseas. The way that these new freedoms were used, though, did not always coincide with state aims and objectives, resulting in new restrictions being introduced on where Chinese investment could go. Similarly, in 2014, getting more Chinese citizens to dip into their extensive savings to invest in the Shanghai stock market became seen as a key means of recapitalizing loss-making enterprises without increasing debt. Companies that needed support were listed on the Shanghai stock exchange, policies were introduced to facilitate trading (including the removal of the previous ban on margin trading), and the state media talked up the prospects of a sound financial future for the country generating considerable financial returns for investors (Fuller, 2016: 59–61). Within a year, a 150 per cent increase in the value of the market, in part built on various legal and not so legal ways of borrowing to finance speculation, was causing concern. A range of new policies were subsequently introduced to first of all stem the flow of borrowing-driven investment, and then to respond to the subsequent rapid fall in market prices as boom turned to potential crash with the value of shares dropping 43 per cent in two months:

> Regulators limited short selling under threat of arrest. Large mutual funds and pension funds pledged to buy more stocks. The government stopped initial public offerings. The government also provided cash to brokers to buy shares, backed by central-bank cash. State-run media continued to persuade its citizens to purchase more stocks. In addition, China Securities Regulatory Commission … imposed a six-month ban on stockholders owning more than 5 percent of a company's stock from selling those stocks. Further, around 1300 total firms, representing 45 percent of the stock market, suspended the trading of stocks. (Zeng Fanhua et al 2016: 415)

Stock markets have failed in many parts of the world and many a government has had to step in to control or stop trading. Even so, the ups and downs of the Shanghai exchange in 2014–16 were a boom and boost 'with Chinese characteristics'. Attempting to use private capital and stock markets to resolve problems in the state sector is a very good example of pragmatically trying whatever 'economic means' (in Deng's language) work best to meet the state's objectives. Using an institution that is 'often considered the epitome of the market model' (Aspers and Kohl, 2016: 58) was seen as a means of strengthening parts of the state sector. The problem was that it didn't work in the way it was thought it would work, and the ability of the market to function had to be curtailed. While it is hard to find accurate ways of measuring the extent of market freedom or influence, it's fair to say that in the case of the Shanghai stock market, it was considerably lower by the summer of 2016 than it had been a year earlier.

The power to guide …

The state does not just try to retain authority by controlling the way that the market functions. At times, the state simply imposes itself in a fashion akin to the old top-down model of state planning. The drive to develop a low carbon economy to deal with severe environmental problems has been driven from the political centre with mandatory targets and plans (Goron, 2018). Environmental targets were also included in the responsibility system which sets targets for local officials that are then used to evaluate their performance. Notably, in the case of the environment, the new targets were given compulsory veto power status (Jin, 2017; Goron, 2018), which means that cadres who didn't meet these targets would be deemed to have failed even if they met all other non-veto targets.[5]

More generally, such target setting linked to cadre evaluation has provided an important way of replacing an element of central power that was previously lost through liberalization and decentralization, and ensuring that the central leadership's priorities are filtered down through the political system to the lowest levels of local government (Gao Jie, 2015). Leading Small Groups that pull together different agencies working in the same broad issue area also play an important role in trying to resolve rivalries and enforce a common position. The strengthening of party committees within all levels of state structures (Gore, 2017) and within private enterprises too (Yan and Huang, 2017) has also created (or recreated) mechanisms through which the party centre's (Xi's) preferences are communicated. The unprecedented length and depth of the anti-corruption campaign initiated by Xi might have also provided new incentives to think twice about imposing individual or local preferences over central ones (Manion, 2016).

This points to the 'intertwined hierarchies' of the party and state in the cascading down of central goals and preferences (Naughton and Tsai, 2015: 1). As another example, it is the party rather than the state that plays a key role in the selection and appointment of key personnel throughout the country; it oversees appointments in government agencies and ministries, SOEs (especially large ones), key financial institutions (especially state owed banks and policy banks, securities commission and other regulators), government-affiliated organization (such as schools, universities, institutes and medical/health organizations), and also most non-government organizations and social organizations (Brødsgaard, 2012, 633–4). The main criteria for selection and promotion are the political quality (especially loyalty to the party) of the candidate, personal qualities such as 'relations with masses', leadership and other professional capabilities, and previous political performance in helping generate economic development. This is why, as noted at the start of this chapter, some have argued that it is the organizational structure of the party, not the state, that establishes the means of turning central objectives into actual policies (Landry, 2008).

Cadre evaluation is linked to residual importance of the Five Year Plan. Although it is now officially called an 'outline programme' (*guihua gangyao*), it generates more than just a programme through the 'network of thousands of sub-plans that evolve into detailed execution instructions' developed by different ministries, at different levels of local governments, and for individual industries (Heilmann and Melton, 2013: 586). Combined with regional development plans, this creates an overarching system of planning that is a major pillar of Chinese industrial policy. The dominance of banks as sources of finance in China has provided an important means of supporting and promoting favoured enterprises and sectors to support the resulting goals. This includes those private enterprises that take on the role of large 'national champions'. Moreover, despite a massive reduction of formally state-owned companies, the state has 'adaptively maintained its authority and control over China's "commanding heights" large state enterprise sector' that shape the very nature of the Chinese market (Li Chen, 2016: 946), and subsidies their activities in a range of different ways. China's most important R&D academies and institutes also remain under central control. When added to the government funded research undertaken at universities, and in the Chinese Academy of Science (which has ministerial standing), then the state remains responsible for R&D and training in a way that Gabriele (2009: 17) argues goes way beyond the 'normal' public sector research activities of other states and societies.

The word 'formally' is used before state-owned in the above because informal and indirect state ownership is even more important than the headline figures suggest. This is because it is not easy to work out who actually owns China's roughly one and a half million Limited Liability Companies (LLCs). While some of these are small independent companies that would be part of the private sector under pretty much any definition, others are part of pyramid type business groups. What look on the face of it like private companies are often subsidiaries of one or more SOE, and have chains of responsibilities that tie them back to the state (Sutherland et al, 2012). As an indication of the what this might mean for an understanding of the state sector in China, in 2010, Naughton (2015: 53) calculated that 23,738 firms could ultimately be traced back to a parent that was one of the roughly 100 SOEs that were owned and controlled by the central government's State-owned Assets Supervision and Administration Commission. When it comes to China's largest companies and national champions, even those that are formally private and independent from the state often receive the sort of state support and external promotion that are normally reserved for state enterprises (Milhaupt and Zheng, 2015). As Wank (1998) argued a number of years ago now, informal relationships can be more important than formal ownership designation in determining who gets state support.

... and the freedom to act

However, while the state might retain important chains of communication that in particular make it easier to do things in times of crises than might otherwise be the case, it does not control what they do on a day-to-day basis. Enterprises of different types can and do behave like market actors pursuing commercial goals in a competitive economy (and in competition with each other) responding to market signals. Millions of private enterprises manage to operate profitably within China's state directed and limited economy, often finding flexible ways of getting round obstacles; for example, using alternatives to the formal banking system to get finance (Hsu, 2012). If we look at the financial system as a whole, we might suggest that it is a very good example of the flexibility, pragmatism and experimentation in findings ways that simply work that has been a core feature of the overarching process of the transition from socialism in China to whatever it is transiting to.

Competition also occurs between China's formal SOEs too. Here it is worth restating that, of the over 100,000 SOEs in China, less than 100 of them are directly owned at the central government level. There can be rather large gaps between the goals and interests of the central leadership and central state apparatus on the one hand, and what local governments want and do on the other hand. Given the diversity of China, there is also not surprisingly rather large gaps between what individual local governments want and do as well, and often intense competition between them to attract investment, develop local champions and so on. Indeed, one of the characteristics of the Chinese political economy that marks it out as somewhat different from previous developmental states is the degree to which the local state is a key actor when it comes to managing the economy. And not just the local as understood as the immediate sub-nation provincial level of authority (including autonomous regions and those municipalities granted provincial level status). The relationship between the party, state, financial institutions and enterprises can be rather intimate the lower down the hierarchy of power you go, where building a close relationship with the local government is a good way of increasing the chances of private enterprises succeeding (Yang Keming, 2012). As Bai et al (2019: 3) argue in a paper that outlines the various types of support that a local government can extend to favoured enterprises: 'The only way for private firms to succeed in China is to obtain a special deal from a local political leader, which allows them to either break the formal rules or obtain favorable access to resources.' The argument that this is the 'only' way of succeeding could be challenged. However, while there is disagreement in the China studies community over the extent and significance of local autonomy, there is more or less unanimity that local governments matter. It has become a common sense of sorts. Yet it bears repeating that this understanding is often missing when it comes to mainstream IR conceptions of what China is and wants.

The contract responsibility system might start at the top, but setting targets is not the same thing as mandating exactly how they should be met. Local leaders are left to work out how best to meet them based on the conditions in their own local territories. When the emphasis was on generating economic growth, this resulted in the creation of a whole range of different ways of boosting local economies. These local plans were typically made in isolation from what other local authorities were doing, and often resulted in competition between them. What made a huge amount of sense for the individual and the locality made little sense at all when aggregated nationally (Whiting, 2004). One consequence was a massive overcapacity in a number of sectors as various local governments sought to encourage the expansion of the same types of economic activity as each other. Local leaders were also often faced with meeting targets in different areas that were very difficult indeed to reconcile (Gao Jie, 2010: 69). This became particularly problematic as the stress shifted from growth alone to 'harmonious' growth in 2013 (Jin, 2017), with local leaders now expected to meet both growth and sustainability targets at the same time. Moreover, as targets pass down through the ladder of authority, new targets and interpretations can be added that are then passed on further downwards:

> The central leaders develop general policy objectives according to their overarching goals for China's socioeconomic development. Local officials then transform these policy objectives into a variety of performance targets in accordance with the local situation and allocate the targets to their subordinates at the next lower level. During this process, local leaders may add extra performance targets that are established to meet the needs of local development plans. As such, as performance targets are allocated downwards through the administrative hierarchy, a target pyramid is formed. (Gao Jie, 2015: 40)

Concern that local governments had too strong a grip on national finances led to tax reforms in 1994 designed to return the balance of fiscal power back to the central government. Since then, however, one consequence has been that localities have been all but forced to find new creative ways of raising money. Not only were the resulting 'normal' sources of income they received often insufficient to meet spending obligations, but on an individual level, leaders wanted to support those projects that would deliver the local growth that they needed to enhance their career prospects (ADB, 2014). Chief among these was the use of land-use rights; not selling the land itself as this remains the property of the (local) state, but the right to utilize it in different ways for limited periods. Over the years, this became the single most important source of income that local governments could directly control themselves. This meant that rising real estate prices and frequent transfers of utilization rights became a good thing for local governments, if not for local residents and insecure tenants of various types.

Even in times of crisis, the centre's control is far from complete. The response to the global financial crisis is an excellent example here. It was the central government that decided to act quickly, not only announcing a stimulus package, but telling the banks to overturn their previous policy of caution and lend China out of a potential recession caused by a collapse of exports to the crisis hit West (Lardy, 2012). But it was local governments that were then were left to deliver growth, establishing thousands of Local Investment Platform Companies (*difang rongzi pingtai gongsi*) which borrowed from the banks to fund local projects (mostly infrastructure ones).[6] Growth was maintained and crisis averted, but at the cost of a further lack of coordination and, more important, an expansion of debt that over a decade later was proving very hard (and impossible in places) to pay off.

Actors, actions and strategy

We could go on. But it is not the intention here to provide anything more than the most basic and limited overview of the nature of China's political economy than is necessary. Rather, the intention is to try and flesh out in the broadest of brushstrokes the symbiotic relationship between state driven control and direction on the one hand, and independent interest and action within the resulting parameters of action on the other. If we ask if the Chinese state sets objectives for economic performance and results that it wants to mobilize the economy and society to achieve, then the answer is yes it does. And if we ask if the Chinese state trusts the market to achieve these goals, then the answer is no. But this doesn't mean that other actors aren't following their own objectives at the same time and/or utilizing the state's strategic concerns to pursue commercial profit-based agendas. Nor does it mean that the state always achieves what it sets out to attain. Different and even conflicting local objectives (and interpretations of central directives) can at times generate dysfunctional outcomes at the aggregate national level.

There is much that the Chinese state can do to control international economic interactions. And more than many other states can do to control what domestic economic actors do, and where they do it. But other objectives can also be pursued by both state and non-state actors. Sometimes these support overall central state objectives and contribute to their attainment. But not always. And to think of a single state interest and single state actor also underestimates the degree of bounded pluralism and the range of actors and interests within the Chinese state itself. As we move to consider Chinese strategies and preferred mechanisms for bringing about global change in the following chapters, it is important to keep the implications of this bounded autonomy in mind.

3

Chinese (Grand) Strategies for (Global) Change

For a number of years, Chinese analysts who studied Chinese strategy found it difficult to find one. The level of fragmentation and the (bounded) plurality of interests discussed in the previous chapter were so great that what they found instead was a rather contradictory set of interests and drivers resulting in a lack of coherence in external action (Wang Jisi, 2011). For example, despite calling his book *Inside China's Grand Strategy*, Ye Zicheng (2011) focused on the myriad domestic problems at home that China had to sort out before it could do anything effective overseas. In particular, he highlighted what he portrayed as the almost impossible task of reconciling the views of 'dogmatic conservatives' on the one hand, and 'extreme nationalists' (of various varieties) on the other. Somewhat earlier, Shi Yinhong (2002: 4) bemoaned an absence of a shared understanding of what it was that China actually wanted to achieve and concluded that

> today's China in her rising is still far from having developed a system of clear and coherent long-term fundamental national objectives, diplomatic philosophy and long term or secular grand strategy ... a rising China is and will probably be for a long time an uncertain and somewhat perplexed China.

In the first decade of the millennium, Men Honghua (2004; 2005) was one of the biggest critics of this lack of coordination. By 2015, while acknowledging that the job was still far from complete, he had become more confident. China was now moving, he argued, towards something that began to look like a truly integrated GS with 'a profound strategic adjustment, gradually forming the future of China's long-term strategic layout' (Men, 2015: 44). Three key reasons are usually given for this progress. The first is the widespread understanding in China that changes in the global environment had resulted in a rather unexpected shift in relative power capabilities, and China now had an opportunity to push for change that was previously lacking. The second is that Xi Jinping had implemented structural changes that facilitated much needed coordination among conflicting foreign affairs actors. The third was that his strategic thinking had established the fundamental objectives and diplomatic philosophy that Shi (2002) and others had argued was previously lacking.

This chapter relies heavily on what has been said in China about Chinese strategic thinking – including what has been said by China's top leaders themselves. While this allows us to try and understand what this strategy is and what it is meant to achieve, it does create significant risks. As noted in the Four Extents, the nature of the political system under Xi means that contradictory voices have been somewhat quieter than in previous years, and what looks like greater consensus can hide considerable silent disagreement. It is easy, then, to assume a level of support and buy-in that exaggerates the real balance of opinion. In addition, and thinking back to the discussion of strategic signalling in Chapter 1, clearly announced strategies might have more to do with establishing a preferred vision of what China is and how it will act as a great power than reflecting what China's leaders really want. Xi's strategic thinking might be better thought of as an exercise in political marketing rather than a real and deliverable guide to action. Talking about a strategy is one thing, what is actually done might be something rather different. As such, it's important to maintain a healthy scepticism over whether what looks like a strategy and is sold as a strategy is really something else instead. Perhaps a tool in the promotion of a preferred non-Western identity as a great power designed to attain other ends (and perhaps hide other strategic goals).

As Zhang Feng (2012: 319) argues, 'a grand strategy can almost always be inferred if one tries hard enough to rationalize it', and it is only fair to accept that the analysis here does include a degree of inference. This entails placing a degree of clarity on 'the conceptual flow' of Xi's strategic thinking that isn't always very clear or fluid in Xi's speeches or interpretations of them. There is a degree of confusion in this thinking and writing over means/actions and ends/aspirations that can make it difficult to work out what leads to what. It is also not wholly clear if there is one single theoretical/philosophical starting point (Marxism-Leninism) or two (Marxism-Leninism and Chinese historical thinking). As such, while the flow of thinking provided in

Figure 3.1 (later in this chapter) makes some sort of sense, it might be a sense that has been imposed on something that is less clear in reality. Finally, the previous chapter has established important caveats regarding different interests and intentions that should also inform the way we think about how the top leaderships' objectives can be attained.

Keeping all of this very much in mind as mediating variables, we can identify ten major strands of what looks like an overall Chinese strategy for change. Some of these ten have been extracted from analysing what Xi and other Chinese leaders have said about what China wants, and how it does and will exercise Great Power Diplomacy with Chinese Characteristics (GPDCC). However, rather than just relying on self-declared strategy, other strands have been inferred from action instead; including in the case of core interests, action that seems to contradict at least one of the supposed principles of China's new type of diplomacy. Do these ten strands combine to form a coherent GS? The answer really depends on what you expect a GS to look like as it is a term that has come to mean different things to different people (Silove, 2018). In its earlier connotations (and some current ones as well), it implied directing and coordinating all national resources to win a war and then control the resulting post-war peace (Liddell Hart, 1954). This idea of China mobilizing to win a battle is perhaps at the back of the mind of those who refer to China's GS in an undefined way. Not necessarily a military conflict, but a more general struggle for global dominance.

A more limited understanding of GS used by Chinese analysts points to the creation of mechanisms for integrating domestic and international security and economic policy making that were previously lacking (Men, 2015). This is useful in pointing to the substantial changes that have occurred in an attempt to redress previous weaknesses and provide joined-up thinking and practice under Xi. It also allows for an understanding of having a set of goals and preferred ways of attaining them, without then also assuming that all that is said and done is necessarily directly controlled and organized by the top leadership. It is also not too distant in conception from neoclassical realist understandings that GS exists at the intersection between the domestic and the international/ structural levels. Here, a GS results from domestic considerations shaping which specific preferences and objectives are prioritized given not only what you want to attain, but also what is attainable given the prior and overarching constraints established by the nature of the international system (Taliaferro et al, 2009; Kitchen, 2010).[1]

Rather than think of a GS with all the different interpretations that follow from capitalizing the G and S, it might be easier to stick with the idea of bounded autonomy within the constraints of the strategic objectives and structures established by the central leadership established in Chapter 2. This allows us to focus on the symbiotic relationship between top-down authority and bounded independent action, and remember that not all that is done by Chinese overseas is done at the central state's direct behest to attain state goals. The drivers of any given relationship can be rather difficult to unravel. Sometimes SOEs and private enterprises are acting on behalf of the state, undertaking projects that Norris (2016) suggests wouldn't be pursued by private economic actors just seeking market access and profits. But sometimes they are not. And although it might not matter as long as these commercially driven actions help attain state determined objectives, evidence suggests that on some occasions, they don't.

Low profile as strategy?

Discussions over Chinese strategy in China over the years have been in part shaped by considerations of language and translation. For example, more than one Chinese scholar has suggested in private discussions that as a GS was something that hegemonic great powers like the US had, there was thus something of a reluctance to talk of China having one too. After all, China's leaders seldom missed the opportunity to declare that 'China will never pursue hegemony or expansion, nor will it seek to create spheres of influence, no matter how the international situation changes, and how China develops itself' (State Council, 2019). This specific quote is taken from the 2019 White Paper on China and the World, but the same basic message has been pushed by consecutive leaders since Deng Xiaoping.

When originally proposed by Hu Jintao and subsequently taken up with gusto by Xi, the Chinese term *renlei mingyun gongtongti* was officially translated in English as a 'Community of Common Destiny for Humankind', and more often, simply described as a 'Community of Common Destiny'. But as Cao Zhiyuan (2017: 42–3) notes, by 2015 the term 'Community of Shared Future for Mankind' (sometimes Humankind) was usually being used instead, and later became the standard translation. This was because the word 'destiny' in English was thought to imply a lack of choice and agency along a pre-determined trajectory of (only) China's making. Presumably the same line of thinking also explains why *zhongguo fang'an* has increasingly been translated in English as the 'China Solution' (CS) rather than a Chinese 'scheme', 'plan' or 'programme' which would be the more normal translation of *fang'an* (and which are still also sometimes used). Indeed, having been widely used in reference to Chinese solutions to global problems at the 2016 Group of Twenty (G20) summit in Hangzhou, mentions of the CS in English seemed to go out of fashion. Similarly, there was what Eliot Chen (2019) called a 'purging' of references to MIC2025 in the Chinese media as a result of negative responses in the US, Germany and elsewhere. Even the idea of 'China's Peaceful Rise' was subsequently changed because it potentially focused external attention on 'rise' rather than 'peaceful' (Suettinger, 2004), and the words Belt and Road in English are now typically followed by 'initiative' (*changyi*) rather than 'strategy' (*zhanlue*).

These examples show the care that has been taken in trying to find a way of establishing Chinese agendas and objectives in ways that do not generate potential harmful responses. Or rather, the care that has been taken some of the time. There have been other times when more assertive representatives of the Chinese state have seemed much less worried about the response to what they have said (and the way they have said it). Interestingly, in all these cases, it was just the language and/or the usage that changed rather than the content/ policy itself. The changes that occurred on the Belt and Road were not a direct consequence of a change in nomenclature from initiative to strategy. They were a result of changing perceptions of the benefits of Belt and Road projects both in recipient states and within China itself. Even when the specific term MIC2025 was not being used, the policies associated with it remained firmly in place. And while the use of the CS might have declined in English language media, debating and promoting the idea of a *zhongguo fang'an* remained a live topic of internet debate on Chinese language internet platforms (Shi-Kupfer and Ohlberg, 2017). As we shall see in Chapter 6, it also took on new dimensions in Chinese language academic literature too, becoming associated with thinking on the superiority of China's developmental path.

These examples highlight one of the key dilemmas in the evolution of China's global posturing. How do you make it clear what you want in ways that do not generate negative responses from others? This dilemma has been a key part of the process of trying to move on from the *taoguang yanghui* philosophy that dominated for much of the post-Mao period towards a more proactive attempt to 'strive for achievements' (Hu Jian, 2012). *Taoguang yanghui* comes from what is usually referred to as a '24 character' phrase promoted by Deng Xiaoping in the post-Tiananmen era when China faced the opprobrium (albeit ultimately short lived) of the international community. In its most popular form, it actually has 28 characters,[2] and although it is normally referred to in English (including in official Chinese translations) as 'Keeping a low profile', a more exact translation of *taoguang yanghui* is 'hide brightness, cherish obscurity'.

As Shirk (2007: 105) notes, 'hide' in the literal translation and associations with Xunzi's *Art of War* led some to conclude that it was a deliberate strategy of obscuring China's true intentions while it was weak, until it was in a position to really try to get what it wanted. Chinese analysts, though, were clear that it was definitely not a deliberate attempt to hide true intentions and to intentionally deceive. Rather, it was a simple guide to action based on the objective reality of Chinese power and China's place in the world. It represented an 'expedient measure to deal with the complex international situation of the time' (Li Qiao, 2007: 41) and 'indicates the strategic direction for our party and state to adjust and implement a more pragmatic and flexible foreign policy in a complicated international situation' (Li Gemin, 2009: 1).

Much of what is written in Chinese on *taoguang yanghui* refers to it as Deng Xiaoping's strategic thinking, strategic diplomatic thinking, or international strategic thought; including both of the articles that the quotes in the previous paragraph come from (which is exactly why they were chosen). It is considered to be strategic as it entailed assessing what could be done given the nature of the world order and China's power capabilities at the time. This again sounds like a neoclassical realist exercise in Grand Strategizing. Buzan also thought that the resulting emphasis on Peaceful Rise and Peaceful Development represented a Chinese GS of sorts:

> It contains a theory about how the world works and how China should relate to that world in the light of its overriding priority to development. It takes military, political, and economic elements into account, and is sensitive to what kind of image China should project to the world. It thus sets a framework for defining China's national interests, and offers a basic principle about how to relate means to ends. (Buzan, 2014: 387–8)

He has a point. Though if this really was a clear idea of how to relate means to ends, the key was to be pragmatic and experimental and to focus on whatever worked in any given situation (Swaine, 2000: 275). So if there was a strategy it was not to have any clearly defined prescriptions or proscriptions at all. Moreover, as the discussion in previous chapters suggests, the diversity of interests and fragmentation in policy making and implementation points to considerable challenges in turning interests into ends.

More power in a changing global order

We have already noted more than once the perceived importance of the global financial crisis in leading to a shift in Chinese thinking on the nature of the global order, and what might be attainable. The resulting change in direction in foreign policy is often identified as occurring at the Central Work Conference on Foreign Affairs in July 2009 which 'adjusted Deng Xiaoping's famous dictum for keeping a low profile ... by putting more emphasis on his injunction to "get something accomplished"' (Yahuda, 2013, 447). It will certainly do as a symbolic turning point even if real change was more evolutionary than immediate and absolute.

Initially, though, rather than creating new opportunities, the perceived power shift created new problems. For Wang Jisi (2011: 68), the speed and extent of the shift took China's leaders by surprise. Having found themselves newly powerful, he argues, China's leaders did not always use this power in effective ways, and instead became 'increasingly assertive'. This generated a negative response from a number of important global actors and 'left both China and its partners underprepared, somewhat confused, and with increased chances for miscalculation' (Shi Yinhong, 2015: 1). The question, then, was how best to take advantage of the opportunities that the global crisis (and other changes) had given China to use its power resources to bring about change in others that best met Chinese interests (Zhu Chenghu, 2011). Or put another way, having power is one thing. How to use it effectively is quite another thing altogether.

Xi Jinping and Chinese strategy

Continuity and change

Although Xi Jinping is largely credited for creating a path out of this uncertainty towards selective global leadership, it is important to take a step back from the idea that all has changed under Xi, or that Xi is responsible for all of that change. This is partly because power transitions are not just about what rising powers do or want. What existing powers do (or don't do) is important too. That Xi's leadership coincided with a Trump Presidency that was perceived to be moving the US away from global leadership, multilateralism and a commitment to an open global trade structure is clearly significant. It created the impression in China that a space had been vacated that China could now seek to fill (Yan, 2019: 10). This was reflected in the way in which Xi tried to establish China as the champion of global free trade and open economies in the face of growing inward looking protectionism elsewhere.

Similarly, as the coronavirus outbreak went global in 2020, there was a concerted effort to identify China as *a* – and maybe *the* – global leader of the response as a result of the US stepping back from the World Health Organization (WHO). With individual European nations seeking their own solutions rather than working collectively through the EU, it was also left to China, so the narrative goes, to provide the emergency support that countries like Italy, Iran and Serbia desperately needed (Sun, 2020). As we shall see in Chapter 5, the opportunity was not grasped very effectively. But the fact that it was there at all – not least given China's role in the early spread of the virus – was much more to do with what Trump and other Western leaders did (and didn't do) than it was a consequence of Chinese strategy. From conflict in the Middle East and north Africa through to missteps in responding to the pandemic via a range of different crises on the way, the roots of many of the challenges to the liberal global order emerged from inside that liberal order itself.

Moreover, China's international policies and strategies did not start anew on 15 November 2012 – the day that Xi formally became General Secretary of the CCP. There is actually a lot in the new thinking that looks like the reaffirmation of now rather longstanding principles that have supposedly been guiding Chinese international interactions since the Panchsheel Treaty of 1954 (which established the Five Principles of Peaceful Co-existence). But even if we focus on the other new turns in Chinese foreign policy under Xi, there is evidence of continuity with the past rather than a fundamental break or change; though we should remember that as Vice President from 2008, Xi was part of the previous power structure as well.

By the time Xi became top leader, Hu Jintao had already played a key role in leading China away from *taoguang yanghui* (Zhao Suisheng, 2010). Moreover, while similarly arguing that Hu's conception of a 'harmonious world' represented the key shift in Chinese global thinking and strategy away from the previous era, Zheng and Tok (2007) argue that Hu's innovations were themselves built on the prior adjustments in thinking and practice made by Jiang Zemin. It was Jiang who spoke of taking advantage of an important period of strategic opportunity (*zhongyao zhanlue jiyu qi*) to make China better off and globally powerful at the 16th Party Congress in 2002 (Jiang, 2002). Fifteen years later Xi was still pointing to the moment of opportunity as being the key to China's global role in the future (Xi, 2017e). Even the aspiration to build a CSFM that has become so associated with Xi's global ambitions was first raised by Hu Jintao (2012) in his valedictory speech at the 18th Party Congress. And discussions of GPDCC uses language that will be familiar to those who have studied previous explanations of how and why China will peacefully rise. China's new 'assertiveness' in the South China Sea and elsewhere had already been identified (Thayer, 2011) and contested (Johnston, 2013) before Xi took control,[3] and a set of 'core interests' were in the process of being established that represented policy red lines that were not open for negotiation with anybody (Swaine, 2010). The decision to actively seek reform of global economic governance had also been formally adopted as a key national strategy before Xi's assumption of power (in Chapter 53 of the 12th Five Year Plan adopted in March 2011). And while Xi might have stepped up the search for (or creation of) an idealized Chinese past that explains how China will behave in the future, it was under Hu that Chinese history and philosophy made the transition from being a 'feudal rot' or a 'meaningless remnants of the backward past' to become a positive foundation of contemporary Chinese thinking and practice (Kallio, 2016: 18).

A Xi change?

So we can trace a continuity not just from Xi to Hu before him, but also back to Jiang Zemin. Indeed, as will be discussed in Chapter 5, there is an evolutionary logic to Chinese perceptions of its place in a changing global order that can be traced back to the response to China's potential international isolation in and after 1989. But whatever the reality of continuities with the past, discussions of China's global role often typically do indeed identify the 18th Party Congress as the start of a new era. As just one example of many, Dong Wen (2018: 64) suggests that:

> Since the inauguration of President Xi Jinping in 2012, the new international relations have demonstrated the greatness of China's peace-loving and win–win development. It has established a great power image of China's non-hegemony and non-expansion, embodying a civilized country, an eastern Great Power, a responsible Great Power and a socialist Great Power.

As Richard Hu (2019, 3) argues, 'leadership matters in foreign policy transformation and Xi Jinping's leadership has played a key role in transforming Chinese foreign policy'. In terms of developing a GS, three major reasons are put forward to support the idea that Xi's leadership is responsible for this transition to a new era.

Linking the internal and the external

The first is bureaucratic and structural reform already hinted at in Chapter 2. The creation of a new National Security Commission (NSC) in 2013 in particular can be seen as representing a fundamental lack of faith in what had become a fragmented foreign affairs decision making (and implementing) power structure over previous decades (Lampton, 2015). The NSC is not a foreign policy institution as such as it has a very strong domestic facing focus (You, 2016), with a particular emphasis on what are typically referred to in Chinese as the 'three evils' or 'evil forces' (*sange shili*) of terrorism, separatism and religious extremism. It also has its philosophical starting point in the conception of 'comprehensive security'. This is the idea that national security is not just about preventing war and inter-state conflict (though this obviously remains very important) but also encompasses a whole range of non-traditional security issue areas as well; the environment, economy, culture and so on (Liu Jianfei, 2018: 24). Its goal is to bring together different elements of the security management apparatus together under a single overarching hierarchy to get a holistic approach, to provide holistic solutions, and also to break down the conceptual barriers between what is a domestic security challenge and what is an international issue (Hu Weixing, 2019; Cabestan, 2017). The idea of comprehensive security has been around for some time, evolving from the rethinking of the nature of security after the end of the Cold War and the introduction of a new security concept (*xin anquan guan*) under Jiang Zemin (FMPRC, 2002). But it is under Xi that this thinking has been transformed into institutional change.

The establishment of a range of functional Leading Small Groups also provides a means of bringing together different bureaucratic actors into single institutional settings where different interests can either be reconciled or subordinated to the wishes of the central leader (Brødsgaard, 2017; Tsai and Zhou, 2019). For students of GS, the most significant result of these changes was that almost for the first time since the revolutionary era, there was now a formal institutional mechanism where internal and external objectives and core interests could be brought together and combined to form a single coherent strategy. This linking of the domestic and international, so the argument goes, is the fundamental starting point for understanding China's new GS. For example, Zhao Minghao (2015: 101) argues that:

> China's grand strategy can be interpreted as an internal-external rebalancing. Such delicate and ambitious rebalancing entails a twofold effort: one is a series of bold internal reforms to regain the economic momentum and upgrade its competitiveness, and the other is to proactively enhance its international position as a global power and satisfy its national security requirements.

and the two dimensions of this double balancing can only be done effectively because of the institutional changes implemented by Xi.

The BRI has been identified as almost the epitome of how to integrate domestic development goals and political economy considerations with external policy. It has its origins in the search for a new growth pattern to replace a previous reliance on exports and domestic investment, while at the same time dealing with the twin constraints caused by chronic overcapacity (particularly in construction related industries) and 'excessive' foreign currency reserves (Wang Yong, 2016: 457). It also had conceptual antecedents in the longstanding desire to rebalance the economy by helping develop western and central regions by creating international linkages that do not have to flow via China's coastal provinces. The BRI should also reduce the previous dependence on oil imports – particularly those that flow through the Straits of Malacca (Wuthnow, 2017). These potential domestic gains were all seen in China (rightly or wrongly) as increasing Chinese political influence overseas at the same time (Swaine, 2015). Indeed, these inside–outside linkages plus the support and commitment of China's top leader have led some to conclude that the BRI is in itself a form of Chinese GS (Zhang Feng, 2015; Clarke, 2020); though from the logic applied it would seem to make more sense for it to form one strategic tool of a grander GS rather than a GS in itself.

Strategic signalling (again)

The second major difference that Xi has made is in signalling his and China's intentions to use power resources in certain ways. This is true both in terms of signalling to an international audience (which we have already discussed in detail) and also to domestic audiences (within the party and within the country more generally). Add all that he has done in explaining Chinese goals and capabilities to these audiences, and it certainly sounds as if he is trying to articulate that China has a GS.

Pang Zhongying (2018: 8) points to Xi's speech at the UN in September 2015 (Xi, 2015) as the first time China's new agenda was outlined to a global audience. And as shown by the analysis of Xi's speeches listed in the Appendix to this book, it is certainly true that Xi was particularly active in establishing China's credentials as a global governance reformer and his commitment to offering Chinese solutions to the world throughout 2015. When you add on the various domestic and national high-level speeches made by Xi and others after the Party Congress and on into 2018 – a particularly active year in Chinese strategic signalling – it is difficult to disagree with Elizabeth Economy's (2018, C3) argument that six years after taking over the leadership of the party, Xi Jinping had effectively 'proclaimed that China has both the intent and the capability to reshape the international order'.

Xi Jinping's strategic thinking

The Appendix provides a selected list of major events and speeches from the 12th Five Year Plan in 2011 through to the celebrations of the 70th anniversary of the PRC in 2019. This is not a complete record, but an annotated log of those official sources that were analysed in preparing this book. It is made up of both major speeches by top leaders at major events (that thus perform an important signalling function) and those sources that are representative of the sorts of arguments being made more generally by Chinese foreign affairs related officials.[4] In Chapter 6, these will be used to provide the textual basis for the analysis of whether there is a coherent China alternative view of world order, and can hopefully provide a shortcut for others interested in Chinese strategic thinking and signalling in this period. Here, the same texts are simply used to show the ways in which Xi (and others) presented China's new positions to domestic and global audiences.

Collectively they build a picture of Xi's idealized vision of the world that he wants China to help build, and explain how China can help build it; though again, sometimes using a rather idealized view of Chinese actions. While just having goals and an understanding of how they might be achieved might be too thin to constitute a GS even by the loosest of definitions, the third reason that Xi has been identified as making a key break from his predecessors is through this strategic thinking. To comprehend how his strategic thinking is on a different level from what others have done, we need to go back to the importance of understanding domestic politics, and the way that theoretical innovations (for example, of Hu and Jiang) are different from theoretical turning points (for example, of Mao, Deng and Xi).

There is an increasingly strong interest in how Chinese history can provide a basis for a future alternative Chinese world order. Including by Xi himself. Nevertheless, Marxism is continually reasserted as the starting point of all Chinese strategic thinking. But this does not mean that Marxism generates the same prescriptions for China under Xi as it did under previous leaders. It has to change to meet the realities of the time. As just one example of this mode of thinking, at the 95th Anniversary of the party's founding in 2016, Xi (2016b) argued that: 'Marxism, and its development in China, has guided the causes of our Party and people with scientific theories that not only run in continuity but are also able to evolve as the times require. ... Marxism is the fundamental guiding thought upon which our Party and country are founded.' Here, the need for Xi's new thinking is explained in ways that echo the distinction between Theory and Thought that was at the heart of both Mao's original reinterpretation of Marxism, and Deng's subsequent reinterpretation of Mao (Sun and Li, 2017; Gao Hong, 2018; Xiao Xinfa, 2018).

Mao's revolutionary strategy was based on rejecting Marxism as a blueprint that explained how revolution *would* happen (through proletarian revolution in advanced industrialized economies) and instead treating it as a theoretical guide to practical action. Theory in the shape of Marxism – or by then, Marxism-Leninism – provided the guiding principles, or what the CCP constitution calls 'the laws governing the development of the history of human society' (CCP, 2017: 1). These laws need to be applied to the concrete specific circumstances of each case to produce actual guides to action that are subject specific and generate practical revolutionary Thought. Thus, because Russia in the 1910s was very different from China in the 1930s and 40s, the application of the same guiding theoretical principles to the two cases produced two very different but equally Marxist revolutionary strategies. Indeed, from this logic it was a misuse of Theory to dogmatically take what had happened in the Russian case as a model for revolution in China because of the very different contexts of the two revolutionary processes. Deng used exactly the same logic to explain why Mao's revolutionary strategy had to be abandoned after his death. Times had changed and the biggest threat to the revolution was no longer unresolved class struggle, so he argued, but poverty and underdevelopment. Thus, it was now entirely right and in keeping with Mao's own approach to abandon the specific policies Mao had proposed and stood for and instead focus on expanding the productive forces.

It would be theoretically wrong, then, to simply keep on following the same development path as the material conditions of the country and the nature of the global order had both changed. Socialism needs to be dynamic and change in response to these and other changes (Yu Chengwen, 2017). Or as Xi (2016b) put it:

> as it is confronted with new trends and requirements in practice, Marxism also needs to be further adapted to China, further attuned to contemporary needs, and further popularized. Marxism does not exhaust truth, but rather paves a path towards it. ... Ideas are born from the times in which we live, and theories originate from practice ... Today, times have changed, and the breadth and depth of our country's development have far surpassed what the authors of the Marxist classics imagined when they wrote their works.

After Deng, other leaders had made their own theoretical contributions. But, so the argument goes, Xi's theoretical contribution was of a different order, as it entailed changing the primary contradiction which is meant to be the very starting point of all subsequent thinking and action. If the primary contradiction isn't correctly resolved by the party, then the revolution and the party will be defeated.[5]

In terms of international relations and China's global role, Xi's theoretical thinking is said to have done two things. First, like Deng Xiaoping before him, he has reflected on the overall nature of the changing global environment, on China's changing position within the global order (its changing relative comprehensive national power), on the successes that the party has achieved, and identified the major challenges that still face it in the future. Second, he has taken Marxist principles as filtered through the innovations of his predecessors and filtered them again through the lessons of China's history and the wisdom of China's ancient philosophies to come up with a new guiding theory for a new age. Or that is how it is meant to be. When looked at in more detail – as it is in Chapter 6 – the way that China's pre-revolutionary past is used looks less like an intervening variable than a separate independent starting point in its own right. In some interpretations, it looks even more important. As a result, it is presented alongside Marxism as a second separate originator of ideas in Figure 3.1, rather than as a subordinate and intervening variable that the logic of the argument suggests that it really should be.

Joined-up thinking? A conceptual strategic flow

At the heart of Xi's new thinking on international relations and global order are four key concepts. Although their abbreviations (and alternative translations) have already been established earlier in this book, it is worth repeating them here as the following section is going to be abbreviation heavy:

NTIR	New Type of International Relations	*xinxing daguo guanxi*
GPDCC	Great Power Diplomacy with Chinese Characteristics[6]	*zhongguo tesede daguo waijiao*
CS	China Solution	*zhongguo fang'an*
CSFM	Community of Shared Future for Mankind[7]	*renlei mingyun gongtongti*

These are not the only ones – far from it. In fact, The China Dream (*zhongguo meng*) has actually been the main focus of external attention and might well have been mentioned more than any of the others. It's certainly literally been the 'poster boy' for new thinking (in that it has been the subject of countless propaganda posters and other forms of visual displays). But following Mattis's (2019) argument that we need to think how different concepts link together to form a logical greater whole, it is these four that have a degree of logical coherence. Collectively, they *might* form the basis of a conceptual flow that links a philosophical and/or theoretical starting point, with a way of putting this into practice to achieve the goal of establishing a new Chinese form of world order, and an understanding of 'what kind of happy ending will emerge at the destination' (Kallio, 2016: 47). The world 'might' is emphasized in the above sentence because it is not always clear what is meant to lead to what, and there is a danger that a logic and order has been imposed on something that is really more messy and confused. The exact nature of the future world when all this has been done is also less than clearly and explicitly outlined and explained (Rolland, 2020).

At first sight, it is fairly clear that the CSFM is the ultimate aspiration for the type of world order China would like to live in. It is an 'idealistic vision for the future' (Wang Jianwei, 2019: 22) and a vision of 'the kind of future mankind should build' (Wang Yi, 2017b). However, as the CSFM was included as the 13th of the 14 essential points of Xi's Thought at the 19th Party Congress, it is thus both part of the guiding thought and one of the things that the guiding thought is meant to attain at the same time. At the risk of causing further confusion, it is also not always clear if the NTIR is a means to achieve the CSFM, or if it is the type of international relations that will exist once the CSFM has been established. In most analyses, the intention is to establish the NTIR as the vehicle. For example, in Section Twelve of his report to the 19th Party Congress where he talks about 'Working to Build a Community of Shared Future for Mankind', Xi stated that:

> we should respect each other, discuss issues as equals, resolutely reject the Cold War mentality and power politics, and take a new approach to developing state-to-state relations with communication, not confrontation, and with partnership, not alliance. We should commit to settling disputes through dialogue and resolving differences through discussion, coordinate responses to traditional and non-traditional threats, and oppose terrorism in all its forms. (Xi, 2017e, 52–3)

But if this is an outline of how we get there, it is also descriptive of what the world will be like when the CSFM has been established; the type of international interactions that will occur once all other countries (and not just China) have adopted the NTIR.

As such it's really not surprising that in some places the CSFM and NTIR are used almost interchangeably. And in many respects, it doesn't matter. After all, as Li Liyan argues (2018: 10), one of the key functions of talking about the CSFM (and talking about it so much) is to signal to the world that China has (or believes it has) new and different international relations ethics that it now wants to promote. So the exact terms that are used to explain what this ethical position entails is not *that* significant as long as the message is delivered and understood. That said, Yuan Peng (2018: 25) makes a distinction between the NTIR as a 'periodic goal' and the CSFM as the 'ultimate objective'. And this idea of intermediate and longer-term goals makes a lot of sense. Moreover, while creating a CSFM might depend on others buying into what China wants, China does have the ability to act in certain ways itself and bring about change by practising GPDCC. In Xi's words: 'major country diplomacy with Chinese characteristics aims to *foster* a new type of international relations and build a community with a shared future for mankind' (Xi, 2017e: 16, emphasis added).

Despite some fuzziness, there does seem to be an attempt to establish a logical conceptual flow. Xi's theoretical innovations and strategic thinking generates (or should generate) a new and different way of acting. New and different compared to what China has done in the past, and different from how other great powers acted in the past and act today. This new diplomatic action is intended to attain both immediate 'core interest' objectives, intermediate changes in the way that international relations are conducted, and grander world order type ultimate objectives (Zhang Hui, 2018). So while accepting that Figure 3.1 provides more clarity and logic than is always evident in Chinese discourses, it provides a rough flow chart for turning ambition and interest into outcomes. What this world that China wants to build might look like is the focus of the analysis in Chapter 6. In addition to the various abbreviations already repeated and clarified above, it is perhaps also worth clarifying here that in Figure 3.1, M-L is short for Marxism Leninism, and of course, XJP stands for Xi Jinping.

Aspiration and practice: Chinese strategy for global change

If we bring the analysis down from the conceptual level to the specifics of what can be done to try to attain Chinese goals, then we can identify ten broad strategic strands. The word 'strands' here is used in its loosest possible definition to allow it to cover a range of different types of actions and objectives. Those that are dealt with in depth in the following chapters are simply noted here, with the detailed explanations left for later.

One example, and the first strategic strand, is the goal of ensuring that China's ideas and preferences are heard in a world where other voices dominate, which is dealt with in detail in Chapter 5 (and to an extent in Chapter 6 as well). This is captured in Figure 3.1 by the term 'China Voice', which is an umbrella term for a variety of different tools that have been deployed to disseminate Chinese narratives. The looseness of the term 'strand' is also evident here, as the China Voice is both a means and an end at the same time. Developing discursive power is seen as a way of changing the way that others think about China, and therefore the way that they respond to China too. At the same time having discursive power is thought of as a defining characteristic of being a great power, and a key determinant of comprehensive national power (Rolland, 2020: 7). To have it indicates that a certain power status has been achieved, and also lays the foundations for attaining other more material objectives.

Figure 3.1: Conceptual flows in 'new thinking'

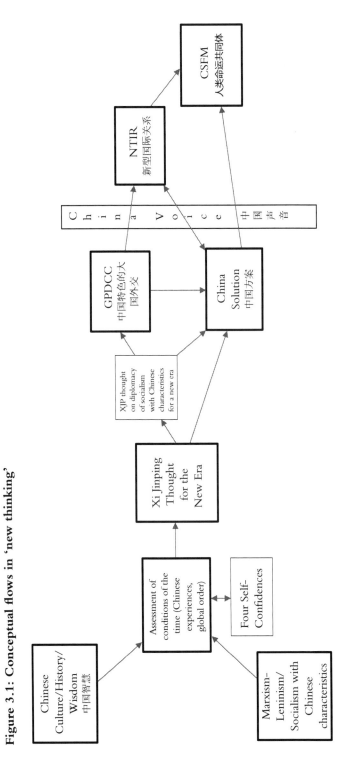

At least, that is the plan. As we shall see in Chapter 5, the way that discursive power has been used has not always led to the sort of response from others that makes it easier for China's leaders to attain other material goals too.

A non-alliance strategy for a non-polar world ...

The second strand is, in the language of GPDCC, to eschew building ideologically based bloc-type alliances, and instead to become the 'first country to make partnership-building a principle guiding state-to-state relations' (Xi, 2017b). In contrast to what is depicted as more traditional modes of alliance building, the claim is that China does not just look to partner only with like-minded states, but instead is pragmatically open to building partnerships with anyone who agrees with a common set of underlying principles:

> the essence of partnerships is the same: treating each other as equals and pursuing win–win cooperation, while transcending differences in social system and development stage. This important practice by China, offering a new option for countries exploring approaches to state-to-state relations is widely recognized and welcomed. (Wang Yi, 2017d)

The specifics of each individual partnership vary depending on that country's/region's specific relationship with China, and where each sits in the global order (Feng and Huang, 2014).

So, for example, we see a partnership based on energy and (non-traditional) security concerns with one of China's backyards in the form of the SCO, albeit one with economic spillovers. With overlaps in both membership and intention, there is another different partnership with the rest of the BRICS with the aim of creating new structures of global economic governance that reflect the shifts in relative power capabilities since the establishment of the Bretton Woods institutions. To these we can add a more paternalistic (shared) development partnership with African states as epitomized by the Forum on China–Africa Cooperation (FOCAC), and a partnership built on shared trade and financial relations (and futures) with the Association of Southeast Asian Nations (ASEAN) as an institution, and Asian neighbourhood states in general. These are all rather different from China's 'strategic partnership' with Europe, which in turn is different from the nature of the great power relationship with the United States, reflecting Chinese perceptions of Europe's and America's contrasting positions in the global order.

The aim, then, is to build a network of different sets of relationships with China at the centre. A form of networked power structure with a 'hub and spoke' approach to building relationships and potential partnerships. This diplomacy was initially primarily based on building comprehensive relations with nations or regional groups. However, Wang Jisi (2011: 75) also identifies another related 'transformation' in Chinese strategy: 'it is becoming less country-oriented and more multilateral and issue oriented. This shift toward functional focuses – counterterrorism, nuclear nonproliferation, environmental protection, energy security, food safety, post-disaster reconstruction – has complicated China's bilateral relationships.' In short, different issues need different types of relationships with different sets of countries. So rather than building a single relationship with European states, for example, they might be potential partners in some areas (like global economic governance reform) but largely oppositional in others (such as human rights) where partnerships with different sets of countries might be more efficacious. As noted in the Introduction, this idea of China as representing a very different type of actor in different policy arenas has now been recognized and articulated by the European Commission (2019) too.

... with an emphasis on some partnerships over others

What Qin Yaqing (2014) calls China's 'strategic design' (*zhanlue buju*) has long operated on this principle of differentiated relationships and emphases. This has typically been captured by variations of the idea that great powers/major countries are the focus (*daguo shi zhongdian*), the neighbourhood is the primacy (*zhoubian shi shouyao*), developing countries are the foundation (*fazhanzhong guojia shi jichu*) and multilateral institutions are the important platform (*duobian guoji zuzhi shi zhongyao wutai*) of this diplomacy. This reflects the ongoing belief that the nature of the relationship with the United States will be the main determinant of both the nature of the international order and what China can do within that order for some time to come. Hence the reason that great powers – and one specific great power in particular – are the main focus of diplomacy at the highest level.

On a day-to-day basis, however, it is China's neighbours and other developing states that occupy special roles, and an emphasis on them can be seen as the third major strategic strand. This is partly because there remains considerable tension in the neighbourhood about Chinese ambitions, and disagreement over territory and sovereignty that might result in tension becoming something else. Hence as Qin Yaqing (2014) also argues, the need to assuage their concerns and build trust and confidence through diplomatic and economic means. It is also partly because while there remains a stated aspiration to build a CSFM that is a truly global community, there is an acknowledgement that some countries are more likely to share Chinese aspirations than others. In fact, in Xi's first incarnation of the CSFM, the emphasis was on building a *regional* community with China's neighbours (again partly as a trust building exercise). It was only later expanded to include other non-Asian developing countries, before finally becoming an aspiration for the global community as a whole (Xie and Zhang, 2018: 58). Even in its global form, Guo Wei (2017: 124) has shown that there is still a heavy emphasis in analysis of Xi's speeches on 'common development with countries in Asia, ASEAN, Africa, and on the Silk Road' and a focus on building relationships with potentially like-minded developing countries rather than liberal ones in the West.

So in addition to the region, there is also a focus on building a range of cooperative arrangements with developing countries to share China's experiences with them, and to provide more concrete ways of encouraging their development. The Belt and Road of course is one of these. Not just the initiative itself, but a range of facilitating sub-initiatives and projects.[8] So too are the various aid and commercial projects that China has established with other developing countries. And we should also add to this the range of 'different multilateral platforms and mechanisms' (Hu, 2019: 10) that China has either established or used to further its agendas; the FOCAC, the China-Community of Latin American and Caribbean States (CELAC) Forum, the BRICs and SCO Summits, the China-Arab States Cooperation Forum, and China's interactions with ASEAN (either on its own or as part of the +3). As we shall see in Chapter 6, this focus on developing countries is even more pronounced when it comes to the CS.

What is the South?

The concept of South-South cooperation (*nannan hezuo*) is often invoked by China's leaders as an important part of China's global strategy. As with the way that the term is used in other settings, it is far from clear which countries actually constitute 'the South'. In the Chinese case, dividing the world up entails a process of double dichotomization. On the one hand, there is a fairly straightforward economic/developmental criterion – though the point at which a country makes the transition from developing to developed is far from clear. On the other are less tangible ideational/ideological/political criteria. In terms of political orientation, we have countries that might not have much in common other than a rejection of the dominance and supposed universalism of 'Western' values and political preferences (as outlined in the Introduction). They are the 'non-West'. And the extent to which economically developing countries align themselves with the West (either in terms of the West's values or more formal political ties) plays a key role in determining how they are perceived in Beijing. So countries with relatively low levels of development might lose a degree of their 'southness' if they ally with Western interests (or states). Conversely, more developed countries like Turkey at times enhance their 'southness' when they position themselves against Western interests and actors.

China's position on human rights is also helpful in identifying the non-West. As Putz (2019) explains, in July 2019 two different letters were sent to the UN Human Rights Commission. The first called for an end to detention of Uighurs in Xinjiang, and the second defended China's right to deal with its own domestic politics and complained about the politicization of human rights issue. A similar division of supporting and opposing letters also followed the introduction of the new National Security Law in Hong Kong in 2020. While there was more overlap in the signature of the two critical letters than in the two supporting ones, if we add them together we can see a rough divide between the types of states that are likely to support and oppose China's insistence that it can do what it wants within its own sovereign territory; and thus who is likely to be considered a friend (and who is not) on related issues in Beijing. There is an emerging group of Western type liberal democracies that are prepared to oppose Chinese policy on the one hand,[9] and (for want of a better all-encompassing term covering a wide variety of political regimes) a group of largely non-Western type regimes that support China on the other hand.[10] As Lawler notes (2020), the majority of the latter group have been recipients of Belt and Road funding, and at the time the Hong Kong letter was signed, many of them were seeking to renegotiate debt repayment schedules with China. So there are trends that really do look like a move towards bipolarity. But it really is a very rough guide, and for the reasons outlined in the Eight Arguments in the Introduction, there are countervailing trends too that make it more sensible to think of bipolar tendencies rather than a bipolar world per se. Notably, there are important absentees from both sets of letters. The US (which is not a member of the Human Rights Commission) is the most obvious but not the only one. Only 16 of the 27 EU member states signed either or both of the two letters criticizing Chinese practice. And while the definition of where Europe starts and ends is a little blurry, even with the addition of five non-EU European states, that still only accounts for roughly half of the continent (in terms of states if not population). Turkey signed neither. Nor did three of China's partners in the BRICS (Brazil, India, and South Africa), or any of the ASEAN member states, or roughly half of the states of Africa.

To add a layer of complication, all of the states that recognize Taiwan are in the broadly defined group of developing non-Western states (with the exception of the Vatican City). However, this does not stop them from receiving aid from China or having commercial relations, as Haiti–PRC relations demonstrate. Indeed, such financial relations have been seen as a means of trying to persuade them to switch recognition to Beijing (Zhu Zhiqun, 2013). Enforcing the one China policy, persuading others to accept the PRC as the legal representation of that one China, and preventing Taiwan from assessing some sort of de facto (if not formal and legal) independent identity as an international actor has been a longstanding international ambition.[11] It is an end that requires developing a range of means to attain; financial statecraft with Taiwan's partners, various initiatives with Taiwan and representatives of global organizations and so on. While it is not a strategy as such, it does entail developing strategic thinking and action (Huang Jing, 2017), and the term 'strategic strand' is deliberately flexible enough for it to count as the fourth of the ten here.

Asymmetric benevolent developmentalism

GPDCC's developmentalism component entails emphasizing key self-identified differences from other/previous international development funders, and represents the fifth strategic strand. China is, according to its own narratives, doing development differently, with a focus on filling the need for greater connectivity and 'integrated development' (Xi, 2018a). It also wants to be seen to be promoting a different understanding of what development is. Or at the very least, promoting a different understanding from Western powers about which development principles should be prioritized. This focus on development is also seen as stemming from a different understanding of the causes of insecurity too:

> much of the conflict and turbulence we see around the world stems from the lack of development. More people have come to the realization that only with development can we remove the breeding ground of global challenges, secure the basic rights of the people, and propel the progress of the human society. (Yang Jiechi, 2018a)

Building on the conception of comprehensive security noted above, what Xi (2017e: 21) called 'common, comprehensive, cooperative, and sustainable security' does not only include development, but a wide range of non-traditional issue areas: economics, politics, culture, society, science and technology, information, resources, and ecological security (in addition to more traditional areas like military security and nuclear safety; Liu Jianfei, 2018: 24). Working out how best to achieve security in each of these domains also requires working out who best to work with on an issue by issue basis. This neatly takes us back to the importance of issue based non-ideological partnerships rather than alliances as a means of attaining security aims, which in turn also counteracts some of the other bipolar features of Chinese strategic thinking.

If development is important – or more correctly, a certain type of development is important – then what can China do to make it happen? China's own developmental experiences have increasingly been seen as something that others can learn from, and thus provide a form of ideational inspiration and/or practical guide. Another oft made argument is that China's major contribution to global peace and development is simply to continue to grow and provide opportunities for others to benefit from this growth (Wang Yi, 2018a; 2018b). The Belt and Road is also often presented as an example of China practising a form of economic and development leadership for the world. This leadership, so the story goes, has a focus on ecologically sound development and the attainment of basic standards of living and making socioeconomic progress. While China has committed to capacity building initiatives (for example, in Africa and along the Belt and Road), it does not focus on building political institutions and democratic practices, or encouraging the sort of 'good governance' reforms associated with more (neo)liberal agendas.

Once again, the emphasis is on Chinese difference from other great powers (past and present). This also entails a very strong insistence that this is not just a case of China doing development *to* others, but rather a case of cooperation *with* fellow travellers. Nevertheless, when you look at the direction of financial flows, the way that China's experiences are viewed within China itself, and the nature of the various multilateral platforms noted above, this does not look like a relationship of equals. Rather, it looks like what we might call a form of asymmetric benevolent developmentalism whereby a superior and successful China disseminates its experiences and (more importantly) disburses its money to other less powerful (and as yet, less successful) developing states.

Finance, development and other interests

China's real intentions for engaging with other developing states have been questioned. Where China emphasizes South-South development cooperation, others see a concerted state effort to secure the things that China needs and wants. Be that hard resources like raw materials or softer diplomatic support for grander Chinese goals and aspirations. Moreover, rather than promoting development, Chinese financial projects overseas have been identified as a new source of debt creating a new form of dependency for a number of developing countries. Rather than being a resource for others to benefit from, the BRI is seen instead as a potential source of what Taylor (2019) calls 'a vector of underdevelopment' and Langan (2018: 89–117) and many others have referred to as establishing a new form of Chinese neocolonialism (though most often works that focus on Chinese neocolonialism tend to go on to debunk the concept rather than support it). There is also the additional question of whether the state is in control of these financial (and other flows), or if other commercial actors and interests are actually taking the lead. These are debates we will return to in Chapter 4 and in the Conclusion to this book.

There might be disagreement over the intended end, and indeed over actors. But there is little or no disagreement that economic diplomacy or economic statecraft is an important part of China's global economic activity, and it thus represents the sixth strategic strand. This is, though, a rather broad term that covers a wide range of activities. It can include truly diplomatic activities undertaken at the state-to-state level – negotiations in multilateral organizations and to establish bilateral free trade agreements for example (Zha, 2015; Zhang Shuxiu, 2016). Or the less formal use of market and financial power that will be discussed in detail in Chapter 4. That analysis will show how Europe and North America became more significant targets for Chinese investors than developing states as Chinese priorities changed. One of the themes that runs through this book is that not all of these changing economic patterns are the result of direct state control, and that other interests play a role too. But the importance of the state in shaping the boundaries of bounded autonomy is another key theme, and it is thus sensible to include supporting the technological upgrading of Chinese industries as a seventh strand of China's strategy for global change.

Governance reform

In promoting the various components of the new thinking on international relations, China's leaders are keen to point to their support for the existing order. China has, for example, shown its commitment to multilateralism through its actions 'within the G20, APEC and other multilateral frameworks' (Xi, 2018a), and has backed up its rhetorical support for the UN system with increased funding and the provision of peacekeepers (Xi, 2015c). China claims to have promoted the resolution of conflict in Iran, Syria, Afghanistan and the wider Middle East through political means and 'diplomatic settlement' rather than through force or one-sided resolutions (Yang Jiechi, 2018a). Wang Yi (2017d) also points to the mediation China provided to solve conflict between Myanmar and Bangladesh over the Rohingya crisis. And Xi was keen to position China as the backbone of the multilateral response to the COVID-19 pandemic (as the US stepped back from leadership), through support for the WHO, cooperation with other G20 members, and through bilateral projects with individual countries (Xi, 2020).

However, as argued in the Introduction, this support for the existing structures of global and regional governance is very much a qualified backing. Of the existing major institutions, the UN, a reformed WTO, and the G20 are the preferred arenas (Foot, 2014; Breslin and Ren 2018). These three are organizations where the power of the US is in turn: mediated by the formal power structure and where China has a veto; where decisions are made through consensus supported by legally based dispute resolution mechanisms; and where there is no formal distribution of power, and rotating host countries possess considerable power to frame the terms of debate for that year. Or put another way, they are all institutions that the US cannot control either on its own, or alongside other Western liberal allies. The same is not true in other institutions and organizations, where there is clear Chinese dissatisfaction with the distribution of power, and some of the norms and principles that underpin the way they work. This dissatisfaction is compounded by a strong feeling that China does not get the respect that it deserves – and indeed, the respect that many Chinese *want* – from the international community.

The result is something of a tension in Chinese objectives and strategies. This tension reveals itself in the eighth strategic strand which we might call a responsible reformist governance agenda. As we have already discussed this in both the Introduction and Chapter 2, we can deal with it briefly here by reminding ourselves of a three-pronged approach; the preference for some bodies over others that we have just discussed, an attempt to reform those power structures that are deemed to be unfair and unrepresentative, and the preparedness and ability to introduce new structures of governance that support Chinese global agendas.

Attempts to become a norm reviser, definer and entrepreneur (Kelly, 2016: 49) might also be thought of as part of this governance reform agenda. Or perhaps part of China's soft power strategy (or indeed, as part and parcel of both). However, it is so important in its own right that it is considered to provide a ninth strategic strand here. In the past, this alternative tended to revolve around the argument that China does not have a normative position at all. More than that, China actively stands against the promotion of a normative position and believes that each country should do what works best for itself given its own specific circumstances. Somewhat ironically, the process of actively promoting this anti-normative national identity (and pitching it as the antithesis of the way that other great powers act) results in it becoming a normative position of sorts in itself.

While this focus on establishing difference with the West remains today, there has been a more proactive turn as well with Chinese thinking and experiences increasingly proffered as providing an alternative for other developing states and for new forms of governance in some issue areas. As this is the focus of the discussion in Chapter 6, it will simply be noted here and left for further discussion later.

Core interests

Much of what is said by China's leaders focuses on righteousness, harmony, cooperation and benevolence in international relations. However, this sits alongside the equally often asserted commitment that China will give no ground whatsoever when it comes to its core interests. As just one example of many similar statements, Wang Yi (2017a) asserted that:

> The Chinese people are not to be bullied, nor will we give
> in to coercion. No country should expect China to trade
> its core interests away or tolerate any infringement on its

sovereignty, security and development interests. Under the leadership of the CPC Central Committee, we have drawn a clear red line on issues concerning national sovereignty, security and other core interests, and have taken firm actions to defend our rights and interests.

For Norton (2015), it is in the establishment of a clear set of core interests, and the development of policies to defend them, that we find the true heart of a coherent Chinese GS. Here, though, it is cautiously considered to be the tenth and final strategic strand rather than a GS in itself. This caution is necessary as it is not a case of core interests establishing a means to attain an end. Rather, getting others to accept China's core interests is the end, and a number of sub-stratagems are deployed to try and gain that acceptance. But the deliberately loose definition of a strategic strand allows it to be counted as one here, even if it might be better thought of as a principle or objective that other strategies are used to attain.

From a core interests perspective, projects like the BRI can be seen as a means of tying regional economies so closely to China that challenging Chinese core interests (for example, territorial claims in the South China Sea) becomes too costly to be viable. This economic diplomacy occurs alongside military developments which are designed to simultaneously signal China's commitment to defend its interests by whatever means possible. And again to make the costs of challenging them unacceptable. A further pillar is diplomatic initiatives designed to allay fears and communicate peaceful intent (as long as these core interests aren't contested). And the last is one of the stated aims of GPDCC; the promotion of softer forms of interactions through the development of people-to-people diplomatic exchanges: 'We must strengthen bilateral and multilateral cooperation in culture, education, tourism, youth, media, health, poverty reduction and other fields. We need to promote mutual learning among civilizations as it will help us build bridges of friendship' (Xi, 2018a). As long as each country recognizes and respects others' core interests and doesn't get involved in affairs that are none of their business, then everything will be fine (Xi, 2017b). Or put another way, if others simply accept China's own self defined core interests, then China can put interest aside and focus on loftier goals and objectives instead. But as Lin (2019: 42–3) asks, what happens if this doesn't happen and China's expressed national interests collide with those of other countries – when both think that the same territory is part of their core interests for example? Given what has been said about not backing down over core interests in China, it is reasonable to assume that China's core interests would be deemed to take precedence over the stated core interests of others. If this does happen, it also seems reasonable to assume that China's perceptions of itself as being defensive and righteous might not correspond with how others understand Chinese actions or interpret Chinese intent.

From strategic thinking to action

This distinction between how Chinese strategy is seen in China and how Chinese action is perceived by others draws attention to three important threads of hesitation that runs through this chapter. One hesitancy emerges from the concern that talking about strategies (grand and not so grand) can lead to an assumption of central coherence, coordination and control that hides the importance of the interest and action of a relatively (if bounded) plural set of Chinese actors. The second hesitancy originates from a very real concern that focusing on what is said can generate an image of China that is at odds with what is actually being done in real life. The idea of what China is and how it acts is an idealized version of a self-identity that is designed to try and convince both domestic and international audiences about Chinese difference and superiority. But this doesn't necessarily mean that this essentialized China is the same as the real China that others encounter in the real world. And the third related hesitancy takes us back to the importance of Chinese military action, and its absence from the analysis in this book.

That said, even if you dismiss what is being said as lacking contact with reality, it does no harm to understand what messages the Chinese leadership wants to send out about itself and about its strategy. In addition, the identification of ten strategic strands in this chapter does not just rely on what the leadership says its strategy is, but also on observations of concrete action. However, the best way of allaying these hesitancies is to move from the study of the rhetoric and discourse to specific grounded case studies. In keeping with the aim of disaggregating different potential sources of Chinese power, this will start with an analysis of sources of economic power in Chapter 4, and then move to softer and ideational dimensions in Chapters 5 and 6.

4

Markets, Technology and Finance: Turning Resources into Power

In September 2019, China was reported to have signed an agreement with Iran to invest something in the region of US$400 billion in oil related industries and industrial infrastructure. In return, China would be able to buy discounted oil and related resources (using currencies other than the US Dollar), and Chinese firms would be given 'first refusal' to run existing or future contracts in all Iranian petrochemical projects without competition. As part of the deal, China was also reported as preparing to send 5,000 security personnel to Iran to protect its citizens and investments (Watkins, 2019).[1] Three weeks later the US Department of State imposed sanctions on six Chinese companies and some of their executive officers for breaking US sanctions on transporting oil from Iran (Pompeo, 2019). The timing of the two announcements was probably coincidental. The sanctions applied to transactions that had occurred before the new deal was announced, so may well have been introduced in any case. But whether they were directly linked or not, these two stories combine to provide an example of one of the themes of the time that emerged as Chinese outward investment grew in the new millennium: the idea that China was using its financial power to get hold of strategic resources in places that others would not (or could not) go. In the process, so the argument went, China was propping up authoritarian states and undermining the attempts of others to promote the protection of human rights and to guarantee national, regional and even global security.

It is hard to escape the conclusion that high politics and strategic objectives loomed large in Chinese economic relations with Iran. Or at various times, with North Korea, Myanmar and Zimbabwe as well.

But this doesn't mean that all Chinese overseas projects are driven by the same goals and delivered in the same ways. On the contrary, there is now a rather large body of research that shows how other actors and interests have driven relationships elsewhere. Even when political considerations are important – for example, in the case of Myanmar – this doesn't mean that the central government is in total control and that commercial considerations are absent.

Given both the reality of China's changing global role and actions, and perceptions of what they were designed to achieve, then a consideration of Chinese finance is an essential component of any assessment of China as a global power. Financial power might include the internationalization of the RMB, and much has been written on the potential for it to challenge or even replace the dollar as the world's most important reserve currency.[2] This would indeed have massive significance for the world. Yet although the RMB was added to the IMF Special Drawing Rights (SDR) currencies in 2016, the subsequent process of reform and liberalization was, at best, patchy. Making the changes that would be required to allow the RMB to be globally used to the extent that it could become a challenger global reserve currency would entail a loss of control over financial flows. This was a price for a form of global financial power that China's leaders were rather reluctant to accept (Lo, 2015). Moreover, while the RMB oscillated between the fifth and seventh most used currency for international settlements in the four years after becoming an SDR currency, the volume of transactions remained relatively small. For example, in January 2020 it accounted for just 1.65 per cent of transactions, three quarters of which were for dealings between mainland China and Hong Kong. If you take out these intra-Chinese payments, then the value of payments made using the RMB would be close to the figure for the Malaysian Ringgit, which is not often spoken about as a major global currency or one destined to replace the dollar.[3] Rather than being destined for currency leadership, Bowles and Wang's (2013) argument that the first target for the RMB is to become a 'normal' currency with an influence relative to the size of the Chinese economy still retains considerable salience a number of years after they first made it.

As such, in the following consideration of the growth and importance of Chinese financial power, the emphasis is on financial flows rather than currency. This is partly because, as has been argued throughout this book so far, financial flows have been something of a game changer in shaping China's profile as a global power. It is also partly because assumptions of the nature of China's political economy have often shaped the way that this COFDI has been understood, confusing corporate intent with state strategy. This is because top-down design establishes conditions which can be utilized by commercial actors, thus making it difficult to parse what intentions lie behind any specific financial interaction except by undertaking individual transaction level analyses.

It is also an excellent example of how the study of China's domestic political economy helps us understand the nature of China's global power resources. Here, it is important to locate the study of China's global ambitions within the understanding of how the state–market relationship works as outlined in brief in Chapter 2. It also makes sense to start with a short consideration of how other sources of potential economic power have been utilized to try and deliver different objectives. This is because they are important in themselves, because one of the concerns about the growth of COFDI is the lack of reciprocity, and also because the way that market and financial power interact is at the heart of broader concerns over how and why China might be trying to attain global technological power and leadership.

National power and transnational production

As I have argued at length before (Breslin, 2005; 2007), although the study of 'commodity chains and global capitalism' (Gereffi and Korzeniewicz, 1994) has long been established as a core endeavour of IPE scholarship, its insights still too rarely intersect with IR studies of power in the global order. Instead, when trying to understand or assign power in global economic relations, many assessments start from statist and national units of analysis. In short, the perspective is still predominantly inter-national even though the nature of globalized production typically isn't, and the way that states interact with non-state economic actors in these production processes means that identifying national based loci of power is not a simple task.

Whether having a trade surplus actually translates into national power has been an issue of contention pretty much since people began to theorize the power dynamics of international trade (Hirschman, 1945). But putting that to one side for the moment, does it make any sense to talk about China's trade surplus with the US in isolation from the trade deficit that China runs with southeast Asian economies (that it imports components from to make the goods that it exports)? If the focus is on China's overall global role and power, then the answer would seem to be no. If it is instead on bilateral relations between the US and China, then the answer is probably yes. But even here we have to consider that part of the US deficit has been produced by US companies locating their production in China, generating profits back in their corporate headquarters, and keeping prices (and inflation) down for American consumers. The statistics that are still used to evaluate national power simply cannot capture the fragmentation and distribution of power that these nationally based statistics hide within them. National level analyses – and particularly bilateral ones – can at best only tell a small part of the story of China's global economic interactions. If China's disruption to pre-existing trade patterns is a source of power, then it is a power that is shared between a number of different types of actors. This includes non-Chinese beneficiaries and power holders, including those who make the investments to produce exports, those who design goods, those who provide intermediary components and materials, those who ship supplies and goods around the world, and those who market, advertise, and distribute the final finished goods in the ultimate markets. It also includes the power that the consumers in those ultimate markets have over what they decide to buy.

None of this is intended to suggest a powerless China in the global political economy. It is just that it is not as easy to assign and understand power in this political economy as might appear at first sight, and as is often asserted by political actors. China's emergence as a major global economic actor was of course facilitated by the actions of the Chinese state – both in its national and local manifestations. Like others before it, the Chinese state did much to create an uneven playing field to encourage and facilitate a certain type of growth. And when the state establishes preferences for new directions, then it has a number of mechanisms available to it to cascade its preferences and goals down through political and economic structures. Moreover, there is clear evidence of state intervention and control of markets that goes beyond the 'normal' activity of economic management (which of course also takes place in China as well). It has the ability, to try and change the nature of the Chinese economy in ways that (importantly for this study) have implications beyond China's borders. And this has created a situation where what happens in China can have massive implications for production and consumption across the world. To be sure, it is relatively easy in some sectors to change how and where any single good is produced if the supply chain is disrupted either by accident or intent. However, the sheer number of commodities that have a Chinese input in the production process means that the global economy as a whole is particularly dependent on Chinese production, and resultingly vulnerable to shocks that disrupt the production or supply of these goods.

In relations with some countries in some sectors, Chinese production is so dominant that there are very clear potential power asymmetries. For example, the US Economic and Security Review Commission (ESRC) argued that there were 'economic and security risks' from dependence on China. At the time of its report in 2019, 13.4 per cent of all drug and biologic imports into the US came from China, and 39.3 per cent of medical device imports. In addition, many of the drug imports from India to the US were themselves dependent on prior supplies from China to India (ESRC, 2019: 8). This made US consumers and the US health system as a whole vulnerable to either dramatic market shifts as a result of a sudden change in global demand, or political tensions disrupting trade flows.

This was exactly what happened as COVID-19 began to spread around the world in 2020. According to the Peterson Institute, the situation was even more acute when it came to personal protective equipment. In 2020 at the start of the coronavirus pandemic when such equipment was needed most, around half of all imports into the EU and the US came from China, and the average for the rest of the world was only slightly lower at 43 per cent. For specialist nose and mouth protectors, the figures were even higher (Brown, 2020). Beyond medical equipment and drugs, a Henry Jackson Foundation report calculated that Australia was 'strategically dependent on China' for 595 different categories of goods, New Zealand for 513, the US for 413, Canada for 367 and the UK for 229. Such strategic dependence was defined as where China controls at least 30 per cent of global production of a good, and where the partner economy is a net importer of it and gets more than half of its supplies from China (Rogers et al, 2020).

Does the dependence of others necessarily result in power for China? Or is it China that is instead vulnerable through dependence on others? Dependent on imported components in the production of exports, dependent on foreign markets for continued export growth, dependent on foreign capital for the production of many exports, and dependent on imported energy supplies? The answer is that the nature of global production means that both are true at the same time. China can indeed deliberately exploit its position to exert influence over those dependent others. Here, any element of Chinese power is contingent on the availability of supplies from elsewhere, and/or the speed at which production facilities can be established/relocated elsewhere. China's overwhelming dominance in the production of rare earths and, as it demonstrated in 2010, its willingness to try to control supply has been touted as the classic example of dependency creating power. Though even here 'market power and political leverage proved fleeting and difficult to exploit' as production increased elsewhere, and technological advances reduced demand for Chinese controlled rare earths (Gholz, 2014: 2).

It also has both power and vulnerability at the same time if others think that it might act in this way in the future. And once more, we are back to questions of trust. A lack of trust can emerge from the sort of fundamental concern about national ambitions and strategies discussed in Chapter 1, from a lack of confidence in an economy's resilience and ability to keep providing what needs to be provided, or from a more pragmatic concern that too many (economic) eggs have been placed in one (national) basket. Moreover, deliberate attempts to utilize dependency for political gain also reduce trust and raise the spectre of it happening again in the future. Such concerns might lead to a desire to keep China happy to guarantee supplies. But they can also lead to the desire to remove vulnerabilities by 'decoupling' from the Chinese economy, thus making the vulnerability China's instead. While moves to do so were already the preference of President Trump before 2020, it's fair to say that the coronavirus pandemic did not increase confidence and trust in China, resulting in calls to rethink the nature and basis of the relationship with China in a number of other Western governments too.

Market power China

Such trust, and the lack of it, also played an important role in conditioning external responses to the adaption of the MIC2025 blueprint for industrial and technological upgrading by the State Council in 2015. It is also a very good example of how the creation of unfair playing fields has significant implications for both those who want to work in China, and those who face the consequences of the internationalization of Chinese economic actors. In terms of the former, it draws attention to the nature of China's 'market power'. Not in the sense that it is used in economic theory (which refers to corporate power within a market) but instead following Drezner's (2007) understanding of how market size is an important tool of state power in international relations. It has been deployed to explain how other large markets have become a source of power for other global actors. For example, Steven Gill (2008: 141) argued that the strategic use of market access was a key means by which the US forced others to accept and internalize its values and preferences. The size of the single market inside the EU has also been described as a key source of its ability to externalize its regulatory preferences onto others. As with the US example, this can include the deliberate coercive enforcement of these preferences in negotiating market access with other countries or regions. But it also occurs indirectly, as external actors independently decide to change their domestic structures to align themselves with EU regulation because the EU economy is deemed be too big and too important to miss out on. Hence the concept of 'Market Power Europe' (Damro, 2012) that this section heading has borrowed from.

In keeping with these arguments, Chinese market power starts from an assumption that the Chinese economy is also too big and important to miss out on. Not just big and important now, but even bigger and more important in the future. It is also an economy that is not freely and openly accessible to outsiders in all areas, with the Chinese state retaining significant control over market access. As such, in order to secure this access (now and in the future) others do things that they would not otherwise choose to do, or do not do things that they might otherwise want to do. This can include, for example, political decisions not to be critical of China to maintain market access and also to gain an advantage on others who are looking to get the same access and contracts. It also includes the acceptance by both states and commercial actors of economic conditions on market entry. Here, once again, we need to emphasize the significance of projected futures in making calculations over whether to accept these restrictions or not. This includes assumptions about future change in the nature of the Chinese regulatory regime (and its convergence to more liberal norms), and assumptions about future growth potentials.

In the past, the restrictions that the Chinese state applied on market access often simply entailed maintaining the profitability of domestic firms that might otherwise be unable to compete in a truly competitive economy. In addition to supporting domestic firms through a range of subsidies and preferential fiscal treatment, this was also facilitated after 1995 through the Catalogue (formally The Catalogue Guiding Foreign Investment in Industry). The Catalogue stipulates on an industry by industry basis where investment is prohibited, restricted, encouraged or permitted, with often quite detailed and specific conditions for each industry. By and large, the direction of travel in various new editions has been towards greater liberalization, though at times there have been reversals in individual sectors (Yu Zheng, 2019). Surveys of foreign economic actors also suggest that what is written down in the Catalogue is often less important than the more informal methods that local governments in particular use to either protect local producers, or to encourage external actors to do certain things that are deemed to be beneficial (or both).[4] With this in mind, although The Foreign Investment Law passed in 2019 (operational from January 2020) was touted as creating a level playing field for foreign actors, it is likely that national level legislation will continue to not always translate into local level action.

Without getting involved in the debates over how far the RMB might have been undervalued in the past (and when this changed), it is safe to argue that the state has also utilized exchange rate and currency controls as a means of economic management to support its economic objectives. Currency policy is also a very good example of the state's ability and willingness to suspend or even reverse liberalization when it deems that national interests are being too harshly affected. Examples include the move to suspend appreciation from 2008–10 as Chinese export growth collapsed in the wake of the global financial crisis, and the depreciation of July 2015 (McCauley and Chang, 2019).

Market power and technological leadership

The MIC2025 blueprint played an important role in increasing concern about the consequences of China's economic rise among those who had previously been less concerned. Of course, there was much more to any change of mind than just MIC2025 alone. It was announced at a time of rising frustration that WTO membership had not led to the liberalization of the Chinese economy that many had expected when China joined in 2001. In 2016, this frustration resulted in China not being recognized as a market economy within the WTO by the US and the EU, even though it had been widely assumed that such a recognition would be automatically extended on the 15th anniversary of China's entry (Miranda, 2018). The announcement of MIC2025 was also just one part of the broader change in strategic signalling outlined in Chapter 1 that pointed to a change in emphasis and direction in Chinese overseas ambitions. And its announcement came at a time of rapid growth in COFDI, particularly in north America and (Western) Europe. But even on its own, the MIC2025 blueprint document made it pretty clear that this was more than just the previous 'normal' protection and support of domestic producers, but something that was also driven by conceptions of a competitive global order: 'Creating an internationally competitive manufacturing industry is the only way for China to upgrade its overall national strength, safeguard national security, and build a world power' (State Council, 2015).

Within China itself, MIC2025 was seen rather differently. China might not have reached the levels of liberalization that others wanted when it joined the WTO, but it had come a very long way in an attempt to conform to standards established by others. Moreover, not ratifying something (Market Economy status) that was assumed to have been promised (with legal force) in 2001 was taken as a sign of arbitrarily moving the goal posts in an attempt to damage China. This was, after all, an era when initiatives like the Trans Pacific Partnership and the Transatlantic Trade and Investment Partnership were seen in China as a direct response to China's growing influence and an attempt to lock China out of much of the global economy (Blanchard, 2019: 82). There were accusations of hypocrisy too. Western developed economies were not only also developing their own new industrial strategies, but MIC2025 was typically explained as being directly inspired by Germany's 'Industry 4.0' programme for developing smart manufacturing. But what was seen as being smart and legitimate action by Germany was instead depicted as underhand and unfair when it was done by China.

At the same time, other developing economies were also making developmental progress, reducing China's previous low-cost advantage in the global economy. This was creating a 'double squeeze' between the developed and developing worlds. Moreover, despite China's rapid economic growth, the MIC2025 blueprint pointed to considerable weaknesses in an economy where the 'manufacturing industry is large but not strong' and 'there is still a big gap compared with advanced countries'. Innovation capability was described as 'weak' with a high dependence on imported components in 'core technologies and high-end equipment', and overall product quality was 'not high'. Global brands were still lacking, resource and energy utilization were low and industrial pollution high, the level of informatization was low, the degree of industrial internationalization not high, and 'the ability of enterprises to operate globally is insufficient' (State Council, 2015).

These different internal and external starting points show how difficult it is to find common ground on some issues, and remind us of the sources and consequences of mutual distrust briefly discussed in Chapter 2. From the outside, Chinese policy appeared to have entered a new phase. Despite the emphasis on weaknesses and the need to 'catch up' in official documents, this seemed to be about something else. This was a concerted pitch for Chinese global technological leadership that 'poses an existential threat to the US monopoly over high-tech sectors' (Yu Jie, 2019: 39). Moreover, while there had been a similar concern about falling behind Japan as it rose to become 'No 1' in the 1970s (Vogel, 1979), the consequences of falling behind to China were viewed as much more dangerous. This might not only change the nature of the global economy but also, through the potential use of these technologies, global security as well (Mussington, 2018). And it was not just the nature of the China challenge that was changing but also who was being challenged (Wübbeke et al, 2016). In addition to competing with other developing economies in low-cost globalized production, the technological dominance of advanced Western economies was now under threat as well.

Financial power: Chinese aid

While the majority of the rest of this chapter is devoted to the drivers and consequences of COFDI, it would be negligent to ignore the role of development assistance. Indeed, it is not always that easy to separate development finance from investment in the first place. This is in part because of the way that both are used to fund similar projects such as infrastructure development. More important, it is because of a lack of a clear distinction between what is traditionally thought of as aid provided to support development in other countries, what is done by states to try to attain strategic national objectives (access to key resources, externalizing excess capacity, the One-China policy and so on), and what is commercial activity designed to generate profits. To add an extra layer of complexity and potential confusion, as China is not a member of the Organisation for Economic Co-operation and Development's Development Assistance Committee (DAC), it does not have to (and doesn't) classify and report its aid activities in ways that conform to DAC's definition of what is Official Development Assistance (ODA). This means that Chinese statistics are not immediately internationally comparable, and can also lack the transparency over terms and conditions that DAC definitions are meant to provide.

The extensive development loans extended by the Eximbank and CDB would normally be reported as portfolio investments by other countries (Dollar, 2016: 3). However, these loans are often extended as part of larger development assistant packages that can include requiring recipient countries to use Chinese companies to deliver projects using Chinese sourced labour and materials (Gallagher and Irwin, 2014). These loans can also be used to 'secure access by Chinese firms to natural resources' (Shapiro et al, 2018: 12), entail part repayment in resources, and/or grant Chinese actors ownership and/or profit sharing rights. As a result, what looks like development finance can sometimes have investment type consequences in terms of gains for Chinese actors. Conversely, COFDI (particularly in infrastructure projects) can have development-aid type consequences for the recipient country even when delivered via commercial projects.

While it does not produce DAC conforming statistics, what the Chinese government has done is publish two White Papers on Foreign Aid (State Council, 2011b; 2014). The first of these made a distinction between three different types of development finance. Grants are the main form of funding for social programmes (hospital and school construction, water projects, technical cooperation, emergency aid, and so on). Interest free loans are also 'social' in nature by supporting public facilities. These are typically for 20-year periods, with repayment starting after year ten. Concessional loans are for productive projects, and most of the money goes to transport, communications and infrastructure programmes, and the development of mineral and energy resources. It is in this final category of concessional loans that the distinction between aid and commerce becomes particularly blurry.

Both White Papers reported that Africa was the main recipient of Chinese Aid (just over half of all aid according to the 2014 report), with Asia accounting for just under a third. However, the picture looks rather different if you add on Other Official Flows (OOF) of finance which contain no or minimal grant elements, and are for commercial projects that generate development-type projects. These are primarily energy related projects, and also include financing in mining and construction, agriculture forestry and fisheries, transportation and communications. The Aiddata project at the William and Mary College calculate that Russia was the main recipient of such OOF by 2014, with the amount of OOF received more than the combined total of the top ten recipients of Chinese ODA (Dreher et al, 2017).[5]

Statistics, evidence and intent

One of the consequences is that it is very difficult to work out exact figures, and even harder to get a set of statistics that is accepted and consistently used by a wide range of observers.[6] Nevertheless, we can say with confidence that China has emerged from being a marginal player on the global stage (though a significant bilateral partner for some individual economies) to a major one in a relatively short period of time, having seen an 'unprecedented acceleration' since the turn of the millennium (Bohoslavsky, 2016: 9). While some calculate otherwise, the Chinese government probably became the world's single biggest source of development finance in the 2010s, 'easily surpassing the IMF or the World Bank' as a result of a massive increase in 'direct loans and trade credits ... from almost zero in 1998 to more than 1.6 trillion USD, or close to 2 percent of world GDP in 2018' (Horn et al, 2019: 3).

Fortunately, the intention here is not to provide a reliable and agreed set of statistics, as an analysis of the literature suggest that this would not be possible. Rather, the aim is to use the case of the evolution of Chinese aid policies as a way of providing examples of the core arguments of this book. In this respect, opacity and contention is rather useful, as it takes us straight to the issue of the way that evidence is sought and presented to support (or reject) key arguments. The lack of transparency provides ample room for interpretation and trust issues to influence the way data is understood and used. For example, Strange et al (2017: 938) suggest that various forms of investment are sometimes bundled together with loans and other development projects to deliberately create 'inflated estimates to demonstrate the challenge that China poses to Western donors'. Alternatively (or additionally), the volume of financial flows can be exaggerated by focusing on what is announced rather than what is actually disbursed. This is also true for straightforward investment rather than just development funding. Brautigam (2015) has shown that much of what is reported as new Chinese land-based investments in Africa never actually comes to fruition. Similarly, in 2017, Chinese investors quietly cancelled 19 investment deals in Europe and North America that had previously been announced with considerable fanfare and publicity (Baker McKenzie, 2018).

Nation branding: doing things differently

More generally, the blurring of investment and aid-type activity feeds into (and is taken as evidence of) suspicions that China is trying to change the world and undermine existing ways of doing things. Here difference is something that doesn't have to be inferred. It is frequently clearly and loudly proclaimed from within China itself. There is a good reason that there isn't the same distinction between commercial and aid relationships with other developing states in the Chinese case, so the argument goes. This is because the nature of China's commercial relationships is not the same as Western ones. They are not built on the same zero-sum calculations that Western ones are said to represent, but instead search for 'win-win' common prosperity outcomes and are built on principles of friendship, equality, mutual benefit and support, common prosperity, and mutual learning (FMPRC, 2006). This is why they often have the developmental type consequences that Western commercial relationships with developing countries typically don't have.

There is also a loudly self-proclaimed different philosophy when it comes to Chinese ODA. China's approach is said to be built on 'principles of not imposing any political conditions, not interfering in the internal affairs of the recipient countries and fully respecting their right to independently choosing their own paths and models of development' (State Council, 2014). The West by implication (and at times explicitly) is associated with linked forms of aid designed to disseminate and promote liberal preferences (Zhang et al, 2015). China's own development experience is also said to give it special insights and a special concern with promoting development elsewhere with a specific focus on 'poverty reduction, infrastructure development, food security, capacity building', and addressing climate change through 'underlying principles of common but differentiated responsibilities, equity and respective capabilities' (FMPRC, 2019). The various documents that outline China's position on development and aid collectively establish a sense of Chinese superiority, both in terms of occupying a moral and ethical developmental high ground (again, compared to other great powers and the West), and in terms of practical contributions. The Belt and Road is portrayed as one of these contributions and is described as 'the largest platform for international cooperation and a popular public good in the world' (FMPRC, 2019).

We might question how true and/or extensive this difference really is. There are in fact conditions attached to taking money from China. As noted above, even though countries that do not recognize the PRC have received emergency aid, the 'One-China Principle' still influences who can get what from China. Accepting the terms of financial deals that typically involve using Chinese resources and/or labour might not at first sight be overt political interference, but they do limit the autonomy of the recipient state to act in ways that they might prefer, and might have greater developmental spillover effects. The extent to which China really has created a new modernity and solved the conundrum of how to industrialize without polluting that others can learn from and follow is also rather contestable (to say the least). But realities do not always shape policies. In terms of the way that China is being marketed, development aid has become a major arena in which an idea of Chinese difference is being constructed. Indeed, it is evolving into something more than just being different. What China does, and how it does it, is being portrayed as fundamentally *better* as well as fundamentally *different*, and Chinese action is resulting in it emerging as a global leader in the provision of development support for others.

That said, there is a certain defensiveness to Chinese positions as well. The two White Papers on Foreign Aid were both in part designed to refute foreign criticisms of what China was doing and establish the 'correct' Chinese version of the truth. The increase of what we might call more 'traditional' aid to developing states in the years preceding the first White Paper can also in part be taken as an attempt to deflect criticisms of more commercially based Chinese economic activities and interests (Davies, 2010: 13). And the amount of times that Chinese development assistance and other financial flows to Africa were said to definitely not constitute a form of neocolonialism at the 2018 FOCAC summit suggest that there was concern in Beijing that the neocolonial argument was indeed gaining purchase.

Development assistance actors

A further consequence of the relative opacity in Chinese development related financing is that it can also aggregate and blur different types of actions pursued by a variety of actors designed to attain diverse goals. In addition to philanthropic goals, we can make a rough and rather blunt distinction between ODA type funding which is intended to make political gains (like building support for grander international objectives), and that which is instead primarily intended to make economic gains (access to strategic resources, exporting excess capacity or just making profits) (Dreher et al, 2018). But even that distinction does not tell the full story.

ODA by definition is 'official' financial flows, and so the hand of the government should be clear and evident. It should also according to DAC definitions be extended to primarily enhance the welfare of the recipient country, and not that of the donor. In the Chinese case, while the state's hand is clearly there, the extent of corporate involvement and gain in the delivery of many projects was exactly why a number of analysts of the early phases of the growth of Chinese aid concluded that it wasn't ODA at all (Hubbard, 2007; Davies, 2010). It was not just that aid projects benefitted commercial actors, but they were often the originators of them as well, working with overseas governments to identify projects that they then requested aid financing to provide (Lancaster, 2007; Kobayashi, 2008; Lönnqvist, 2008).

The role of the state needs to be unravelled too. As noted in Chapter 2, there has also been overlap and competition between different state agencies in the delivery of different types of development support. Until 2018, China had no central state aid agency. Various incarnations of China's trade ministry (now MOFCOM) held formal authority after 1952, but faced 'a long history of internal competition' from the FMPRC (Zhang Denghua, 2018). Individual ministries also initiate specific forms of aid within their areas of competence – for example, Health, Science and Technology, Education, Agriculture and Communications. The ministries of Civil Affairs and Defence are involved in disaster relief, and the major financial agencies (Ministry of Finance, Eximbank, CDB, SAFE) all play roles in funding overseas assistance and/or facilitating flows of money (Varrall, 2016; Zhang and Smith, 2017).

The China International Development Cooperation Agency was designed to deal with the resulting problems of coordination, and prevent inter-agency rivalry by taking responsibility directly under the State Council (rather than via MOFCOM). It describes its own mission as 'to formulate strategic guidelines, plans and policies for foreign aid, coordinate and offer advice on major foreign aid issues, advance the country's reforms in matters involving foreign aid, and identify major programs and supervise and evaluate their implementation'.[7] Its creation also might be an attempt to separate out ODA type activities from more commercially related projects with development consequences, such as special development loan projects funded by the CDB and Eximbank and other financial agencies (Cheng, 2019).[8] This latter type of financing includes state-provided financing specifically designed to fund projects along the Belt and Road. Key among them is the Silk Road Fund which received initial funding from SAFE (65 per cent of the total), the CDB (5 per cent), the Eximbank and the CIC (15 per cent each). As the BRI vastly increased the number of Chinese actors involved in overseas projects, it is a relatively safe bet to suggest that the diversity of (economic) actors and interests is not going to disappear any time soon, even if the balance of importance among them shifts over time.

This rather short diversion into the political economy of Chinese overseas aid hopefully highlights how even something that is very clearly state driven entails the interaction of different types of interests from a relatively wide range of Chinese overseas actors. It is also an example of how the state provides the overarching policy framework that economic actors are constrained by, but which also often puts them in an advantageous position to succeed in some parts of the world relative to other national actors (Chen Muyang, 2018). This is even more evident when the focus turns towards the drivers and consequences of the growth of COFDI.

Financial power: Chinese Outward Foreign Direct Investment

According to the 2019 White Paper, China in the World in a New Era, 'in 2018, China's overseas investment reached US$143 billion, up by a factor of 53 since 2002, a yearly average growth of 28.2 percent' (State Council, 2019). In a document that is not short of impressive statistics, at first sight this is not *that* impressive by comparison with the expansion of other types of Chinese economic activity. Foreign trade, for example, had increased 223-fold. Moreover, cumulative outward investment remained dwarfed by the US$2 trillion worth of non-financial inward FDI (White & Case, 2017: 12–13). The key, though, is the starting point. While other figures in the section on 'interaction with the world' start from the beginning of the reform process in 1978, the statistics for COFDI only start in 2002. This is because it was only then that COFDI began to be a significant component of China's global economic profile.

Perceptions of the initial first wave of COFDI after 2002 tended to focus on Chinese investments in other developing countries, with a specific emphasis on relations with authoritarian ones. The state was widely argued to be supporting its SOEs to go to places that others either wouldn't or couldn't go, to gain political support and strategic raw material resources. This was variously referred to as 'a love affair with rogue states' (Fish, 2010) and 'Dictatorship Diplomacy' (Kleine-Ahlbrandt and Small, 2008).[9] For Halper (2010) it was this use of 'no string attached' finances to support other illiberal states and gain support for its own illiberal political and economic model that represented the real 'Beijing Consensus', rather than the more appreciative identification of an innovative and open China in the earlier book of the same name by Ramo (2004b).

Others, though, found different realities. At the same time as the idea of a state driven strategy was gaining purchases in the years around the global financial crisis, investigations on the ground in recipient countries typically discovered different stories. Nobody denied the importance of the state in opening doors and facilitating interactions. But the picture that emerged was of companies taking the lead in a search for commercial objectives rather than following top-down commands for strategic purposes (Downs, 2007; 2010). Those involved in energy and raw material industries did not have to simply send resources back home but could sell them on the open global market. Moreover, resource seeking investments were said to be less important than commonly understood. In Africa at least, manufacturing rather than mining was the main target of COFDI in these early years (Brautigam, 2008; 2009). Such non-resource seeking investment decisions were often driven by the failure to make profits at home in an overcrowded market (Rosen and Hanemann, 2009), particularly by small and medium enterprises who found it particularly difficult to compete with dominant SOEs in the domestic market (Gu, 2011).

South-South COFDI remains an issue of interest and concern. However, attention has also turned to investments in more developed economies, raising questions of the long-term wisdom of allowing Chinese ownership of strategic industries; be they directly related to national defence considerations or economically strategic ones. One common question cuts across both periods though. Rather than reflecting commercial logic driven by business interests, is the Chinese state instead driving COFDI, and using it as an instrument of 'economic statecraft' (Norris, 2016) to achieve its nationally defined goals and ambitions? And if the answer is yes (as it often is), the next question is whether these ambitions go beyond narrow economic goals.

Given all that has come before in this and previous chapters, it should be no surprise that my answer to both questions is the same. Sometimes, but not always. The picture that emerges is one of both considerable residual state control and influence, and also considerable divergence and plurality of objectives and interests too. These two apparently contradictory findings can be reconciled by making a distinction between the 'overall executive discretion' (Hurst, 2011) of the (central) state on the one hand, and the agency of individual commercial and local state actors to pursue their own goals within the boundaries that this executive discretion sets on the other.

Chinese Outward Foreign Direct Investment: what the statistics don't tell us[10]

COFDI did not begin in 2002. There were outward flows in the 1970s and 1980s, and what Blanchard (2019: 79) refers to as a dramatic increase in the 1990s, with accumulated overseas stocks at US$30 billion by the end of the decade. By international comparative standards, though, this was a tiny amount, and what could be invested where and by whom was very tightly controlled by the state. This only began to change with the announcement of a '*zou chuqu*' or 'go out' strategy to encourage Chinese companies to look to invest overseas in 1999. Even then it wasn't formally initiated until the following year, with full national statistics only collated and published from 2003 (for the previous year's activity). Hence the White Paper starts its growth calculations from 2002.

That the White Paper statistics for 2018 don't match those produced by MOFCOM (US$143 billion and US$129.83 billion respectively) might be a result of subsequent recalculations of the earlier MOFCOM figures as more information came to light. Such reassessments often occur with investment statistics in both directions. But it points to a bigger problem of finding a set of statistics that is widely accepted as being as close to the truth as possible, and which is widely trusted and used by non-Chinese analysts. Indeed, rather than recording a growth of any kind in 2018 (as both the White Paper and MOFCOM statistics did), the Heritage Foundation calculated a 30 per cent year on year decline instead. This was based on the Global Investment Tracker, which is widely used by those who do not trust official Chinese government data.[11] These statistics too, though, have to be revised as investment actually occurs rather than being announced (or most often, doesn't occur in its entirety). So it is quite possible to find different analyses that use the same source, but cite different figures as a result of when they consulted the data.

There is a general feeling from those who study the numbers in detail that official Chinese statistics tend to understate the real extent of Chinese overseas holdings for two reasons. The first is that they do not include profits made by Chinese companies overseas that are directly re-invested without ever being repatriated to Chinese parent companies (Gallagher and Irwin, 2014). The second is that they find it difficult to account for small scale investments like cross-border ones carried out predominantly by local and private actors (Luo et al, 2017: 144). The China Global Investment Tracker also only includes investments of over US$100 million, so it too does not factor in these smaller investments. These small flows do not really make that much difference to the overall picture, but can have specific micro level implications. For example, while official Chinese statistics calculated that US$315 million had gone to Mongolia by 2007, Mongolia claimed that it had received close to three times as much (US$900 million; Tan, 2013: 750). This gap between the two sets of statistics has little overall importance for students of the big picture of COFDI, but is a very significant issue for those who instead focus on COFDI in specific individual locations (such as Mongolia).

The real picture is further muddied by the fact that around two thirds of all COFDI from 2002 to 2018 went to just three places: Hong Kong, the Cayman Islands and the British Virgin Islands. And quite simply we don't know where this money eventually ended up. Some of it will have gone to third countries, and shown up on global investment statistics as investment from the intermediary recipient rather than from China (particularly from subsidiaries in Hong Kong). But some of it is recycled as inward investment back into China to take advantage of incentives offered to foreign investors. By some calculations around a quarter of all COFDI is 'round tripped' in this way (Casanova et al, 2015). So while most studies of statistical anomalies in COFDI suggest that the official figure underestimates the total, the actual amount of COFDI that is ultimately invested in final projects outside of China might really be less than the official figures suggest as a result of this round tripping.

Analysing short-term changes over a relatively small time period is particularly challenging. On the one hand, what looks like an ineluctable trend can end up being an aberration because one or two individual investment projects are so big that they skew the figures. A good example is ChemChina's massive US$43 billion takeover of Syngenta in 2017, which was enough to turn a 22 per cent year on year reduction of Chinese investment in Europe without the deal into a 76 per cent increase with it (Baker McKenzie, 2018). Changes in the Chinese regulatory and incentive structure can also have very dramatic effects that create new patterns almost overnight (and sometimes stop existing patterns as well). In this chapter, for example, there is a specific focus on the 44 per cent jump in COFDI in 2016, and the subsequent sharp contraction the following year. What might have easily been mistaken for a new trend turned out to be a blip instead. Many of the findings of the very good research on the first wave of COFDI – where it went and what it was trying to do – were simply not replicated by studies from about 2012 onwards. They remain very useful studies of the first generation of investments,[12] but many of their original conclusions have been overtaken by time. It will also take many years to fully understand the consequences of the COVID-19 pandemic on Chinese investment flows, so studying what happened in 2020 alone tells us little to nothing about longer-term consequences. So the warning that it is often too early to tell in the study of China in general is particularly pertinent when it comes to the study of COFDI.

What the figures can tell us

Perhaps the best we can do is stick to a common set of statistics, hope that the flaws within them are relatively consistent across years, and look for general trends. We can then try and see if the same general trends can be observed using other sets of data as well. And fortunately, they can. Unless otherwise cited, the data below comes from MOFCOM, either directly through its own publications and web resources, or indirectly as reported by the National Development and Reform Commission (NDRC). The simple headline is that China went from being pretty much insignificant to becoming a major source of outward investment in the space of a decade and a half. To put more flesh on this, we can see an average annual growth rate of 35.8 per cent from 2002 to a high point of COFDI in 2016, before a rather large decrease in 2017.[13] This resulted in the overall stock of Chinese overseas investment rising from 25th in the world in 2002 to sixth. In terms of annual flows, the highpoint 2016 figure of US$196 billion placed China as second only to the US as a source of outward investment that year, accounting for 13.5 per cent of all global flows (compared to being 26th and providing 0.5 per cent of all flows in 2002; NDRC, 2017: 3–4).

For reasons that we shall return to later, after 14 years of continued annual growth, COFDI fell back rather dramatically in 2017. Initial Chinese figures suggested by almost 30 per cent to US$120.08 billion (MOFCOM, 2018), though later revised ones calculated a 19.3 per cent drop instead (MOFCOM, 2019a). Both calculations put China back down to third in the global league table behind both the US and Japan (MOFCOM, 2018). And it is interesting to note just how important Japanese FDI still is given the focus on China's growth in recent years. Given the way these statistics change, it is not wholly clear if COFDI then rose again in 2018 or not. It depends on whether you use the early or later MOFCOM figures as a starting point, and then whether Chinese or external statistics are used for the following year. But everybody agrees that whatever happened in 2018, there was a further drop in 2019, with the highest figures for 2019 of US$110.6 billion over 40 per cent below the 2016 figure (Ernst and Young, 2020). So even though it is difficult to be precise with the statistics, we can again say with confidence that having reached a high point in 2016, there was subsequently a significant drop off over the next three years. We will never know if this then would have stabilized into a consistent pattern of flows under normal circumstances because what happened to the global economy in 2020 was far from normal.

So why did COFDI grow so quickly in and before 2016, only to subsequently fall off? The answer is found by analysing the evolution of state objectives and the policy reforms implemented to help attain these goals alongside a consideration of how various actors responded to these changes to pursue their own individual interests. Interests which at time coincide and contribute to the attainment of state goals, but which also sometimes don't.

Chinese Outward Foreign Direct Investment: from permitting to encouraging

Despite being encouraged to go global around the turn of the millennium, it wasn't actually that easy to do so for many. Initially, COFDI had to be approved by the NDRC, the inheritor of previous state planning functions and China's major macroeconomic management and control institution. This changed as the system was reformed and decentralized (Tan, 2013). By 2014, only investments of over US$1 billion (as well as those in sensitive countries) had to be approved rather than simply reported and registered, and local governments had become responsible for investments under US$300 million (Casanova et al, 2015; Sauvant and Nolan 2015). SAFE played (and continues to play) an important role in controlling and approving overall financial flows, as well as being a major provider of funds for overseas projects itself. But it was the NDRC's Department of Foreign Capital Utilization that was responsible for approving investment projects which entailed large scale transfers of currency out of China. Though they still needed to give approval for funding for large scale projects, policy changes in 2006, 2008 and 2009 gradually made it easier for companies to get hold of foreign currency to be used in overseas projects (Rosen and Hanemann, 2009: 11). For many enterprises, these changes made it easier to invest overseas. For others – especially for small and medium sized enterprises – it was not so much a case of making it easier, as making the virtually impossible now possible.

If the first stage saw the state *allowing* COFDI, the subsequent (overlapping) stage was to actively *promote* the benefits of going overseas; from facilitation to encouragement. Rather than just making it possible to move money offshore, a range of special funds were established to support projects in various parts of the world. This is one of the areas where the distinction between commercial investment and state promoted development assistance becomes rather indistinct. Incentive projects also targeted firms hoping to acquire advanced technology and knowhow, and to move up the global value chain (Amighini et al,

2013). This included 'soft' types of support such as providing guidance and training to companies that often had little or no experience of operating outside China's borders (Knoerich, 2017). A range of more concrete support and promotion mechanisms were introduced over the years as well, and as Sauvant and Nolan (2015: 897) have provided a comprehensive list of them, it is easiest to reproduce that list here rather than paraphrase it, even though it is relatively long:

> subsidies (including financial and fiscal support); priority access to loans; expedited approval; priority access to foreign exchange; tax rebates on (or waivers for) the export of goods (e.g., equipment); priority regarding overseas financing, investment consulting, risk assessment, risk control, and investment insurance; and priority treatment regarding information questions, consular protection, customs exit and the entry of personnel, expatriate personnel approval, registration and the domestic coordination of import–export operation rights, and international communication.

Individual ministries and agencies also developed a range of measures designed to help companies in their areas to gain from overseas investment. For example, in 2016 the Ministry of Industry and Information Technology produced a plan specifically designed to help small and medium enterprises to go overseas (Ernst and Young, 2017).

Changing investment patterns

Not surprisingly, the regulatory changes had a profound impact on who was investing, and where they were investing. As already noted, initially it was the activities of large state enterprises investing in developing countries that first raised concerns about the consequences of this new Chinese global role. But rather than just searching for resources, other considerations played a role too among early responders. Establishing branch offices overseas to support exports was also a characteristic of this first wave of investment (Yeung and Liu, 2008: 68). But the extent of investments in other developing economies looked so out of odds with 'normal' investment patterns from other states that it created a debate over whether Chinese firms perceived risk differently from their counterparts in other countries (particularly developed ones).

The consensus answer to this question was a qualified 'yes'. The evidence did indeed point to considerable Chinese investments in 'risky' countries, and relatively more so than from other major investing economies (Ramasamy et al, 2012). However, the most commonly argued position was that Chinese companies did not actively seek them out in preference to more stable ones, but that they were simply less concerned about the nature of the regime of the host country than was the case with investors from elsewhere (Dollar, 2016). This was particularly true for SOEs, either because they expected the Chinese state to bail them out should things go wrong (Duanmu, 2012), and/or because of the 'risk-reduction effect of good political relations' (Li and Liang, 2012). That other companies from other countries were disinclined to invest in such places also suggests that there were fewer existing and entrenched foreign companies to compete with, thus making the prospects of success for new Chinese entrants somewhat higher than in more mature and saturated markets.

But things change – and often very quickly. As investment responded to these changes in state regulations and incentives, the nature of COFDI underwent a quite dramatic transformation. By 2017, the relative importance of investment in unstable developing states in the overall profile of COFDI was much diminished and the geographical spread of Chinese investments now looked much less abnormal than a decade earlier. Rather than focusing on Chinese difference, the 2017 IMF annual report on China was referring to the drivers of COFDI as '*the traditional desire* for new markets and technology' (IMF, 2017b: 25, emphasis added), and Chalmers and Mocker (2017) were happy to conclude that the era of 'exceptionalism' was already over.

Becoming 'normal'?

These changes to the outward investment regime eventually resulted in five key changes in China's investment profile. First, while promoting exports had been a driver of COFDI from the beginning, this type of investment increased as Chinese companies set up affiliates overseas to help sell things; for example, investing in textile production in a range of states to sell into the US and European markets. Second, mergers and acquisitions (M&A) replaced brownfield (energy related) investment as the main way of investing overseas, accounting for around two thirds of all COFDI in 2018 (MOFCOM, 2018). Third, the nature of M&A activity changed too. While resources and materials accounted for two thirds of overseas purchases from 2005 to 2013, the subsequent focus was on buying brands and technology and knowhow, and establishing overseas operations. This fed into the overall COFDI profile to leave the tertiary (service) sector accounting for just under 80 per cent of the total stock of COFDI by 2017 'mainly in leasing and business services, finance, wholesale and retail, information transmission/ software and information technology services, real estate, transportation and warehousing' (NDRC, 2017: 26).

Fourth, the above changes all combined to result in a shift in destinations too. To be more correct, multiple shifts. Originally focusing on resource rich economies in the developing world, there was first a move to resources acquisitions in the developed world (mainly Canada, Australia and the US), and then to other investment activities in developed economies. As a result, 'by 2015, high-income economies were capturing two-thirds of all Chinese M&A by value' (White & Case, 2017: 4) with Europe and North America emerging as the two most popular destinations. The following year, they accounted for close to half of all COFDI (not just M&A activity) with investment to these two destinations more than doubling (and investment to the US alone almost tripling). But just as it seemed possible to conclude that Europe and North America were now the favoured investment sites, subsequent changes in the Chinese regulatory system combined with US–China friction and concerns about future investment screening to change things again. According to the Rhodium Group's statistics, COFDI to the US fell from US$46 billion in 2016 to US$29 billion in 2017, and then fell again to just US$4.8 billion in 2018 (Hanemann et al, 2019). By 2019, M&A activity in Europe and North America had fallen back to roughly the levels they had been at in 2014 and 2012 respectively, with Asia now the most popular destination (Ernst and Young 2020).

Fifth, the number of Chinese actors engaging in overseas activities also increased. Investments by large centrally owned SOEs initially dominated, but by 2018 accounted for just under a third of the annual value of COFDI (MOFCOM 2019b). We need to add on to this investment by SOEs owned by local governments to get an overall understanding of the importance of the state sector. But then we immediately have to separate them out again as local SOEs do not act in the same way as national level ones. Then we have the additional problem of the role of the state in individual LLCs noted in Chapter 2, which means that some of them wouldn't be thought of as truly non-state actors in other economies, but which nevertheless are a different type of entity than those directly owned by the state (at whatever level). And just to add one more extra layer of fuzziness, there are also a handful of non-state enterprises that are thought of as national champions, and get the sort of state support that formally state-owned companies might have in other countries. Huawei and the HNA group are two very good examples (Rühlig, 2020).

Keeping this lack of clarity in mind, the statistics (just about) show a significant increase in the role of the non-state sector in a relatively short period of time as a result of all the other changes noted above. Accounting for just 19 per cent of all COFDI in 2006, it overtook the state sector in either 2015 or 2017 depending on which figures you use, reaching 57.4 per cent of all COFDI in 2018 (MOFCOM, 2019b). Larger centrally owned SOEs tend to be involved in big projects that have strategic aims, and thus have the sort of potential political implications that those who have wider concerns about Chinese ambitions look out for (Naughton, 2015). The size of these projects can also result in SOE investment exceeding that from non-state sectors in individual years. But it is instructive that having assessed the direction of travel over a number of years, Ernst and Young (2017: 17) concluded that small and local enterprises had become 'the backbone of China's outbound investment'.

Perhaps it is best to put specific statistics aside and try and come to general overall conclusions. Although its dominance has declined, the state sector remains crucially important, and more important than is the case in the overseas investment activities of more mature freer market economies. It is even more important than appears at first sight if LLCs are treated as state-related actors (Hubbard, 2016), and national champions are considered to be state linked if not state owned. While it has declined in relative importance, the way that investment has been used to gain control of and/or access to major resources remains significant. So too is the fact that a significant amount of COFDI is supported by loans from the state banks. While this is particularly important for energy and natural resource investments (Gallagher and Irwin, 2014: 839), Bo and Gallagher (2017) have shown how the Eximbank and the CDB have also been (overwhelmingly) more important than commercial banks in funding COFDI in general; certainly more important than state banks funding for investment in other economies. Overall, the extent of state involvement and support that all types of investors receive to different extents helps create what Ramamurti and Hillemann (2018) call a 'government created advantage' for Chinese investors that goes beyond what other governments typically offer to support their favoured investors.

Not surprisingly, in terms of what they invest to achieve, and where they do it, there are significant differences between different types of investors. Amighini et al (2013) found that private companies were much more likely to go overseas to gain technology and markets, while SOEs were more likely to seek out the things that the Chinese state thinks China needs for long-term development (such as energy and other resources). As already noted, there can also be big difference between the large central SOES, which tend to conform more to this politicized understanding of strategically (resource) driven investment, and locally owned SOEs. The latter in general tend to 'fulfil more profit-oriented development objectives of their local owners' (Li et al, 2014). As such, while still being very much part of the state system, their behaviour is 'closer in character to non-state enterprises' than to the larger more strategic central SOEs (Luo et al 2017, 156). Add this all together, and as Buckley (2017) argues:

> The argument that in an authoritarian state 'politics trumps economics' does not however seem to be the case with an overall explanation of Chinese OFDI. Government does interfere but this interference is differential—across ownership groups (SOEs and private companies may be both encouraged/subsidised and impeded/discouraged), sectors, Provinces and types of firm.

Oliveira et al (2017: 423) make the simple argument that 'to treat all Chinese OFDI as equal would be a mistake'. What is most interesting about this statement is the need to make it at all – why on earth would all investment from a country as large as China be treated as a single entity in pursuit of a single goal? The fact that it is often treated this way says a lot about the way China is perceived and its ultimate objectives understood by some international observers. And it's fair to say that under Xi Jinping, the way that China has presented itself to the world has not exactly undermined the idea of a centralized leadership – or even one man – in charge and in control.

The limits of bounded autonomy

Given the argument made above about the potential pitfalls of assessing data for any single year, it might then seem strange to focus on 2017 as warranting specific attention. Particularly (as also noted above) as it was in many ways the preceding rapid growth that was abnormal rather than the subsequent drop. However, the state's response to this abnormality is rather illuminating, and highlights a key dilemma for Chinese policy makers that echoes the analysis in Chapter 2. How do you liberalize and facilitate the outward investment regime while at the same time maintaining enough control to make sure that investors invest where you want them to?

The explosion of investment in 2015 and 2016 was facilitated by the state's administrative and regulatory reforms. The central agencies responsible for controlling financial flows deliberately let go of much of their previous control over who could invest and where they could invest it. This was seen as the best way of helping small and medium sized Chinese companies do what they needed to do from both macro and micro perspectives. Having facilitated greater freedoms, though, it did not take long for concern to appear over the way in which these new freedoms were being utilized. This included anxiety about the financial viability of some of them, about the possibility of using investment as a disguised means of capital flight, and evidence that some recipient countries were responding negatively to what had been a very rapid increase of COFDI in a very short period of time (Miller, 2019: 236).

In order to rebalance the overall profile and partly regain the control that the state had previously ceded, new capital control restrictions were reintroduced in late 2016 followed by regulations aimed at 'guiding' and regulating COFDI the following year (State Council, 2017). This guidance included revising China's sectoral discrimination policy to clarify encouraged sectors (notably those designed to increase connectivity along the Belt and Road),[14] restricted ones (specifically 'investment in real estate, hotels, cinemas, entertainment industry and sports clubs'),[15] and prohibited sectors. This last grouping includes investments that 'endanger or may endanger national interests and national security',[16] which is imprecise enough to include anything that the central authorities deem to be damaging.

The drop in investment in 2017 points to the success of these measures. So too does the fact that MOFCOM (2018) could report that 'no new projects were added in real estate, sports and entertainment areas'; a line that was repeated in subsequent annual reports too. So rather than being restricted sectors as should have technically been the case, they in practice became prohibited ones. This shows the extent of the state's ability to shape overseas investment activity through regulatory tools, and also through the other means that is has of communicating its preferences. But while the fact that it *could* and *did* intervene suggests an active and vigilant state, the fact that it *had to* intervene in this way shows that it is not always an all-powerful and all controlling state. The state creates opportunities and possibilities, but the easier it makes it for a range of actors to act relatively freely (be that at home or overseas) then the less able it is to ensure that these actors respond in the ways that the state wants them to. When they (or the market more broadly) doesn't do what they are expected or desired to do, then they have to be brought back under control.

Follow the leader?

If stopping certain types of investment in specific places is one side of bounded autonomy, the flip side of the coin is responding to incentives to follow leaders' preferences. Here, the example of investment flowing along the Belt and Road might seem to provide an excellent example. Even as overall COFDI dropped in 2017, the fact that it increased by 3.5 per cent to Belt and Road countries suggests that a number of Chinese companies had allowed themselves to be guided by the state into its – and in this case, Xi Jinping's – preferred projects. This is really not surprising given how much the state has done to try and make such investments attractive to its commercial actors. In addition to the financing available through specific funding pots and export and credit insurance for investors – the normal sort of Chinese state support for investors – it has tried to facilitate and encourage investment in a number of ways. For example, it has signed over 60 bilateral investment treaties with Belt and Road countries (Ferguson et al, 2018), made steps towards expanding currency swaps and transnational currency settlements (OLGBRI, 2017), and established various forms of economic development and cooperation zones to facilitate COFDI.

It is rather difficult to gauge the specific importance of these policies as we don't know how much investment would have occurred without them and without the BRI. We also need to remind ourselves of the close relationship between loans and investment noted above, and the fact that money extended by the state banks, the specialist Silk Road Fund, and the AIIB can generate contracts for Chinese companies and thus have corporate investment type effects. As a result, the actual investment type activity of Chinese companies along the Belt and Road will be greater than the raw COFDI investment figures suggest. Even so, given that BRI countries collectively accounted for over 60 per cent of the world's population and around a quarter of global GDP, then attracting 13.6 per cent of all COFDI in 2019 does not look particularly remarkable.

Changing our minds? Responding to Chinese economic power

In many respects, though, the real figures are less important politically that the sort of signalling and perceptions discussed in Chapter 1. The

BRI fanfare has been heard and understood in a number of foreign capitals as sign of China's strategic intent. The growth of COFDI has also been felt and understood in certain ways too. A Pew survey of the broadly defined Asia region in 2019 found a majority in each country perceiving the growth of COFDI as a 'bad thing' (even in those countries where Chinese economic growth in general was predominantly seen as being 'good') (Obe, 2019). There has also been a rethink of the consequences of China's growth in some of the more developed Western economies that have only relatively recently become major recipients of significant Chinese financial flows.

Perceptions of what the growth of COFDI might mean do not exist in isolation from other shifts in how countries have interacted with a changing China. In the US, for example, the decision to impose tariffs on Chinese exports in 2018 was initially driven by the argument that bilateral trade surpluses in China's favour had disadvantaged the US for a number of years. This fed into (or built on) other concerns about Chinese technology theft, and the potential for some form of military conflict in the future. Even so, Tingley et al (2015: 29) argue that the growth of Chinese M&A activity in the US from less than US$1 billion in 2000 to US$14 billion in 2013 played a key role in raising anxieties about China, with national security arguments often masking more fundamental apprehensions about 'losing out'. The use of the Committee on Foreign Investment in the United States (CFIUS) to investigate (and at times block) proposed investment deals from China goes back as far as 1990. According to Zimmerman (2019), the introduction of the Foreign Investment Risk Review Modernization Act in 2018 to update the jurisdiction and scope of CFIUS activity was a direct result of 'increased fear regarding China's growing strategic and economic clout and the potential loss of American technology supremacy'. This suggests that while the growth of COFDI was not the only source of a harder line on China, it certainly played a role.

As with the CFIUS, new EU regulations establishing a framework for investment screening in 2019 were not just a response to Chinese challenges alone. But also as with the CFIUS example, the growth of COFDI was a significant driver of the policy change (Anthony et al, 2020: 19–20). Indeed, given that concerns about the consequences of China's rise had previously been generally less pronounced in Europe, the growth of COFDI arguably played an even more significant role in a more significant re-framing of thinking in Europe than it did in the US. To be sure we don't know for sure what was cause and what was effect. Did the changed economic relationship reshape views of China's global governance ambitions, or was it instead the proactive Chinese promotion of a governance reform agenda that led to a rethink of the benefits of attracting Chinese investment? What is clear, as reflected in the EU's new strategy paper on relations with China in 2019, is that a very significant rethink took place in some European capitals (and at the EU level as well) after 2015: 'there is a growing appreciation in Europe that the balance of challenges and opportunities presented by China has shifted. In the last decade, China's economic power and political influence have grown with unprecedented scale and speed, reflecting its ambitions to become a leading global power' (European Commission, 2019: 1).

Ongoing financial difficulties in South, Eastern and Central Europe created opportunities for Chinese investments, with the establishment of the 16+1 process in 2012 providing a new platform for relation between China and a group of Central and Eastern European Countries towards the western end of the Belt and Road. This became 17 with the addition of Greece in 2019.[17] Not surprisingly, what was seen as an opportunity in central and eastern Europe was seen as a potential threat in other places. As a European Parliament Briefing put it in 2018:

> The 16+1 format is an attractive tool for China to increase its political influence on CEECs [Central and Eastern European Countries], as it is one of China's main platforms to push its BRI vision forward. Since the BRI raises high expectations with CEECs for future Chinese investment and funding, the 16+1 format allows China to mould CEECs into political allies willing to support Chinese core interests at EU level. In recent years, some CEECs have in some instances given priority to Chinese political interests over EU interests. (Grieger, 2018: 3)

This concern was compounded by growing anxiety in Europe about allowing Chinese ownership in strategic sectors. As Thorsten Benner argued in an interview in the *Financial Times*:

> There used to be a belief that Germany and China were perfectly complementary partners. Now we have realised that China has become a core competitor and that it uses investment in a very strategic manner to copy technology and accelerate the catch-up. And there is a realisation that Chinese investment has an impact on national security. (Buck, 2018)

It is important to retain a sense of balance. The speed of the growth of COFDI and the way that it was been reported resulted in an inflated understanding of how significant it actually was. For example, investment from China to the US increased by over a third between 2013 and 2018, second only to the increase of investment from Argentina, but with a much greater consequential stock (US$60.182 billion compared to US$4.9 billion). This is clearly important and substantial. But it still left China with only 1.4 per cent of the total stock of foreign investment in the US, in 13th place and just above South Korea. Ireland (with a population of less than five million) had invested more than six times the figure from China, and the UK in first place nearly ten times more (SelectUSA, 2019). These statistics are based on the ultimate beneficiary: where the money originates from rather than the location of the final investor (for example, via tax havens in the Caribbean). Similar calculations in the UK put China 17th in a league table of investors at the end of 2017 with £7.9 billion. This put China just below India, at half of the figure for 15th place Ireland, and with about a tenth of the investment in the UK that originated from fifth placed Japan (ONS, 2019). In Germany, China was the 13th biggest investor at the end of 2018, and even if *all* investment from Hong Kong (in 12th place) was added to that from the PRC, it would only lift the combined China-Hong Kong total up one place above South Korea to tenth place (DB, 2019: 28–30). It was a similar story in Australia too, with Chinese investment growing rapidly for the best part of a decade, but still only ranking 9th in terms of total stock of holdings in 2018, with 1.8 per cent of the total (Dfat, 2019). Hong Kong was fifth with 3.4 per cent, some way behind the US (26.7 per cent), the UK (16.4 per cent), Belgium (9 per cent) and Japan (6.5 per cent).

To reiterate, the growth of COFDI and where it is going really is important. The speed of the rise of investment from China really is important too. It's just that the aggregate and overall importance is not quite as high in many countries as most of the headlines and 'common sense' understandings of Chinese significance might suggest. At the same time, the residual importance of investment from other sources can be overlooked. Partly because they have been global investment actors for longer, and also partly because these countries are trusted in ways that China isn't.

Coronavirus and the future of China's economic power

One conclusion of this chapter is that things change so quickly that it is hard to say anything about the future with any certainty. New patterns of investment might well have emerged in normal circumstances as a result of changing Chinese priorities, and also changing perceptions of the benefits of taking Chinese money. But as already noted, 2020 proved to be anything but normal as the coronavirus pandemic led to economies across the world going into various degrees of suspended animation. When it comes to tracing long-term evolutions of trends in a whole range of different economic arenas, the changes from 2019 to 2020 across a range of indicators will be more dramatic than those that resulted from the global financial crisis.

Rather than try to establish certainties about Chinese economic power in a post pandemic world, it is more realistic to be somewhat cautious and point to a range of potential scenarios instead. The drive to make domestic consumption ever more important as a source of Chinese growth had been ongoing before the pandemic. As Li Keqiang (2020) noted in his Government Work Report in 2020, the combined impact of the domestic close down and a dramatic slump in global economic growth created – or exacerbated – a whole range of economic challenges: 'Domestically, consumption, investment, and exports have declined. Pressure on employment has risen significantly. Enterprises, especially micro, small, and medium businesses, face growing difficulties. There are increasing risks in the financial sector and other areas. The budgetary imbalances of primary-level governments have intensified.' One scenario for dealing with these challenges is a rebalancing away from overseas projects and an emphasis on investing at home to return to growth. As one of a series of *People's Daily*'s front-page commentaries on the pandemic put it, 'shifting part of the foreign trade production capacity to the domestic market' and increasing domestic investment to 'drive the expansion of the consumer market' were the most effective way of trying to recover from the economic dimension of the pandemic crisis (*People's Daily*, 2020c).[18]

Even before the pandemic began to spread, a number of investment projects along the Belt and Road had already faced problems generating enough money to pay for themselves. This had generated considerable debate on both the political utility of debt relationships for China, and whether it was an intentional strategy to actually promote financially unsustainable projects in the first place. A fuller discussion of the nature of 'debt diplomacy' follows in the Conclusion.

Here, the point is simply to suggest – rather uncontrovertibly – that global economic turmoil will make things worse. This can actually create opportunities for China. For example, those countries that are 'friendly with us' might get preferential treatment when it comes to debt relief according to one Chinese think tank analyst (Kynge and Yu, 2020). But rescheduling debt payments is likely to cast further doubt on the wisdom of investing in projects that are based more on the political logic of promoting the BRI than on sound economic fundamentals.

If these first two outcomes suggest a turn away from global investment, there are potentially countervailing factors at play to. As was the case in and after the global financial crisis, the coronavirus crisis could see major overseas companies and resources available at knock-down prices. Indeed, in response to the possibility of Chinese purchases of suddenly rather cheap European firms, in April 2020, the EU Commissioner for Competition, Margrethe Vestage, urged European governments to do exactly what her office normally tried to stop; to protect domestic companies and prevent takeovers from foreign government backed entities, including via partial nationalization of them if necessary (Esponiza, 2020). There might be opportunities in developing economies too that lose markets in (and finance from) the West. An increase in debt in developing countries will also impact on their financial relationships with China. And yet another scenario is that the force of decoupling arguments might be enhanced: 'the Covid-19 crisis has forced many corporates to think about relocating their manufacturing bases and factory outlets out of China. Beijing will face a great challenge in convincing companies and investors to stay engaged with its industries and market' (Panda, 2020).

These are not necessarily mutually contradictory scenarios at all. There could be less overall COFDI, but what is invested might take advantages of the opportunities that the pandemic ultimately offers. A concerted effort to continue production in strategic sectors throughout the pandemic combined with the problems facing other countries could put China in a strong position to push ahead with MIC2025 objectives 'to move China up the manufacturing value chain, expand its global market competitiveness, and reduce its reliance on foreign firms and their intellectual property' (Sutter et al, 2020). And/or more COFDI might occur alongside a reduction of flows into China and a form of de-engagement, as governments and companies think through the costs and benefits of reliance on China. As one of the arguments established in the Introduction is that we need time to know what the long-term implications of anything really is, then it is reasonable to repeat here that it really is too early to tell, and will be for quite some time. In terms of thinking about the future, though, it is rather likely that pre-existing perceptions of the nature of Chinese objectives, of the autonomy of Chinese actors, and of the consequences of Chinese action, will all help shape the impact of the pandemic on China's global economic power as well.

Ideas, Voice and Attraction

Before 2004, it was extremely rare to hear the words 'China' and 'soft power' spoken in the same sentence (Gill and Huang, 2006). In the following five years, the study of Chinese soft power generated enough scholarship to put it on the way to becoming part of any mainstream analysis of the Chinese power. Predominantly China's potential regional power but also influence and attraction in other parts of the world too.[1] In a remarkably short period of time, it was a topic that went from being pretty much non-existent to become a 'theme of the time' of sorts.

It is no real coincidence that this rather rapid change of focus coincided with the initial boom in COFDI discussed in the previous chapter. In addition to the general growth of financial flows, the establishment of China's new sovereign wealth fund (the CIC in September 2007) provided a focal point for those already concerned that the Chinese state was now prepared to use its financial resources in strategic ways that could harm the national interests of major Western powers. Not just by buying up strategic assets in the West, but also by trying to buy friendship and support in the developing world. It also provided an example within China of how (mis)perceptions of what the country wanted could result in actions to block Chinese activity (Wu and Seach, 2008: 47). Hence the importance of trying to assuage these potential concerns by 'cultivating a benign reputation abroad' (Shirk, 2007: 106).

There were other reasons too though. In 2007, Hu Jintao's report to the 17th Party Congress had included a specific call to increase Chinese soft power as a source of both national cohesion and global competition:

> In the present era, culture has become a more and more important source of national cohesion and creativity and a factor of growing significance in the competition in overall national strength, and the Chinese people have an

increasingly ardent desire for a richer cultural life. We must keep to the orientation of advanced socialist culture, bring about a new upsurge in socialist cultural development, stimulate the cultural creativity of the whole nation, and enhance culture as part of the soft power of our country. (Hu, 2007)

This not surprisingly resulted in interest in what those soft power cultural resources might be, and how they could be utilized to bring about change. Equally unsurprisingly, it generated a new interest in soft power from among Chinese scholars as well, with Wang Yiwei (2008: 258) noting the following year that 'few Western international relations phrases have penetrated as deeply or broadly into the Chinese vocabulary in recent years'.

The Beijing Olympics in 2008 also helped shape the soft power agenda, and responses to it. The Games were seen in China as a great chance to bring people to the country and to showcase China to a global audience. It was given an even greater significance in China because of the feeling that the country had been slighted in 1993 when the millennial Olympic Games were awarded to Sydney. There had been a widespread expectation (and not just in China) that Beijing would win, and this would be a signal of China's re-acceptance into the international community despite both the hangover from Tiananmen and anti-Beijing lobbying from human rights groups and by some US politicians. After all, Tokyo had been awarded the Olympics less than 20 years after it had been on the 'wrong' side of history in the Second World War, so why should China have to wait any longer? Moreover, for much of the previous year, winning and preparing for the Olympics had become a major domestic political campaign, rallying the people round what was expected to become a successful endeavour. As a result, not winning the games (despite gaining most votes in all but the very last and decisive round of voting) was not only taken as a way of punishing China internationally, but also threatened to damage the leadership's credibility domestically (Chen Yanru, 1998).

The 2008 Games were thus seen not just as a validation of China and its progress, but also as a partial righting of previous wrongs. As the Chinese academic Pang Zhongying (2008) argued at the time:

China was extremely excited, honoured, and satisfied to host such a world event because it desires to be acknowledged as an indispensable member of the international community.

The Chinese elites proclaimed the Beijing games a 'century old dream' of the Chinese people, which mainly meant that the Chinese people want their achievements and progress to be universally recognized.

2008 was also the year that the Lehman Brothers filed for bankruptcy in the US and the failing Northern Rock bank was nationalized in the UK, and what started out as a crisis of a certain type of financial regulation (or indeed, the lack of it) spread out across the globe. This crisis of neoliberalism gradually turned attention to whether China might provide an alternative ideational model of development for a post-Western World.

While this chapter touches on issues relating to China's normative power, a full discussion is left to Chapter 6, which focuses on what looks like a clearer attempt than ever before to establish Chinese preferences and experiences as the basis for alternatives; alternative ways of organizing the world and providing forms of global governance, and an alternative way of promoting development and modernization. The main purpose of the current chapter is to establish what exactly it is that we are talking about (which is not as straightforward as it might sound), what the Chinese leadership is trying to achieve, and the resources that it thinks that it has available to it. As I have covered the last of these purposes elsewhere (Breslin, 2020), to avoid repetition the emphasis here is tilted towards the other objectives.

Much of the discussion in both academic and more popular forums of Chinese attempts to influence the way that others think uses the language of 'soft power'. Indeed, it is a term that has been used throughout the earlier chapters of this book. While it is a term that has been widely used in IR scholarship for a number of years, it is a concept that can mean different things to different people. This general lack of agreed meaning gets stretched even further when applied to the Chinese case. So in keeping with the overarching inspiration of this study to try and disaggregate different sources of Chinese power, the chapter will begin by unpicking different sources of Chinese influence. However, while the desire is to separate out different power resources, there is also an underpinning recognition that this is often very hard to do. Some think that it is actually impossible (Li Mingjiang, 2008b). In particular, the way in which China projects itself as a new and different type of financial partner explicitly blurs harder financial resources with softer ideational ones. The material and the ideational are inextricably linked. To reflect this, the chapter concludes with examples of issues that show the importance of hard economics in arenas that are sometimes considered to be ideational and soft.

This final section includes a discussion of Chinese 'crisis diplomacy', with a specific focus on what was done and said during the COVID-19 pandemic in 2020. Here the analysis draws on the understanding of bounded pluralism and autonomy established in previous chapters, and focuses on the mixed messages that emerged as different Chinese actors did different things; for example, trying to control the discourse of who to blame for the crisis at the same time as providing medical supplies. This example also highlights the contradictions that can emerge between establishing narratives for domestic consumption on the one hand, and for international audiences on the other; and between different types of international audiences too.

What is soft about Chinese soft power?

Maybe if Hu Jintao had used a different term than *ruanshili* in 2007, then we might have subsequently been talking about something else rather than soft power. Maybe a range of different non-hard power sources rather than just one. But we are where we are. In many ways, it is a term that provides a very useful antidote to just focusing on the potential hard military challenge that a rising China might pose in the future. The problem is that it has become something of an umbrella concept covering anything and everything that isn't hard military power. This includes offering or threatening the sort of financial, economic and diplomatic inducements and punishments that the original architect of the soft power concept thought were part and parcel of normal harder sources of power and influence in international politics; the very elements of power politics that his understanding of soft power was defined against in the first place (Nye, 1990; 2000; 2004).

If the constituent elements of soft power create one definitional conundrum, another emerges from how it is transmitted. Soft power was originally conceived as the idea that others will align themselves to you and your policy preferences because they are attracted to your political and social system and values. But actual real-world policies are important too, as it is these that directly impact on others and illustrate whether underpinning values are truly held and acted on, or simply empty propaganda-type ideas. So for Yan Xuetong (2019: 13), effective 'political leadership' is the key to having soft power, as culture and values only inform policy decisions, while leadership generates the actual 'deeds' that lead to attraction (or not). As such, you could argue that soft power in itself and on its own is not something that needs to be specifically and deliberately promoted, but should instead result from the successful pursuance of other policies; something that a country develops as a result of all that it says and does. At an extreme, maybe actively promoting soft power might be an indication that you don't have it organically and naturally. It might not even be something that a national government can control at all. Is attraction to the American way of life more about wearing Nike, eating McDonalds and driving a Ford to see the latest Hollywood movie than it is about an attraction to anything that is done by the US government?

To be sure that is a rather extreme interpretation and few countries simply leave everything to chance. A wide range of countries have used an even wider array of methods to promote their own preferred idea of what they are and what they stand for: official international media groups, the state promotion of national cultural actors and artefacts overseas, educational exchanges, tourism and so on. Even straightforward state funded advertising on transnational and overseas media networks designed to promote tourism, investment and trade serves the broader goal of establishing an overall national identity. And China is not alone in utilizing the hosting of major global events to promote a preferred national image and identity. Not only is the concept of deliberate and proactive 'nation branding' now well established as a key element of public diplomacy, but it is also seen as an important dimension of soft power in general (Olins, 2005).

It was this active construction and promotion of an idea of China through a concerted top-down political effort that emerged as a synonym for 'soft power' in discourses within China itself (Wang Yiwei, 2008). Yet terms like 'China's soft power offensive' (Torres, 2017), 'China's Soft Power Wielding' (Ding, 2008b) and China's 'Stealth "Soft Power"' (Luqiu and McCarthy, 2019) all point to intentions and objectives that seem rather hard and harsh, even though they all contain the word 'soft' within them. As others are doing it too, perhaps it is unfair to ask if the state promotion of Chinese soft power means that it isn't really soft in any meaningful way. It might be particularly unfair given the strong feeling in China that it has to try harder than the existing powers to get its voice heard as 'the right to speak internationally is largely in the hands of Western countries headed by Europe and the United States' (Shi Jianping, 2017: 10). Hence, the importance of projecting the China Voice that was briefly mentioned in Chapter 3, and which we will return to in Chapter 6. Nevertheless, and accepting this potential accusation of inequity is a valid one, there is something rather odd about considering a well-funded state-led effort to promote its own understanding of itself in competition with others as being 'soft'.

One frequent response to questions about the extent of true softness of Chinese soft power is that China is different. Concepts evolve, so the argument goes, and also mean different things in different settings. Soft power with Chinese characteristics is simply different from soft power as originally conceived of by Nye because the Chinese cultural, historical and political setting is very different from the US in the 1990s (or indeed any Western country at any time). Zanardi (2016: 431), for example, argues that because 'in Chinese culture, military force has traditionally been used for non-military purposes', there is no contradiction in contemporary Chinese strategy in thinking of military action as forming part of a soft power agenda.

This is fair comment. But the problem is that concepts that we want to use to analyse and understand international politics need to have some intersubjective meaning. If we have to work out what any concept or idea means in its own specific and unique context before we can use it, then we lose the building blocks of a comparative way of thinking about the world and how it is organized. As will be discussed in the following chapter, the same is true if norms and theories have to be 'nationalized' as well, and can only be understood within a specific cultural framework that generates different meanings of the same term. As such, rather than thinking of a single ideational component of Chinese global power, the suggestion is that it makes sense to disaggregate different components of what is typically thought of as Chinese soft power. In particular, the aim is to distinguish between two elements of non-hard power. The first is soft power as originally understood by Nye focusing on the latent power of attraction. Here, the stress is on what it is that others see of China that they are attracted to. The emphasis is on the perception and the perceiver. This is separate from the proactive projection of a preferred national image by the Chinese state: a project that is variously thought of as constituting national branding (Pu Xiaoyu, 2019), or public diplomacy (d'Hooghe, 2005), or international political marketing (Sun, 2007). The focus here is on the methods that the state uses to try and get its message across, as well as what that message actually is. The two are clearly linked. However, separating them out in this way illustrates potential gaps between the message that the state wants to send out, and the way that messages are understood, with the suggestion that the nature of the state project can actually undermine China's appeal and attractiveness in some audiences, rather than enhance it.

Discursive power and Chinese objectives

While the specific focus on Chinese soft power might have its origins in and around 2007–8, the recognition in China of the importance of shaping narratives and debates has a much longer history. Shambaugh (2013) traces the specific use of soft power back to 1993 in an article by the then Fudan University Professor Wang Huning, who would eventually become head of the Leading Group for Propaganda and Ideology Work under Xi Jinping in 2017. Even before then, the importance of shaping the way that China was thought of and spoken about overseas had become a policy priority given the more critical international environment that China faced in the wake of Tiananmen, and the beginning of the end of the Cold War. An initial concern that China might face international isolation soon gave way to new concerns that rapid economic growth might also create problems. This became articulated in discussions over the 'China Threat Thesis' (*zhongguo weixie lun*) – the idea that hostile forces China were seeking to 'demonise China wherever possible' (Liu and Liu, 1997). In order to do so, they would find whatever 'evidence' they could of Chinese malevolent intent. This would then be presented to policy makers to convince them to take China's threat to the existing global order and/or national interests seriously, and to develop policies designed to prevent China's continued rise (Wang Yunxiang, 1996).

If projections of China's continued rise were problematic for China, so too were projections of an alternative; the idea that the CCP would inevitably fail and that China would collapse (Liu Xiaobiao, 2002; Shambaugh, 2013: 219). But whether talking about inevitable failure or inevitable and inexorable rise, these discourses had one key thing in common. They were dominated by voices from outside China. Thus, there was a pressing need to develop and disseminate indigenous voices to prevent others from having a monopoly on shaping understandings of China (Glaser and Murphy, 2009: 24). This started out as an attempt to deflect criticism of China's domestic political structures and processes. For example, in 1991, the State Council Information Office (formed the previous year) produced China's first White Paper, and included an English language version for international audiences. This elucidated exactly how Chinese people enjoyed human rights (in contrast to the dominant interpretation pushed by foreigners), and explained why in the Chinese case ensuring the right to subsistence was a more urgent task than the sort of political rights that richer Western liberal democracies prioritized (State Council, 1991).

Issuing White Papers has subsequently become a well-established means of establishing what the official and preferred Chinese view of a range of different issues actually is (Wang Hongying, 2003). These include what have become the fairly regular issuance of Defence White Papers that are closely studied for signs of new directions and ambitions. Many of them are reactive in nature, written in response to perceived negative external discussion and/or condemnation of specific China related issues. The initial Human Rights White Paper turned out to be the first of a series on issues that chronicled Chinese practice (and successes) over the years and specific changes in issues like judicial protection, religious freedom, and the relationship between development and rights. There has also been a specific White Paper on Human Rights in Xinjiang, and criticism of Chinese policy there also resulted in White Paper responses on 'historical matters', 'cultural protection', 'terrorism and extremism' and 'vocational training' in the region.[2]

Deflecting criticism and explaining China's future

The Xinjiang example shows that the goal of deflecting criticism by establishing Chinese versions of truths remains an important goal today. While not formally called a White Paper, the release of a timeline outlining the release of information on the outbreak of the coronavirus in Wuhan in 2020 (Xinhua, 2020b) fulfilled a similar defensive/ deflective function. A second type of approach is to assuage concerns over what China's ever-increasing power will mean for the Asian region in particular, and the world in general. The specifics of the message have changed as Chinese perceptions of its own relative power have changed. But even within the more proactive promotion of Chinese alternatives that will be discussed in Chapter 6, the underlying message has remained the same. China has, according to the White Paper on China's Peaceful Development (State Council, 2011a) 'broken away from the traditional pattern where a rising power was bound to seek hegemony' and won't behave like other rising and great powers in the past. Not only do others have nothing to fear, but China's rise will bring peace, stability and growing wealth for the region and the world.

While shaping narratives remains the main reason for adopting a proactive discursive power agenda, it is not the only one. For example, there is an important domestic dynamic to the way that China's leaders project themselves and the country as well (Ni, 2012). Being seen to be a great power on the global scene visiting and receiving other global leaders and participating in major global events shows that China is taken seriously and has the respect of others (Deng, 2008; Shambaugh, 2015). On one level, it shows the success of the party in overcoming previous humiliations, and restoring China to its rightful place at the top table of global politics; it is the sort of global role that the Chinese people have been told that China *should* have, and historically did have (Scobell, 2012). Hence the emphasis on China's 'rejuvenation' under Xi rather than just rise.

On another level, being treated as a global power by others is taken as external validation of the CCP's successes (Edney, 2015). This creates a form of self-reinforcing logic of validation, because those who criticize China must either simply not know the full true facts, or be deliberately trying to paint falsely negative pictures of China for their own narrow ends (Callahan, 2015, 244). This helps explain why so much effort was taken to show external support and validation for the Chinese response to the COVID-19 outbreak in 2020. Given that even within China there was a strong feeling that mistakes had been made in the early days of the outbreak, external endorsements provided a corrective. Hence the importance of showing that 'the international community generally believes' that China has 'set a model' for others through its 'outstanding leadership, coping ability, organizational mobilization capability, and implementation ability' to redress the balance.[3] It is the CCP's way of saying 'you don't need to take our word for it'.

Having soft power as end and means

While having soft power is a means to attaining other ends, it is also partly seen as being an end in itself. Quite simply, you cannot be a truly proper global great power if you don't have soft power. So having it is a key indicator of having attained great power status. New great powers should promote themselves to global audiences just as other great powers did in the past and still do today. Their films and art and literature should be seen and read by others. Their languages should be disseminated and even in the long run become a medium of international interactions, and their media groups should talk to the world. This understanding of soft power as end is also built on a conception of a competitive global arena where others have for too long been able to impose their cultural influence without significant competition.

Soft power as difference

Talking about soft power – rather than having it – also serves as a way of showing Chinese difference. All great powers might promote their soft power, so the argument goes, but China is specifically well suited to doing so in a way that makes it very different from others. Hagström and Nordin (2020), for example, show how Xi Jinping located China's modern emphasis on soft power as originating in traditional Chinese thinking and practice that has passed through the generations into the hands of current leaders. More generally, one of the common features of the Chinese language literature on the CS that will be discussed in the following chapter is that China today bears the hallmarks of its ancient past.

Soft power is seen in China as being China's domain. It is what China does and one of the reasons that it has been so eagerly accepted in China is because it is what China has always done. The specific term might be Western, but in many ways soft power is simply seen as the modern incarnation of China's traditional philosophical influences and historical actions (Wu You, 2018). Even when China has had the ability to enforce its preferences through harder source of power, including through military supremacy, this understanding of history emphasizes the decision to use 'integrity and grace to influence, educate and guide' instead (Yang and Li, 2018: 5). Moreover, for some it is not so much a case of Chinese choosing not to use force, but of Chinese being incapable of doing so as they 'do not have the genes of aggression against others' (Liu and Wang, 2017: 15). The flip side of this argument is the idea that unlike China and the Chinese, Western powers and Westerners not only have the ability to be aggressive, but have historically chosen to use hard power, 'strongman politics' and hegemony to get their way (Liu Jianfei, 2018: 18).

In the 1970s, François Duchêne (1972) proposed the idea that the then European Community was, or would become, a 'civilian power'. It would not seek to spread its influence through military means as great powers normally did, but by finding other ways of promoting its values of tolerance, justice and equality instead. Others prefer the idea of 'normative power' (Manners, 2002), but similarly stress the significance of promoting values and ideas through peaceful means as a hallmark of how the EU (and its predecessors) differs as a global actor from other great powers (including a number of individual European states).

In the same vein, using soft power as the main means of trying to influence others also emphasizes China's difference. We could even think of taking the European starting point and refer to 'civilian power China' or 'normative power China' to go alongside the idea of 'Market power China' also borrowed from Europe in Chapter 4. Or maybe given the language used in China, we should use 'soft power China' instead. Whatever, the specific term, though, the goal is clear. Talking about China's soft power credentials and predilections is expected to generate that soft power itself by persuading others that China will not act as others acted before, or how others now suggest China will act in the future. The discourse itself becomes a source of what the discourse is meant to achieve. Well, that's the way that it should work in theory. In practice, the way that China's soft power has been promoted has often had the opposite effect instead.

Soft power as attraction

When it comes to soft power defined as attraction, Chinese preferences are irrelevant. Attraction is in the eye of the beholder. To be sure, there are things that can be done to make certain things clearer to see than others (or to be seen in specific ways). But as argued throughout this book, that still doesn't ensure that they will be seen in the way that the transmitter wants them to be seen. The emphasis in Chapter 1 was predominantly on the way that the BRI and other Chinese signals have been perceived in the West. But of course, talking about the West as a single thing is rather problematic. People born and educated in the West can and do find things in China that attracts. Neither Martin Jacques' (2009) *When China Rules the World* nor Daniel Bell's (2015) *The China Model* are wholehearted and uncritical affirmations of CCP rule. But both see elements of how China is organized and its global preferences as worth applauding and supporting, and also as potential improvements on dominant Western practices and preferences. As Dreyer (2015: 1015) notes, it is actually Westerners rather than Chinese scholars or officials who have most often argued that the 'the solution to the ills of the post-modern world, beset with problems derived from rampant inter- and intra-state competition' can be found in China's past and what she calls the 'Tianxia trope'.

The desire for successful and workable alternatives to the Western way plays an important role in shaping the way that China is perceived. Sometimes simply not being the West and not being associated with military interventions is enough to make China look like an attractive international relations actor. Not being the West also plays a role in generating attraction to China in economic terms too. We have already noted the idea of the attempt to portray China as a different type of economic partner for other developing states. But in terms of how others perceive China (rather than how it is projected), it is the way that China has developed and grown that has been the main focus of attention. As I have argued elsewhere, a case can be made for arguing that what has become widely referred to as the China Model is neither Chinese nor a model in its very essence (Breslin, 2011). On one level, it is difficult to see how the specifics of what has happened in China are replicable in other settings (so it is not really a workable model). On another, if we strip back the specifics to try and reveal fundamental principles that might be replicable, then we end up with ideas and practices that have been around for quite some time, and contain elements that students of economic planning in the US in the 19th century might find familiar (so it's not specifically Chinese). Like attraction, though, what the Chinese model is or isn't is in the eye of the beholder. If it is seen as a coherent and successful model, and others choose to learn from it, then it becomes real in terms of the impact it has.

In itself, the simple speed and extent of Chinese growth is very impressive. So too is the amount of people that have been pulled out of poverty in the process. Viewed from certain perspectives, the way that it has been achieved is also impressive. China is widely understood to have followed its own path and not done the things that proponents of (neo)liberal development suggest that economies should do. Once again, whether things have in reality been done as differently as this simple broad-brush overview suggests is often irrelevant. This idea of how China's development project has evolved has become something of a mini theme of the time, and the Chinese experience has come to be understood as an example of what you can achieve if you do things your own way, and don't follow neoliberal prescriptions. It is not so much a case of what China is and has done that is attractive here, as what China isn't and hasn't done by rejecting the previously dominant developmental orthodoxy.

That said, some really do focus on the details. At times this might include the manifestation of Chinese economic success in the form of modern city skylines, impressive construction feats, and a vastly expanded modern infrastructure. But at times it includes the specific policies and thinking that has brought about these transformations too. It is difficult to say with confidence the extent to which China's development really has led to attraction, rather than just admiration. What we can say with confidence, though, is that China's economic transformation has provided the basis for what might become soft power. It has created reasons for admiring and respecting achievements that might lead to attraction, and maybe even something more.

Disseminating Chinese narratives

Diplomacy-type tools

Issuing White Papers replicates domestic methods of getting the party's message across through the externalization of propaganda work (Brady, 2008; Edney, 2014; Shambaugh 2015). The way that set-piece grand events are used to transmit the latest message to the Chinese people have also been emulated and externalized too. Big picture thinking on China and its global role are included in primarily domestic facing mega events: party and state congresses, annual plenary meetings, high days and holidays and special anniversary events and so on. And the more powerful China is thought to have become, then the more foreign analysts scrutinize these major statements for signs of intent and policy change.

In addition, a host of international forums and meetings have been used (and established) to push the message to international audiences. We need to be careful not to suggest that everything is new. UN sessions, for example, have provided the opportunity to present an official view of China since the PRC replaced the Republic of China as the Chinese representative in 1971. Overseas trips by China's leaders and reciprocal visits back to China have also provided ample opportunities over the years to make high-profile speeches and to expose visitors to the China that its leaders want foreign dignitaries to see. That said, it is notable that who China's leaders interact with has changed somewhat, with increased visits to and from African states since Hu Jintao took power (Eisenman and Shinn, 2018: 159). And the number of opportunities has also increased as a result of China's embracing of multilateral organizations such as Asia Pacific Economic Cooperation (APEC), G20, ASEAN +3 summits and so on. We can add to this those institutional groupings that China has either initiated or played an important role in establishing; the SCO, the BRICS, FOCAC, the 16/17+1 Process and so on.

While simple participation is often enough to provide a platform for disseminating the Chinese story, these events are deemed to be particularly important when held on Chinese soil. Foreign Minister Wang Yi first referred to this as 'host diplomacy' when it was China's turn to host both the APEC Summit and the Conference on Interaction and Confidence Building in Asia in 2014. The key here is 'the ability to set and execute agendas' rather than just participating in agendas established by others (Jia, 2017). The G20 Hangzhou Summit in 2016 is a particularly good example, as it was here that Xi really pushed the idea of a CS for global governance, and has been taken as the moment that China first announced to the world its ambitions to take on global leadership roles (Gracie, 2016). And then there are the events that China itself creates and uses as mechanisms for promoting its preferred narratives. These include the South-South Human Rights Forum, the World Peace Forum, The World Internet Forum, The Understanding China Conference, and the Bo'ao Forum for Asia, where Zheng Bijian first explained the 'Peaceful Rise of China' to the world in 2003. We have already noted the significance of the 2008 Olympics as a means of showcasing China, to which we can add the 2010 Shanghai Expo (Nordin, 2012) and the attempt to demonstrate China's commitment to an open global economy through the 2018 Import Expo in Shanghai.

The task of national image promotion, then, has taken on something of the air of a Chinese political campaign. It is the international equivalent of the type of mobilization to achieve an end that has become an integral part of the way the Chinese political system functions. These campaigns are usually built around having a simple and clear message to repeat that can often come down to a very basic slogan. In terms of China's international public diplomacy, the most persistently used of these over the years has been China's peaceful rise, and its resulting mutation into 'Harmonious World', 'Peaceful Development', and other forms of peace and harmony. China as a 'responsible great power' also had a degree of longevity too. But there are many others. The promotion of the 'democratization of international relations' under Jiang Zemin has been echoed by subsequent leaders. And under Xi, at times it seemed as if any problem that the world faces entails building a CSFM to resolve it.

Diplomacy by other means

Finding the boundary between the state and non-state is not always easy. For example, individual Chinese think tanks have varying degrees of relationships with the state ranging from those that are directly research institutions for ministries and other party and state agencies, to those that have no formal political master. And it is simply incorrect to suggest that all members of Chinese think tanks are simply following and espousing the official government position. If you get the chance to participate in think tank events in China, then it is certainly not unheard of for the members to disagree among themselves or to be critical of official policy. So it is with some unease that they are included as representatives of diplomatic intention here. They are partly included as the ability to speak remains contingent on the speaker not crossing over into politically taboo areas. Not contradicting the official line can be helpful too. And some independent groups have taken it on themselves to become supporters and promoters of leaders' preferences and strategies (Wang and Xue, 2017). The way that various think tanks have repeated the official view of what the BRI is and is meant to achieve in their interactions with non-Chinese partners is a particularly good example here (Vangeli, 2019). However, they are mainly included because of intent. Even many of the more independent ones only exist because Xi Jinping announced that having more of them was a good thing (Menegazzi, 2017). The point of expanding think tank interactions in the minds of the Chinese leadership was to directly insert Chinese voices and narratives into debates and discussions (Brady, 2017: 10). They are thus a tool that the leadership thinks that it has available to it, even if individual members of individual think tanks might not always simply be agents of the official message.

There is considerably less unease in referring to China's international media as a diplomatic tool, as they are explicitly tasked with expanding China's communicative capacity (Sun Wanning, 2015; Keen, 2016). In launching the China Global Television News (CGTN) service in December 2016,[4] for example, Xi Jinping explicitly urged it to 'tell China's story well, spread China's voice well, let the world know a three-dimensional, colourful China, and showcase China's role as a builder of world peace' (Xinhua, 2016). And if there was any further doubt over the political starting point of these operations, in 2018 CGTN and China Radio International were merged into a new China Media Group, and their overarching superior authority was shifted from the State National Radio and Television Administration to the party's Central Propaganda Department. Partly as a result of these changes, in 2020, the US State Department formally designated Chinese media operations in the US as 'Foreign Missions', meaning that they were considered to be direct agents of the Chinese party-state rather than even quasi-independent media actors.[5] Alongside the foreign language print media, most notably the *China Daily* and the *Xinhua* news agency (and maybe the *Global Times*), they provide the official stories of China that the leadership wants outsiders to hear. Since around 2009, they have been actively extending their profile in terms of both the locations they operate in, and the foreign languages they use (Thussu et al, 2017). This includes not just direct broadcasting and publication, but also providing content and inserts for other foreign broadcasting and print media providers (Lim and Bergin, 2018).

Chinese media organizations are keen to point out that they play an important role in getting other voices and stories heard as well as Chinese ones. For example, they claim to emphasize stories about Africa produced from the African regional production centre in Nairobi, that are depicted as the antithesis of either neglect or negative reporting from mainstream Western media groups (Thussu et al, 2017). In this respect, in addition to disseminating narratives, they are also a tool of presenting China as being a different type of global actor and great power than other (Western) ones. They also serve a third purpose in trying to increase familiarity with China by including not just news stories, but also showcasing traditional Chinese culture, China's (peaceful) history, food and cooking, and tourist destinations.

Familiarization and people-to-people interactions

Such a familiarization strategy is at the heart of many other forms of interactions too, with Xi Jinping highlighting his desire to increase 'people-to-people' exchanges and 'cross cultural interactions' as important arenas of interaction (Xi, 2019c; 2019d). Familiarization is presumably based on the understanding that it will result in not just understanding, but also empathy, affinity and if not outright support, then at least a greater willingness to listen. Notably, there is a strong historical focus to much activity that emphasizes an idealized view of China's past and, where appropriate, peaceful and mutually prosperous historical transnational interactions. While these clearly operate at a different level to diplomatic type campaigning, they are not as isolated from the state's control and interests than the language of people-to-people relations might suggest. The very fact that Xi identified them as important soft power tools is significant in itself. When the Ministry of Culture and the China National Tourism Administration merged to form a new Ministry of Culture and Tourism in 2018 (responsible for many broadly defined people-to-people activities), one of the explanations was that the new agency would be a more effective way of 'enhancing the country's soft power and cultural influence' (State Council, 2018); the state as facilitator of people-to-people interactions.

Clearly, the many people and institutions that are involved in such interactions are not under direct state control on a day-to-day basis. But equally as clearly, the hand of the state is never too far away. What individual overseas Chinese tourists do, for example, is not the result of a daily edict or instruction from a state agency telling them where to go and what to do. But the government does issue guidance on behaviour, and also makes it easier or harder to go to certain places based on political considerations. The Ministry of Culture and Tourism's Bureau for External Cultural Relations is a key actor in the organization of events overseas, and in bringing foreigners to China for cultural exchanges. These visitors will not be micromanaged 24 hours a day, but anybody who goes to China to attend events should be aware that the Chinese media often reports them in ways that serve broader political ends. Either that attendance implies a validation of what China does or that China has wisdom to offer the world (or both). Moreover, visas can be and are denied if the visitor is deemed to be unwelcome for whatever reason.

The role of Confucius Institutes (CIs) has come under particularly close scrutiny from both students of Chinese soft power and also policy makers in a number of countries. So much attention, in fact, that what they do and why does not need repeating in detail here.[6] They are unashamedly and clearly part of a state project, originally organized by an agency of the Ministry of Education (the *hanban*), and extolled by China's leaders as performing important roles in spreading positive stories and images of China (Lo and Pan, 2016). It should come as no surprise whatsoever to those who host CIs overseas that in addition to providing language training, there is an overarching goal to promote a particular idea of China. This is part of their fundamental mandate and the reason that they were established in the first place.

Yet concern that they are agents of telling only partial stories of China has resulted in numerous complaints, and become a focus of negative reporting and attention. This might be because of concerns that this selectivity extends beyond the walls of the CIs themselves, and into their host institutions to censor issues that the Chinese authorities deem to be sensitive or negative. It is also probably because CIs have come to be seen as the most visible and concrete manifestations of a wider Chinese 'United Front' strategy designed to influence what can and cannot be said about China in other countries, and build coalitions of pro-Chinese forces. And maybe they have become synonymous with attempts to influence domestic political debates that go beyond just simply discussing China too (Brady, 2017; Suzuki, 2019). As their governance structures typically dictate who can and cannot be employed – including banning those who have participated in Falun Gong activities – there has also been considerable disquiet over the extension of Chinese legal and political preferences into other countries; and indeed the legality of allowing this to happen.

Or perhaps it simply comes down to the fundamental lack of trust that we are returning to again and again, which means that anything the Chinese state does is met with suspicion. This means that what individual CIs do or don't do in their local host communities often has less impact on how they are perceived at a political level than a pre-existing and more general understanding of the intentions and virtue of the state authority behind them. Because CIs are identifiable entities (as opposed to other less tangible instruments of ideational influence), opposing them has become a key means of challenging the spread of Chinese influence in general. A number of governments have put pressure on host universities to think again. For example, the 2019 National Defense Authorization Act in the US removed Department of Defense funding to support Chinese language programmes at any 'institution of higher education that hosts a Confucius Institute' (US Congress, 2018); not just within the CI itself, but within the wider university as a whole. Individual universities have also independently decided to end their CI partnerships. The governance issues noted above are often cited as a key factor. The potential reputational damage of having a CI also plays a role. Even when there is no evidence at all of undue influence, the perception that connections with China *might* influence their research agendas has unsettled scholars in those universities. Particularly, but not only, researchers of China and China related issues.

Media focus on responses to CIs has tended to be on the US – partly because of the extent of government opinion and action, and in part because of the broader significance of the US–China bilateral relationship. And partly because that's where the biggest number of CIs have closed. However, the first CIs to close were in Canada and France in 2013, and Sweden was the first country to close all of its *hanban* funded institutes in 2020. At the time of writing, CI arrangements had also been cancelled in Germany, the Netherlands, Belgium and Denmark, and a Confucian classroom scheme operating in 13 schools was also cancelled by the New South Wales government in Australia. And of course, we don't know how many offers to open CIs have been turned down because of one or more of the concerns outlined above.

This antagonism resulted in the reorganization of the delivery of Chinese language overseas in June 2020, designed to 'disperse the Western misinterpretation that the organization served as China's ideological marketing machine' (Chen Xi, 2020). The *hanban* was rebranded as the Ministry of Education Centre for Language Education and Cooperation, and CIs were moved out of the state system and placed under a new 'non-governmental' organization; the Chinese International Education Foundation. This foundation was an alliance of 27 institutions and companies with an interest in international education, including a number of China's leading universities. Given that universities are ultimately responsible to higher state agencies – directly to the Ministry of Education, to specialist central departments and agencies, to local governments and so on – this still leaves room for those who are already sceptical to question its 'non'-governmental status. And given the pre-existing scepticism and suspicion of the role of CIs, it is unlikely that this move will have a significant impact on how they are viewed.

Add all this together and at best, CIs have failed to improve China's image and standing in North America, Western Europe and Australasia. And there is considerable evidence to suggest that the overall impact has been a negative one. So rather than working on rebranding, the Chinese government might be better served focusing its attentions (and money) on places where it is more likely to reinforce pre-existing positions, rather than trying to change minds in places where such attempts in themselves are seen as part of the problem, rather than a solution.

Soft power or something harder?

The study of CIs sometimes forms part of a wider interest in international educational exchanges, and language study in particular.[7] While there is a consensus that education can have an impact on perceptions and views, there is no guarantee that spending time learning a language (either at home or overseas) has positive results. More than one language student has ended up frustrated and alienated rather than with a deep affection for one of the places that the language is natively spoken in. And even those who do end up with a deep love for a country do not necessarily also love its politicians, or come to align themselves with state objectives. Moreover, we cannot just assume that the number of people studying a language or a country is a consequence of attraction and a proxy indicator for support and empathy. Students and researchers often have more tactical reasons for learning about a country. The desire to know more about an enemy for example was an important driver of the evolution of Asian area studies during the Cold War (Cumings, 1997). The commercial opportunities that China presents (and might present in the future) are also important too. This brings us back to the relationship between economic sources of power and other non-hard factors. Or put another way, is it simply China's economic (and particularly market) power that is the reason that others change their behaviour and actions rather than anything to do with ideas, discourses and culture? Or, despite the best intentions of the analysis in this chapter, is it really possible to make a distinction between them?

In order to explore these questions in a little more detail, this chapter finishes by exploring three dimensions of China's potential power and influence where economic and other factors interact. The first, the role of tourism, typically is included as one source of people-to-people interactions that can influence the way that a country (and its goals) is perceived. The second, the role of consumer choice, is considered to be an important element of a number of different types of interaction; part of tourism itself, the consumption of film, art and music and so on. The focus here though is slightly different and centres on when consumers decide to punish foreign actors by boycotting what they are selling. The third is the way that the flow of resources and the dissemination of narratives interacted during and after the spread of the COVID-19 pandemic in 2020.

Tourism: state strategy, people-to-people interaction,
or market power?

As with the study of international education, there is a widespread (though not a universally held) understanding that international tourism 'may act as a positive force for stimulating peace through reducing tension and suspicion' (Timothy and Kim, 2015: 414). The number of foreigners visiting China is both significant and somewhat less important than headline tourism figures might suggest at the same time. Significant because of the scale: over 14 million visitors in both 2018 and 2019 generated just under US$130 billion in revenue each year. This number is somewhat dwarfed by the impact of domestic tourism within China with over six trillion such tourist trips in 2019 generating six times more in revenue than international travellers. Even so, the figure for foreign visitors is still considerable, second only to the US in a global league table, and contributing an amount equivalent to roughly half of Vietnam's total GDP for the same year. However, numbers for inbound international arrivals provided by the Ministry of Culture and Tourism include business and family trips as well as cross-border trips made by residents of Hong Kong for work purposes.[8] Less than half of the 2018 visitors included an overnight stay in the PRC, and of those that did, half were from other 'Chinese' territories (Hong Kong, Macao and Taiwan). In terms of the overall number of visitors, only 12.5 per cent of all incomers came from Europe and 7.9 per cent from America with the overwhelming majority (76.3 per cent) from these other Chinese territories and the rest of Asia. So if we move from numbers and finance to other less tangible cultural and familiarization impacts, then we might reasonably assume that a large number of these visitors were already rather familiar with Chinese culture and history (to different degrees).

Regional states occupy eight of the top ten destinations for Chinese outbound tourism too – nine if Russia is included in a wider definition of the regional backyard with the US as the only exception.[9] Given the fragility of some regional relations, it is not surprising that there is at times a connection between high politics and tourist flows. For example, Kim et al (2016: 81) have noted a correlation between periods of Sino-Japanese political tension and reductions in two way flows of tourists (albeit short-lived ones). After the South Korean government decided to deploy the US Theater High Altitude Area Defense system against Chinese wishes in 2017, there was a 61 per cent reduction in Chinese tourists over the previous year in the main key tourist months of March to October (Jennings, 2018). Chinese package tours can only go to countries that have negotiated an 'Approved Destination Status' with China (Tse, 2013). This has allowed the state to use bilateral tourism deals as a disciplining tool in its relations with other countries, signing agreements with those that are deemed to be friendly and stopping tours if China's interests are deemed to be harmed. In this case, the then Chinese National Tourist Administration simply stepped in to prevent the sale of package tours to South Korea. Similarly, in 2005, China withdrew from the China-Canada Bilateral Tourism Agreement negotiations in response to the then Canadian Premier's meeting with the Dalai Lama (Fan, 2010: 256).

The ability to control tourism changed as regulations on individual travel were relaxed. While large groups of often first-time travellers on organized tours still can be found at many tourist destinations, the growth in outward tourism has being driven by individual, independent and repeat travellers.[10] Diplomatic agreements are still important as the ease (or otherwise) of getting a visa and the availability of direct flights can be important facilitators of (or blocks on) travel. The desire to attract Chinese tourists also crosses the line into considerations of Chinese financial/market power rather than just global people-to-people engagements. If exposing others to Chinese culture is a means of increasing sympathy for Chinese national interests and objectives, then inward tourism should be the most effective mechanism. Yet perhaps counter intuitively, the increased knowledge and understanding of China that the government is craving might result from the growth of outward tourism instead.

China became the number one source of foreign tourists (by spend) in 2012. In 2017, these tourists collectively spent close to twice as much as tourists from the US (second in the list) – US$257.7 billion compared to US$135.2 – accounting for close to a quarter of the total global tourist spend (UNTWO, 2018). Whether this growth of tourism is a source of positive people-to-people cultural diplomacy or not remains rather debatable. While Wu You (2018) argues that it helps paint an image of Chinese prosperity and modernity, it is rather easier to find reports of rude and inappropriate behaviour by Chinese tourists than positive stories; particularly, but not only, in Japan, Vietnam, Hong Kong and other favoured East Asian regional destinations. This is why the China National Tourism Agency produced the above noted guidance on how to behave overseas in 2013.

However, there are other cultural spillovers too. For example, those wishing to attract Chinese visitors in a competitive international market need to learn more about the different preferences of different Chinese age and societal groups, and how to market themselves to potential Chinese tourists (King and Gardiner, 2015). If you want to tap into this new market, then it becomes more or less essential to be findable on the Chinese *baidu* search engine, to have the sort of Chinese language website that Chinese surfers are familiar with using, to developing a good e-reputation on Chinese travel forums, and get the support of important Chinese travel 'influencers'.[11] This points to not only increased knowledge of potential Chinese tourists, but also the likely increased global significance and use of the Chinese language as a medium of transnational communication in tourist industries.

Consumer power, hurt feelings and negative soft power

What this suggests is that Chinese consumer choice is resulting in change in others. The same is true when it comes to education. Once again, while the emphasis in China might be on the consequences of getting more foreign students to China, what others do to attract potential Chinese students provides another example of the way in which the financial resources of individuals and families is influencing behaviour overseas. So does this translate in power for China and support the Chinese state project?

There is a suspicion that the answer is yes and that some universities are moderating what they say and teach about China so as not to put off potential students who share their government's positions and concerns. However, clearer evidence is available in the commercial world where producers and retailers have been punished for hurting the feelings of Chinese consumers. For example, Dolce and Gabbana saw its Chinese market all but disappear after a series of adverts which were taken as mocking China, and leaked messages that were taken as a further insult (Williams, 2019). In 2019, tweets in support of the Hong Kong protestors by the General Manager of the Houston Rockets basketball team, Daryl Morey, not only resulted in their merchandise disappearing from Chinese online sites, but a wider punishment of the National Basketball Association in general with 'almost every Chinese sponsor of the league, plus others associated directly with the team' suspending their support (Dreyer, 2019).

The hand of the state is rarely totally absent in any of these cases. In some, the state has taken direct action, as was the case when Marriott International fell foul of cyber legislation for appearing to imply that Hong Kong and Taiwan were not part of the PRC. In others, the reporting of incidents by the state media has been a major catalyst for subsequent consumer and online action. But China's online community has been hyper alert and hypersensitive to slights too, and has become an independent guardian of Chinese sovereignty and hurt feelings. Versace faced a consumer boycott for a shirt that was taken as suggesting that Hong Kong was a separate entity from China. In response, 'Chinese internet users began scouring websites in an online witch hunt for any international fashion companies active in mainland China which did not list Hong Kong, Taiwan, or Macau as being part of China', resulting in in a range of companies being 'exposed'. Versace, Coach, Givenchy, ASICS, Samsung, Calvin Klein, Swarovski and Fresh subsequently apologized and removed the offending products or remedied their mistakes (Koetse, 2019). American Airlines, Delta, Marriott, Ray-Ban, Zara and others have also all issued formal apologies at one time or another for referring to (or allowing it to be inferred that) one or more of Hong Kong, Macao and Taiwan were individual countries. But no matter how the issue gains momentum, fears of the impact on sales in China (and thus the power of Chinese consumers) plays an important role in dictating the response to the outcry. And once more, what the Chinese market might become in the future, rather than just what it is today, also feeds into considerations.

So the importance of the Chinese market now and in the future results in foreign companies aligning their practice and language to conform to Chinese expectations. It also potentially externalizes Chinese preferences as well. For example, freedom of speech in the US and the freedom to protest in France and other European countries allows people to say what they want about Hong Kong or Tibet or the nature of the Chinese political system. If individuals chose not to utilize these freedoms because of calculations of financial gain and loss, then that in itself might be cause for concern for those who support these freedoms. But it is up to them to make a calculation of the costs and benefits and to come to a final decision. If they are ordered not to by others, then it becomes another order of concern altogether.

Crisis diplomacy and the coronavirus: mixed messages and responses

Crisis diplomacy is another issue area where material resources play a large part in trying to build attraction and a positive image of China. But rather than just leave the support and aid to speak for itself, there is typically a concerted campaign to make sure that Chinese action is recognized and appreciated. Providing supplies and personnel to help others is a basic starting point. But to rise above other countries, China has to do (and be seen to be doing) something special and/or different. This might entail doing things that are beyond what other countries with similar levels of development are doing. Or in the case of Chinese aid to Haiti after the 2010 earthquake, putting humanitarian concerns above politics by providing extensive relief even though Haiti had diplomatic relations with Taipei rather than Beijing. Or it might entail being seen to do things that others can't or won't do, or doing it better. Providing UN peacekeepers might not fall into a strict definition of crisis diplomacy or disaster response. But it is somewhat related, and the fact that China provides more peacekeeping troops than the other UN Security Council permanent members has been noted more than once by Chinese politicians and analysts. The increase in Chinese numbers (and financing for peacekeeping operations too) is contrasted to the 'reluctance' of Western states to send their troops to dangerous places, and an overall reduction in the desire to lead by the US (He, 2019). And it is not just in China that this has resulted in the understanding that 'China is surpassing the United States as the leader in UN peacekeeping' (Pauley, 2018).

In addition to providing aid and relief, learning from what China has done at home in responding to various disasters can play a role too. Particularly if China's political system can be shown to produce more effective responses than those of liberal democratic states. Here, we have to keep in mind the discussion above about the domestic dimension of reputation and discourse management. The importance of being seen to be more effective than others – and in particular, gaining external praise and validation for this effectiveness – might have external salience, but has more utility in reinforcing the message of confidence in the regime and the leadership at home.

Attraction, medical diplomacy and the COVID-19 pandemic

On a number of levels, the coronavirus pandemic provided an excellent opportunity for China's leaders to further the soft power agenda; to deploy medical diplomacy, to make reputational and leadership gains at the expense of others, and to get external validation and thanks for its actions to show to a domestic audience. Problems encountered in various different national responses provided negative cases to contrast Chinese successes against, and to offer China's experiences as something for others to learn from. Shortages of supplies in a number of countries also created the opportunity for China to step in and send provisions to the needy. Not just the 'normal' recipients of Chinese medical aid in the developing world, but to Western powers as well. The suspension of funding from the US for the WHO contributed to the creation (or expansion) of a gap in global health leadership for somebody to fill. And with the basis of the whole European project questioned as individual European states looked out for themselves rather than each other, there was a wider chance of being seen to be promoter and protector of multilateralism and solidarity more generally.

These opportunities were not passed up. The merits of China's 'centralized, unified and efficient "wartime pandemic command system"' under the leadership of Xi Jinping (*China Daily*, 2020: 23) was indeed explained as the source of success.[12] These achievements were said to be not just for China itself, but for the world too. They provided important lessons for others on how best to respond, and also (so the argument went) resulted in a crucial delay in the global spread of the virus that created a space for others to prepare. This was a space which many were subsequently explained as having wasted. With a particular eye on domestic audiences, there was also an emphasis on reporting outsiders' validation of Chinese policy choices. Reporting on Xi's phone calls with foreign leaders, the *People's Daily* (2020a) said that the UK Premier Boris Johnson 'congratulates the Chinese government and people on the remarkable achievements they have made in epidemic prevention and control with strenuous efforts and enormous sacrifices' and that 'Britain has been studying and learning from China's useful experience'. Similarly, French President Emmanuel Macron was reported as appreciating the 'courage and decisive measures' of the Chinese government and people which meant they had 'effectively contained the disease in a short period of time'. While praise from Western liberal leaders is very welcome, it helps when 'Western' criticisms of China are also debunked by external validation. For example, in reporting the 'expert' view of the President of the Africa WorldWide Group think tank (in an interview with a Russian news agency, thus showing the independence of the position), the *People's Daily* (2020b) reported Sire Sy as rejecting criticisms of China, lauding China's approach over those of 'some Western countries', and concluding that 'if there is a prospect that emerges, it is that, at present, China shows the best public health system in the world'.

As President Trump first discussed suspended funding for the WHO and then subsequently acted to do so, China donated US$20 million on 11 March 2020 and a further US$30 million on 23 April. Chinese supplies were donated to the WHO as well as to a range of individual countries by the government, charitable foundations (such as the Jack Ma Foundation and the Tsai Foundation), and private companies (such as Huawei). There were also significant transfers on commercial terms too from a vast array of Chinese companies. The gratitude of recipient states was also widely publicized in China. In addition, the General Information Department of the Chinese Foreign Ministry was particularly active on Twitter showcasing Chinese action, rebutting claims of political motivations rather than altruism, and retweeting the thanks of recipients to the Chinese government and people. As Twitter is banned in China, it would seem fair to suggest that this was not simply intended for a domestic audience within China.

Here, what China was seen to be doing was contrasted with what others either couldn't or wouldn't do. Serbia proved to be one of the most publicly thankful recipients, with President Vucic arguing that 'China is the only country that can help' in the absence of European and international solidarity after announcing a State of Emergency (Vuksanovic, 2020). In Latin America, China was depicted as 'stepping in to fill a void left by President Trump, who has alienated long-time partners and undermined the country's standing in Latin America and the Caribbean', supplying medical materials to Mexico and Argentina at the same time as the US was seen to be trying to divert supplies intended for others to itself (Angelo and Chavez, 2020). By doing what others wouldn't, China was not only providing much needed practical help – a sign in itself of the flexibility of the Chinese economic model in being able to respond quickly to changed circumstances[13] – but also occupying a sort of moral and ethical high ground that had either been evacuated by others, or which they could simply not occupy given their inferior political and ethical structures.

Defensive triumphalism

As a result, a number of observers were quick to argue that, whether they thought that it was deserved or not, China was 'winning the coronavirus propaganda war' (Karnitschnig, 2020). Helped by the 'glaring absence of US leadership', it was having 'notable success in reshaping its image as a leader' (Borger, 2020). Given the way that US policy making evolved during the pandemic, it is not surprising that China's position and possible gains were often viewed in the context of what was being done (or not as the case may be) and said in Washington. But while China's rise and the decline of the US is often explained in the language of a zero-sum game, in reality things look rather more complex. The early conviction that China was winning soon gave way to more negative assessments of the consequences of this broadly defined medical diplomacy, particularly (but not only) in Europe (Cabestan, 2020). This was because while the crisis provided China with the opportunities outlined above, it also highlighted or exacerbated three key problems that China had to face as the pandemic spread.

Who's who at the WHO

The first of these related to the WHO. Despite widespread international condemnation of the US withdrawal of funding, President Trump was not alone in thinking that the WHO – and in particular its Director General Tedros Adhanom Ghebreyesus – had been rather quick to endorse China's own official version of its virus response. In addition, Beijing's insistence that Taiwan should not be given any sort of indication that it was being accepted as an independent sovereign actor through participation in WHO activities did not always play well with global audiences. Taiwan was allowed observer status in the World Health Assembly of the WHO in 2009, in part because its absence during the SARS outbreak of 2003 meant that one of the territories that most needed to be involved was excluded from the formal international response. However, the invitation to attend as an observer was not extended in and after 2017 because of the perception in Beijing that under President Tsai Ing-Wen, there was a greater appetite to push for Taiwanese independence. Or short of independence, to take part in more activities that were usually reserved for sovereign states and to gain a greater de facto international acceptance of being an independent entity.

Given that Taiwan was widely considered to have developed one of the world's most effective responses to the pandemic, excluding it from the WHO did not convince everybody that the right thing was being done for the global effort. As Marlow (2020) argued at the time, '[f]ew governments around the world are likely to emerge from the pandemic with a stronger standing than before. Taiwan is one of them – and that's not good for China.' In a small way, then, the pandemic might have worked against the realization of Beijing's objectives in relation to Taiwan's global role and identity. For example, in an article titled 'Let Taiwan into the World Health Organisation', *The Economist* (2020a) argued that:

> Taiwan's performance is remarkable. Even more remarkable is that the country is not a member of the World Health Organisation. The simple reason is that a bullying China refuses it entry … When Taiwan wrote to the WHO in late December asking whether there was human-to-human transmission in the virus outbreak in Wuhan, the WHO, the body now admits, did not reply.

In the US, the new 'Taiwan Allies International Protection and Enhancement Initiative (TAIPEI) Act' mandated the US to 'advocate, as appropriate – (A) for Taiwan's membership in all international organizations in which statehood is not a requirement and in which the United States is also a participant; and (B) for Taiwan to be granted observer status in other appropriate international organizations' (Gardner, 2020). Although it was passed during the pandemic, the act was first tabled in May 2019 and thus reflects longer standing broader changes in thinking and policy in the US. But as argued in the Introduction, the pandemic played a role in concentrating and accelerating what was already changing. In keeping with the new bill's objectives, the US Department of State announced that a special 'virtual forum' had taken place on 31 March to find ways of sharing Taiwan's 'successful and internationally lauded' response to the crisis, by 'expanding Taiwan's participation on the global scale' (US Department of State, 2020).

Aid, trade and reliability

A second problem area was the nature of the supplies that were being provided. The issue here was partly the nature of the supplies themselves, and partly the way in which their provision became politicized. Taking the former first, there were complaints from a number of countries that the materials that they were receiving from China either did not work, or were unsuitable for the specific purpose that they had been ordered. As just one example, the head of the Finnish government emergence supply agency had to resign after face masks ordered (via a Finnish agent) from China proved to be 'unsuitable for hospital use' (Reuters, 2020). As argued in Chapters 2 and 4, state control over economic activity in China is far from complete. In the response to the pandemic, the number of Chinese economic actors in the medical equipment sector increased dramatically. For example, in total there were an astonishing 3,000 extra new producers of medical face masks in the first quarter of 2020 alone. These included large SOEs like Sinopec, companies with significant state holdings like the car producer SAIC-GM-Wuling, public national champions like BYD, large foreign owned companies such as Foxconn, and hundreds of small scale local producers too (Ren, 2020).

Not surprisingly, the quality of what was being produced by these new actors was not always up to scratch. And not just when it came to face masks. On 1 April 2020, new regulations came into force mandating that exporters must have a PRC Medical Device Product Registration Certificate as well as the right certification required by the host country (Wu and Xie, 2020). But as this would have resulted in a massive potential drop off in exports when they were most needed in a number of countries, restrictions on testing kits and other supplies were soon relaxed to ensure a greater flow. While the Chinese regulatory system responded rapidly twice as events moved very quickly, the association of China with faulty supplies proved easier to establish than to break down.

Shaping narratives, deflecting blame

In many respects, though, it was the political narrative that accompanied the supply of materials that was more damaging for China than the quality of the goods, and this was the third major problem China faced. There was also a general feeling that China was talking up its benevolence by placing an undue emphasis on aid, while most of what was being sent to developed countries was on a commercial basis at market prices (*Economist*, 2020b). The support that China was offered from the rest of the world in the early days of the outbreak was also absent in many Chinese stories. But the bigger issue was the combination of defensiveness and aggressiveness that informed some responses to criticisms and complaints both in the Chinese media and in the speeches and writings of a number of Foreign Ministry representatives. This defensiveness also went far beyond simply deflecting criticism of the reliability of Chinese medical supplies.

The idea that the Chinese government was exaggerating the extent of its philanthropy formed part of a wider concern with the way in which it was trying to control narratives of the crisis for political purposes. At the most basic level, this originated from the idea that the government was trying to get respect and thanks for controlling the virus without taking any responsibility for what it did to allow it to spread in the first place. While some pointed to assumed origins of the virus and what might have been done to prevent it becoming a human one in the first place, the main external focus was on what happened next. Even if its origins eventually did turn out to lie somewhere else, there were still crucial government and governance failings that allowed the virus to spread in and from Wuhan when it might have been contained. The silencing of Chinese doctors who tried to raise the alarm, the time taken to inform others that human-to-human infections were taking place, and the failure to stop travel from the epicentre of the outbreak in Wuhan until after five million people had already left (CGTN, 2020) were the three most oft cited examples. Lack of trust in the official Chinese figures for infections and deaths also played a role too.

The primary response from China was that politicians (primarily, but not only, in the US) were trying to deflect criticism of their own failings by trying to blame others instead. And there is probably some truth in this. It also made sense for China's leaders to try to establish a narrative of its crisis response that highlighted the things that helped bring it under control rather than action and inaction that allowed it spread in the first place. But if it's not surprising that China's leaders acted in this way, neither was it surprising that this attempt to manage the discourse was met with resistance and even hostility outside China too. If it did not feel right to be expected to be thankful for Chinese 'sacrifices' or Chinese supplies that would not have been needed if there had been no crisis in the first place, then this unease became something else on those occasions when the language that was used to defend China crossed over from defensiveness to a sort of triumphalism.

In most cases, trying to deflect blame simply entailed arguing that trying to identify origins did not help find solutions. Politicians should leave it to scientists to work out what happened in the future, so the argument went, rather than trying to appropriate blame for political reasons while the virus was still spreading. However, there were more forceful responses as well. Much of it repeated the idea that any criticism of China was simply and only motivated by political factors aimed at 'stopping China from becoming stronger' by 'promoting more hate against China from across the world'.[14] Particular vitriol was reserved for those who used the terms 'China virus' or 'Wuhan virus', as President Trump and US Secretary of State Michael Pompeo did respectively. But various other agents of this 'western' project were also accused of 'stigmatizing', 'slandering', and 'defaming' China (among other things). This included those who, through their criticisms, were accused of the 'vilification' of 'the tremendous efforts and huge sacrifices made by China and its people', and denying 'China's significant contribution to global public health and safety'.[15] For the Chinese ambassador to London, if there was a need for an apology, it was not *from* China but *to* China; an apology for the West's 'campaign of stigmatisation' (Liu Xiaoming, 2020).

At times, Chinese officials went even further. The Chinese ambassador to Canberra suggested that if the Australian government pushed for an investigation into the outbreak of the pandemic, then the Chinese people might respond by questioning why they bought Australian goods; a threat of the sort of 'boycott diplomacy' discussed in the previous section (Lim and Ferguson, 2020). On 12 March 2020, Zhao Lijian (2020a), Deputy Director of the General Information Department of the Foreign Ministry, tweeted that the US military might have brought the virus to Wuhan. The following day he called for others to 'read and retweet' an article suggesting that the outbreak might have started in a US military laboratory at Fort Detrick, and been transmitted to China by participants in the World Military Games in Wuhan in October 2019 (Zhao Lijian, 2020b). The article in question (Romanoff, 2020) was published on the website of the Canadian based Center for Research on Globalization, which presumably was thought of as providing credibility as it came from an independent non-Chinese source. The Center, though, has not been averse to providing heterodox views of global politics since its founding in 2011, including, for example, the argument that the September 11 attacks on the US were a result of 'a military-intelligence ploy'. Its author had also previously referred to those who confronted the military forces in Beijing in 1989 as 'mercenaries', and argued that the protests were in reality an American instigated, organized and resourced 'color revolution' (Romanoff, 2019).

Zhao did not subsequently appear at public briefings for almost a month. When he did, he pulled back from his previous position to an extent, noting that his tweets were purely personal and not the position of the Foreign Ministry. He also provided a sort of 'heat of the moment' justification that his comments were 'a response to US politicians' stigmatization of China, which also reflects the righteous anger of many Chinese people over these stigmatizing acts' (*Global Times*, 2020b). By then though, the idea of a US origin had been widely repeated. Moreover, the first (and at the time of writing, the only) user-posted comment that was published underneath the semi-retraction actually reinforced the original suggestion: 'Zhao is absolutely correct. He raises valid questions that need to be answered. The rabid attacks against China are suspicious. Are they an attempt to divert attention from their (US) incompetence? Or are they trying to hide something?' (*Global Times*, 2020b). As a comment, it cannot be counted as an official position. But as a comment that was allowed to be posted by an official media organization, and one that remained online afterwards, it cannot have been an observation that was deemed worthy of immediate removal for spreading fake rumours.[16]

There were also intimations that the virus might have had other non-Chinese origins. Just over a week after Zhao pointed to the US, the *Global Times* (2020a) tweeted that: 'Italy may have had an unexplained strain of pneumonia as early as November and December 2019 with highly suspected symptoms of COVID19, reports said'. It did not directly say that this meant that the pandemic started in Italy. However, neither did it say what those 'reports' actually were, let alone what they said. Furthermore, in addition to trying to avoid blame, China's successful crisis response was increasingly contrasted against Western ones in ways that looked rather celebratory; an approach that fits into the idea of an Occidentalist normative strategy that will be discussed in more detail in the following chapter. One example is the promotion of the idea of morally superior China that was only concerned with saving lives through its international response versus a politicized West that was instead motivated by power politics and points scoring. In addition, not only could China's political system respond more quickly and effectively than democracies, but there was something about Western culture that was problematic too: 'Asian countries, including China, have been particularly successful in their fight against Covid-19 because they have this sense of community and good citizenship that is lacking in Western democracies' (Anon, 2020a). This quote was from a post by an unnamed Chinese diplomat working in the Chinese embassy in Paris. A similar anonymous posting on the same embassy website became the focus of even greater anger, and not just in France. This was in part because of is overall tone, but specifically because of its suggestion that nursing staff in French care homes 'abandoned their jobs overnight, deserted collectively, leaving their residents to die of hunger and disease' (Anon, 2020b). This is perhaps the most extreme example of a sort of Chinese position that resulted in Josep Borrell, the EU high representative for foreign policy, arguing that what had started as a local crisis in Hubei province had evolved into a situation where it was Europe that was now being 'stigmatized' by China in a 'a global battle for narratives' (Borrell, 2020).

Discursive power, Chinese narratives and attraction

This brief analysis of the competition to narrate the COVID-19 pandemic provides a snapshot of what happened over a very short period of time in the first quarter of 2020. As such, it cannot be taken as establishing an immutable set of positions. Neither in terms of Chinese policies and stances, nor external responses to them. That said, it is not easy to see how those that have been alienated by Chinese rhetoric can be persuaded to change their minds. To be sure, China's leaders have responded in the past to international criticism and pushbacks by changing their policies or language (or both), and this might happen again. There is also always the chance that attentions will turn to other sources of other as yet unknown problems in the future. Or that US policy will become the bigger story in the long run. But when the international response to the new National Security Law in Hong Kong is added to the impact of some of the things that were said and done during the pandemic, then it is unlikely that 2020 will be viewed by historians as a highpoint in the history of Chinese attempts to win friends and gain followership.

In reality, it was only a rather small number of individuals who were actively involved in pushing this mixture of self-protection and superiority through discourse management. Most notably, different elements of the Foreign Ministry were very energetic in using foreign language media of various sorts to get the message across. This included embracing Twitter as a means of disseminating views, with Zhao Lijian and Hua Chunying becoming particularly prominent participants (Gill, 2020). The *Global Times* also had an important role to play in promoting the message in English language mediums (including via its own Twitter account as well as through its own platforms). While this more proactive approach might have become more evident during the pandemic as a result of the extent of the crisis and the potential long-term damage for

China, it was not a consequence of responding to COVID-19 alone. The call for a more 'fighting spirit' from diplomats in defending China had been made the previous year in light of criticism of Chinese policy in Xinjiang and the demonstrations in Hong Kong. This in turn was a response to Xi Jinping's already noted earlier call to tell good (and Chinese) stories about China to counteract the dominance of foreign views and news sources in global discussions.

In truth, though, it only takes a few people if they say the right (or wrong) sorts of things in the right places. A couple of Foreign Ministry spokespeople, the editorial writers of a couple of newspapers and the odd Chinese diplomat overseas is enough. Moreover, as Cabestan (2020) argues, the Chinese state tried to do too many things too quickly. This resulted in an incoherent message with one part of the effort emphasizing Chinese aid, solidarity and responsibility while others were simultaneously seeking to deflect blame from China, blaming others, and asserting Chinese superiority. Doing so might have had utility (or been essential) for a domestic audience and legitimation purposes, but looked triumphalist and uncaring from other perspectives.

So the position taken by some representatives of some parts of the Chinese state should not be taken as representative of a monolithic Chinese view. Indeed, this 'Wolf Warrior Diplomacy'[17] was criticized by leading Chinese IR scholars (such as Shi Yonhong and Yan Xuetong) as being counterproductive and creating a 'huge gap between what is intended and what is achieved' (Wong, 2020). It is probably not even representative of the views of all of those in the highest echelons of the Chinese party-state itself. The hard and defensive-aggressive tone of many official statements certainly stands in very stark contrast to the actions of individual Chinese who reached out with true compassion to help friends and strangers overseas, and watched what was happening in other countries with real empathy and sadness.

Even in 'normal' times, and when done in more nuanced ways, trying to control narratives and to enhance the China Voice has often been far from successful. The fact that the state is trying to get its message across at all can lead to a focus on what the regime and leadership is prepared and able to do. The focus is often on the overall intention behind the effort and also sometimes – for example, via CIs – on the means of its delivery. In the process, the actual content of the message can be overlooked or discounted as disingenuous.

Even though there has been an overarching attempt to show Chinese responsibility and commitment to global peace and prosperity, China's self-image promotion towards other developing countries is built on its difference to the West and previous great powers. So it's not really surprising that this does not always find a sympathetic reception in those Western states that are being negatively 'othered'. Conversely, the idea that China's public diplomacy has been more welcomed and embraced in Africa and parts of Latin America than in other parts of the (Western) world has become something close to an accepted truth (even if it is sometimes based on assertion and assumption rather than on firm evidence). During the pandemic (and at other times too), the treatment of African residents and traders in China did not exactly result in non-Western solidarity. Somewhat true to form, Zhao Lijian (2020c) tried to explain this as a consequence of US interference and misreporting trying to drive a wedge between China and Africa, rather than any problem with Chinese origins. But the response from a number of African governments suggested that they thought the problem was indeed China's and not the West's.

This suggests that we need to take care not to simply assume that attitudes to China break down along clear West versus non-West lines. Nevertheless, there is a clear intention on the part of China's leaders to try and convince fellow non-Western states that they are all fellow travellers. And under Xi, the emphasis has titled a little away from being a stakeholder in the existing order towards pushing this idea of China as an alternative to Western liberal principles. This turns our attention to the way in which Chinese wisdom is being touted as providing Chinese solutions for the world. Which not by accident is the focus of the analysis in the following chapter.

Normative Power? China Solutions for the World

Just as the initial driver of the desire to tell positive stories and increase Chinese soft power was a defensive one, so too was the Chinese rejection of the truly universal nature of dominant norms and practices of international politics. Rather than consider China against supposedly universal definitions and concepts, the aim was to 'Sinify' them. To establish understandings and definitions that emerged from China's own history and thinking and reflected China's specific developmental experiences. This would then generate specific China relevant definitions that should provide the basis for any consideration and/or evaluation of Chinese policy and practice rather than using those developed and deployed by others that had emerged from Western philosophies and histories.

The logical extension of this thinking, continually repeated by Chinese leaders and scholars, is that all countries need to do the same to develop individual bespoke nationalized norms and theories. The same reasoning applies to political systems and economic models as well. So, for example, just as China developed its own developmental path and did not follow any other pre-existing model – even socialist models explored elsewhere – so 'other countries should not copy the Chinese model' (Xiao Xinfa, 2018: 26). They should not follow the specifics of what China did, but instead copy the same methodology and 'embark on a political development path that suits its own national conditions and conforms to its own characteristics' (Zhou, 2018: 13). The outcome should be a system of normative, theoretical and developmental anarchy. Anarchy is used here in its IR theoretical meaning of an absence of a higher form of authority above the sovereign state where no interpretation dominates, and each country pursues its own development path and defines its own set of national norms and principles. The result should be a global order characterized by massive diversity, with the common nature of values, norms and principles stripped back to very basic elements and only the most basic components of the 'common values' of existence (Yan Shuhan, 2018: 20).

The need to embrace diversity is one of the core principles of the CSFM, and marks it out as a very different type of global ambition than those that conceive of building a community of common (liberal) values. But in the very process of endorsing diversity, are Xi and other Chinese leaders somewhat ironically privileging Chinese preferences and elevating Chinese views and interests above those of others? There has certainly been a shift of sorts in thinking about how China's own experience might provide concrete lessons for others to follow. While all countries might be unique, there is something about China's uniqueness that make it rather special. Some Chinese – apparently including Xi Jinping – believe that Chinese wisdom (*zhongguo zhihui*) can create developmental lessons that have gone beyond outdated and often failing western theories and prescriptions to provide new options for developing economies. Chinese wisdom can also provide the basis for reform of the global order to resolve current governance deficits and power inequalities.

There is a prima facie case, then, for arguing that the long-expected Chinese attempt to change the fundament principles that underpin the way that the world is organized is now underway. As such, one of the aims of this chapter is to investigate why China's experiences and thinking are now thought of as having salience for others beyond China's borders, potentially providing the basis for an alternative way of thinking about IR, development and global governance. And why now? It then moves to explain what the content of any normative alternative might be, and identifies the main governance areas that have been identified as being potential areas where China might lead. There is an emphasis throughout on the idea of 'Occidentalism' that has been established in previous chapters, and the construction of an idealized vision of China by first constructing an idea of the West that China is the polar opposite to.

Before that, though, it is important to clarify what can be shown and claimed given the research methods that have been used. The analysis in this chapter is built on two key sets of sources. The first is the same set of speeches of China's top leaders that were used to identify China's strategy for global change in Chapter 3 (which are detailed in the Appendix). It is important to remember that much of what is said in these is intended to influence a domestic audience, and this might explain not only much of the content, but also the way that it is expressed. For example, talking about the four self-confidences is at least as much an attempt to convince the Chinese people to be confident as it is the externalization of pre-existing confidences into a global reform agenda. What looks at first sight like the celebration of self-confidence is probably instead a tool for dealing with the lack of it.

The second is Chinese academic writings written in Chinese, with a particular focus on those that try to unpick the theoretical basis and logic of the 'new' thinking. As noted in the Introduction, it is not always clear if what is written represents a real and committed belief, or instead is the result of a more pragmatic research strategy shaped by the state's attempt to ensure that academia reflects and emphasizes the official party line on key issues (Minzner, 2019). At the same time, those who hold contrary opinions to those that are politically favoured might choose to keep quieter than they would in different circumstances. So there is no claim here that those writings that have a strong Occidentalist approach and/or actively promote Chinese alternatives are representative of all Chinese writing and all Chinese thinking. Far from it. Indeed, a number of the sources cited in this chapter are from rather obscure academic journals that are not even widely read within China. In this respect, this chapter might be seen as an example of the sort of 'opinion shopping' discussed in Chapter 2. It is a deliberate attempt to cherry pick to prove a point. That said, given that the strand of thinking these opinions represent has proximity to the views of China's leaders, they need to be taken seriously, no matter how firmly held or representative of all Chinese scholarship they really are.

China's changing ideational challenge

The idea that China might provide an ideational alternative to the West is nothing new. Be that an alternative to the liberal West or other forms of European derived political preferences for organizing how people and countries interact. While the lure of opening the Chinese market historically played an important role in shaping the way China was approached and engaged, fascination with Chinese cultural, societal and philosophical differences played a role too. Japan might have emerged as the major representation of a Yellow Peril in the late 19th and early 20th centuries (not least because of its military successes), but China too was seen as a potential source of a threatening shift of global power to the East. Even when the Western powers themselves were exerting their own power over China in the years after the Opium Wars, the idea of a Chinese 'reawakening' garnered significant attention, pointing to the potential consequences of what might happen once China was strong enough to assert its preferences again (Fitzgerald, 1996).

The nature of a Chinese alternative looked rather different after 1949, with Mao's version of communism extolled as providing a radical alternative not just to Western capitalism, but also to what parts of the left in Europe saw as the more routinized, conservative, de-radicalized variety practised and promoted by the Soviet Union (Bourg, 2012). This was an alternative that the Chinese authorities actively promoted overseas through their links with revolutionary groups and others who might be sympathetic to Chinese goals. It was also supported by what would now be called a soft power strategy. For example, by promoting the message in specialist foreign language publications like *The Peking Review*, *China Pictorial* and *China Reconstructs*.

Not surprisingly, this changed as the nature of the Chinese state and Chinese ideology itself changed. The Chinese communist alternative after Mao was no longer a radical revolutionary one, but instead a potentially economic modernizing one. Perhaps even the much hoped for 'third way' between capitalism and old-style communist party rule (either the state planning kind or the more radical Maoist version). The desire to find an effective developmental alternative to capitalism – or more correctly, its neoliberal manifestation – has influenced the way a number of people have looked at and interpreted China's political economy ever since. So too has the fear that China might provide this alternative from those who see it as a less than positive prospect.

Socialization or strategic silence?

That said, the idea of China as a source of ideational contributions of any kind rather diminished in the late 1980s and 1990s. The hope for a bright Chinese alternative was first punctured by the way that the Chinese state responded to calls for further change in Tiananmen Square in 1989. This was a response that made this version of Chinese political authority look very much like many other repressive authoritarian political systems rather than something new. It was then further diminished by a process of economic reform in the mid and late 1990s that saw China becoming entwined with the capitalist global economy. Economic reforms at home might have fallen a long way short of the big bang economic shock therapy undertaken elsewhere, but still privileged other interests over those of China's industrial working classes. It might have been the ruling communist party that was driving a transition towards neoliberalism rather than the more usual alliance of pro-liberalization capitalist forces, but just because China's version of neoliberalism was a state-led one didn't mean that it was something radically and fundamentally different (Hart-Landsberg and Burkett, 2004; Wang Hui, 2005).

This was also a period when alternatives to the dominant form of neoliberal capitalism were looking rather thin on the ground. The collapse of communist party rule elsewhere saw a number of former communist countries and territories become democratic and make rather quick transitions to new capitalist forms. Economic crises in East Asia and Latin America starting in the late 1990s not only undermined the appeal of stronger state forms of capitalism but also, through the conditions attached to aid packages, further facilitated and consolidated neoliberal preferences. Neoliberalism at the turn of the millennium was looking strong and lacking obvious challenges. China's membership of the WTO in 2001 was seen as a further sign of China's commitment to the neoliberal status quo, and also as a key means of ensuring that China moved ever closer to status quo norms in the future. China looked much less likely to change the world than to itself become ever more socialized into the existing dominant global economic order. Not (immediately) politically so, but economically ever more 'normal'. In September 2005, shortly after meeting the architect and mouthpiece of China's Peaceful Rise narrative, Zheng Bijian, the then US Deputy Secretary of State Robert Zoellick (2005) argued that China was no threat to the existing order at all as:

> It does not seek to spread radical, anti-American ideologies.
>
> While not yet democratic, it does not see itself in a twilight conflict against democracy around the globe.
>
> While at times mercantilist, it does not see itself in a death struggle with capitalism.
>
> And most importantly, China does not believe that its future depends on overturning the fundamental order of the international system. In fact, quite the reverse: Chinese leaders have decided that their success depends on being networked with the modern world.

Indeed, for Zoellick, China now had the opportunity to be become more than just a 'responsible stakeholder' in the current order. Alongside other great powers, it could develop a special responsibility to sustain and support it as well.

This idea of convergence was not universally held. Ramo's (2004b) identification of a 'Beijing Consensus' was responsible for a renewed focus on an alternative Chinese development model. Some thought that this provided a much more fundamental challenge to both capitalism and liberalism than Zoellick had suggested (Barma and Ratner, 2006). As noted at the very start of this book, there was also a relatively strong school of thought that economic growth would eventually see China emerge as a superpower, and when it was more able to try to push for change, then it would. Any relative silence and acquiescence from China was thus only temporary and perhaps even a deliberate expedient measure designed to allow it to grow under the radar of extensive international scrutiny. Here, there is a clear overlap with the idea of *taoguang yanghui* as strategy discussed in Chapter 3.

If this was the aim, it was aided by the granting of Permanent Normal Trade Relations to China by the US in 1999 (operational from 2000) in the run up to China's WTO entry in 2001. This took away the need to debate China's access to the US market each year, and thus removed the annual opportunity for those critical of China (for whatever reason) to voice their concerns in a high-profile political setting. In this respect, the process of WTO entry in part depoliticized China's trade relations – which is probably one of the reasons that China's leaders sought it in the first place. While some saw China being socialized as a victory for a US policy of engaging China, others saw it as creating the basis for an ever-stronger China to challenge the US and the global order in the longer term (Christensen 2006). And to be fair to Zoellick (2005), he was in many ways trying to encourage China to choose the path of responsibility and normalcy in the future rather than asserting that this was an inevitability, noting that '[u]ncertainties about how China will use its power will lead the United States – and others as well – to hedge relations with China. Many countries hope China will pursue a "Peaceful Rise", but none will bet their future on it.'

These debates provide an example of the argument made in Chapter 1 that discussions about China in the US are often as much about US power and policy than they are about China. In addition to the question of the efficacy of US policy towards China itself, there was also the suggestion that the US focus on fighting enemies in North Africa and the Middle East had created a space for China to occupy. Most of the focus was on the China challenge to US power in China's own backyards. What Keller and Rawski (2007: 5) called an 'apparent US disengagement from Asia' had coincided with

China's turn towards multilateral cooperation with Southeast Asia. In addition to increased economic ties of various sorts, Chinese support for sovereignty and non-intervention resonated with the normative preferences of many regional elites (Shambaugh, 2005). For early identifiers of a Chinese soft power challenge to the US – albeit using a rather broad definition of what soft power was – this was where it was most evident:

> The United States has underestimated China. Washington hawks remain focused on China's potential 'hard' power, with many fearing that Chinese military modernisation has progressed further and faster than previously thought. But it is America's 'soft' power—that is, its cultural, economic and diplomatic clout—that China is now challenging. Through a combination of trade, aid and skilful diplomacy, Beijing is laying the foundations for a new regional order with China as the natural leader and the United States as the outsider. (Windybank 2005: 28)

The dominance of an Asia focus in these early debates made sense. It was here that China was most active economically and also in terms of trying to convince others of its peaceful intent (Gill and Huang, 2006: 24). But it was not just in the region where US policy after 2001 was seen to have 'opened new opportunities for China's emerging security diplomacy to succeed' (Gill, 2007: 2). Thompson (2005) pointed to a reluctance to accept the conditions on development assistance by Western dominated institutions as one of the reasons that Chinese soft power increased in Africa (alongside other factors like the growth of Chinese medical assistance to the continent). In North Africa and the Middle East, opposition to intervention and in many respects simply not being associated with the 'war on terror' was enough to increase the idea of China as an attractive international ally promoting a set of principles and preferences that stood in stark contrast to those on offer from the major Western powers (Lampton, 2008).

Norms for China or norms for the world?

The emergence of 'new' thinking

Previous chapters have already established the importance of the global financial crisis in changing perceptions of China's global role. This is also the case when it comes to studying the emergence of new

Chinese governance proposals and concepts. The crisis was said to have revealed the fallacy of liberal supremacy and disproved the 'end of history thesis', while the ineffective response to the crisis 'exposed the multiple defects' and inflexibility of the old order in dealing with its own problems (Li Sixue, 2017). It was not so much that there was an *opportunity* to challenge the status quo ante, but an absolute *need* to provide new post and/or non-Western ones to replace failing liberal orthodoxies. From this starting point, it took a number of years to move from calling for reform of extant global governance institutions, through the provision of supplementary new ones, to possessing and articulating a clear idea of what such reform should achieve. Rather unsurprisingly, Xi Jinping's ascension to power at the 18th Party Congress in 2012 is often seen as representing a key moment in the transition to this third phase.

Xi made his first significant foray into the world of IR concepts by proposing a 'new type of great power relations' with the US in 2012; a notion that was at the heart of his first formal leader-to-leader meeting with President Obama the following year. In 2013, Foreign Minister Wang Yi referred to 'Great Power Diplomacy with Chinese Characteristics' (Wacker, 2015: 66) and spoke of the importance of 'China's Solution', 'Chinese wisdom' and 'China's Voice' in promoting new governance agendas when commenting on Xi's contribution to the G20 meeting in St Petersburg (FMPRC, 2013a). It was also in Russia that Xi first expanded the need for a new type of great power relations into a broader and more generic need for a 'new type of international relations' per se.

While he had previously spoken about a CS for cross straits relations and for China's neighbourhood, the first time that Xi referred to a CS for the world was at a speech at the Körber Foundation in Berlin in the spring of 2014. In November of the same year, he convened a Central Foreign Affairs Work Conference to lay out his new vision for China's global role. And according to Ruan Zongze (2015), this for the first time clearly established China's 'diplomatic identity' (*waijiao shenfen*) as a global governance reformer. If it is possible to find a single event that starts a new era, perhaps this was it. More often, China's hosting of the G20 Summit in 2016 is identified as the moment that China took its place on the world stage committed to a global governance reform agenda – including norm and thought reform (Guo Wei, 2017). Though rather than try to be precise, we can say with more confidence that between the 18th and 19th Party Congresses, China emerged as a clearly (self) identified force for global governance reform. A force that was prepared to take global leadership in selected policy domains, willing and able to provide more global public goods, and also ready to promote new ideas, norms, theories and definitions that could underpin the transition to a new global polity.

Nationalizing norms and models

The importance of 'nationalizing' norms has most often been discussed in light of China's emphasis on how specific national conditions shape understandings of the most relevant and important human rights in any national setting. But it goes much further than this. The suffix 'with Chinese characteristics' (or prefix in Chinese – *you zhongguo tesede*) was originally designed to explain how China's new form of socialism under Deng Xiaoping was still socialist despite embracing certain capitalist measures and methods. It has subsequently been used to qualify an extensive set of ideas, norms, theories, and practices to highlight their specific (and at times unique) qualities and contents when they are manifest in a Chinese context. Such a Sinification is meant to imply a difference in emphasis within broadly shared norms, rather than representing the establishment of contending rival Chinese positions. For example, using the concept of International Law with Chinese Characteristics suggests that there is no need for 'a new paradigm of international law' to reflect Chinese interests and preferences, as this can be done by emphasizing certain elements of the existing paradigm (such as state sovereignty and non-intervention) and paying less attention to others (Chatham House, 2016: 3). From this understanding, China is not challenging the status quo per se, but just questioning the way that certain parts of the status quo are interpreted, emphasized and implemented.

However, as argued in the Introduction, it's not entirely clear that all of the subsequent interpretations really do only represent a difference in emphasis rather than something more substantial and fundamental. Many Chinese discourses of human security, for example, lose a focus on the individual as the main referent point which should be at the very heart of what human security is all about (Breslin, 2015). To be sure, it has been described as a 'slippery' concept (Paris, 2001) and, as Chinese analysts often point out, one that did not even have a shared and agreed definition when it was first introduced in the UN's 1994 Human Development Report. In this respect, then, it might not immediately stand out as a particularly good example to use. But it is notable that the Chinese term that is most often used to describe the 'human' in human security discourses is *renlei*, which refers to humankind as a whole in Chinese rather than individual human beings.

As a result, what human security means when discussed in Chinese language forums does not always have the same commonality with those discourses that the preferred English translation of the Chinese terminology suggests.

But whatever this European observer might think, the message from China is clear. Promoting Chinese thinking is not a revisionist act, but a reformist one. Indeed, it is typically depicted as a restorative process. Rather than being new, China privileges those basic ordering principles that not only laid the foundations for a new world order after the end of World War Two but also, as Xi (2017b) argued, go back to 'the principles of equality and sovereignty established in the Peace of Westphalia over 360 years ago'. From this logic, it is not China that is challenging basic principles, but the imposition of liberal arguments and neoliberal economic models that were a deviation from an older set of norms that China now seeks to restore.

This idea is reflected in what the CSFM is meant to be all about. It is promoted as the antithesis of Western approaches to constructing a preferred future world order in two ways. First, it is fundamentally philosophically different. It is not about building a single world polity as favoured by cosmopolitan thinking, nor about the imposition of the preferences of Western great powers under the guise of universalism. Rather, it aims to build 'a consensus of different civilizations' (Xie and Zhang, 2018: 61) 'where diverse civilizations and development models coexist' (Zhang Jun, 2018). This is a world where each should simply do what works best based on national conditions, and China's aim is to create an order where this is not only tolerated but encouraged (Bu, 2018; Xiao Xinfa, 2018). Second, the methods that China will use to attain its idealized future world order are different too. The argument that China will never try and impose its will and visions on others has been repeated time and time again. It also become one of the core principles of Xi Jinping's 'Thought on Diplomacy' that is supposed to guide Chinese actions (Yang Jiechi, 2018a). Embracing diversity is not just an ethical or moral position, but a practical one as well, as the imposition of policies, preferences and paradigms is seen as a key cause of both instability and disorder within states, and also international tension and disharmony (Yang Jiechi, 2018b).

Through the externalization of the benefits of China's ongoing growth by allowing access to the Chinese market and also through the promotion of the BRI, China is said to have shown that its development provides massive opportunities for others. These successes are seen to be particularly impressive when compared both with those countries that have either followed the neoliberal path with disastrous consequences, or resisted them and been punished by the West for such defiance. In the process, China's developmental successes have not only disproved the end of history argument by showing that alternatives to liberalism are very much alive and thriving, but have also disproved the China Threat Thesis too (Guo Wei, 2017). From this perspective, once more, the Western logic of threat is turned on its head. It is not China that provides the threat, but rather the West that is threatening when it imposes itself on others in ways that China never will:

> No matter how far China develops, it will not dominate and will not expand. To put it bluntly, the 'China Solution' in the new era is not a threat to world development. On the contrary, the 'Western Program' based on the 'Washington Consensus' by Western powers is a real threat to world development. (Wu et al, 2018: 5)

Internationalizing norms and models

There is now a clear appetite for establishing Chinese preferences and ideas as the basis for governance arrangements that go beyond China's own borders and China's own domestic issues. As just one example of many of the type, State Councillor Yang Jiechi (2017) has argued that 'the Chinese Communists and Chinese people are fully confident of offering Chinese input to human exploration of better social systems'. Moreover, in the form of the CS, it appears as if thinking is changing on the willingness and wisdom of promoting China's own development experiences as something for others to follow as well. Or maybe more correctly, the understanding of the type of lessons that can be learnt from studying China's experiences appears to be changing.

Let's start with the example of human rights. Wang Yi (2017c: 5) has argued that 'we need to promote human rights through development. The right to development is the primary human right for developing countries'. Even though the reference to the 'right to development' takes us back to the importance of each country doing what is best for it in terms of development strategies, this is not simply a statement of China doing something at home and letting others do whatever they want to do too. It is a clear statement of a Chinese understanding that China's leaders think should be externalized. It is not saying that the right to development is the primary right for China, but it is the primary human right for all developing economies.

Similarly, the declaration of the first South-South Human Rights Forum held in Beijing in December 2017 affirmed the importance of each country developing its own specific and discrete development path and conception of rights. But at the same time, it declared that 'the right to subsistence and the right to development are the primary basic human rights', and argued that the 'international community should take the eradication of poverty and hunger as the primary task, and strive to solve the problem of insufficient and unsustainable development and create more favorable conditions for the realization of the people's right to development especially in the developing countries' (SSHRF, 2017). Again, this suggests that in both understandings of development and human rights, there are bottom line principles that apply to more than just China. It is not just that China's position on human rights is one of many different nationalized interpretations but also, as Titus Chen (2019: 2) argues, one that is claimed to constitute the basis of a 'new universal value'. It is also a position that is now often said in Chinese discourses to be 'superior' to Western ones.

Beyond human rights, this new China-derived universalism is embedded throughout the language of building a CSFM. And it has had a moderate degree of success in being accepted by others too. For example, in renewing the mandate of the UN Assistance Mission in Afghanistan in 2017, the UN Security Council for the first time passed a resolution that reflected Xi's new thinking when it stressed 'the crucial importance of advancing regional cooperation in the spirit of win–win cooperation as an effective means to promote security, stability and economic and social development in Afghanistan and the region to create a community of shared future for mankind' (UN, 2017a: 1). The resolution also explicitly referred to the Belt and Road as one of the mechanisms that could bring about this greater regional cooperation and 'urged' further efforts to increase its impact' (UN, 2017a: 9). The same year, the UN General Assembly '[r]eaffirmed that practical measures should be examined and taken in the search for agreements to prevent an arms race in outer space in a common effort towards a community of shared future for humankind' (UN, 2017b: 28). Similarly, in 2018, a UN Economic and Social Council resolution on a new partnership for Africa referred to 'the spirit of win–win cooperation and to create a shared future, based upon our common humanity' (UN, 2018: 11). Not surprisingly, these have been presented in China as not just international acceptance of Xi's ideas, but the embrace of them and the creation of a new international or global 'consensus'.[1] The Chinese media is particularly keen on reporting statements of support from international observers (particularly academics and even more particularly politicians) as evidence of a broad buy-in to Chinese initiatives.

Emphasizing diversity versus China-derived universalism

This creates a potential dilemma. One fundamental Chinese position is that all countries have their own unique histories and cultures and so by definition all have their own unique characteristics. (Sun and Li, 2017: 12). A second is that the imposition of models and preferences on other countries is wrong. So does this mean that it is also wrong to promote Chinese experiences and preferences to others too? Does the creation of a new international consensus contradict the emphasis on a community of diversity for example? If all experiences are nationally valid, then how can China set benchmarks for what are the primary human rights? The answer is that there is no necessary inherent contradiction in principle, but there can be in execution and dissemination.

In theory, China does not provide any sort of model for others, but simply an example of what can be done. This is both true when it comes to thinking about norms and principles, and also when it comes to working out how best to develop. Here, what China has done shows the importance and effectiveness of avoiding the prescriptions of the neoliberal model and instead finding a relationship between state and market that works:

> The proposal of the China Solution fully demonstrates that the post-modernized countries can have better social institutional arrangements that do not copy the Western model, and can promote the development of the global governance system while maintaining stable development, and bring maximum benefits to the people. (Gao Hong, 2018: 110)

From this understanding, China's successes become a referent point for others looking for new solutions rather than a model that should (or indeed, can) be followed. And if others do decide to look at China and emulate some of the specific things that China did along the way, then that's entirely up to those autonomous actors to do, and nothing to do with Chinese influence or power (Yang Guangbin, 2016). To be sure, some Chinese might think that China has something to offer. But this is not the same as *insisting* that China's lessons must be learnt and implemented by others.

Similarly, while China might have ideas that 'other countries can learn from and adopt in order to solve the international problems in global governance', this is simply a case of suggesting ideas and principles that others might learn from (Shi Jianping, 2017: 11).

China does not force others to listen or to buy into concepts like the CSFM. This is shown to be in stark contrast to the way that Western powers previously imposed liberal norms and preferences on others, and would still do today if they could. The message is that China won't ever colonize weaker states and impose new political systems on them. Or build new rules and governance structures that penalize and/or omit those that don't accept Chinese preferences. Or make developmental assistance and other economic interactions dependent on others falling in line. Support for Chinese initiatives, so the argument goes, instead comes from independent external validation of them because they resonate with the aspirations of non-Chinese around the world.

And there is truth in this. After all, the stated goals of the CSFM are all quite general and quite difficult to oppose. Moreover, there are plenty of people (including, but not limited to, leaders of other developing non-Western states) who want the future to be different from the past, and for the influence of existing Western powers to be less pronounced in that future. Nor does actively promoting Chinese experiences and predilections *necessarily* contradict the non-imposition strategy. The argument is that China cannot just sit back and expect others to make the decision to look to China for wisdom on their own. This is because the knowledge of what China is promoting remains very patchy (at best) outside China. While this may be only natural given that the clear articulation of Chinese solutions is still at a very early stage, it is made more urgent because of the perceived dominance of others (Shi, 2017: 10). Hence the need for proactivity. From this viewpoint, China must try to create as many channels as possible for increased interactions (particularly among developing states) and to promote 'mutual learning among civilizations' (Xi, 2018a) rather than just leave potential influence to emerge more organically. This includes promoting new international institutions (forums, conferences, regional groupings and so on) to provide innovative ways of getting the story across (Song, 2017: 12) in addition to the sort of nation branding strategies outlined in Chapter 5.

Even this proactivity in itself and a greater confidence in talking about China's successes marks a significant shift from 'China's previous diplomatic practice' (Pang 2018: 8). However, at times the language that is used sounds like something more than just presenting China's experiences and preferences and letting others decide how to respond to them. In addition to the above-mentioned human rights example, China's new thinking and new proposals are argued to have 'transcended' a number of previous orthodoxies: 'the traditional Western theories of international relations for the past 300 years' (Wang Yi, 2017c), Western global governance thinking and practice, and also outdated and failed Western thinking on development (Ruan, 2015; Zhang Yu, 2016; Sun and Li, 2017; Wang Yi, 2017a; Yan Shuhan, 2018; Yang Li, 2018). China is now is also said to 'occupy the moral high ground' compared to Western powers (Wang Yi, 2017c). So at times, the rhetoric sounds like something more than just putting Chinese ideas and experiences out there, and then stepping back and leaving it to others to decide what to do with them.

Why is China special?

Power and responsibility

Even if it is just a case of China providing an example of what can be done rather than a clear blueprint for global change, what is it about China that makes it such a good example for others to follow? One rather straightforward answer is found in the argument that China's relative power capabilities have, in Xi's (2015a) words, 'achieved a historic leap'. As a result, China now has the ability to challenge the previous dominance of the West in a way that others simply can't. In addition to the logic of power and capability, Chinese thinkers add duty as second explanation. The logic here is that great powers have a special responsibility to provide global solutions that don't fall on other smaller and less powerful states. In the past, developing states (including China) have been excluded from the way that global governance has been organized and their voices are still not heard as they should be even as the distribution of global power has shifted. As such, it is particularly incumbent on China as the most powerful of the developing states to act as a representative of them all and become what Pang Zhongying (2018: 7) calls a 'coordinator' between the great powers and developing countries in promoting change.

A third answer that this is not a case of China imposing its solutions on others, but that others actively want China to provide its solutions based on its wisdom and experiences (Sun, 2018; Xie and Zhang, 2018). Or in Xi's own words, 'the international community is looking forward to hearing China's voice and seeing China's Solution. China cannot be absent' (Xi, 2015f). They want China to lead not only because it has the power to do something, but also because it has lessons that others can learn from. It is worth taking a step back here to remember the context in which the CSFM and the CS came about. For many years, it wasn't Chinese leadership that was seen as the problem, but rather the lack of it. It was accused of benefitting from the global public goods provided by others while not being prepared to supply any itself. In 2014, President Obama complained that China was a 'free rider', and had been so for decades, focusing on growing economically while others provided the peaceful global environment that facilitated this growth (Saich, 2015: 314). Promoting the CS, then, in a proactive and forceful way was in part a response to these claims of being absent, and designed to provide an antidote to them and silence international criticism (Wang Qiuyi, 2018: 56; Xu Jin, 2018: 5).

Success and superiority

This leads us directly to the fourth reason and the simple idea that China has something special to offer because it has been successful. For the most part the study of success focuses on economics, and a comparison of China's continued growth with the failing liberal project. But there is also an increasing focus on the superiority of China's political system too (Tobin, 2018). Chinese-style deliberative democracy (*xie shang min zhu*) is explained as providing the stability that China needed when making complex and rapid transformations (Bu, 2018), and avoiding the instability that the competition in multi-party liberal democracies 'inevitably' brings (Luo and Yang, 2017: 37; Lei, 2019). It is a system that is argued to be particularly effective in responding to crises. Li Keqiang (2020), for example, explains how the political system allowed for an effective response to the COVID-19 pandemic:

> Under the leadership of the Party Central Committee, the central leading group for covid-19 response has made timely decisions and plans; the central guidance group has provided effective guidance and supervision; the State Council inter-departmental task force has coordinated the response efforts; all local authorities and all government departments have fulfilled their respective duties, and people from every walk of life have given their full support. Together, we have waged an all-out people's war against the virus.

Of course, the political system responded to the very early days of the response in Wuhan in far from effective ways. But irrespective of the reality, this is the discourse, explanation and logic that the Chinese state has decided to promote. And for very understandable reasons.

Reflecting confidence or building it?

A common theme that runs through much of what is written in China is an emphasis on the 'four self-confidences' (*sige zixin*); confidence in China's road or path, theory, system, and culture. Chinese successes are said to have come about despite considerable international criticism of Chinese policies and approaches, and numerous predictions over the years that the Chinese way was unsustainable and China would collapse (Wu et al, 2018: 5). China has also succeeded despite a number of the major global powers acting in ways that were not exactly designed to facilitate China's growth. Or at least that's the way it is argued by some. As a result, the Chinese people should have great confidence in the development path that they have taken, the theoretical and cultural foundations that have generated this path, and the political system that has allowed the correct decisions to be made and implemented effectively. And of course, it is the party that is behind all these correct theories and approaches.

As Kelly (2018) notes, promoting these self-confidences became a major focus of the official state media, with the primary audience very much a domestic one. It was also supported by the sort of poster campaign that is rather familiar to anybody who has studied the Chinese propaganda processes, or simply spent a long time in China. So rather than *emerging* from self-confidence, the promotion of Chinese thinking and Chinese solutions might instead be a project in *establishing* self-confidence. Emphasizing China's achievements is a key means of consolidating support for the architects of these successes in the past, and having confidence that they will do what is best in the future too (Bandurski, 2018). Moreover, that China now has something that others are said to want to learn from shows just how successful China's leaders have been, which should only 'strengthen our confidence in China' (Tian, 2018: 126). Being impressed by China's achievements shows admiration for what has been done. Wanting to learn from China says something deeper about how it has been done as well.

History and theory

It is not just China's recent history that marks it out as having a special role. China's ancient history does too. Chapter 3 outlined the way in which Xi Jinping is said to have re-evaluated China's experiences, goals, and power capabilities and resources for 'the new era'. This 'comprehensive and dialectical assessment' (Bi, 2017: 18) is widely credited – extremely widely so in China – with laying the foundations for the ability to think about and create Chinese solutions for the world. In the conceptual flow that was also presented in Chapter 3, Chinese experiences were presented as one of the starting points for this theoretical innovation. This is because Xi has placed a specific emphasis on the importance of historical legacies that go back much further than the founding of the CCP, or the writings of Marx and Engels. China's 'unique advantage', he argues, results from a 'distinctive ideological system' that is the result of 'the intellectual wisdom and rational speculation that the Chinese have accumulated for thousands of years' (Xi, 2016a) with the current party leadership simply 'the curator of a 5,000 year-old civilization' (Xi, 2016b).

In that same conceptual flow chart, Marxism-Leninism is presented as a second and separate theoretical starting point alongside Chinese historical experiences. This is technically theoretically incorrect as Marxism-Leninism should be *the* single starting point. As Xi (2015a) has explained, the process of reflection and analyses that has led to his theoretical change is a dialectical materialist process which has its fundamental starting point in Marxism. The very basic mode of analysis that has generated his new thinking is itself firmly grounded in Marxism, and thus so is everything that flows from it. He has also repeatedly restated the Marxist origins of China's successes. As just one example, it is described as 'the fundamental guiding thought upon which our Party and country are founded. Were we to depart from or abandon Marxism, our Party would lose its soul and its direction' (Xi 2016b).

Xi has also argued that it is essential to go right back to the original Communist Manifesto and 'the basic theory of Marxism' to find the solutions to the 'practical problems of contemporary China' (Xinhua, 2019b).[2] But even in doing so he also argued that the 'general principles elaborated in the Communist Manifesto are correct in the whole, but they cannot be used to provide ready-made answers to all the specific questions raised by the Communist Manifesto for the development of human society 170 years later'. In order to answer these questions and those that have arisen in the intervening years, it is essentially to be constantly innovative:

> We must understand the times and grasp the trend of the times, stand at the forefront of human development, actively explore major issues concerning the future and destiny of mankind, and contribute China's wisdom and China Solutions in response to the global challenges facing the world today and to solve common problems facing humanity.

As argued in Chapter 3, this logic means that the policies and actions that drive the party forward today are not only very different from those that originally inspired Marx and Engels, but also from those that were pursued by China's previous CCP leaders in different times. It is entirely Marxist to be doing things today that would have been unthought of by different Marxist thinkers and communist party politicians in different eras. More than that, it would be *anti-Marxist* to simply carry on thinking what they thought and doing what they did in a different era.

From this understanding, the identification of two sources of current thinking is a mistake. However, with the exception of the mode of analysis, it is not always wholly clear that Marxism, rather than something else, really is it the heart of Xi's innovations. The concept of class struggle certainly does not loom large in discussions of the NTIR or CSFM or the CS. Given that Mao Zedong was not much of an economic determinist, it makes it rather difficult to use determinism as a benchmark to judge subsequent varieties of Chinese Marxism against too. But the emphasis in Xi's thinking on the ability of culture and ideas to shape material change (rather than the other way round) does not always sound as if it has much of a materialist or determinist base. Certainly, in general, the emphasis on the significance of China's pre-revolutionary and somewhat un-Marxist historical philosophical precedents can leave the original Marxist-Leninist laws rather diluted and at times hard to pinpoint.

Reading academic exegeses of Xi's thinking doesn't always help either, as collectively this work creates a somewhat confused picture. Does China's past constitute a national context that universal laws need to be applied to, or does it provide an alternative set of truths that have been combined and melded together with Marxism under Xi to form something new? Sometimes it is the former and sometimes the latter, and sometimes both in the same piece of writing. Although it is a very blunt way of measuring influence, it is worth noting that in explaining how 'China's Development of an Ecological Civilization' could be taken to a new stage, Xi (2019f) spent one paragraph outlining the Marxist origins of Chinese efforts, and three on the significance of ancient Chinese thinking and practice.

Whatever the case, Xi Jinping's theoretical thinking and innovation has found new ways of translating this past into future action and aspiration, and this provides a fifth reason why China's experiences, thinking and practice are considered to have special resonance for others. While it might sound like a contradiction, China's unique history is explained as having relevance for others exactly *because* it is unique. The length of China's unparalleled 'uninterrupted civilization' (Sun, 2018: 107) means that it is only China of all the world's civilizations that has witnessed, experienced, survived and learnt from every possible challenge that can befall countries and leaders over the centuries. It is thus specially and uniquely placed to give what it has learnt to the rest of the world:

> Standing at the height of human history, we can easily find that although human beings have created a large number of different civilizations in different periods, there is only one civilization that has survived the storms and snows, and that is the Chinese nation. It can be said that the Chinese nation has witnessed all the inheritance of human civilization from the beginning to the present, and it is a civilization with mission and responsibility. (Liu Ling, 2018: 86)

Moreover, this longevity is explained as having established much stronger and longer lasting cultural traditions than is the case in other (much younger) countries and civilizations.

More important (and more frequently argued), China is said to have something akin to a cultural DNA that permeates through the ages and all but forces Chinese today to seek harmony (Yang Li, 2018). From this starting argument, China's different ambitions and philosophies as an international actor today are explained as emerging from traditional Chinese ethics that emphasized harmony, benevolence, righteousness (Zhao Xiaofeng, 2018) and the Chinese practice of pursing 'harmony between all nations' (Ai, 2018: 7). Indeed, rather than emerging from Marxism, the CSFM is sometimes depicted as a return to past ways after a period of Western-centricism and a new version of the peaceful *Tian Xia* tradition when China was last a (regional) great power (Yang and Li, 2018: 3).

Before China's past can be presented as the basis for its present and future actions, an idealized version of that past first has to be constructed. This entails a rather eclectic and selective use of different (and at various times, conflicting and oppositional) Chinese philosophical traditions to create a form of what Yan Xuetong (2018: 8) calls 'traditionalism'. There is then a mixing of 'facts with myths through selective use of China's vast historical and cultural experiences' (Zhang Feng, 2013, 45) to emphasis the parts of Chinese history (real or mythical) that support current and future agendas. For example, the tributary system has been re-interpreted and presented as representing an era when China's exceptional (in both usages of the word) values and principles established a regional order that guaranteed peace and development for all. This then is projected as the basis for a new era of regional prosperity and security under a neo-tributary system (Pan and Lo, 2017). It also entails glossing over or ignoring those parts of China's past where the influence of the idealized pacific and benign historical values and practices were harder to discern; including quite a few periods of China's more recent history.

Challenging universalism: promoting Occidentalism

Crucially, these guiding 'genes and blood of the Chinese nation' are depicted as the direct opposite of those that guide the action of Western great powers (Yang Li, 2018: 7). This forms part of a larger effort to establish that China has a very different personality 'from the one followed by the traditional powers' (Wang Yi, 2018a) through the Occidentalist project that has been referred to throughout preceding chapters. This entails the carefully constructed dissemination of an essentialization of Western thought and practice to compare an idealized and essentialized idea of China against.

Here, the five 'nos' established by Xi Jinping (2018b: 2) as the basis for China's relations with Africa provides a good example. These are:

> No interference in African countries pursuit of development paths that fit their national conditions; No interference in African countries' internal affairs; No imposition of our will on African countries; No attachment of political strings to assistance to Africa; No seeking of selfish political gains in investment and financing cooperation with Africa.

Putting the question of the veracity of these claims to one side, on their own, these nos are somewhat facile and are not particular noteworthy. The oft repeated argument that China favours peace, partnerships and dialogue is equally glib as well. They only have significance and importance if somebody else does do what you promise not to do, and isn't partial to peace and friendship. Similarly, there would be no need for Xi (2018a) to say that China will: 'refrain from seeking dominance and reject the zero-sum game. We must refrain from beggaring-thy-neighbor and reject power politics or hegemony with the strong bullying the weak' if others *don't* refrain from acting in this way. Unsurprisingly, others are indeed depicted as behaving in exactly that way. And equally unsurprisingly, those others are either Western countries or the West as some sort of aggregated whole. As an indicative example of the many arguments made in a very similar vein, in explaining the Chinese cultural wisdom that lies behind the CSFM, Li Liyan (2018: 9) contends that:

> The culture of Western countries that advocates hegemony is the way of thinking that stems from this 'zero-sum game'. This culture believes that the enhancement of a country's ability and the increase of wealth can freely humiliate other countries and at the same time cause the decline of wealth in other countries. Under the influence of this culture, Western countries impose themselves at will on others in international exchanges, leading to frequent tragedies of plunder and war around the world.

Moreover, Li argues that this is the 'diplomatic guiding ideology' of 'most countries'. So here we see 'the West' combined into a single thing, with a single modus operandi and a single philosophical and theoretical basis of action. Of course, this is not a universal position and many Chinese scholars and foreign policy officials would be very unhappy with such an aggregation of all things Western into one single entity. But it is an idea and methodology that is not hard to find, often alongside references to the 'outdated Cold-War mentality and zero-sum mindset' that guides Western states. This specific quote comes from previous Foreign Minister and at the time State Councillor, Yang Jiechi (2018a). So it can hardly be thought of as a fringe opinion held only by a handful of scholars publishing in obscure journals.

At the same time, we see the essentialization of China into a single entity too. This China operates from an entirely different and indeed opposite way from the West, inspired by an entirely different and opposite set of motives. This entails defining China in ways that sometimes do not easily correspond with witnessed realities. The idea of China pursuing a development model that places environmental good over economic gain is one example here. Notwithstanding important shifts in Chinese environmental policy in recent years, the rapid growth that is touted as one sign of China's successes was not always accompanied by a concern with the environmental consequences of this growth. And even a shift in emphasis is not the same as solving the environmental problem once and for all. Indeed, there is still a very long way to go. There is also an insistence that Chinese people are inherently inclined to seek harmony and peace and 'do not have the genes of aggression against others' (Liu and Wang, 2017: 15). This might surprise students of Sino–Indian relations. Or of 20th century Chinese history. And students of 19th century Chinese history as well. And those of the Qing Dynasty's replacement of the Ming, or the fragmentation of the Han Dynasty and the Three Kingdoms, or of the Warring States period. Unless, of course, it only refers to violence against others, and internal conflict doesn't count (and the Mongol conquests don't count either because of the Mongols' ethnicity). Here, we should note not only the peaceful 'cultural gene' that Chinese have, but also the implication (and sometimes more than that) that others do not have them. Or even more fundamentally, that others *cannot* have them because they are not Chinese.

The result of this essentialization is the juxtaposition of the Western and Chinese positions, and the philosophical starting points that generate these polar opposite positions. Zhao Kejin and Shi Yan (2018: 38), for example, argue that there are actually two different Western international relations 'models': 'the power politics model led by European countries, which is dominated by the sphere of influence and colonial expansion … [and] the hegemonic political model in which the United States and the Soviet Union were in ideological confrontation and hegemonic struggle after the end of the Second World War'. Even so, these 'traditional' models share the same essential philosophical starting points, and these starting points are the exact opposite of where Chinese thinking and practice starts from. In the traditional 'Western' model, the 'sovereignty principle' is 'mutual equality'. In the NTIR it is 'mutual respect'. While the old 'value principle' is power balancing, the new value is 'fairness and justice'. The old 'Interest Principle' of 'You lose I win' (or zero-sum gains) is replaced by a 'win-win' philosophy. And while the traditional model assumes a 'Relationship Nature' that sees others as enemies, in the NTIR others are seen as partners (Zhao and Shi, 2018: 42). Hence the argument that China has both transcended traditional thinking and also now occupies a new moral high ground.

While this dichotomization between the West and China primarily occurs at a state level of analysis, it bleeds into other levels too. For example, we have already noted the self-proclaimed success of the Chinese political system in dealing with crises. The key here is that the implication is not just that Western democratic models *didn't* respond in the same way, but for some reason they *couldn't*. This is partly explained by looking at those political structures and hierarchies that either allow or prevent quick and decisive action, and comparing states' abilities to control and mobilize key economic resources. It is also partly explained in societal terms too. Here the emphasis often moves from a binary China–West divide to a broader Asia–West one that has clear echoes of previous debates over Asian values. This argument has been made both by Chinese diplomats (Anon, 2020a) and respected Chinese academics like Jia Qingguo (in an interview with Ma Guochan 2020):

> The citizens of these [Asian] countries emphasize self-discipline, and are more rational and pragmatic in their work. They are not as casual and romantic as Europeans and Americans. Compared with Europe and the United States, East Asian society generally pays more attention to group interests ... From the perspective of East Asians, the interests of the group define the interests of the individual, and the interests of the group can only be protected if the interests of the group are protected.

Here, just as lauding Chinese successes works best if less successful Chinese examples are disregarded, Asian superiority also looks more superior if the success of liberal democracies like New Zealand in responding to the crisis are similarly overlooked.

Chinese solutions and governance ideals

So what exactly is it that is being offered as an alternative to these Western ways? As we have already covered the NTIR, GPDCC, and the CSFM in Chapter 3, we do not need to detain ourselves too long on their content here. In many respects, their fundamental essence can be summed up by one rather long quote from Xi's speech at the 19th Party Congress when he argued that China must:

> stay on the path of peaceful development, and continue to pursue a mutually beneficial strategy of opening up. We will uphold justice while pursuing shared interests, and will foster new thinking on common, comprehensive, cooperative, and sustainable security. We will pursue open, innovative, and inclusive development that benefits everyone; boost cross-cultural exchanges characterized by harmony within diversity, inclusiveness, and mutual learning; and cultivate ecosystems based on respect for nature and green development. China will continue its

efforts to safeguard world peace, contribute to global development, and uphold international order. (Xi, 2017e)

As a brief recap of the major components of the new thinking, countries should resolve differences through dialogue, consultation and mutual understanding rather than through conflict, and multilateralism with the UN system at its heart should be promoted to ensure security, rather than unilateral action by the strong (Xi, 2015c). Partnerships rather than alliances should be the order of the day (Wang Yi, 2017d). Rather than try and dominate others and seek to gain an advantage from them, international relations should instead emphasize 'fairness, justice, and win-win cooperation' (Xi, 2017e), with righteousness always winning out over interest in any international interaction (Xu Jin, 2018, 9). While there is cooperation in the existing traditional Western way of doing international relations, competition is seen as the primary impulse, with any cooperation a secondary consequence of competitive impulses. By contrast, for China cooperation is the primary impulse that should come above all else (Liu Jianfei, 2018: 20).

Global governance reform should build institutions that are truly democratic and give all countries – including small and developing countries – an equal say and allow their voices to be truly heard (Xi, 2017b). And all 'countries should adhere to environmentally friendly development and not sacrifice the environment for one-sided pursuit of economic benefits' (Dong Wen, 2018: 62). The three key underpinning starting points of this new IR thinking are 'mutual respect' (*xianghu zunzhong*), 'fairness and justice' (*gongping zhengyi*), and 'cooperation and win-win' relationships (*hezuo gongying*) (Du, 2017: 97).

The China Solution for global governance

When Xi first spoke about the CS in Germany in 2014, it was in the form of a rather general reference to China's contribution to resolving global issues, and in particular, to remedying global governance deficits: 'we will contribute China's wisdom in dealing with contemporary international relations, contribute a China Solution to the improvement of global governance, and contribute to the human society's responses to the challenges of the 21st century' (Xi, 2014). In the first instance, it was the first part of this – the idea of a CS for global governance – that gained most attention and fed into existing debates about China's global ambitions and desire and ability to change the world (Kelly, 2017a; 2017b). It was taken as a statement of intent, with the G20 summit in

Hangzhou in 2016 seen as a key moment when China began to take the lead in promoting its new solutions at a multilateral forum (Liu Chenguang, 2017: 28). As is often the case, the original rather general idea was subsequently given more substance is it began to be defined by Xi, other leaders, and Chinese scholars as they proposed solutions to problems in a range of specific issue areas.

One of the first was Xi's call for internet governance to be built around 'cyber sovereignty' at the first Wuzhen Internet Summit in November 2014 (Liu Xinru, 2016); an example of the sort of China-established international forums to promote Chinese preferences that have become increasingly more commonplace. This argument has a lot in keeping with the defensive intent that has informed Chinese critiques of universalism more generally. Indeed, rather than look like a new agenda for global governance, it looks more like an agenda for not having governance at the global level at all, but instead seeking to establish the highest source of authority at the national level. The proposals might thus be thought of as a block on the ambitions of others to establish other forms and structures that place ultimate governing authority above the nation state.

Perhaps the absence of higher forms of authority and the lack of governance at the global level does constitute a form of global governance in itself. Particularly if its non-existence at the global level and its location elsewhere is agreed by all and there is a shared understanding that the national level is the most appropriate and/or effective site of governance. Or agreed by most if not by all. Unless, that is, sovereign nation states independently decide to transfer authority to a higher body on certain specific policy areas. Governing climate change and the environment might be one example here where there is a willingness in China to see global agreements provide a form of governance (if not the creation of enforceable global authority). Or if, in the case of the reformed UN that China wants to see, the whole point of that higher-level authority is to ensure that sovereignty isn't impinged on without consent.

It is notable that cybersecurity is an issue area where there is no strong pre-existing governance structure, meaning that China can 'actively participate in the formulation of governance rules' (Du, 2017: 100) from the ground up. Other new and as yet ungoverned 'frontier areas' where China might be able to exploit first mover advantages include 'deep sea, polar regions and outer space' (Yang Jiechi, 2018a). Climate change was another early self-identified area where China could make a leading contribution. At the 19th Party Congress, Xi (2017e) argued that '[t]aking a driving seat in international cooperation to respond to climate change, China has become an important participant, contributor, and torchbearer in the global endeavour for ecological civilization'. Studying the climate change and broader environmental governance agenda allows us to put flesh on the general arguments for why China is specially placed to offer solutions that have been outlined above. First, as a great power it can act in ways that others can't. For example, being a great power propelled China into discussions with the US that would not be available to others. The agreement with the US in 2014 on Climate Change and Clean Energy Cooperation (White House, 2014) is proposed as one concrete example of what only cooperation between two great powers can bring about. Second, Xi positioned China as both the representative and defender of developing countries as a whole, pointing to the principle of 'harmony without uniformity' and the different capabilities, responsibilities and goals of developed and developing countries, with the latter having 'legitimate needs … to reduce poverty and improve their people's living standards' (Xi, 2015d).

Third, even before the emergence of CS discourses, China's contemporary commitment to environmental solutions was explained as originating in its ancient traditional culture and thinking, and the emphasis on harmony between man and nature that can be found in Confucianism, Buddhism and Daoism (Pan, 2006). Fourth (and with the scepticism noted above in mind), there is an emphasis on China's recent experiences and successes in 'following a path of green, low-carbon and sustainable development' (Wang Yi, 2019c) and constructing a new ecological civilization that supposedly transcends the previous developmental experiences of earlier developers.[3] This has resulted in a self-assigned moral authority to talk, and also a range of practical policies that others can potentially learn from. We could also add another component here in the way that the withdrawal of the US from the Paris Climate Change agreement created even greater opportunities for the assertion of Chinese global environmental leadership.

Domestic success is also important elsewhere. China's self-declared success in dealing with the COVID-19 pandemic, for example, was touted as providing examples for others that China actively shared through various mechanisms. Notwithstanding the missteps and mistakes that were made in China when the virus was first identified, the pandemic was also thought to have created the opportunity for a greater Chinese global leadership role as well. Not least because of the withdrawal of US support (and funding) for the WHO, and the missteps and mistakes made in the US (and elsewhere) in forming domestic responses. Given the number of people who were once living in poverty in China, it's not surprising that poverty reduction has been given a particular strong focus by China's leaders (Xi, 2015c). Chinese growth successes are thought to give it a degree of legitimacy in the eyes of others, as well as giving China the ability to actively promote development overseas as well. It is also an area where China has one of its longest established formal mechanisms to facilitate 'South-South' learning and share its experiences in the shape of the International Poverty Reduction Centre established in collaboration with the United Nations Development Programme (UNDP) in 2005 (Wu Zhong et al, 2010). Indeed, in a detailed analysis of all of Xi's speeches from 2013–16, development was by far the most mentioned of all the major global issues where China is said to have a leadership role to play (Guo Wei, 2017).

By becoming a major development actor, China is not only showing that development can be done differently – for example, by prioritizing connectivity through what Xi (2018a) called 'integrated development' – but also trying to set agendas for how we conceive of what development actually means. Or more correctly, what it shouldn't mean; the movement towards liberal democracy, the promotion of individual political rights and freedoms, good governance agendas and so on. Here too, China has already put in place institutions designed to provide not just monetary flows, but forms of governance that reflect this philosophy and definition of development through assistance and lending principles. These include the various forums that have been established to coordinate and showcase development relationships with different parts of the world that have been discussed in previous chapters (FOCAC, China-CELAC Forum, the 16/17+1 process, and so on).

The China Solution for development dilemmas

Despite this focus on global governance solutions (externally at least), the example of poverty reduction and development more generally also point to a second understanding of the CS. Here the emphasis is on how the success of the Chinese developmental project provided a direct refutation of Fukuyama's 'End of History' argument. Non-Western and non-neoliberal alternatives were not only alive and well, but generating tremendous developmental successes by ignoring neoliberal prescriptions (Yang Guangbin, 2016). This generated a strand of CS thinking where China's developmental experiences are said to have 'transcended the popular dogma of the capitalist market economy based on private ownership in theory and practice' (Zhang Yu, 2016). As a result, they might now guide development projects in other countries too. Within Chinese discussions of the CS, this second emphasis gained more purchase after Xi's speech on the 95th anniversary of the founding of the CCP in 2016 where he referred specifically to 'a Chinese solution for the exploration of a better social system for mankind'.

Strong state developmentalism did not originate in China. Indeed, as argued elsewhere, it is possible to trace linkages from China today back through the Asian developmental states to German development under Bismarck, and from there back to the American System of the early decades of the1800s (Breslin, 2011). Clearly, there are massive differences between all of these. The Chinese developmental state is very different from the Asian ones that evolved and thrived during the Cold War and even more different still from Germany and the US in the late and early 19th century respectively. But there are strands of logic and broad-brush policy preferences that have filtered down as the lessons of earlier developmental states have been studied in later ones. If the market 'dogma' that China is said to have transcended – a word that comes up time and time again in writing on the CS – really is an accepted truth (as a dogma must be), then it is an only relatively recently accepted one. Taking a broader historical perspective suggests that China is less exceptional in favouring and deploying certain types of economic management and planning than might appear at first sight. And certainly, less exceptional than much of the CS literature often suggests. From this perspective, while the Chinese example does indeed challenge neoliberal assumptions and preferences, in doing so it renews and reinforces the basic starting points of other developmental orthodoxies.

To treat China as different and abnormal gives a false impression of what the normal is that it differs from. In truth, historically, forms of strong state capitalism are much more normal than the dominance of neoliberalism since the late 1970s might lead us to think. So if the goal is to discuss the relative merits of neoliberal approaches compared to more statist forms of capitalism, then it makes sense to view China as just one example (of many) of state developmentalism. But if the goal is instead to create more nuanced understandings of different types of developmental states, then there are big differences between China and previous versions, and it might indeed occupy a category all on its own. In terms of how the CS is spoken of in China – and in the eyes of some who look at China as well – it certainly is treated this way. And when it is pitched as a standalone type or model, then there are three main ways in which the Chinese developmental experience is argued as potentially providing inspiration to others.

The first is to view China as an example of what you can do if you do the same thing that China did. China as inspiration. This is very significant in itself as a means of discrediting the idea of convergence towards a single (neo)liberal model of development. It is also the main way in which China's model has been explained as having salience for others. So here it is not the specifics of Chinese policies that matter, but the simple fact of the model's existence and its perceived success. The second then layers another learning process on top. In the process of working out what works best for you, it might make sense to have a look at some of the specific things that China has done and see if they might have salience for you too. Bearing in mind what has been said above about other developmental states, this might include things that China did that were previously done by others. But in the CS story, these earlier experiences are put to one side, and it is the specifics of the Chinese developmental process that are seen as potentially providing specific concrete lessons.

The third is to treat China's experience as providing something more than just inspiration and options, and as providing a basic starting point that other developmental experiences can build on. As we have already noted above, it is not always as easy to see the roots of previous forms of Marxism in this newly innovated thinking. Nevertheless, there are a number of Marxist theorists in China who do see it in Marxist terms and argue that China's developmental experiences today are the latest endpoint of the evolution of scientific socialism from Marx's original position. Through theoretical and practical innovations, the argument is that China has moved Marxist thinking into a new stage: 'The "China Solution" not only embodies the basic principles of Marxism, but also reflects the characteristics of today's world era and China's development practice. It is a concrete embodiment of Marxism in China and the era, and an important symbol of Marxist theoretical innovation' (Xiao Xinfa, 2018: 26). This could simply take us back to China as an example of what you can do if you too innovate. But in some discourses at least, what China has done means that others no longer need to go back to the original starting point at all.

The guiding ideology for the CCP is Marxism-Leninism rather than the thoughts of Marx and Engels. This is because the original thinking had already been filtered through the Soviet experience by the time that the CCP was formed. Thus, the ideology that Mao (and others) began to apply to Chinese circumstances was not the unadulterated original, but its already adapted and innovated Marxist-Leninist form. The way the CS is sometimes being presented and promoted applies a similar logic. For example, Wu Yuanhua et al (2018: 5) argue that '[h]istorical experience also shows that the road of socialism with Chinese characteristics expands the way for developing countries to modernize by taking into account the development experience, value, and spirit of the socialist road with Chinese characteristics, and combining the actual characteristics of each country'. Just as the Soviet experience filtered Marxism and gave the world a new Marxism-Leninism to build new domestic thinking on, so China now provides that same prior filter for even later developers. What China has done has provided a short cut for others. They can benefit from the way that these original truths have already been filtered through the Chinese experience, and start from there. They can now apply their own concrete circumstances to the truths that China has revealed and develop their own China-influenced (or filtered) guides to action. The first two ways of learning from China imply developing separate and parallel developmental thinking and practice, albeit in version two with lines of influence and emulation that connect them. Figure 6.1 shows that in the third version, there is a direct linear flow that establishes China's path to development as directly providing the basis for others to build their own development paths on. It is not just a case of using the same methodology but directly building on Chinese lessons and successes.

There might be a fourth learning process too. Or perhaps it's a mechanism. One way in which learning takes place is for others to look at China and then adopt one of the three learning and emulation processes. But for all the reasons outlined in this and previous chapters, there is a strong feeling that the major channels of global communication – both formal and informal – do not work in China's favour. Hence the need to expand the China Voice to get positive stories of China across to those who might want to hear them. In this respect, talking about the CS might serve as a means of delivering the message rather than just analysing it. But more specific, concrete and targeted methods are also used as well. In addition to the general articulation of stories of Chinese successes, researchers at the Center for International Knowledge on Development are trying to identify what they think are the most pertinent lessons and messages for other developing countries and disseminating them to target audiences. This process is based on the understanding that it is not the whole China experience that can or should be promoted to others. Rather,

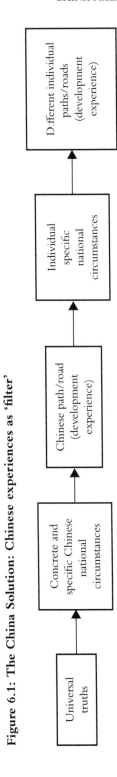

Figure 6.1: The China Solution: Chinese experiences as 'filter'

Universal truths → Concrete and specific Chinese national circumstances → Chinese path/road (development experience) → Individual specific national circumstances → Different individual paths/roads (development experience) specific parts might work on a case by case basis with different lessons for different countries.

Despite this targeted approach, the Chinese argument remains that suggesting things is still very different to enforcing them on unwilling recipients. Quite so. But when added to other forms of knowledge sharing, then the idea that the China Model is actively being touted does begin to have more credence. Particularly when knowledge sharing overwhelmingly entails knowledge only going one way. This might still fall short of actively exporting the model, but it is also more than just passively waiting to see if others want to learn and follow or not.

Towards a Chinese normative order?

Despite having spent considerable time reading the various papers that have informed the discussion above, trying the ideas out at conferences, workshops and seminars, and then writing up this chapter, it's hard to lose the nagging thought that none of it really matters at all. This is partly because the ideas and arguments presented in this chapter would be challenged by other Chinese scholars. It has not tried to be fully representative of the overall nature of the discourse, but to show one part of it that points to a greater Chinese proactivity and a greater appetite for leadership. It is also partly because much of what is being spoken about remains somewhat vague, referring to general aspirational principles that are easy to agree with but rather difficult to concretize.

But more important, talking and doing are not always the same thing. We have already noted above, for example, that despite considerable efforts that have brought tangible results, a new Chinese ecological civilization is still more of an aspiration than a reality. Indeed, in 18 months from the beginning of 2018, the increase in China's coal generated energy supply was greater than the combined reduction in the rest of the world over the same period (Ambrose, 2019). It is only right to applaud successes when they are deserved, and this includes the many positive steps taken towards finding solutions to environmental problems in China. But it is rather premature to claim that the battle has already been won and a new Chinese concept of modernity has emerged as a result.

Moreover, as Lam (2018: 390–91) argues, there is more than one 'strategic narrative' coming from China, and they do not all point in the same direction:

> In speeches on international affairs written for the international community, China projects the soft image of a peace-loving nation, intent on contributing to world peace and sustainable development. However, when the speech topic concerns sensitive issues, such as Chinese sovereignty and security clashes with US and Japanese interests, the tone becomes sharper and more assertive.

As one example, Lin (2019: 42–3) notes that at the same time as Xi was promoting the construction of a CSFM at the 19th Party Congress, he also argued that 'we must put national interests first'. Despite the emphasis on righteousness as the basis of China's international exchanges, this is conditional on others recognizing and accepting China's core interests. And this is quite a big condition. There is also an absence of any sort of notion of what you do if and when the desired for peace and harmony isn't forthcoming. How do you deal with conflict and confrontation if dialogue and discussion doesn't resolve it? Or if two or more countries don't share an acceptance of what are legitimate and accepted core interests? Or if different core interests conflict with each other? If the aspired for world order and type of international relations falls short of reality, then what?

And then we come to the gaping hole in this book; China's military modernization and power capabilities. Despite the insistence that military expansion and modernization is only ever for defensive intent, the size and increased technological basis of China's military forces give it the ability to act in ways that could be less than peaceful. Certainly, for those countries that do not share China's definition of the limits of its sovereign core interests, the expansion of China's military presence in the South China Sea might not presage a future of peace and harmony for all. So there is evidence to suggest that China's behaviour as a great power could be less different from other great powers than the preferred discourse suggests.

Maybe in the short term, though, this is enough. The point is not to construct a working model of global governance overnight. Or maybe even ever. Organizing the world would likely turn out to be a time consuming and expensive endeavour. Rather, it's about sending out messages. Presumably in an ideal world, Xi and the rest of the Chinese leadership would want others to associate themselves with China's goals and buy into China's views of itself. But if that doesn't happen (immediately or at all), then the process of Occidentalism highlights the failings of the status quo ante and the need to find alternatives to it. It represents the rejection of the existing dominant way of doing things and its replacement by a non-Western non-universal and even an anti-universal position.

There is a hierarchy of norms in Chinese thinking with sovereignty at its apex. In certain issue areas, this points to governance being defined and practised at the national level, rather than having any higher-level uniformity of understanding or authority. So even if they do not result in a Sinocentric world order, these initiatives and innovations certainly undermine the ability of others to impose their preferred world view and to build their preferred instruments of global governance. What this suggests, then, is a future of contention in some areas, with China leading the critique of what it depicts as Western-imposed universalism. Not a bipolar future as such, but one where conflict and contention are ever more pronounced. And understanding how the West is being essentialized in this Occidentalist agenda is one of the reasons that a study such as this one maybe does matter.

Another reason that it matters is that studying what is being said in China about the world helps us understand Chinese domestic politics a little bit better as well. The process of Occidentalism entails essentializing China as well as the West. And this essentialized China is one that is increasingly explained as not just unique (as all countries are from this mode of thinking), but uniquely unique. At times it is almost as if there is a genetic difference. Certainly the idea that Chinese think differently from others is now a common assertion at international conferences without any explanation of where this difference might come from. If those others are critical of China it is either because of this difference in thinking, or a lack of understanding, or some sort of combination of both. It is not quite a case of having to be Chinese to understand China, but in extreme cases it can get quite close. Studying Chinese discourses, then, and focusing on extreme cases and examples, might not tell us what the future will be. But it does point to one potential outcome that has a number of backers within the upper echelons of the Chinese political system.

Conclusion

One of the themes that runs through this book is that, every now and again, something is said about China that resonates with an audience and gains popularity through repetition. It crystallizes an emerging but often ill-defined viewpoint or sentiment to become the sort of 'theme of the time' discussed in Chapter 1. Joshua Ramo's identification of a 'Beijing Consensus' is an excellent example. First proposed in an op ed in the *Financial Times* in May 2004 (Ramo, 2004a) and subsequently elaborated in an expanded format for the Foreign Policy Centre in London (Ramo, 2004b), it captured a general feeling, refined it, gave it a hook, and fed it back to a largely receptive audience. Those who looked in detail at what Ramo described as the fundamental elements of the Beijing Consensus were largely unconvinced that it was an accurate reflection of how China's political economy actually worked (Kennedy, 2010). The model as described by Ramo looked more like the aspirations that China's leaders were espousing for what a future model might look like, rather than an accurate reflection of the nature of the political economy at the time. But in some respects, the actual content of the Beijing Consensus was irrelevant. The Beijing Consensus, and the notion of a 'China Model' that succeeded it, both summed up the growing feeling that China might have something that others could learn from to provide an alternative to neoliberal development prescriptions. Moreover, it spoke to more than one audience. Those who had been hoping for an alternative to neoliberalism welcomed it, while supporters of liberal projects – and not just neoliberal ones – were concerned by it. It even started a debate within China itself over whether there really was a replicable model or not.

A revived China threat

Another example is the emergence of the argument that China deliberately deploys a form of 'debt-trap diplomacy'. After Sri Lanka ceded control and ownership of Hambantota Port to China in 2017 after being unable to pay back loans, Brahma Chellaney (2017) argued that this was the result of a deliberate Chinese state strategy. China, he argued, had deliberately made loans so easy to get, and on cheaper terms than those offered by more traditional funders, that a number of developing countries had been lured into overextending themselves. Once the realities of borrowing from China became clear, they had no choice other than to renegotiate their repayment obligations, which resulted in the loss of resources and even sovereignty. In the Sri Lanka case, Chellaney claimed that this took the form of China taking control of a strategically important site on foreign soil that 'straddles Indian Ocean trade routes linking Europe, Africa, and the Middle East to Asia'. And it was an asset that China would not have been able to secure through other diplomatic or financial means.

The idea of a Chinese 'debt trap' existed before 2017. Chellaney (2015) had even used it himself two years earlier quoting the Sri Lankan President's fears of what might happen as reliance on Chinese finances grew. In the intervening two years, however, perceptions of China had shifted in many parts of the world, and its second airing caught the 'zeitgeist' of the moment (Ferchen, 2018) and became an accepted and reproduced 'meme' (Brautigam, 2020). It was even repeated by US Vice President Pence (2018) in October 2018 in a speech on the administration's China policy, when he suggested that the Hambantota Port might 'soon become a forward military base for China's growing blue-water navy'. This suggests that this specific theme of the time had become part of the US government's strategic thinking informing Washington's policy towards China. The announcement by the US administration of the International Development Finance Corporation in October 2018 as a new mechanism for delivering foreign aid (in part to counter China's growing economic influence) suggests that it might also have informed US policy towards other parts of the world as well as to China itself.

The 'debt trap' argument fed into wider concerns over the consequences of Chinese investment in developing economics, and was taken as evidence that this investment represented a form of neocolonialism. This argument had been around since at least the mid-2000s in academic debates,[1] but was given a boost in popular discourses with the then US Secretary of State Hilary Clinton's warnings of new colonial dangers for Africa in 2011 (though not specifically mentioning China by name; Quinn, 2011). The idea of a debt trap was also consistent with a broader apprehension over how the BRI might be used to further Chinese geopolitical agendas. If you were already concerned, then Hambantota provided confirming evidence of why you were right to be concerned. And it also both built on and contributed to a growing sense that there was an appetite to push back against Chinese initiatives in the US and in some of the countries along the Belt and Road (Rolland, 2019).

So it was not so much a case of debt trap diplomacy emerging as a new theme of the time as it acting as a vehicle for the resurrection of a longer standing theme: the idea of a China Threat. To be sure, it is not always clear what China is being identified as a threat to; perhaps a different type of threat to different things for different people. But again, precision doesn't really matter. These themes and memes are never exact and precise or have a shared meaning. Indeed, the more pervasive ones are pervasive exactly because they sound right to people who have different interests and different concerns.

The arguments revisited

The debt-trap discourse provides a useful way into revisiting a number of the core arguments that were identified in the introduction and have (hopefully) been evident throughout the previous chapters. For example, it fits squarely with the idea that location matters. It might simply be a coincidence that Chellaney is a renowned Indian strategist and policy researcher, and that the Indian government has long been anxious about Chinese objectives in India's own neighbourhood, and keen to convince others to be anxious too. But it probably isn't. Moreover, while there might in general be an increased focus on the idea of China as a threat or challenge, that doesn't mean that it is thought of this way everywhere. And even where it is, the nature and extent of that threat and challenge differs from place to place, as does the range of responses that are being proposed.

The way that China's leaders have signalled their intentions has also helped shine a new light on them. Both 'them' in terms of the leaders and 'them' in terms of the intentions. While this might have led some to rethink their positions on China, pre-existing starting points also play a role too. If you already had suspicions, then the way that intentions have been signalled will not have exactly assuaged them. Maybe China could not have simply gone on with a low-profile strategy while simultaneously increasing its global economic reach and significance under the radar. Surely people would have noticed this presence eventually. But the whole point about articulating plans as loudly and frequently as possible, and asking others to endorse them, is to get those others to take what you are saying seriously. And they have. The problem for the Chinese leadership is the serious consequences that have often subsequently been inferred are not always the ones that they wanted to signal and imply. It is an example that also suggests that the location of the perceiver matters.

In addition, although there are already many real consequences of COFDI and development-type economic assistance to study, this remains a discourse that is as much about the future as it is about the present. It is about constructing an idea of what the future will look like unless things change now; an attempt to construct an image of the future to shape current policy. The extrapolation of current patterns into future realities is thought of as feasible and likely because the rhetoric of Chinese ambitions is supported by the reality of how China's material global role and impact has changed in recent years. In particular, the growth of COFDI, the speed of this growth, and changes in where this investment goes (or wants to go) has been the biggest reason that the consequences of China's continuing rise have been rethought in some parts of the world.

The debt trap hypothesis should also make us think about the way that evidence is sought and found to prove hypotheses. That's because it's really not that easy to find the firm evidence necessary to prove this somewhat problematic concept despite its popularity (Brautigam, 2020). This is not an attempt to dismiss all or any concerns with the way that Chinese loans and other projects are being funded and implemented along the Belt and Road and elsewhere. Far from it. There are a number of clear and very important problems and consequences of the growth of Chinese aid and development related financing (including BRI endeavours). A number of countries' debts really have increased as a result of their financial relationship with China. Laos is a particularly notable example, with the IMF raising the risk of it facing 'external debt distress' from moderate to high in 2017, largely as a result of external borrowing from China (and also from Thailand; IMF, 2017a). Hurley et al (2018) suggest that eight countries on the Belt and Road became 'severely vulnerable' to debt distress as a direct result of funding from projects that were specifically identified as Belt and Road ones. And it is probably much more of a problem than the official figures suggest. The opacity of Chinese overseas financing data and the blurring of commercial and aid projects means that there is considerable 'hidden debt' in a number of recipient countries that could shape their relations with China in the future (Horn et al, 2019). There is also clear evidence that a number of countries are facing problems repaying loans, seeking ways of renegotiating obligations, and pulling out of previously agreed projects. All of this is true. But none of this is evidence in itself of a deliberate debt-trap diplomacy strategy rather than problems that emerge from other causes. Assuming a deliberate debt-trap diplomatic strategy results in a focus on the wrong drivers and at times the wrong actors. Outcomes are assumed to be intentional, and consequence is mistakenly presented as evidence to support a pre-existing perception of intent that can result in misguided predictions of future action; and as a result, misguided policy too.

In the failed attempt to find evidence that might support the debt trap hypothesis, a couple of issues emerged that not only have wider salience for the study of Chinese power in this book, but also might be useful for other studies of China's global role and impact as well. On one level, at an extreme, just concentrating on what China wants and does can lead to the agency of the recipient state being underestimated or even discounted. While there is no denying the power that the Chinese side have given the financial resources that they are prepared to use, there is evidence from on the ground research to show that local recipient actors are far from powerless and passive. Rather, studies spanning a number of years now show how the recipients' interests instead play very important roles in shaping the nature of the relationship (Brautigam, 2009; Bunte, 2019; Corkin, 2014). As such, if we want to focus on why projects are accepted that don't make financial sense in the long run, we need to turn our attention to matters other than just Chinese objectives or the development desperation of China's partners. There are a range of other motivations that draw recipient countries into dealing with China, including the consequences of distributing resources, domestic electoral fortunes, and straightforward personal gain. If we want to know how Chinese interests might change the world, then of course we have to try and identify what those interests are and how they might be pursued. But we also need to think what others want too, and how they respond to Chinese initiatives.

On another level, different conclusions can be a result of different focuses of analysis, and can result from answering different questions. If you are primarily interested in the consequences of interaction with China, then maybe the cause of those consequences doesn't matter that much. But, while the debt-trap thesis sees the failure of projects as the successful utilization of Chinese financial power and strength, studying Chinese debates and discourses reveals a stronger emphasis on Chinese weakness and at times policy failure. Not every China funded project that faces financial difficulties results in Chinese ownership of previously sovereign assets. Quite often, the outcome is that losses are written off by the Chinese partner, and proposed future projects are cancelled by the now hesitant recipient state. The Rhodium Group found that when defaults occur, Chinese leverage is actually often very limited. Asset seizures are very rare compared to other means of refinancing and even debt forgiveness, and 'many of the cases reviewed involved an outcome in the favor of the borrower' (Kratz et al, 2019). If this was a coherent and deliberate strategy, then we might expect Chinese voices to clamour for more projects that will fail, thus leading to an increased overseas debt dependency on China. The reality is that there has instead been a move towards rethinking 'overseas lending practices' to try to prevent the expansion of 'the debt burdens of developing countries' (Hornby, 2019), and to strengthen oversight and due diligence procedures to avoid further failures and financial problems in the future. The creation of a new China International Development Cooperation Agency in April 2018 was largely a response to the previous lack of coordination (including between different state agencies), but also partly because of the proliferation of risky (and at times illegal) practices in failing overseas projects (Rudyak, 2018). The goal is to *reduce* the possibility of defaults, not to increase them.

There might indeed be overarching objectives for making it easier to move money overseas, and a grand desire for what the BRI might lead to in the end. But this does not mean that each and every project is initiated by the state to bring about these goals, and is directly controlled by it. Where the debt-trap understanding sees strategy and coherence, if you study China from the inside out then the picture that emerges is rather different. Policies might be better coordinated than before Xi came to power (particularly domestic and foreign ones) but it is still not hard to find uncoordinated scattergun and haphazard exuberance. Political considerations (gaining friendship and support through 'prestige projects') or a desire to take advantage of perceived BRI opportunities (or both) have resulted in projects that were developed too quickly by a diverse set of actors. Many of them had little or no knowledge of the countries they were dealing with or experience in investing overseas, resulting in inadequate planning, risk assessment, and project management (Akpaninyie, 2019).

There is another issue too. While not denying (again) that it is important to focus on what Chinese are doing and what they want, there is a risk that this can make it seem as if China is the only actor. And whatever it is that is being looked at, it's unlikely that this is the case. For example, while a number of Pacific island states have considerable debt burdens, China is the minority creditor for all except Tonga, with Japan and multilateral institutions the major source of loans and grant aid (Rajah et al, 2019). If we are worried about the causes and consequences of debt in these countries, then China is *part* of the story and part of any potential solution. But not all of it. Chinese investment on the African continent at the end of the 2010s was also less than that originating from (in rank order) France, the United States and the UK (UNCTAD, 2019). The relative importance of China and other states can vary from year to year, but the overall message is the same. China is not even the biggest single source of investment on the continent, let alone the only one. And as noted in Chapter 4, China's stock of FDI in the UK, Germany, Australia and the US does not (yet) put it in the top ten in any of them, despite significant increases over a relatively short period of time. That others are doing it too might sound so obvious that it doesn't need to be mentioned at all. But after reflecting on the nature of some discussions of China's global impact in some venues over recent years, then devoting a paragraph to outlining what should be obvious does seem appropriate here.

Shaping the debate? Constructing a national image

After finding no evidence to support the debt trap diplomacy argument in BRI transport projects, Jing and Sheng (2019) concluded that its origins, popularity and potential longevity lay not so much in economic activity as in public relations. If they are right – and the evidence suggests that they are – this suggests that all the efforts that have been put into telling a good story of China have failed. Once more, and with apologies for repeating this, it is important to qualify this statement by adding that this is the case in some parts of the world at least. And this suffix should be taken as read now as a qualifier for the other broad brushstroke statements made in the rest of this conclusion. These efforts might indeed have persuaded some about Chinese intent and ambition. But it's not easy to find people who were previously concerned about the consequences of China's rise (particularly in the West) who have changed their mind.

Perhaps that was never really possible. But it's not just that Chinese soft power initiatives have failed to impose Chinese narratives over dominant discourses about China's rise. It's that the general tone of the debate has moved in the opposite direction, and there is even more suspicion and concern about Chinese intent now than before China's leaders embraced a nation branding strategy. This is in no small part a result of changes in the way that material economic relations with China have changed for many states. China does not always look like a new and different type of great power pursuing win-win outcome based on righteousness rather than national interest in some of places that have received Chinese finance. And even less so where there is a perceived potential security challenge from China too. Moreover, it is not just on the Belt and Road or in debt vulnerable developing economies that flows of Chinese money have become increasingly significant and increasingly politicized too. When viewed in light of Chinese commitments to change the nature of the domestic economic growth model and to achieve leadership in key technological sectors, COFDI can look very much like a means of increasing China's resources in a global competition for comprehensive national power.

And ironically, this nation branding and self-titled soft power strategy in itself has been one of the causes of this shift. The problem here is not so much the message as the messenger. The very fact that it is a concerted and well-funded state project simply refocuses attention on the state and pre-existing assumptions about what it wants. Within China, it is seen as being a defensive and corrective necessity, emerging from China's relative weakness and the dominance of others in controlling global media agendas and political discourses. From the outside, it is taken as a sign of China's new strength and confidence. At an extreme, not just an attempt to shape discussions and insert Chinese voices into debates over issues like Xinjiang or Tibet, but also to prevent these issues from even being discussed at all.

Material sources of discursive power

Why does this matter? If you don't agree with a particular narrative of China, then disseminate and promote an alternative. If you are really worried about certain institutions, then close them down or don't renew the arrangement. This is exactly what has happened with a number of CIs. Or deploy the sovereignty principle and ensure that what is being said and done accords with national laws and regulations. This is what happened when CGTN was accused of breaching UK media regulations on impartiality over the reporting of the political turmoil in Hong Kong in 2019. So why worry if China is trying to promote itself in certain ways, or trying to establish its preferred narratives or parameters of debate in different places?

It matters because the ideational is connected to the material. Or rather, it is widely assumed to be connected to the material.

Censuring China can and does lead to Chinese displeasure. So if CIs are closed down, or Chinese broadcasters punished or banned, or if strong counterarguments are made in opposition to favoured Chinese discourses, or if China's 'soft power' strategy in itself is criticized, then this might have other consequences. The emphasis here is on *might*, as there is no strong evidence that hurting the feelings of the Chinese people does have significant economic penalties over the longer term for countries. But it can in the short term, and has had real consequences for those companies discussed in Chapter 5. If these concerns about the consequences of displeasing China result in self-censorship, then Chinese policy has been successful. Chinese discursive power has increased both in terms of the ability to prevent discussions of things China doesn't want discussing, and also in reducing criticism of Chinese practice (particularly criticism of China's domestic political regime). Crucially, though, it is not the specific attempt to increase this discursive power through the soft power agenda that has generated this success. To reiterate the argument made above, this has been counterproductive. Rather, it is Chinese material power that has generated these consequences. Or if there is an ideational dimension to this power, it is through external projections of what China's power will look like in the future producing action and/or inaction, rather than the specific things the Chinese state itself has done in the ideational sphere. Talking about Chinese power and assuming it in the future has become a source of that power in itself.

Towards a non-Western world order?

The success of the attempt to promote China Solutions and an alternative vision of future global order is rather difficult to assess. It is not surprising that there is an appetite for change. The global financial crisis and the consequences of intervention in the Middle East and north Africa would have been enough on their own to raise questions about the morality and efficacy of the status quo ante even without any Chinese action. Moreover, it's not just in China where there is a feeling that the rules have been written by others, and that these rules reflect world views, histories, philosophies and interests that are not as universal as they are often claimed to be. The desire to keep others out of domestic political and economic systems is not unique to China either. And the election of President Trump and the subsequent step back from US multilateral commitments created a gap in some global governance forms as well. As argued in Chapter 6, it's also quite hard to argue against the sort of things that are being proposed by China's leaders. Who wouldn't want to live in a world of peace and harmony where morality and righteousness guide actions towards mutually beneficial outcomes? It would certainly be a brave leader that proposed the goal of constructing a world built on hegemony, inequity, conflict and submission instead.

Maybe just not being the West is enough to make China's world view attractive. Or if not enough in itself, then maybe actively constructing an essentialized idea of what that West is and what it stands for serves the purpose. At the very least, it might undermine support for the status quo and make it harder for others to promote and/or impose their preferences, even if this does not automatically translate into active support for Chinese alternatives. Indeed, once you start thinking about what it actually is that Xi and others are proposing, it's difficult to go much beyond the aspirational. It really is not clear what can and should be done to find remedies and solutions to conflicts if the desired for peaceful CSFM doesn't come about. Similarly, as I have argued before, if there is something that we can clearly identify as a Chinese Model, again it's best thought of as establishing what China is not, and thus what others don't have to be as well:

> it is not big bang reform and shock therapy; it is not a process where economic liberalization necessarily leads to democratization; it is not jettisoning state control over key sectors; it is not full (neo-)liberalization (particularly in financial sectors); it is not the western way of doing things; it is not following a model or a prescription; it is not being told what to do by others; and it is not telling others what to do. (Breslin, 2011: 1338–9)

The COVID-19 pandemic and (studying) China's rise

Although the coronavirus outbreak became the overwhelmingly dominant issue in Chinese politics in 2020, it doesn't seem quite right to refer to it just as another theme of the time. This is in part because it might trivialize what became a tragedy for millions of people across the world. And even those who were not personally touched by tragedy in the real meaning of the world suffered distress, uncertainty and often financial loss. To call it a 'theme' simply doesn't capture the scale and depth of the impact of the pandemic, nor the fact that this impact will be felt in many different ways for many years to come. And as the scale of the catastrophe clearly illustrates, this was not just a China story. It might have started as one.

In some tellings, it finishes as a China story as well as well, as the search for explanations of what happened (and why) return to Wuhan. But for many, the immediate questions that were being asked as the pandemic spread were about different national responses (and failings) rather than what China did (or just what China did alone).

However, while the scale and importance of the pandemic means that it is more than just another theme of the time, it does share some of the features of the other era defining themes that have been considered in this book. As well as being too important in itself simply to overlook, as with the example of the debt-trap, the outbreak also acts as another excellent case study for exploring the main arguments and understandings that have underpinned the analysis throughout.

The coronavirus outbreak was an example of how an unexpected exogenous shock can rock the political system and raise questions over its resilience and fitness for purposes. Indeed, to call it exogenous to the political system itself might not be correct at all. The system did not incubate the virus itself, but it did incubate the political culture that resulted in the early attempts to warn of an impending crisis being silenced. Li Wenliang was one of those who tried to raise the alarm only to be accused of making 'false comments' that could disturb 'the social order'. His death on 7 February 2020 from the virus did not pass unmarked, with China's online community not only expressing grief, but many of them calling for more freedom of speech. Over the years, a number of other shocks and scandals have similarly led to questions being asked about the ability of the regime to protect its people: either through inadequate procedures that allowed corners to be cut and/or regulations to be ignored (for example, the contaminated baby milk crisis of 2008, the Wenzhou train crash of 2011, and the faulty vaccines scandal of 2018); trying to suppress the real extent of a problem (SARS in 2003); or to hide the real cause of them (the Fanglin school explosion of 2001 and the Wenzhou train crash again); or through preventing the aggrieved from organizing to find out the truth and seek justice (after the Wenchuan earthquake in 2008); or through a combination of any or all of the above.

In the past, these reactions have typically been short lived and very much focused on individual events. Questions have been asked about what caused the specific problems in each case, rather than about the nature of the political system more generally. Moreover, as often noted, the Chinese word for 'crisis' is a combination of the characters for danger (*wei*) and opportunity (*ji*).[2] As Xiao Yuefan (2013) has shown, the CCP has become quite adept at using crises to its own advantage by controlling the narrative. The party – and particularly the central party leadership – emerges as the solution to problems that were outside its ability to previously control because they were a result of natural causes, or because of things that people in other (lower) parts of the administrative hierarchy were doing wrong. Or in the case of the global financial crisis, the result of inferior and ineffective financial governance in advanced Western economies.

In the case of the coronavirus, once it was clear that there really was an urgent issue that needed addressing, it was addressed with considerable urgency. A joint Chinese and WHO report on the response to the outbreak noted Xi Jinping's leadership of the outbreak response, and referred to it as 'perhaps the most ambitious, agile and aggressive disease containment effort in history' (WHO, 2020: 16). It also argued that this response provided 'vital lessons for the global response', but that 'much of the global community is not yet ready, in mindset and materially, to implement the measures that have been employed to contain covid-19 in China' (WHO, 2020: 19). While some outside China expressed concern about undue Chinese influence over WHO, the Chinese media was keen and quick to report it as external praise and validation for the state's response. As we saw in Chapter 5, it also trumpeted what China was doing to support the pandemic response elsewhere, and the media and Ministry of Foreign Affairs went on the offensive to defend China from external criticism; particularly, but not only, from the US.

So does the coronavirus outbreak reveal fundamental weaknesses in the Chinese political system (or its political culture), or the state's ability to flexibly respond to unexpected challenges through the mass mobilization of people and resources (in ways that others can't)? Or does it point to the emergence of Chinese aspirations for a form of Chinese global health leadership? The answer is all three of these at the same time. Where the emphasis is placed in any analysis depends on the sort of questions that the analyser wants to ask and the primary focus of their intellectual agenda. Questions about China lead to a focus on the first two possibilities while questions about the impact of China on the world lead to a focus on the third. Pre-existing starting points also play a role; for example, in shaping which side of the dichotomized understanding of the political system you come down on – fundamentally flawed or effective? Or influencing whether you think Chinese global health leadership could be a good thing or not.

Events can make fools of any soothsayer, and inevitable futures can turn out not to be inevitable at all. But ultimately, we will probably think of the pandemic as acting as a magnifying glass rather than a microscope.

Rather than allowing us to identify something we couldn't see without the microscope, the magnifying glass makes things that we had already identified much clearer and/or bigger than they had appeared before. For example, it has hardened negative perceptions of China among those who were already negative, and given the increasingly sceptical something more to be sceptical about. So might the pandemic ultimately represent the ordering moment that Kupchan (2012: 182) argues has been absent in the transition from unipolarity? The sort of moment normally provided by post-war settlements over the centuries, but in the case of the end of the Cold War was a less precise but similarly defining moment. A moment when alliances and preferences become hardened and fixed in a new world order? A moment when Chinese triumphalism and Occidentalism creates clearly defined and fixed global schisms? Possibly. But despite the identification of a number of cleavages between China and the West (whatever that means) in the previous chapters, the eighth argument of the introduction still sounds about right.

Alastair Iain Johnston (2019) has gone further than most in trying to identify what the China challenge might mean in different policy arenas. The patchiness he identifies in part reflects differential levels of Chinese (dis)satisfaction with different parts of the global order. Or in Johnston's conception, rather than different elements of a single order, with a variety of different governance orders. It also in part reflects the broader international environment within which China's rise is taking place. Unlike during the Cold War, there is no need for states to choose a partner and to stick with it in a holistic alliance or bloc. It is very possible to develop a security alliance with the US, for example, but to still develop strong and deep economic relations with China. Or for countries that are rather concerned about China's territorial claims and military action in the South China Sea to be major recipients of Chinese money. Or for India and China to work together with others to establish the BRICS New Development Bank while continuing to view each other with suspicion in the security realm and over relations with Pakistan; and at times even to fight each other.

What this suggests, then, is not the transition to a Chinese world order – whatever that might be – anytime soon. Rather, it suggests an ongoing process of multiple challenges, negotiations and shifting constellations of alliances and power across different issue areas. Certain constellations of power and interest are likely to be seen across these policy domains in ways that might have some elements of a bipolar order. But they will coexist with elements of a multipolar one. And indeed, with some elements of a depolarized and more fragmented order too. This might not be a world that China can easily lead or dominate. However, it is likely to be one where Chinese decisions and objectives will be an important determining factor. And because of this, it will be a world where it will be very hard indeed for others to lead and dominate instead.

APPENDIX

China's New Thinking: An Annotated List of Key Sources

Date	Event	Relevance/Message	Source
March 2011	12th Five Year Plan	Established participating in global economic governance as a long-term development strategy.	Bi (2017)
Nov 2012	18th Party Congress	Hu Jintao calls for the creation of a global CSFM.	Hu Jintao (2012)
March 2013	Xi's Talk at Moscow Institute of IR	Xi advocates 'new type of international relations with win-win cooperation at the core'.	FMPRC (2013a); Liu Jianfei (2018)
Sept 2013	Wang Yi's Comments on Xi's participation at St Petersburg G20 Summit	Refers to Xi's 'important discourse about the governance of the world economy' and promises more Chinese wisdom and solutions for the world's problems.	FMPRC (2013b)
Oct 2013	Conference on Neighbourhood Diplomacy	First ever conference on the theme; Xi calls for a regional CSFM to 'take root'.	FMPRC (2013b)
March 2014	Xi's Speech at Körber Foundation in Berlin	Xi's first use of 'China Solution'.	Xi (2014)
Nov 2014	Central Conference on Work Relating to Foreign Affairs	Xi establishes goals for a new role in world affairs; emphasis on becoming a global governance reformer; promotion of policy of partnerships rather than alliances.	Ruan (2015); Hu (2019)

Date	Event	Relevance/Message	Source
Jan 2015	Xi's Speech at 20th collective study group of the 18th Central Political Bureau	On the need for constant theoretical reflection and innovation in the face of changing domestic and international circumstances.	Xi (2015a)
March 2015	Xi's Speech at Bo'ao Forum	Calls for a Community of Common Destiny for Asia.	Xi (2015b)
Sept 2015	Xi's Speech at UN General Assembly	Promotion of CSFM; Commitment to UN being at the heart of any new governance structure.	Xi (2015c)
Sept 2015	Xi's Speech as host of the Roundtable on South-South Cooperation at UN headquarters in NY	Importance of South-South collaboration and 'uniting and cooperating with the vast number of developing countries is the unshakable foundation of China's foreign relations'. Announcement of a number of development assistant packages.	FMPRC (2015)
Oct 2015	Communique of 5th Plenum of 18th CC	first proposed the term 'institutional discourse power' (*zhiduxing huayuquan*) and the need to increase it in global economic governance.	CCP (2015)
Oct 2015	Xi's Keynote Address to High-Level Forum on Poverty Reduction, Beijing	China will provide Chinese wisdom and a China Solution to help reduce global poverty.	Xi (2015c); Wu, Wu and Li (2018)
Nov 2015	Xi at Paris Climate Change Summit	China's Commitment to effective climate change governance through domestic reform and the promotion of 'harmony without uniformity' allowing developing countries to pursue their own solutions.	Xi (2015d)
Dec 2015	Xi's Talk at New Year's Tea Party of the National Committee of the Chinese People's Political Consultative Conference	The importance of promoting China's voice and a China Solution and new contributions to peace and development.	Xi (2015e)

Date	Event	Relevance/Message	Source
Dec 2015	Xi's New Year's Eve Message	Refers to a demand for a China Solution from the international community.	Xi (2015f)
May 2016	Xi's Speech at Symposium on Philosophy and Social Sciences	On the 'unique advantage' China has because of its cultural tradition 'distinctive ideological system', 'intellectual wisdom and rational speculation' 'accumulated for thousands of years'.	Xi (2016a)
July 2016	Xi's Speech at 95th Anniversary of Founding of CCP	On the need for continuous innovation in Marxist theory to meet the reality of the times, and on promoting core cultural values and national spirit. China's 'sacred duty' to 'promote the peaceful development of the world' and 'contribute Chinese wisdom for improving global governance' and build a CSFM.	Xi (2016b)
Sept 2016	Xi at G20 Summit in Hangzhou	A total of 17 speeches and statements establishing China as a global governance reformer, including a commitment to G20 as a vehicle for change and an open global economy and CSFM.	Xi (2016c)
Jan 2017	Xi at Davos	Commitment to open global trading system, innovation should be the driver of global economic growth; 'we should develop a model of fair and equitable governance'.	Xi (2017a)
Jan 2017	Xi at UN Office in Geneva	Importance of sovereign equality as the basis for global order; 'China is the first country to make partnership-building a principle guiding state-to-state relations'.	Xi (2017b)

Date	Event	Relevance/Message	Source
Feb 2017	UN	CSFM written into a UN resolution for the first time on the social dimension of the new partnership for Africa's development.	Yuan Peng (2018)
March 2017	UN Human Rights Council 37th Session, Geneva	UN adopts two resolutions (on the realization in all countries of economic, social and cultural rights and the right to food) which include calls to build a CSFM.	Yu (2018)
May 2017	Xi at Belt and Road Forum	The importance of policy coordination with other states and their plans and objectives; the importance of innovation driven growth.	Xi (2017c)
July 2017	Yang Jiechi on implementing Xi's Thought	Xi tapped into Chinas unique culture and history; importance of communicating Chinese ideas to the world; emphasis on four self-confidences.	Yang Jiechi (2017)
Sept 2017	Xi at Xiamen BRICS Summit	BRICS as a 'champion of development'; BRICS countries have responsibilities to uphold peace and security and take part in global governance.	Xi (2017d)
Sept 2017	Wang Yi in *Study Times*	CSFM an 'overarching aspiration' that started for the region but now expanded to the world; Xi's thought based in Marxism and has 'transcended' Western theories of IR.	Wang Yi (2017a)
Sept 2017	Wang Yi at UN General Assembly	NTIR and CSFM Xi's vision for the future order China wants; UN is central but needs to be more democratic and promote equality.	Wang Yi (2017b)

Date	Event	Relevance/Message	Source
Oct 2017	Xi at 19th Party Congress	Major country diplomacy with Chinese characteristics a key element of The Thought on Socialism with Chinese Characteristics for a New Era, 'which aims to foster a new type of international relations and build a community with a shared future for mankind'. Building a CSFM 13th out of 14 in the essence of Xi Jinping thought; origins of the new approach in Chinese history and culture and the Five Principles of Peaceful Co-existence.	Xi (2017e)
Dec 2017	Wang Yi at opening ceremony of the first South-South Human Rights Forum, Beijing	'[W]e need to promote human rights through development. The right to development is the primary human right for developing countries.'	Wang Yi (2017c)
Dec 2017	'Beijing Declaration', at the First South–South Human Rights Forum, Beijing	Each state should do what works for it: 'The right to subsistence and the right to development are the primary basic human rights.'	SSHRF (2017)
Dec 2017	Wang Yi at Opening of Symposium on International Developments and China's Diplomacy in 2017	The importance of building functional partnerships (and not alliances) and building a new type of international relations. China already practising what it promotes. A commitment to protecting Chinese nationals and economic interests overseas; CSFM has origins in 5,000 years of history.	Wang Yi (2017d)
Jan 2018	Wang Yi at China-CELAC Forum	China as sharing its 'developmental dividends' with others; China's continued growth a developmental contribution to others.	Wang Yi (2018a)

Date	Event	Relevance/Message	Source
May 2018	Xi at Bo'ao Forum for Asia	The importance of 'top level planning' to consider new circumstances and develop new practices; the bankruptcy of Cold War mentality and zero-sum thinking; build a CSFM; on China being open to increased imports.	Xi (2018a)
May 2018	Xi at the National Conference on Environmental Protection	Outlines targets for taking the 'Development of an Ecological Civilization to a New Stage'.	Xi (2019f)
June 2018	Xi at SCO Summit in Qingdao	SCO has 'achieved a major breakthrough in the theories and practices of international relations' and 'created a new model for regional cooperation'; move towards a NTIR.	Xi (2018b)
June 2018	CCP Foreign Affairs Work Conference	'Xi Jinping thought on diplomacy of socialism with Chinese characteristics for a new era' becomes fundamental guideline for international interactions; Xi affirms a readiness to take a leadership role in reforming global governance. CSFM to 'make the global governance system fairer and more reasonable'.	FMPRC (2018); Yang Jiechi (2018a)
July 2018	Yang Jiechi at Seventh World Peace Forum, Tsinghua University, Beijing	China as anchor and engine of global growth; China taking concrete action in aiding development and seeking settlements to conflicts; cyberspace, deep sea, polar regions and outer space as new arenas of governance.	Yang Jiechi (2018a)
July 2018	Vice Minister of Foreign Affairs Le Yucheng at Seventh World Peace Forum, Tsinghua University, Beijing	CSFM a 'blueprint' designed by Xi for mankind built on Chinese history and civilization; UN system and G20 key vehicles for global governance reform.	Le (2018)

Date	Event	Relevance/Message	Source
July 2018	Xi at BRICS Business Forum in Johannesburg	Importance of developing country views being heard when creating new governance rules for innovation, trade and investment, intellectual property protection, cyberspace, outer space and the polar regions; commitment to China's openness to the global economy.	Xi (2018c)
Sept 2018	Xi at FOCAC Summit	Friendship first in seeking cooperation; China has a 'mission' to make contributions for mankind; 'China will share more of its development practices with Africa'; announces a range of different cooperation initiatives.	Xi (2018d)
Sept 2018	Wang Yi at UN General Assembly	China's growth as a key contribution to global development.	Wang Yi (2018b)
Oct 2018	Vice Minister of Foreign Affairs Zhang Jun in *China Daily* on Human Rights	China's own history of poverty and development gives it key insights; right to development the most important human right.	Zhang Jun (2018)
Oct 2018	Yang Jiechi at Valdai Discussion Group	Cold War mentality still too dominant; values should not be exported and imposed; respect for cultural diversity the key.	Yang Jiechi (2018b)
Nov 2018	Xi at Import Expo in Shanghai	'New Era, Shared Future' the slogan of the expo; importance of opposing anti-globalization and staying open to others and a commitment that China will open further; G20, APEC, SCO and BRICS should play a greater role in building a fairer and more equitable global economic governance system.	Xi (2018e)

Date	Event	Relevance/Message	Source
Dec 2018	Wang Yi at Symposium on The International Situation and China's Foreign Relations	Importance of South-South cooperation for China; China has a 'mission' to take global responsibility.	Wang Yi (2018c)
Jan 2019	Wang Yi at FMPRC New Year Reception	China's commitment to openness 'on the right side of history', and China an 'important upholder of the international order' in the face of unilateralism and protectionism; 'Building partnerships is a creative approach China has adopted in developing state-to-state relations'.	Wang Yi (2019a)
April 2019	Xi at Second Belt and Road Forum	Emphasis on consultation and joint development, green and 'high standard' cooperation; infrastructure the 'bedrock' of connectivity; strong focus on giving greater foreign access to the Chinese economy and protecting intellectual property.	Xi (2019a)
April 2019	Xi at Belt and Road Leaders' Roundtable	Emphasis on 'working with all parties' as BRI evolves and 'the principle of extensive consultation, joint contribution and shared benefits'.	Xi (2019b)
May 2019	Xi at Conference on Dialogue of Asian Civilizations	Rich historical experience of cross-cultural interactions; importance of inclusivity, diversity, cooperation and mutual learning in Asia; key role for people-to-people interactions, including through tourism.	Xi (2019c)

Date	Event	Relevance/Message	Source
June 2019	Xi at SCO Heads of State Meeting	Calls for more cooperation in more areas – digital economy, e-commerce, AI, big data, culture, education, tourism, sports and media, and people-to-people exchanges (particularly among the young and women).	Xi (2019d)
June 2019	Xi at Conference on Interaction and Confidence-Building Measures in Asia	Repeats China's commitments to peace and development; calls for conclusion 'at an early date' of the Regional Comprehensive Economic Partnership and other forms of regional integration.	Xi (2019e)
June 2019	Wang Yi at FOCAC follow-up meeting	Rejects neocolonialism and debt-trap accusations as an unfounded attempt to vilify and undermine Sino-African relations; reaffirms five 'no' policy towards Africa.	Wang Yi (2019b)
June 2019	Xi Jinping at Osaka G20 Summit	'Reform and innovation the impetus for growth'; need for WTO reform; Belt and Road as a means of breaking 'development bottlenecks'.	Xi (2019g)
July 2019	Wang Qishan at Beijing World Peace Summit	Chinese development a source of world peace; existing global order needs reforming rather than 'cast it aside and start all over again'.	Wang Qishan (2019)
Sept 2019	Wang Yi at UN Climate Action Summit	Chinese commitment to Paris Agreement and improving global climate change governance; China pursuing high quality low carbon growth.	Wang Yi (2019c)
Sept 2019	Wang Yi at UN Forum on Sustainable Development	Commitment to 'scale up' South-South Cooperation.	Wang Yi (2019d)

Date	Event	Relevance/Message	Source
Sept 2019	Wang Yi at UN General Assembly	China stands for independence, equality among nations, equity and justice and mutually beneficial cooperation, and opposes protectionism and multilateralism; 'Development is the master key to solving all problems'.	Wang Yi (2019e)
Sept 2019	Wang Yi Article in *People's Daily* celebrating 70th Anniversary of the PRC	Outlines China's successes and global contributions to global peace and cooperation and as 'protector of the international order'; GPDCC defined as leadership of the CCP, independence and autonomy, concern for the global common good, equity and justice, and win–win results; China to lead in global governance reform.	Wang Yi (2019f)
Sept 2019	Position Paper on China and the UN	Commitment to multilateral system built around the UN and WTO; outlines China's contributions to UN objectives; China 'spearheads' international development cooperation; 'Rights to survival and development are the primary, basic human rights'.	FMPRC (2019)
Sept 2019	White paper on 'China and the World in the New Era'	Outlines China's growth and global contributions; China's growth as major source of global stability and prosperity; diversity the key but China provides 'experience and reference' to other developing countries.	State Council (2019)

Notes

Introduction

1. Referring here to the Gramscian idea that certain beliefs become so widely and unquestionably accepted as being true that questioning them becomes non-sensical.
2. One of the earliest I could find was by Slovakian President Gašparovič (2013).
3. Because it was a crisis of a certain form of finance and capital rather than a universal one; albeit a crisis that had global implications, including impacting severely on Chinese exports.
4. Examples include Walter and Howie (2012) and more recently McMahon (2018).
5. Examples include Beardson (2013), Abrami et al (2014), Fenby (2014) and Magnus (2018).
6. The most consistent proponent of this view is Gordon Chang (2011).
7. This project is ongoing and now hosted at www.correlatesofwar.org/
8. Total population, urban population, iron and steel production, primary energy consumption, military expenditure and military personnel ratio. The most often cited reference to the index of Singer's many publications is Singer et al (1972).
9. Hu was later to be the subject of considerable online criticism for claiming that China had surpassed the US as the world's No.1 economic and technological power in 2018.
10. I made this argument and expanded on it in detail in Breslin (2017).

Chapter 1

1. Interestingly, Dan Lynch (2015) found a very similar disconnect in domestic and international specialists within China itself. The difference in predictions for China's future were so great that one reviewer noted that it was like reading about two different countries.
2. As noted by Herrmann et al (1997: 408).
3. This quote is taken from the introduction to the project's first meeting at Chatham House on 12 December 2019: www.chathamhouse.org/event/national-narratives-and-rise-china-us-europe-and-future-international-order
4. Hunt was foreign secretary for just over a year from July 2018. These statements were made in the first of a three part BBC documentary called 'China: A New World Order', first broadcast on 29 August 2019. Sophie Richardson's (Human Rights Watch) condemnation of the lack of international action over Xinjiang can also be found in the same documentary.

[5] Examples of these works include Gertz (1999; 2002), Timperlake and Triplett (1999; 2000), Triplett (2004) and Babbin and Timperlake (2006).

[6] This is not a government body. It is a cross party committee made up of MPs from all parties in rough proportion to their overall parliamentary position. At the time, this was six Conservatives, four from Labour and one Scottish Nationalist.

[7] Good examples of this research focus include, but are not limited to, Bachman (1986) and Dittmer (1990).

[8] One exception that while still starting from a strategic balance position tried to parse different Chinese perspectives and interests was Pollack (1984).

[9] Examples include Eckstein (1975), Terrill (1977) and Wu (1981).

[10] For the idea of a Chinese financial deterrence more generally, see Drezner (2009).

Chapter 2

[1] For details, see Li (2008), Cho and Jeong (2008), Wuthnow (2008) and Glaser and Murphy (2009).

[2] This specific quote is from Yang Jiechi (2017) but it is repeated time and time again in Chinese writings.

[3] Zhang wasn't endorsing this idea of Chinese superiority, but simply reporting it.

[4] As perhaps most clearly exemplified by Chen Yun's birdcage theory where the statist cage provided the constraints within which the market could operate. The bars on the cage needed to be wide enough not to squeeze the bird to death, but not so wide that the bird could fly away. See Coase and Wang (2012: Chapter 4).

[5] Veto targets over the years have included maintaining social stability and hitting family planning targets (Edin, 2003).

[6] The People's Bank of China's investigation into the resulting level of debt referred to a total of over 10,000 of them at all levels of sub-national local governments (PBOC, 2011: 6).

Chapter 3

[1] Ye Didi (2019) and Tsang (2019) specifically talk of Chinese GS in neoclassical realist terms, with the latter arguing that the party's interests are the core mediating consideration that shapes the calculation of what can and should be done (and how) within the structural determinants of the time.

[2] These translate as 'calmly observe, secure your position, deal with things calmly, hide brightness and cherish obscurity, protect our advantages, never seek leadership, attain some achievements'. Chen and Wang (2011) suggest that Deng didn't actually say all of these things at the same time, but instead the 28 characters emerge from his thinking in the late 1980s and early 1990s and represent his overall strategic thinking of the time.

[3] Although he found no across the board pattern of increased assertiveness, Johnston did accept that the exception seemed to be in Chinese actions in the South China Sea. Although published after Xi became leader, the analysis in the paper was up to and including 2010.

[4] A more rigorous analysis is provided by Guo Wei (2017), who provides a detailed analysis of 43 major speeches from Xi between 2013 and 2016 which they argue are collectively the most important manifestation of Xi's new thinking.

[5] The new primary contradiction was 'between unbalanced and inadequate development and the people's ever-growing needs for a better life' (Xi, 2017e).

6   Sometimes referred to as Great Power Diplomacy with Chinese Characteristics for the New Era.

7   The CS is sometimes called China Plan or Programme in English, and the CSFM was previously typically translated as a Community of Common Destiny.

8   For example, at the Belt and Road Forum in 2017, Xi (2017c) referred to the Belt and Road Science, Technology and Innovation Cooperation Action Plan consisting of a Science and Technology People-to-People Exchange Initiative, the Joint Laboratory Initiative, the Science Park Cooperation Initiative and the Technology Transfer Initiative; a liaison office for the Forum's follow-up activities; the Research Center for the Belt and Road Financial and Economic Development; the Facilitating Center for Building the Belt and Road; the Multilateral Development Financial Cooperation Center in cooperation with multilateral development banks, and an IMF-China Capacity Building Center.

9   Australia, Austria, Belgium, Canada, Denmark, Estonia, Finland, France, Germany, Iceland, Ireland, Japan, Latvia, Lithuania, Luxembourg, the Netherlands, New Zealand, Norway, Sweden, Switzerland, and the UK signed both. Belize, Palau, Slovakia, Slovenia, the Marshall Islands and Liechtenstein only signed the Hong Kong letter, and Spain only signed the Xinjiang one.

10 The Democratic Republic of the Congo only signed the Xinjiang letter. Algeria, Angola, Bahrain, Belarus, Bolivia, Burkina Faso, Burundi, Cambodia, Cameroon, Comoros, Congo, Cuba, Egypt, Eritrea, Gabon, Kuwait, Laos, Myanmar, Nigeria, North Korea, Oman, Pakistan, Philippines, Qatar, Russia, Saudi Arabia, Somalia, South Sudan, Sudan, Syria, Tajikistan, Togo, Turkmenistan, United Arab Emirates, Venezuela, and Zimbabwe signed both. Antigua and Barbuda, Central African Republic, Djibouti, Dominica, Equatorial Guinea, Gambia, Guinea, Guinea-Bissau, Iran, Iraq, Lebanon, Lesotho, Mauritania, Morocco, Mozambique, Nepal, Nicaragua, Niger, Papua New Guinea, Sierra Leone, Sri Lanka, Suriname, Syria, Yemen, Zambia and the Palestinian authority only signed the Hong Kong letter.

11 More than one analyst has also suggested in private that Xi has ambitions to return Taiwan to Chinese sovereignty and pointed to Deng Xiaoping's overseeing of Hong Kong's return as a sort of comparative contribution to Chinese state building.

Chapter 4

1   The China National Petroleum Corporation pulled out of a planned project the following week (Faucon, 2019), reminding us that high-profile announcements of plans aren't always followed up by actual financial flows.

2   Much of which is reviewed in Germain and Schwartz (2017).

3   In overall terms, it was sixth behind the US Dollar (40.81 per cent of all settlements), the Euro (33.58), the British Pound (7.05), the Japanese Yen (3.32) and the Canadian Dollar (1.84). If intra-Eurozone settlements are excluded, then the RMB comes in behind the Australian Dollar and Swiss Franc as well with only 1.1 per cent of the global total. Data for currency transactions is available from the Society for Worldwide Interbank Financial Telecommunication RMB tracker which provides monthly updates: www.swift.com/our-solutions/compliance-and-shared-services/business-intelligence/renminbi/rmb-tracker

4   Such surveys are undertaken annually by the American and EU Chambers of Commerce in China and can be accessed via their respective websites: www.amchamchina.org/ and www.europeanchamber.com.cn/en/home.

5   The data is available from https://china.aiddata.org/. They also include a third category of Vague Official Finance for projects where there is not enough information available to determine if it is ODA or OOF.

6   For details of different methods and a calculation that results in lower figures than normal, see Kitano (2018a).

7   On its own website: http://en.cidca.gov.cn/2018-08/01/c_259525.htm

8   For a detailed explanation of the various agencies still involved in aid related activity, see Kitano (2018b).

9   Though we should note that they were arguing that China was moderating its previous policy and trying to force its partners 'to become more acceptable to the international community' rather than actually supporting such rogue states.

10 The following section builds on the analysis of the same data that I used in Breslin (Forthcoming).

11 The data is available alongside analyses of it: www.aei.org/china-global-investment-tracker.

12 Of this literature, Buckley et al (2007) is largely regarded as a classic example and in many respects a pathbreaker in the study of COFDI decision making.

13 World Bank data shows the same trends but with different figures for individual years: https://data.worldbank.org

14 Also for high-quality equipment and the general upgrading of industries, to enhance R&D and manufacturing capacities, in areas where China had an energy shortfall, promote the upgrading of industries, and agricultural cooperation overseas.

15 And also investment in sensitive or war torn countries, or those without diplomatic relations with China, investment projects that are not related to specific industrial projects, using outdated equipment, or investment that does not meet the environmental or other standards of the host country.

16 And also military investments, those that contravene any international laws that China is party to, pornography and gambling.

17 Twelve of the 17 are EU members; the other five are candidate countries. With the exception of Greece, they were all either formerly Communist Party States, or constituent parts of larger ones.

18 The Center for Advanced China Research tracked this series of commentaries: www. ccpwatch.org/single-post/2020/04/20/Weekly-Report-326-4112020-4172020

Chapter 5

1   Examples of this early scholarship include Huang and Ding (2006), Kurlantzick (2007), Bronson (2007), Sun (2007), Cho and Jeong (2008), Ding (2008a, 2008b), Lampton (2008), Li (2008a), and Wang Yiwei (2008).

2   The full text of all White Papers are available from www.china.org.cn/e-white

3   These quotes are taken from an editorial in Qiushi (2020) but there are many other examples of similar arguments citing the admiration and thanks of foreign leaders and experts.

4   To replace the previous China Central Television (CCTV) 9 and CCTV News English Language Services that had been operating since 2000.

5   Xinhua, CGTN, China Radio International, and the companies that distribute the *China Daily* and the *People's Daily* in the US. CCTV as a whole, the China News Service, *People's Daily* and the *Global Times* were added to the list in June 2020.

6   In addition to those cited elsewhere in this chapter, examples include Paradise (2009), Lahtinen (2015), Wang and Adamson (2015) and Hartig (2015, 2017),

7   On education and exchanges more generally, see Pan (2013), Metzgar (2015) and Bislev (2017).

8   Only a third were designated as coming for sightseeing and leisure, though a rather large 30 per cent were described as 'other'. These figures are from the Ministry of Culture and Tourism via the TravelChina website, www.travelchinaguide. com/tourism. Even though they originate from the same place, statistics vary in different reports. Partly because they tend to be readjusted as time goes by, and partly because of the definition of different regions (such as Europe). Figures for 2020 are not comparable to previous years because of the consequences of the pandemic on global travel.

9   In order, Thailand, Japan, Vietnam, Singapore, Indonesia, Malaysia, America, Cambodia, Russia and the Philippines. There were just under 150 million overseas trips in 2018.

10 According to the China Outbound Tourism Research Institute, in 2017 'The Chinese outbound travel market is currently composed of approximately 40 per cent fully-FIT [Free Independent Travellers] travellers, 40 per cent modular 'semi-FIT' travellers (who choose to book small parts of their trip in small 'modular' packages) and the remaining 20 per cent of the market being made up of package tourists' (COTRI, 2017).

11 These examples are all taken from Marketing to China: www.marketingtochina. com/independent-chinese-travellers-can-attract/

12 This is from a *China Daily* special report that provides a useful overview of the various measures taken as well as performing a form of victory celebration.

13 As an example, the *China Daily* (2020: 20) reported that 'in just a month, the daily allocation of medical protective suits jumped from 21,000 to 270,000, and KN95 masks from 72,000 to 562,000'.

14 These quotes are taken from a *Global Times* (2020c) editorial that is representative of many with the same message. It was chosen simply by randomly looking at what was being said in the *Global Times* on the day of writing (28 April 2020).

15 This is taken from a Xinhua (2020a) report on the Chinese embassy in the UK's response to the UK media, but is typical of many similar responses.

16 Zhao repeated his call for an investigation into Fort Detrick's links with COVID-19 on 6 July 2020 (Zhao Lijian, 2020d).

17 Named after the 2015 Chinese film 'Wolf Warrior', which became a symbol of a newly powerful and confident China that was ready to take on anything that came its way.

Chapter 6

1   The China Society for Human Rights Study has a website devoted to this new consensus and support for Chinese ideas: www.chinahumanrights.org/html/special/20180612/

2   This speech was actually made at the fifth collective study of the 19th Central Committee Political Bureau in April 2018 but only published in November 2019 to coincide with the promotion of a new work plan for 'Party Member Education and Training'.

3   For an overview of the discourse of ecological civilization, see Marinelli (2018).

Conclusion

1 Early examples include Sautman and Yan (2006), Tull (2006), Keet (2008), and Utomi (2008). All but Tull actually end up arguing against the neocolonial idea, and much of what is written on Chinese neocolonialism is written to deny it. Zhao (2014) provides a good overview of negative perceptions of China's presence in Africa – though even here there is an emphasis on the range of potential negative consequences rather than just on neocolonialism per se.

2 Normally in combination with another character; *jihui* or *jiyu* or *shiji*. *Ji* is a rather flexible character, and can also mean machine or aircraft or engine.

References

Abrami, R., Kirby, W. and McFarlan, W. (2014) *Can China Lead? Reaching the Limits of Power and Growth*, Boston, MA: Harvard Business School.

Acharya, A. and Buzan, B. (2007) 'Why is there no non-Western international relations theory? An introduction', *International Relations of Asia Pacific*, 7(3): 285–6.

ADB (2014) *Money Matters: Local Government Finance in the People's Republic of China*, Manila: Asian Development Bank.

Akpaninyie, M. (2019) 'China's "Debt Diplomacy" is a misnomer. Call it "Crony Diplomacy"', *The Diplomat*, 12 March, https://thediplomat.com/2019/03/chinas-debt-diplomacy-is-a-misnomer-call-it-crony-diplomacy/

Alden, C. and Alves, A.C. (2008) 'History and identity in the construction of China's Africa policy: the 'new' face of China-African co-operation', *Review of African Political Economy*, 35(115): 43–58.

Alden, C. and Hughes, C. (2009) 'Harmony and discord in China's Africa strategy: some implications for foreign policy', *The China Quarterly*, 199: 563–84.

Allison, G. (2017) *Destined for War: Can America and China Escape Thucydides's Trap?*, New York: Houghton Mifflin.

Ambrose, J. (2019) 'China's appetite for coal power returns despite climate pledge', *The Guardian*, 20 November, www.theguardian.com/world/2019/nov/20/china-appetite-for-coal-power-stations-returns-despite-climate-pledge-capacity

Amcham China (2017) *China Business Climate Report*, Beijing: American Chamber of Commerce in China/Bain and Co.

Amighini, A., Rabellotti, R. and Sanfilippo, M. (2013) 'Do Chinese state-owned and private enterprises differ in their internationalization strategies?', *China Economic Review*, 27: 312–25.

Angelo, P. and Chavez, R. (2020) 'Gracias China!!!', *New York Times*, 21 April, www.nytimes.com/2020/04/21/opinion/china-latin-america-covid.html

Anon (2020a) 'Systèmes politiques et lutte contre l'épidémie: le grand dilemma [Political systems and the fight against the epidemic: the great dilemma]', Embassy of the People's Republic of China in France, 28 March, www.amb-chine.fr/fra/zfzj/t1762848.htm

Anon (2020b) 'Rétablir des faits distordus: observations d'un diplomate chinois en poste à Paris [Restoring distorted facts: observations of a Chinese diplomat stationed in Paris]', Embassy of the PRC in Paris, 12 April, www.amb-chine.fr/fra/zfzj/t1768712.htm

Anthony, I., Zhou Jiayi and Su Fei (2020) 'EU security perspectives in an era of connectivity: implications for relations with China', SIPRI Insights on Peace and Security, www.sipri.org/sites/default/files/2020-03/sipriinsight2003_0.pdf

Aspers, P. and Kohl, S. (2016) 'Economic theories of globalization' in B. Turner and R. Holten (eds), *The Routledge International Handbook of Globalization Studies: Second Edition*, London: Routledge, pp 41–59.

Babbin, J. and Timperlake, E. (2006) *Showdown: Why China Wants War with the United States*, Washington, DC: Regnery.

Bachman, D. (1986) 'Differing visions of China's post-Mao economy: the ideas of Chen Yun, Deng Xiaoping, and Zhao Ziyang', *Asian Survey*, 26(3): 292–321.

Bai Chong-En, Hsieh Chang-Tai and Song Zheng (2019) 'Special deals with Chinese characteristics', *NBER Working Paper* (25839), www.nber.org/papers/w25839

Baker McKenzie (2018) 'Chinese FDI squeezed in 2017 by regulatory crackdowns at home and abroad', 17 January, www.bakermckenzie.com/en/newsroom/2018/01/chinese-fdi-2017

Baldwin, D. (2002) 'Power and international relations', in W. Carlsnaes, T. Risse, and B. Simmons (eds), *The Handbook of International Relations*, Thousand Oaks, CA: Sage, pp 177–91.

Bandurski, D. (2018) 'China's crisis of overconfidence', *The Diplomat*, 18 December, https://thediplomat.com/2018/12/chinas-crisis-of-overconfidence/

Barma, N. and Ratner, E. (2006) 'China's illiberal challenge', *Democracy: A Journal of Ideas*, 2 (Fall): 56–68.

Baum, R. (1996) *Burying Mao: Chinese Politics in the Age of Deng Xiaoping*, Princeton, NJ: Princeton University Press.

Beardson, T. (2013) *Stumbling Giant*, New Haven, CT: Yale University Press.

Beckley, M. (2011/12) 'China's century? Why America's edge will endure,' *International Security*, 36(3): 41–78.

Bell, D. (2015) *The China Model: Political Meritocracy and the Limits of Democracy*, Princeton, NJ: Princeton University Press.

Benner, T., Gaspers, J., Ohlberg, M, Poggetti, L. and Shi-Kupfer, K. (2018) 'Authoritarian advance: responding to China's growing political influence in Europe', Global Public Policy Institute and Merics Report, February, www.merics.org/sites/default/files/2018-02/GPPi_MERICS_Authoritarian_Advance_2018_1.pdf

Bi Qiu (2017) 'Quanqiu zhili de zhoungguo fang'an de huayu liubian ji lishi qishi [Discourse evolution and historical enlightenment of China's global governance programme]', *Shandong Xngzheng Xueyuan Xuebao [Journal of Shandong Administration College]*, 5: 17–22.

Bislev, A. (2015) 'The Chinese dream: imagining China', *Fudan Journal of Humanities and Social Sciences*, 8(4): 585–95.

Bislev, A. (2017) 'Student-to-student diplomacy: Chinese international students as a soft-power tool', *Journal of Current Chinese Affairs*, 46(2): 81–109.

Blanchard, J.-M. (2019) 'Chinese outward foreign investment (COFDI): a primer and assessment of COFDI research', in Ka Zeng (ed), *Handbook on the International Political Economy of China*, Cheltenham: Edward Elgar, pp 76–97.

Bo Kong and Gallagher, K. (2017) 'Globalizing Chinese energy finance: the role of policy banks', *Journal of Contemporary China*, 26(108): 834–51.

Bohoslavsky, J.P. (2016) 'Report of the independent expert on the effects of foreign debt and other related international financial obligations of states on the full enjoyment of all human rights, particularly economic, social and cultural rights on his mission to China', Human Rights Council, Thirty-first Session, 1 March, www.ohchr.org/EN/HRBodies/HRC/RegularSessions/Session31/Documents/A.HRC.31.60.Add.1_AEV.docx

Bondes, M. and Heep, S. (2013) 'Conceptualizing the relationship between persuasion and legitimacy: official framing in the case of the Chinese Communist Party', *Journal of Chinese Political Science*, 18(4): 317–34.

Borger, J. (2020) 'US AWOL from world stage as China tries on global leadership for size', *The Guardian*, 29 March, www.theguardian.com/world/2020/mar/29/us-awol-from-world-stage-as-china-tries-on-global-leadership-for-size

Borrell, J. (2020) 'The coronavirus pandemic and the new world it is creating', Statement by the High Representative for Foreign Policy, 24 March, https://eeas.europa.eu/delegations/china/76401/eu-hrvp-josep-borrell-coronavirus-pandemic-and-new-world-it-creating_en

Bourg, J. (2012) 'The red guards of Paris: French student Maoism of the 1960s', *History of European Ideas*, 31(4): 472–90.

Bowles, P. and Wang Baotai (2013) 'Renminbi internationalization: a journey to where?', *Development and Change*, 44(6): 1363–85.

Brady, A.-M. (2008) *Marketing Dictatorship: Propaganda and Thought Work in Contemporary China*, Lanham, MD: Rowman and Littlefield.

Brady, A.-M. (2017) 'Magic weapons: China's political influence activities under Xi Jinping', Washington, DC: Wilson Center, 18 September, www.wilsoncenter.org/article/magic-weapons-chinas-political-influence-activities-under-xi-jinping

Brady, A.-M. (2019) 'A strategic partnership: New Zealand–China relations in the Xi Jinping era and beyond', in A.-M. Brady (ed), *Small States and the Changing Global Order: New Zealand Faces the Future*, Cham: Springer, pp 127–44.

Brautigam, D. (2008) 'China's foreign aid in Africa: what do we know?', in R. Rotberg (ed), *China into Africa: Trade, Aid and Influence*, Washington, DC: Brookings, pp 197–216.

Brautigam, D. (2009) *The Dragon's Gift: The Real Story of China in Africa*, Oxford: Oxford University Press.

Brautigam, D. (2015) *Will Africa Feed China?*, Oxford: Oxford University Press.

Brautigam, D. (2020) 'A critical look at Chinese "debt-trap diplomacy": the rise of a meme', *Area Development and Policy*, 5(1): 1–14.

Brautigam, D. and Tang Xiaoyang (2012) 'Economic statecraft in China's new overseas special economic zones: soft power, business, or resource-security?', *International Affairs*, 88(4): 799–816.

Breslin, S. (2005) 'Power and production: rethinking China's global economic role', *Review of International Studies*, 31(4): 735–53.

Breslin, S. (2007) *China and the Global Political Economy*, Basingstoke: Palgrave.

Breslin, S. (2011) 'The "China model" and the global crisis: from Friedrich List to a Chinese mode of governance?', *International Affairs*, 87(6): 1323–43.

Breslin, S. (2015) 'Debating human security in China: towards discursive power?', *Journal of Contemporary Asia*, 45(2): 243–65.

Breslin, S. (2017) 'Leadership and followership in post-unipolar world: towards selective global leadership and a new functionalism?', *Chinese Political Science Review*, 2(4): 494–511.

Breslin, S. (2020) 'China's global cultural interactions', in D. Shambaugh (ed), *China and the World*, Oxford: Oxford University Press, pp 137–55.

Breslin, S. (Forthcoming) 'China goes out', in L. Dittmer (ed), *China's Political Economy*, Singapore: Nova Science.

Breslin, S. and Ren Xiao (2018) 'China and global governance', in T. Weiss and R. Wilkinson (eds), *International Organization and Global Governance*, Abingdon: Routledge, pp 325–35.

Brødsgaard, K.E. (2007) 'China studies in Europe', in D. Shambaugh, E. Sandschneider and Zhou Hong (eds), *China–Europe Relations: Perceptions, Policies and Prospects*, London: Routledge, pp 35–64.

Brødsgaard, K.E. (2012) 'Politics and business group formation in China: the party in control?', *China Quarterly*, 211: 624–48.

Brødsgaard, K.E. (2017) ' "Fragmented authoritarianism" or "integrated fragmentation"?', in K.E. Brødsgaard (ed), *Chinese Politics as Fragmented Authoritarianism: Earthquakes, Energy and Environment*, New York: Routledge, pp 38–55.

Bronson, P. (2007) *The Dragon Looks South: China and Southeast Asia in the New Century*, Westport, CT: Praeger.

Brooks, S. and Wohlforth, W. (2015/16) 'The rise and fall of the great powers in the twenty-first century: China's rise and the fate of America's global position', *International Security*, 40(3): 7–53.

Brown, C. (2020) 'COVID-19: China's exports of medical supplies provide a ray of hope', Peterson Institute for International Economics Trade and Investment Policy Watch, 26 March, www.piie.com/blogs/trade-and-investment-policy-watch/covid-19-chinas-exports-medical-supplies-provide-ray-hope

Bu Chengliang (2018) 'Zhongguo fang'an: fazhan zhongguo jia zuoxiang xiandaihua de xin xuanze [The China Solution: a new choice for developing countries' modernization]', *Jiangsu Xingzheng Xueyuan Xuebao [Journal of Jiangsu Administration Institute]*, 5: 76–82.

Buck, T. (2018) 'Germany toughens investment rules as China concerns build', *Financial Times*, 19 December, www.ft.com/content/568183dc-038e-11e9-99df-6183d3002ee1

Buckley, P. (2017) 'Internalisation theory and outward direct investment by emerging market multinationals', *Management International Review*, 58(2): 1–30.

Buckley, P., Clegg, J., Cross, A., Liu X., Voss, H. and Zheng P. (2007) 'The determinants of Chinese outward foreign direct investment', *Journal of International Business Studies*, 38(4): 499–518.

Bunte, J. (2019) *Raise the Debt: How Developing Countries Choose Their Creditors*, Oxford: Oxford University Press.

Buzan, B. (2014) 'The logic and contradictions of "peaceful rise/development" as China's Grand Strategy', *Chinese Journal of International Politics*, 7(4): 381–420.

Cabestan, J.-P. (2017) 'China's institutional changes in the foreign and security policy realm under Xi Jinping: power concentration vs. fragmentation without institutionalization', *East Asia*, 34(2): 113–31.

Cabestan, J.-P. (2020) 'China's battle with coronavirus: possible geopolitical gains and real challenges', Aljazeera Center for Studies, 19 April, https://studies.aljazeera.net/en/reports/china%E2%80%99s-battle-coronavirus-possible-geopolitical-gains-and-real-challenges

Callahan, W. (2015) 'History, tradition and the China dream: socialist modernization in the world of great harmony', *Journal of Contemporary China*, 24(96): 983–1001.

Callahan, W. (2016) 'China's "Asia dream": BRI and the new regional order', *Asian Journal of Comparative Politics*, 1(3): 226–43.

Cao Shuai and Xu Kaiwei (2018) 'Niquanqiuhua langchao xia quanqiu fengxian shehui de zhili kunjing yu zhongguo fang'an [The governance dilemma of global risk society under the tide of reverse globalization and the China Solution]', *Lilun Tansuo [Theoretical Exploration]*, 6: 69–74.

Cao Zhijian (2017) 'Renlei mingyun gongtongti shijiao xia de quanqiu renquan zhili: Renlei mingyun gongtongti suo mianlin de renquan tiaozhan [Global human rights governance from the perspective of the community of shared future for mankind: human rights challenges faced by the community of shared future for mankind]', *Renquan [Human Rights]*, 2: 40–47.

Casanova, C. Garcia-Herrero, A. and Xia Le (2015) 'Chinese outbound foreign direct investment: how much goes where after roundtripping and offshoring?', BBVA Working Paper (15/17), www.bbvaresearch.com/wp-content/uploads/2015/07/15_17_Working-Paper_ODI.pdf

CCP (2017) *Constitution of the Communist Party of China*, 24 October, www.xinhuanet.com//english/download/Constitution_of_the_Communist_Party_of_China.pdf

CGTN (2020), 'Five million people left Wuhan before the lockdown: where did they go?' *China Global Television News*, 27 January, https://news.cgtn.com/news/2020-01-27/5-million-people-left-Wuhan-before-the-lockdown-where-did-they-go–NACCu9wItW/index.html

Chalmers, A. and Mocker, S. (2017) 'The end of exceptionalism? Explaining Chinese national oil companies' overseas investments,' *RIPE*, 27(1): 19–143.

Chang, G. (2011) 'The coming collapse of China: 2012 edition', *Foreign Policy*, 29 December, www.foreignpolicy.com/2011/12/29/the-coming-collapse-of-china-2012-edition

Chatham House (2016) 'Exploring public international law and the rights of individuals with Chinese scholars – Part 3', Royal Institute of International Affairs International Law Programme Roundtable Meeting Summary, March, www.chathamhouse.org/sites/default/files/publications/research/2016-03-05-Roundtable3-summary.pdf

Chellaney, B. (2015) 'China's silky Indian Ocean plans', China US Focus, 11 May, www.chinausfocus.com/finance-economy/chinas-silky-indian-ocean-plans

Chellaney, B. (2017) 'China's creditor imperialism', Project Syndicate, 20 December, www.project-syndicate.org/commentary/china-sri-lanka-hambantota-port-debt-by-brahma-chellaney-2017-12

Chen Dingding and Wang Jianwei (2011) 'Lying low no more? China's new thinking on the tao guang yang hui strategy', *China: An International Journal*, 9(2): 195–216.

Chen, E. (2019) '"Made in China 2025" unmade?', *Macropolo*, 20 August, https://macropolo.org/analysis/made-in-china-2025-dropped-media-analysis/

Chen Muyang (2018) 'Between State and Market: China's Development Banking in Comparative Perspective', unpublished PhD thesis, University of Washington, Seattle.

Chen, T. (2019) 'A flamboyant mandarin in a declining liberal order: China's revisionist agenda in global human rights institutions', SSRN, http://dx.doi.org/10.2139/ssrn.3403037

Chen Xi (2020) 'New NGO to operate China's Confucius Institutes', "disperse misinterpretation"', *Global Times*, 5 July, www.globaltimes.cn/content/1193584.shtml

Chen Yanru (1998) 'Setting a nation in action: the media and China's bid for 2000 Olympics', in D. Ray Heisey and Gong Wenxiang (eds), *Communication and Culture: China and the World Entering the 21st Century*, Amsterdam: Brill, pp 289–310.

Chen Zhimin (2005) 'Coastal provinces and China's foreign policy making', in Yuefan Hao and Su Lin (eds), *China's Foreign Policy Making: Societal Force and Chinese American Policy*, Aldershot: Ashgate, pp 187–208.

Chen Zhimin and Su Changhe (2014) *Fudan Quanqiu Zhili Baogao 2014: zengliang gaijin – quanqiu zhili tixi de gaijin he shengli* [*Fudan Global Governance Report 2014: Incremental Improvement – Upgrading and Improving the Global Governance System*], Shanghai: Fudan University School of International Relations and Public Affairs.

Cheng Cheng (2019) 'The logic behind China's foreign aid agency', Carnegie Endowment for International Peace, 21 May, https://carnegieendowment.org/2019/05/21/logic-behind-china-s-foreign-aid-agency-pub-79154

China Daily (2020) 'China's fight against COVID-19', China Daily China Watch Institute, Tsinghua University Institute of Contemporary China Studies and Peking Union Medical College School of Health Policy and Management, 21 April, www. chinadaily.com.cn/pdf/2020/Chinas.Fight.Against.COVID-19-0420-final-2.pdf

Cho, Y.N. and Jeong, J.H. (2008) 'China's soft power: discussions, resources, and prospects', *Asian Survey*, 48(3): 453–72.

Christensen, T. (2006) 'Fostering stability or creating a monster? The rise of China and U.S. policy toward East Asia', *International Security*, 31(1): 81–126.

Christensen, T. (2012) 'More actors, less coordination? New challenges for the leaders of a rising China', in G. Rozman (ed), *China's Foreign Policy: Who Makes It and How Is It Made?*, Basingstoke: Palgrave, pp 21–37.

Christensen, T. (2015) *The China Challenge: Shaping the Choices of a Rising Power*, New York: Norton.

Clarke, I. (2011) *Hegemony in International Society*, Oxford: Oxford University Press.

Clarke, M. (2020) 'Beijing's pivot west: the convergence of Innenpolitik and Aussenpolitik on China's "Belt and Road"?', *Journal of Contemporary China*, 29(123): 336–53.

Coase, R. and Wang Ning (2012) *How China Became Capitalist*, Basingstoke: Palgrave Macmillan.

Collier, A. (2017) *Shadow Banking and the Rise of Capitalism in China*, Basingstoke: Palgrave.

Cooper, A., Higgott, R. and Nossal, K. (1991) 'Bound to follow? Leadership and followership in the Gulf conflict', *Political Science Quarterly*, 106(3): 391–410.

Corkin, L. (2011) 'Redefining foreign policy impulses toward Africa: the roles of the MFA, the MOFCOM and China Exim Bank', *Journal of Current Chinese Affairs*, 40(4): 61–90.

Corkin, L (2014) *Uncovering African Agency: Angola's Management of China's Credit Lines*, Farnham: Ashgate.

COTRI (2017) 'FITs drive Chinese outbound traveller growth in 2017: China outbound pulse', China Outbound Tourism Research Institute (COTRI), 15 November, https://china-outbound.com/2017/11/15/fits-drive-chinese-outbound-traveller-growth-in-2017-china-outbound-pulse/

Creemers, R. (2015) 'China's constitutionalism debate: content, context and implications', *The China Journal*, 74: 91–109.

Cumings, B. (1987) 'The origins and development of the northeast Asian political economy: industrial sectors, product cycles, and political consequences', in F. Deyo (ed), *The Political Economy of the New East Asian Industrialism*, New York: Cornell University Press, pp 44–83.

Cumings, B. (1997) 'Boundary displacement: area studies and international studies during and after the Cold War', *Bulletin of Concerned Asian Scholars*, 29(1): 6–26.

Damro, C. (2012) 'Market power Europe', *Journal of European Public Policy*, 19(5): 682–99.

Davies, M. (2010) 'How China is influencing Africa's development', OECD Development Centre Background Paper, April, www.oecd.org/dataoecd/34/39/45068325.pdf

DB (2019) *Direktinvestitionen lt. Zahlungsbilanzstatistik Für den Berichtszeitraum 2015 bis 2018* [*Direct Investment According to Balance of Payments Statistics for the Reporting Period 2015 to 2018*], Berlin: Deutsche Bundesbank.

Deng Yong (2008) *China's Struggle for Status: The Realignment of International Relations*, Cambridge: Cambridge University Press.

Deng Yongheng, Morck, R., Jing Wu and Yeung, B. (2011) 'Monetary and fiscal stimuli, ownership structure, and China's housing market', National Bureau of Economic Research Working Paper (1687), www.nber.org/papers/w16871

Dfat (2019) 'Statistics on who invests in Australia', Australian Government Department of Foreign Affairs and Trade, May, www.dfat.gov.au/trade/resources/investment-statistics/Pages/statistics-on-who-invests-in-australia

d'Hooghe, I. (2005) 'Public diplomacy in the People's Republic of China', in J. Melissen (ed), *The New Public Diplomacy: Soft Power in International Relations*, Basingstoke: Palgrave, pp 88–105.

Ding Sheng (2008a) *The Dragon's Hidden Wings: How China Rises with Its Soft Power*, Lanham, MD: Lexington.

Ding Sheng (2008b) 'To build a 'harmonious world': China's soft power wielding in the global south', *Journal of Chinese Political Science*, 13(2): 193–213.

Dittmer, L. (1990) 'Patterns of elite strife and succession in Chinese politics', *The China Quarterly*, 123: 405–30.

Dollar, D. (2016) 'China as a global investor', Brookings Asia Working Group Paper 4, May, www.brookings.edu/~/media/research/files/papers/2016/05/china-as-aglobal-investor-dollar/china-as-a-global-investor_asia-working-paper-4.pdf

Dong Wen (2018) 'Lun xin shidai xinshi guoji guanxi [On a new type of International Relations in the new era]', *Xue Lilun* [*Theory Study*], 8: 62–4.

Downs, E. (2007) 'The fact and fiction of Sino-African energy relations', *China Security*, 3(3): 42–68.

Downs, E. (2010) 'Who's afraid of China's oil companies?', in C. Pascual and J. Elkind (eds), *Energy Security: Economics, Politics, Strategies, and Implications*, Washington, DC: Brookings Institution Press, pp 73–102.

Dreher, A., Fuchs, A., Parks, B., Strange, A. and Tierney, M. (2017) 'Aid, China, and growth: evidence from a new global development finance dataset', AidData Working Paper (46), 10 October, www.aiddata.org/publications/aid-china-and-growth-evidence-from-a-new-global-development-finance-dataset

Dreher, A., Fuchs, A., Parks, B., Strange, A. and Tierney, M. (2018) 'Apples and dragon fruits: the determinants of aid and other forms of state financing from China to Africa', *International Studies Quarterly*, 62(1): 182–94.

Dreyer, J.T. (2015) 'The 'tianxia trope': will China change the international system?', *Journal of Contemporary China*, 24(96): 1015–31.

Dreyer, M. (2019) 'China NBA: how one tweet derailed the NBA's China game plan', BBC News, 10 October, www.bbc.co.uk/news/world-asia-china-49995985

Drezner, D. (2007) *All Politics Is Global: Explaining International Regulatory Regimes*, Princeton, NJ: Princeton University Press.

Drezner, D. (2009) 'Bad debts: assessing China's financial influence in great power politics', *International Security*, 34(2): 7–45.

Du Zhengai (2017) 'Tuidong goujian xinxing guoji guanxi goujian renlei mingyun gongtongti [Dynamically construct a new type of international relations and build a community of common future for mankind]', *Xingzheng Guanli Gaige [Administrative Management Reform]*, 11: 97–100.

Duanmu, J-L. (2012) 'Firm heterogeneity and location choice of Chinese multinational enterprises (MNEs)', *Journal of World Business*, 47(1): 64–72.

Duchêne, F. (1972) 'Europe's role in world peace', in R. Mayne (ed.) *Europe Tomorrow: Sixteen Europeans Look Ahead*, London: Fontana, pp 32–47.

Eckstein, A. (1975) 'China's trade policy and Sino-American relations', *Foreign Affairs*, 54(1): 134–54.

Economist (2020a) 'Let Taiwan into the World Health Organisation', *The Economist*, 26 March, www.economist.com/asia/2020/03/26/let-taiwan-into-the-world-health-organisation

Economist (2020b) 'Thanking Big Brother: China's post-COVID propaganda push', *The Economist*, 16 April, www.economist.com/china/2020/04/16/chinas-post-covid-propaganda-push

Edin, M. (2003) 'State capacity and local agent control in China: CCP cadre management from a township perspective', *The China Quarterly*, 173: 35–52.

Edney, K. (2014) *The Globalization of Chinese Propaganda: International Power and Domestic Political Cohesion*, Basingstoke: Palgrave.

Edney, K. (2015) 'Building national cohesion and domestic legitimacy: a regime security approach to soft power in China,' *Politics*, 35(3–4): 259–72.

Eisenman, J. and Shinn, D. (2018) 'China's strategy in Africa' in J. Eisenman and E. Heginbotham (eds), *China Steps Out: Beijing's Major Power Engagement with the Developing World*, New York: Routledge, pp 134–69.

Ernst and Young (2017) 'Sound risk management builds a solid foundation for Chinese enterprises to navigate the global landscape', *Ernst and Young China Go Abroad*, Fifth Issue, April, www.ey.com/Publication/vwLUAssets/ey-china-overseas-investment-report-issue-5-en/$FILE/EY-china-overseas-investment-report-issue-5-en.pdf

Ernst and Young (2018) 'How does geopolitical dynamics affect future China overseas investment?', *Ernst and Young China Go Abroad*, Eighth Issue, November, www.ey.com/Publication/vwLUAssets/ey-china-overseas-investment-report-issue-8-en-new/$File/ey-china-overseas-investment-report-issue-8-en.pdf

Ernst and Young (2020) 'Overview of China outbound investment in 2019', *Ernst and Young*, 13 February, www.ey.com/cn/en/newsroom/news-releases/news-2020-ey-overview-of-china-outbound-investment-in-2019

Espinoza, J. (2020) 'Vestager urges stakebuilding to block Chinese takeovers', *Financial Times*, 12 April, www.ft.com/content/e14f24c7-e47a-4c22-8cf3-f629da62b0a7

ESRC (2019) 'Exploring the growing U.S. reliance on China's biotech and pharmaceutical products', US Economic Security Review Commission (ESRC), 31 July, www.uscc.gov/sites/default/files/2019-10/July%2031,%202019%20 Hearing%20Transcript.pdf

European Commission (2019) 'EU–China – a strategic outlook', High Representative of the Union for Foreign Affairs and Security Policy Joint Communication to the European Parliament, the European Council and the Council, 12 March, https:// ec.europa.eu/commission/sites/beta-political/files/communication-eu-china-a-strategic-outlook.pdf

FAC (2020) 'Viral immunity: the FCO's role in building a coalition against COVID-19', House of Commons Foreign Affairs Select Committee, 2 April, https:// committees.parliament.uk/committee/78/foreign-affairs-committee

Fallon, T. (2015) 'The new Silk Road: Xi Jinping's grand strategy for Eurasia', *American Foreign Policy Interests*, 37(3): 140–47.

Fan Shih-Ping (2010) 'The effects of China's tourism diplomacy and a "United Front"', *China: An International Journal*, 8(2): 247–81.

Fasslabend, W. (2015) 'The Silk Road: a political marketing concept for world dominance', *European View*, 14(2): 293–302.

Faucon, B. (2019) 'China pulls out of giant Iranian gas project', *Wall Street Journal*, 6 October, www.wsj.com/articles/china-pulls-out-of-giant-iranian-gas-project-11570372087

Fearon, J. (1997) 'Signaling foreign policy interests: tying hands versus sinking costs', *The Journal of Conflict Resolution*, 41(1): 68–90.

Fenby, J. (2014) *Will China Dominate the 21st Century?*, Cambridge: Polity.

Feng Huiyun and He Kai (2019) 'Why do Chinese IR scholars matter?', in Feng Huiyun, Kai He and Yan Xuetong (eds), *Chinese Scholars and Foreign Policy*, London: Routledge, pp 3–20.

Feng Zhongping and Huang Jing (2014) 'China's strategic partnership diplomacy: engaging with a changing world', European Strategic Partnership Observatory Working Paper No 8, http://fride.org/download/WP8_China_strategic_ partnership_diplomacy.pdf

Ferchen, M. (2018) 'China, Venezuela, and the illusion of debt-trap diplomacy', *AsiaGlobal Online*, 16 August, https://carnegietsinghua.org/2018/08/16/ china-venezuela-and-illusion-of-debt-trap-diplomacy-pub-77089

Ferguson, D., McKenzie, J. and Ng, F. (2018) 'A practical guide to Chinese investor protections along the Belt and Road', *HKTDC Research*, 21 August, http://china-trade-research.hktdc.com/business-news/article/The-Belt-and-Road-Initiative/ A-practical-guide-to-Chinese-investor-protections-along-the-Belt-and-Road/obor/ en/1/1X000000/1X0AEZ03.htm

Fewsmith, J. and Nathan, A. (2018) 'Authoritarian resilience revisited: Joseph Fewsmith with response from Andrew J. Nathan', *Journal of Contemporary China*, 28(116): 169–79.

Fish, I.S. (2010) 'China's love affair with rogue states', *Newsweek*, 13 January.

Fitzgerald, J. (1996) *Awakening China: Politics, Culture and Class in the Nationalist Revolution*, Stanford, CA: Stanford University Press.

Fitzgerald, J. (2018) China in Xi's 'new era': overstepping down under', *Journal of Democracy*, 29(2): 59–67.

FMPRC (2002) 'China's position paper on the new security concept', Foreign Ministry of the People's Republic of China, www.mfa.gov.cn/eng/wjb/zzjg/gjs/gjzzyhy/2612/2614/t15319.htm

FMPRC (2006) 'Zhongguo dui feizhou zhengce wenjian [Paper on China's policy towards Africa]', Foreign Ministry of the PRC, www.fmprc.gov.cn/chn/pds/ziliao/tytj/zcwj/t230612.htm

FMPRC (2013a) 'Xi Jinping calls for the building of new type of international relations with win-win cooperation at the core in a speech at the Moscow state institute of international relations', 23 March, Foreign Ministry of the People's Republic of China, www.fmprc.gov.cn/mfa_eng/topics_665678/xjpcf1_665694/t1024781.shtml

FMPRC (2013b) 'Wang Yi talks about Xi Jinping attending the eighth G20 leaders' summit in St. Petersburg', Foreign Ministry of the People's Republic of China, 7 September, www.fmprc.gov.cn/mfa_eng/topics_665678/xjpfwzysiesgjtfhshzzfh_665686/t1076482.shtml

FMPRC (2015) 'Xi Jinping zai nannan hezuo yuanzhuo hui shang fabiao jianghua chansu xinshiqi nannan hezuo changyi qiangdiao yao ba nannan hezuo shiye tui xiang geng gao shuiping [Xi Jinping delivered a speech at the roundtable on South-South cooperation, expounding the South-South cooperation initiative in the new era, stressing the need to push South-South cooperation to a higher level]', Foreign Ministry of the People's Republic of China, 27 September, www.fmprc.gov.cn/web/ziliao_674904/zyjh_674906/t1300907.shtml

FMPRC (2019) 'China and the United Nations: position paper of the People's Republic of China for the 74th session of the United Nations General Assembly', 18 September, www.fmprc.gov.cn/mfa_eng/wjdt_665385/2649_665393/t1698812.shtml

Foot, R. (2013) 'Introduction: China across the divide', in R. Foot (ed), *China Across the Divide: The Domestic and Global in Politics and Society*, Oxford: Oxford University Press, pp 1–15.

Foot, R. (2014) ' "Doing some things" in the Xi Jinping era: the United Nations as China's venue of choice', *International Affairs*, 90(5): 1085–100.

Freeman, C. and Yuan, Wen Jin (2011) 'China's exchange rate politics: decoding the cleavage between the Chinese Ministry of Commerce and the People's Bank of China', *Centre for Strategic and International Studies*, https://csis-prod. s3.amazonaws.com/s3fs-public/legacy_files/files/publication/110615_Freeman_ ChinaExchangeRatePolitics_Web.pdf

Friedberg, A. (1993–94) 'Ripe for rivalry: prospects for peace in a multipolar Asia', *International Security*, 18(3): 5–33.

Fuller, D. (2016) *Paper Tigers, Hidden Dragons: Firms and the Political Economy of China's Technological Development*, Oxford: Oxford University Press.

Gabriele, A. (2009) 'The role of the state in China's industrial development: a reassessment', MPRA Paper (1455), http://mpra.ub.uni-muenchen.de/14551/1/ MPRA_paper_14551.pdf

Gallagher, K. and Irwin, A. (2014) 'Exporting national champions: China's outward foreign direct investment finance in comparative perspective', *China and World Economy*, 22(6): 1–21.

Gao Hong (2018) 'Zhongguo fang'an de xingcheng jichu, bijiao youshi yu lilun luoji [The basis, comparative advantage and theoretical logic of the China Solution]', *Gaoxiao Makesezhuyi Lilun Yanjiu [Academic Research on Marxist Theory]*, 2: 102–10.

Gao Jie (2010) 'Hitting the target but missing the point: the rise of non-mission-based targets in performance measurement of Chinese local governments', *Administration and Society*, 42(1S): 56–76.

Gao Jie (2015) 'Political rationality vs. technical rationality in China's target-based performance measurement system: the case of social stability maintenance', *Policy and Society*, 34(1): 37–48.

Gardner, C. (2020) 'Taiwan allies international protection and enhancement initiative (TAIPEI) act of 2019', S.1678 – 116th Congress (2019–2020), 26 March, www. congress.gov/bill/116th-congress/senate-bill/1678/text

Gašparovič, I. (2013) 'Slovak president meets the Chairman of the National People's Congress of China,' Press Department of the President, 20 September, www. prezident.sk/?press-department&news_id=18118

Gereffi, G. and Korzeniewicz, M. (eds) (1994) *Commodity Chains and Global Capitalism*, Westport, CT: Praeger.

Germain, R. and Schwartz, H.M. (2017) 'The political economy of currency internationalisation: the case of the RMB', *Review of International Studies*, 43(4): 765–87.

Gertz, B. (1999) *Betrayal: How the Clinton Administration Undermined American Security*, Washington, DC: Regnery.

Gertz, B. (2002) *The China Threat: How the People's Republic Targets America*. Washington, DC: Regnery.

Gholz, E. (2014) 'Rare earth elements and national security', Council on Foreign Relations Energy Report, October, www.cfr.org/sites/default/files/pdf/2014/10/ Energy%20Report_Gholz.pdf

Gill, B. (2007) *Rising Star: China's New Security Diplomacy*, Washington, DC: Brookings.

Gill, B. (2020) 'China's global influence: post-COVID prospects for soft power', *The Washington Quarterly*, 43(2): 97–115.

Gill, B. and Huang Yanzhong (2006) 'Sources and limits of Chinese "soft power"', *Survival*, 48(2): 17–36.

Gill, S. (2008) *Power and Resistance in the New World Order (Second Edition)*, Basingstoke: Palgrave Macmillan.

Glaser, B. and Murphy, M. (2009) 'Soft power with Chinese characteristics: the ongoing debate', in C. McGiffert (ed), *Chinese Soft Power and Its Implications for the United States*, Washington, DC: Center for Strategic and International Studies, pp 10–26.

Global Times (2020a) 'Italy may have had an unexplained strain of pneumonia as early as November...', Twitter, 22 March, https://twitter.com/globaltimesnews/status/1241559268190343168

Global Times (2020b) 'Outspoken Chinese diplomat says tweet on COVID-19 origin was response to US stigmatization of China', *Global Times*, 8 April, www.globaltimes.cn/content/1184903.shtml

Global Times (2020c) 'Political motives behind China smears', *Global Times*, 28 April 2020, www.globaltimes.cn/content/1186941.shtml

Goh, E. (2013) *The Struggle for Order: Hegemony, Resistance and Transition in Post-Cold War East Asia*, Oxford: Oxford University Press.

Goodman, D. (2017) 'Australia and the China threat: managing ambiguity', *The Pacific Review*, 30(5): 769–82.

Gore, L. (2017) 'The Communist Party-dominated governance model of China: legitimacy, accountability, and meritocracy', *Polity*, 51(1): 161–94.

Goron, C. (2018) 'Climate Revolution or Long March? The Politics of Low Carbon Transformation in China (1992–2015): The Power Sector as Case Study', unpublished PhD thesis, University of Warwick.

Gracie, C. (2015) 'China and "the Osborne doctrine"', BBC News, 15 October, www.bbc.co.uk/news/world-asia-china-34539507

Gracie, C. (2016) 'Hangzhou G20: China's ambitions for global leadership', BBC News, 2 September, www.bbc.co.uk/news/world-asia-china-37241315

Green, D. (2020) 'Our approach to China may now have to be more like our attitude to Russia during parts of the Cold War', Conservative Home, 31 March, www.conservativehome.com/platform/2020/03/damian-green-coronavirus-huawei-and-what-to-do-about-china-in-the-long-term.html

Grieger, G. (2018) 'China, the 16+1 format and the EU', Members' Research Service PE 625.173, 7 September, www.europarl.europa.eu/RegData/etudes/BRIE/2018/625173/EPRS_BRI(2018)625173_EN.pdf

Gu Jiping (2011) 'The last golden land? Chinese private companies go to Africa', *IDS Working Paper* 365. www.ids.ac.uk/go/idspublication/the-last-golden-land-chinese-private-companies-go-to-africa

Guo Jiping (2019) 'Da bianjuzhong de zhongguo yu shijie [China and the world in an era of great change]', *Renmin Ribao* [*People's Daily*], 25 September, http://paper. people.com.cn/rmrb/html/2019-09/25/nw.D110000renmrb_20190925_5-01.htm

Guo Sujian (2013) 'Introduction: political science and Chinese political studies – the state of the field', in Guo Sujian (ed), *Political Science and Chinese Political Studies: The State of the Field*, Heidelberg: Springer, pp 1–8

Guo Wei (2017) 'Quanqiu zhili de zhongguo fang'an yu zhongguo huayu de jiangou [The China Solution of global governance and the construction of the Chinese discourse]', *Zhejiang Shehui Kexue* [*Zhejiang Social Sciences*], 5: 121–7.

Hagström, L. and Nordin, A. (2020) 'China's "politics of harmony" and the quest for soft power in international politics', *International Studies Review*, 22(3): 507–25.

Halper, S. (2010) *The Beijing Consensus: How China's Authoritarian Model Will Dominate the Twenty-First Century*, New York: Basic Books.

Hameiri, S. and Jones, L. (2015) 'Rising powers and state transformation: the case of China', *European Journal of International Relations*, 22(1): 72–98.

Hanemann, T., Gao, C. and Lysenko, A. (2019) 'Net negative: Chinese investment in the US in 2018', Rhodium Group, 13 January, https://rhg.com/research/ chinese-investment-in-the-us-2018-recap/

Hart-Landsberg, M. and Burkett, P. (2004) 'China and socialism: market reforms and class struggle', *Monthly Review*, 56(3): 1–116.

Hartig, F. (2015) 'Communicating China to the world: Confucius Institutes and China's strategic narratives', *Politics*, 35(3–4): 245–58.

Hartig, F. (2017) *Chinese Public Diplomacy: The Rise of Confucius Institute*, London: Routledge.

Hay, C. and Rosamond, B. (2002) 'Globalization, European integration and the discursive construction of economic imperatives', *Journal of European Public Policy*, 9(2): 147–67.

He Yin (2019) 'China takes the lead in UN peacekeeping', *China Daily*, 26 September, www.chinadaily.com.cn/a/201909/26/WS5d8bfa01a310cf3e3556d7f3.html

Heilmann, S. (2009) 'Maximum tinkering under uncertainty: unorthodox lessons from China,' *Modern China*, 35(4): 450–62.

Heilmann, S. and Melton, O. (2013) 'The reinvention of development planning in China, 1993–2012', *Modern China*, 39(6): 580–628.

Herrmann, R., Voss, J., Schooler, T. and Ciarrochi, J. (1997) 'Images in international relations: an experimental test of cognitive schemata', *International Studies Quarterly*, 41(3): 403–33.

Hirschman, A. (1945) *National Power and the Structure of Foreign Trade*, Berkeley, CA: University of California Press.

Ho, B. (2014) 'Understanding Chinese exceptionalism: China's rise, its goodness, and greatness', *Alternatives: Global, Local, Political*, 39(3): 164–76.

Hoffman, A. (2002) 'A conceptualization of trust in international relations', *European Journal of International Relations*, 8(3): 375–401.

Horn, S., Reinhart, C. and Trebesch, C. (2019) 'China's overseas lending', NBER Working Paper No. 26050, http://papers.nber.org/tmp/47603-w26050.pdf

Hornby, L. (2019) 'China "rebalances" overseas lending on debt burden concerns', *Financial Times*, 29 January, www.ft.com/content/c0c3b840-238d-11e9-8ce6-5db4543da632

Hsu, S. (2012) 'Role of informal finance in China's continuing economic development', *The Chinese Economy*, 45(1): 28–45.

Hu Angang and Men Honghua (2002) 'The rising of modern China: comprehensive national power and Grand Strategy', https://myweb.rollins.edu/tlairson/china/chigrandstrategy.pdf

Hu Angang, Zheng Yunfeng, and Gao Yuyu (2015) 'Dui zhongmei zonghe guoli de pinggu (1990–2013 nian) [On the comprehensive national power of China and the United States (1990–2013)]', *Qinghua Daxue Xuebao [Journal of Tsinghua University]*, 1: 26–39.

Hu Jian (2012) 'Cong taoguang yanghui dao jiji zuowei – zhongguo waijiao siwei, zhanlue yu celue de zhuanbian chu lun [From taoguang yanghui to active conduct – the transformation of China's diplomatic thinking, strategy and tactics]', *Lilun Dakoan [Theoretical Guide]*, 4: 107–109.

Hu Jintao (2007) 'Hold high the great banner of Socialism with Chinese Characteristics and strive for new victories in building a moderately prosperous society in all respects', Report to the 17th National Congress of the Communist Party of China, 15 October, www.gov.cn/english/2007-10/24/content_785505.htm

Hu Jintao (2012) 'Firmly march on the path of Socialism with Chinese Characteristics and strive to complete the building of a moderately prosperous society in all respects', Speech at 18th National Congress of the Communist Party of China, 27 November, www.china-embassy.org/eng/zt/18th_CPC_National_Congress_Eng/t992917.htm

Hu Weixing (2019) 'Xi Jinping's "big power diplomacy" and China's Central National Security Commission (CNSC)', *Journal of Contemporary China*, 25(98): 163–77.

Huang Jing (2017) 'Xi Jinping's Taiwan policy: boxing Taiwan in with the One-China framework', in L. Dittmer (ed), *Taiwan and China: Fitful Embrace*, Oakland, CA: University of California Press, pp 239–48.

Huang Yanzhong and Ding Sheng (2006) 'Dragon's underbelly: an analysis of China's soft power', *East Asia: An International Journal*, 23(4): 22–44.

Huang Yasheng (2011) 'Rethinking the Beijing Consensus', *Asia Policy*, 11: 1–26.

Hubbard, P. (2007) 'Aiding transparency: what we can learn about China ExIm Bank's concessional loans?', Center for Global Development Working Paper 126, www.cgdev.org/sites/default/files/14424_file_AidingTransparency.pdf

Hubbard, P. (2016) 'Reconciling China's official statistics on state ownership and contribution', EABER Working Paper Series No. 120, www.eaber.org/node/25575

Hui, C. (2004) 'Toward a dynamic theory of international politics: insights from comparing ancient China and early modern Europe', *International Organization*, 58(1), 175–205.

Hurley, J., Morris, S. and Portelance, G. (2018) 'Examining the debt implications of the Belt and Road initiative from a policy perspective', Center for Global Development Policy Paper No. 121, March, www.cgdev.org/sites/default/files/examining-debt-implications-belt-and-road-initiative-policy-perspective.pdf

Hurst, L. (2011) 'Comparative analysis of the determinants of China's state-owned outward direct investment in OECD and non-OECD countries', *China and World Economy*, 19(4): 74–91.

Ikenberry, J. (2008) 'The rise of China and the future of the West: can the liberal system survive?', *Foreign Affairs*, 87(1): 23–37.

IMF (2010) 'People's Republic of China: 2010 Article IV consultation', IMF Country Report No. 10/238, 17 June, www.imf.org/external/pubs/ft/scr/2010/cr10238.pdf

IMF (2017a) 'Lao People's Democratic Republic staff report for the 2016 article IV consultation: debt sustainability analysis', *International Monetary Fund*, 6 January, www.imf.org/external/pubs/ft/dsa/pdf/2017/dsacr1753.pdf

IMF (2017b) 'The People's Republic of China: selected issues', IMF Country Report No. 17/248, August 2017, www.imf.org/~/media/Files/Publications/CR/2017/cr17248.ashx

International Crisis Group (2012) 'Stirring up the South China Sea (I)', *International Crisis Group Asia Report*, No 223, 23 April, www.crisisgroup.org/~/media/Files/asia/north-east-asia/223-stirring-up-the-south-china-sea-i.pdf

Irvine, R. (2016) *Forecasting China's Future: Dominance or Collapse*, London: Routledge.

Jacques, M. (2009) *When China Rules the World: The End of the Western World and the Birth of a New Global Order*, London: Penguin.

Jaros, K. and Tan Yeling (2020) 'Provincial power in a centralizing China: the politics of domestic and international "development space"', *The China Journal*, 83: 79–104.

Jennings, R. (2018) 'Why it hurts less now as China punishes South Korea with tourism cut', *Forbes*, 4 March, www.forbes.com/sites/ralphjennings/2018/03/04/china-keeps-punishing-south-korea-with-tourism-cuts-for-now/#645da352366c

Jervis, R. (1970) *The Logic of Images in International Relations*, Princeton NJ: Princeton University Press.

Jervis, R. (1982/83) 'Deterrence and perception', *International Security*, 7(3): 3–30.

Jia Qingguo (2020) 'China's diplomatic response to COVID-19', *East Asia Forum*, 17 May, www.eastasiaforum.org/2020/05/17/chinas-diplomatic-response-to-covid-19/

Jia Wenshan (2017) 'Host diplomacy for a new world order', *China Daily*, 8 August, www.chinadaily.com.cn/opinion/2017-08/08/content_30366170.htm

Jiang Zemin (2002) 'Build a well-off society in an all-round way and create a new situation in building Socialism with Chinese Characteristics', Report to 16th National Party Congress, 8 November, www.fmprc.gov.cn/mfa_eng/topics_665678/3698_665962/t18872.shtml

Jin Zhen (2017) 'Environmental management system in China: the target achieving process' in H. Kitagawa (ed), *Environmental Policy and Governance in China*, Tokyo: Springer, pp 69–88.

Jing Kong and Shen Kongrong (2019) 'Zhongguo qiye dui yidai yilu yanxian guojia de jiaotong touzi xiaoying: Fazhan haishi zhaiwu xianjing [The effect of Chinese enterprises on the transportation investment of countries along the Belt and Road: development effect or debt trap]', *Zhongguo Gongye Jingji [Industrial Economics]*, 9: 79–97.

Johnston, A.I. (2013) 'How new and assertive is China's new assertiveness?', *International Security*, 37(4): 7–48.

Johnston, A.I. (2019) 'China in a world of orders: rethinking compliance and challenge in Beijing's international relations', *International Security*, 44(2): 9–60.

Jones, L. and Zeng Jinghan (2019) 'Understanding China's "Belt and Road Initiative": beyond "Grand Strategy" to a state transformation analysis', *Third World Quarterly*, 40(8): 1415–39.

Kallio, J. (2016) 'Towards China's Strategic Narrative', unpublished PhD thesis, University of Lapland, Rovaniemi.

Kang, D. (2003) 'Getting Asia wrong: the need for new analytical frameworks', *International Security*, 27(4): 57–85.

Kaplinsky, R., McCormick, D. and Morris, M. (2007) 'The impact of China on Sub-Saharan Africa', University of Sussex Institute of Development Studies Working Paper No. 291, www.ids.ac.uk/files/Wp291.pdf

Karnitschnig, M. (2020) 'China is winning the coronavirus propaganda war', *Politico*, 18 March, www.politico.eu/article/coronavirus-china-winning-propaganda-war/

Keen, M. (2016) 'Going global or going nowhere? Chinese media in a time of flux', *Media International Australia*, 159(1): 13–21.

Keet, D. (2008) 'The role and impact of Chinese economic operations in Africa', in D.-C. Guerrero and F. Manji (eds), *China's New Role in Africa and the South: A Search for a New Perspective*, Oxford: Fahamu, pp 78–86.

Keller, W. and Rawski, T. (2007) 'Asia's shifting strategic and economic landscape', in W. Keller and T. Rawski (eds), *China's Rise and the Balance of Influence in Asia*, Pittsburgh, PA: Pittsburgh University Press, pp 3–13.

Kelly, D. (2016) 'The CCP's acceptance of market principles', in S. Kennedy (ed), *State and Market in Contemporary China: Toward the 13th Five-Year Plan*, Lanham, MD: Roman and Littlefield, pp 48–50.

Kelly, D. (2017a) 'The "China Solution": Beijing responds to Trump', *Lowy Interpreter*, 17 February, www.lowyinstitute.org/the-interpreter/china-solution-beijing-responds-trump

Kelly, D. (2017b) 'Winding back the China Solution', *The Interpreter*, The Lowy Institute, 6 July, www.lowyinstitute.org/the-interpreter/winding-back-the-china-solution

Kelly, D. (2018) 'Seven Chinas: a policy framework', CSIS Project on Chinese Business and Political Economy Paper no.3, February 2018, https://csis-prod.s3.amazonaws.com/s3fs-public/publication/180205_Kelly_SevenChinasAPolicyFramework_Web.pdf

Kennedy, S. (2010) 'The myth of the Beijing Consensus', *Journal of Contemporary China*, 19(65): 461–77.

Kim S., Prideaux, B. and Timothy, D. (2016) 'Factors affecting bilateral Chinese and Japanese travel', *Annals of Tourism Research*, 61: 80–95.

King, B. and Gardiner, S. (2015) 'Chinese international students: an avant-garde of independent travellers?', *International Journal of Tourism Research*, 17(2): 130–39.

Kirshner, J. (2010) 'The tragedy of offensive realism: classical realism and the rise of China', *European Journal of International Relations*, 18(1): 53–75.

Kitano, N. (2018a) 'Estimating China's foreign aid using new data', *IDS Bulletin*, 49 (3), https://bulletin.ids.ac.uk/idsbo/article/view/2980

Kitano, N. (2018b) 'China's foreign aid: entering a new stage', *Asia-Pacific Review*, 25(1): 90–111.

Kitchen, N. (2010) 'Systemic pressures and domestic ideas: a neoclassical realist model of Grand Strategy formation', *Review of International Studies*, 36(1): 117–43.

Kleine-Ahlbrandt, S. and Small, A. (2008) 'China's new dictatorship diplomacy: is Beijing parting with pariahs?', *Foreign Affairs*, January–February, www.foreignaffairs.com/articles/asia/2008-06-01/chinas-new-dictatorship-diplomacy

Knoerich, J. (2017) 'Has outward foreign direct investment contributed to the development of the Chinese economy?', *Transnational Corporations*, 23(2): 1–48.

Kobayashi, T. (2008) 'Evolution of China's aid policy', Japan Bank for International Cooperation Working Paper 27, www.jica.go.jp/jica-ri/IFIC_and_JBICI-Studies/jica-ri/english/publication/archives/jbic/report/working/pdf/wp27_e.pdf

Koetse, M. (2019) 'Hong Kong protests: brand "witch hunt" takes over Chinese internet', BBC News, 15 August, www.bbc.co.uk/news/world-asia-china-49354017

Koike, Y. (2015) 'The AIIB key to Beijing's new economic order', *The Japan Times*, 1 June, www.japantimes.co.jp/opinion/2015/06/01/commentary/japan-commentary/the-aiib-key-to-beijings-new-economic-order/#.V8XznvkrLIV

Kratz, A. (2015) 'One belt, one road: what's in it for China's economic players?', *European Council on Foreign Relations China Analysis*, June, https://www.ecfr.eu/page/-/China_analysis_belt_road.pdf

Kratz, A., Feng, A. and Wright, L. (2019) 'New data on the "debt trap" question', *Rhodium Group*, 29 April, https://rhg.com/research/new-data-on-the-debt-trap-question/

Kupchan, C. (2012) *No One's World: The West, The Rising Rest, and the Coming Global Turn*, New York: Oxford University Press.

Kurlantzick, J. (2007) *Charm Offensive: How China's Soft Power Is Transforming the World*, New Haven, CT: Yale University Press.

Kydd, A. (2005) *Trust and Mistrust in International Relations*, Princeton, NJ: Princeton University Press.

Kynge, J. (2009) *China Shakes the World: The Rise of a Hungry Nation*, London: Phoenix.

Kynge, J. and Yu Sun (2020) 'China faces wave of calls for debt relief on "Belt and Road" projects', *Financial Times*, 30 April, www.ft.com/content/5a3192be-27c6-4fe7-87e7-78d4158bd39b

Lahtinen, A. (2015) 'China's soft power: challenges of Confucianism and Confucius Institutes', *Journal of Comparative Asian Development*, 14(2): 200–26.

Lai Hongyi and Kang Su-Jeong (2014) 'Domestic bureaucratic politics and Chinese foreign policy', *Journal of Contemporary China*, 23(86): 294–313.

Lake, D. (2017) 'Domination, authority, and the forms of Chinese power', *The Chinese Journal of International Politics*, 10(4): 357–82.

Lampton, D. (2008) *The Three Faces of Chinese Power: Might, Money, and Minds*, Berkeley, CA: University of California Press.

Lampton, D. (2015) 'Xi Jinping and the National Security Commission: policy coordination and political power', *Journal of Contemporary China*, 24(95): 759–77.

Lams, L. (2018) 'Examining strategic narratives in Chinese official discourses under Xi Jinping', *Chinese Journal of Political Science*, 23(3): 387–411.

Lancaster, C. (2007) 'The Chinese aid system', Center for Global Development Working Paper, www.cgdev.org/content/publications/detail/13953/

Landry, P. (2008) *Decentralized Authoritarianism in China: The Communist Party's Control of Local Elites in the Post-Mao Era*, Cambridge: Cambridge University Press.

Langan, M. (2018) *Neo-Colonialism and the Poverty of 'Development' in Africa*, Basingstoke: Palgrave Macmillan.

Lardy, N. (2012) *Sustaining China's Economic Growth after the Global Crisis*, Washington, DC: The Peterson Institute.

Lardy, N. (2014) *Markets over Mao: The Rise of Private Business in China*, Washington, DC: The Peterson Institute.

Lardy, N. (2019) *The State Strikes Back: The End of Economic Reform in China?*, Washington, DC: The Peterson Institute.

Lawler, D. (2020) 'The 53 countries supporting China's crackdown on Hong Kong', Axios, 3 July, www.axios.com/countries-supporting-china-hong-kong-law-0ec9bc6c-3aeb-4af0-8031-aa0f01a46a7c.html

Lei Chunfang (2019) 'Zhongguo turang shengzhang de weida zhengzhi chuangzao' [Chinese soil nurtures 'the great political creation'], *Qiushi*, 1 April, www.qstheory.cn/dukan/qs/2019-04/01/c_1124302946.htm

Leung, N., Ngai, J., Seong, J.M. and Woetzel, J. (2020) 'Fast forward China: how COVID-19 is accelerating 5 key trends shaping the Chinese economy', McKinsey, 6 May, www.mckinsey.com/featured-insights/asia-pacific/fast-forward-china-how-covid-19-is-accelerating-five-key-trends-shaping-the-chinese-economy

Li Chen (2016) 'Holding "China Inc." together: the CCP and the rise of China's Yangqi', *The China Quarterly*, 228: 927–49.

Li Gemin (2009) 'Lun Deng Xiaoping "taoguangyanghui, yousuo zuowei" de guoji zhanlue sixiang [On Deng Xiaoping's strategic thinking of keeping a low profile and striving for achievements]', *Dangdai Sheke Shiye* [*Contemporary Social Science Perspectives*], 1: 1–8 and 14.

Li Keqiang (2020) 'Report on the work of government', Report to the Third Session of the 13th National People's Congress, 22 May, http://english.www.gov.cn/premier/news/202005/30/content_WS5ed197f3c6d0b3f0e94990da.html

Li Liyan (2018) 'Renlei mingyun gongtongti de zhongguo wenhua zhihui [Chinese cultural wisdom of the community of shared future for mankind]', *Qianxian [Frontline]*, 10: 8–11.

Li Minghu, Cui Lin and Lu Jiangyong (2014) 'Varieties in state capitalism: outward FDI strategies of central and local state-owned enterprises from emerging economy countries', *Journal of International Business Studies*, 45(8): 980–1004.

Li Mingjiang (2008a) 'China debates soft power', *The Chinese Journal of International Politics*, 2(2): 287–308.

Li Mingjiang (2008b) 'Soft power and the Chinese approach', *Chinese Security*, 4(3): 4–6.

Li Mingjiang (2019) 'China's economic power in Asia: the Belt and Road Initiative and the local Guangxi government's role', *Asian Perspective*, 43(2): 274–95.

Li Mingjiang and Lee Dongmin (2014) 'Local liberalism: China's provincial approaches to relations with Southeast Asia', *Journal of Contemporary China*, 23(86): 275–93.

Li Qiao (2007) 'Deng Xiaoping "taoguang yanghui, yousuo zuowei" de guoji zhannlue sixiang ji xin fazhan [New developments in the international strategic thought of Deng Xiaoping's keeping a low profile and striving for achievements]', *Dalian Ganbu Xuekan [Dalian Officials' Journal]*, 7: 41–3.

Li Quan and Liang Guoyong (2012) 'Political relations and Chinese outbound direct investment: evidence from firm and dyad-level tests', Indiana University Research Center for Chinese Politics and Business Working Paper 19, https://papers.ssrn.com/sol3/papers.cfm?abstract_id=2169805

Li Sixue (2017) 'Xi Jinping zhongguo fang'an sixiang ruogan wenti yanjiu [Research on several issues relating to Xi Jinping's China Solution thought]', *Shehui Kexue Jia [Social Scientist]*, 8: 35–40.

Liddell Hart, B. (1954) *Strategy*, London: Faber and Faber.

Lieberthal, K. (2006) 'Why the US malaise over China? Awareness of the complexities could produce a win-win outcome', *YaleGlobal*, 19 January, http://yaleglobal.yale.edu/content/why-us-malaise-over-china

Lieberthal, K. and Wang Jisi (2013) 'Assessing US–China strategic distrust', John L. Thornton China Center Monograph Series Number 4, www.brookings.edu/wp-content/uploads/2016/06/0330_china_lieberthal.pdf

Lim, D. and Ferguson, V. (2020) 'China's "boycott diplomacy" over calls for coronavirus inquiry could harm Australian exporters', ABC News, 24 April, www.abc.net.au/news/2020-04-29/china-boycott-diplomacy--coronavirus-comes-more-government/12194482

Lim, L. and Bergin, J. (2018) 'Inside China's audacious global propaganda campaign', *The Guardian*, 7 December, www.theguardian.com/news/2018/dec/07/china-plan-for-global-media-dominance-propaganda-xi-jinping

Lin Chun (2013) *China and Global Capitalism: Reflections on Marxism, History, and Contemporary Politics*, Basingstoke: Palgrave Macmillan.

Lin Zhimin (2019) 'Xi Jinping's "major country diplomacy": the impacts of China's growing capacity', *Journal of Contemporary China*, 28(115): 31–46.

Lind, J. and Press, D. (2018) 'Markets or mercantilism? How China secures its energy supplies', *International Security*, 42(4): 170–204.

Liu Chenguang (2017) 'Shilun zhongguo fang'an de hexi yaoyi [Summary of the core of the China Solution]', *Xinjiang Shifan Daxue Xuebao – Zhexue Shehui Kexue Ban [Journal of Xinjiang Normal University – Philosophy and Social Sciences Edition]*, 3(5): 21–33.

Liu Congde and Wang Xiao (2017) 'Xi Jinping xinxing guoji guanxi sixiang zhong de zhonghua youxiu chuantong wenhua jiyin [The excellent Chinese traditional cultural gene in Xi Jinping's thinking on a new type of international relations]', *Shehui Zhuyi Yanjiu [Socialism Studies]*, 3: 9–17.

Liu Jianfei (2018) 'Xinxing daguo guanxi jiben tezheng chutan [The basics characteristics of the new type of international relations]', *Guoji Wenti Yanjiu [International Relations Research]*, 2: 17–29.

Liu Ling (2018) 'Zhongguo fang'an yingdui quanqiu tiaozhan de youshi ji qishi' [The advantages and insight of the China Solution in dealing with global challenges], *Xueshu Qianyan [Academic Frontier]*, 10: 84–7.

Liu Ming (2016) 'BRICS development: a long way to a powerful economic club and new international organization', *The Pacific Review*, 23(3): 443–53.

Liu Xiaobiao (2002) *Chang shuai zhongguo de bei hou: cong weixie lun dao bengkui lun [The Background to China's Song of Decline: From the China Threat Theory to the China Collapse Theory]*, Beijing: China Social Sciences Press.

Liu Xiaoming (2020) 'China has valuable lessons for the world in how to fight COVID-19', *Financial Times*, 28 April, www.ft.com/content/ad61f0ea-8887-11ea-a109-483c62d17528

Liu Xiguang and Liu Kang (1997) *Yaomohua zhongguo de beihou [Behind the Demonization of China]*, Beijing: China Social Sciences.

Liu Xinru (2016) 'Zhongguo fang'an de shidai yunhan [The implication of the era of the China Solution]', *Jiefangjun Bao [PLA Daily]*, 27 July, http://theory.people.com.cn/n1/2016/0727/c40531-28588084.html

Lo, C. (2015) *China's Impossible Trinity: The Structural Challenges to the 'Chinese Dream'*, Basingstoke: Palgrave Macmillan.

Lo, J. and Pan, S.-Y. (2016) 'Confucius Institutes and China's soft power: practices and paradoxes', *Compare: A Journal of Comparative and International Education*, 46(4): 512–32.

Lönnqvist, L. (2008) 'China's aid to Africa: implications for civil society', INTRAC Policy Briefing Paper 17, www.intrac.org/wpcms/wp-content/uploads/2016/09/Briefing-Paper-17-Chinas-Aid-to-Africa.pdf

Luo Jiangwen and Yang Xishuang (2017) 'Lunxiang shijie gongxian zhongguo fang'an de jiben neirong ji qi yiju' [On the basic content and contribution of the China Solution to the world]', *Fujian Jiangxia Xueyuan Xuebao* [*Journal of Fujian Jiangxia College*], 7(3): 34–42.

Luo Limin, Qi Zhen and Hubbard, P. (2017) 'Not looking for trouble: Chinese overseas investment by sector and ownership', *China Economic Review*, 46: 142–64.

Luqiu, L.W.R. and McCarthy, J. (2019) 'Confucius Institutes: the successful stealth 'soft power' penetration of American universities', *The Journal of Higher Education*, 90(4): 620–43.

Lynch, D. (2015) *China's Futures: PRC Elites Debate Economics, Politics, and Foreign Policy*, Stanford, CA: Stanford University Press.

Ma Guochan (2020) 'Jia Qingguo: yiqing jiasu shijie zhixu zhong gou, qu quanqiuhua zou butong [Jia Qingguo: the epidemic accelerates the reconstruction of the world order and de-globalization will not work]', *Caijing*, 18 March, https://finance.sina.com.cn/review/jcgc/2020-03-18/doc-iimxxsth0003067.shtml

Madrid-Morales, D. (2017) 'China's digital public diplomacy towards Africa: actors, messages and audiences', in K. Batchelor and Zhang Xiaoling (eds), *China–Africa Relations: Building Images through Cultural Co-operation, Media Representation and Communication*, London: Routledge, pp 129–46.

Magnus, G. (2018) *Red Flags: Why Xi Jinping's China Is in Jeopardy*, New Haven, CT: Yale University Press.

Maher, R. (2018) 'Bipolarity and the future of US–China relations', *Political Science Quarterly*, 133(3): 477–525.

Mahoney, J. (2014) 'Interpreting the Chinese dream: an exercise of political hermeneutics', *Journal of Chinese Political Science*, 19(1): 15–34.

Manion, M. (2016) 'Taking China's anticorruption campaign seriously', *Economic and Political Studies*, 4(1): 3–18.

Manners, I. (2002) 'Normative power Europe: a contradiction in terms?', *Journal of Common Market Studies*, 40(2): 235–58.

Marinelli, M. (2018) 'How to build a 'beautiful China' in the Anthropocene: the political discourse and the intellectual debate on ecological civilization', *Chinese Journal of Political Science*, 23(3): 365–86.

Marks, S. (2020) 'Coronavirus ends China's honeymoon in Africa', *Politico*, 16 April, www.politico.com/news/2020/04/16/coronavirus-china-africa-191444

Marlow, I. (2020) 'Taiwan emerging from pandemic with a stronger hand against China', *Bloomberg*, 29 April, www.bloomberg.com/news/articles/2020-04-29/taiwan-emerging-from-pandemic-with-a-stronger-hand-against-china

Mattis, P. (2019) 'The Party Congress test: a minimum standard for analyzing Beijing's intentions', Texas University War on the Rocks, 8 January, https://warontherocks.com/2019/01/the-party-congress-test-a-minimum-standard-for-analyzing-beijings-intentions/

McCauley, R. and Chang Shu (2019) 'Recent renminbi policy and currency co-movements', *Journal of International Money and Finance*, 95: 444–56.

McMahon, D. (2018) *China's Great Wall of Debt: Shadow Banks, Ghost Cities, Massive Loans, and the End of the Chinese Miracle*, New York: Houghton Mifflin Harcourt.

McNally, C. (2012) 'Sino-Capitalism: China's re-emergence and the international political economy', *World Politics*, 64(4): 741–76.

Mearsheimer, J. (2006) 'China's unpeaceful rise', *Current History*, 105(690): 160–62.

Men Honghua (2004) 'Ruhe jinxing da zhanlue yanjiu – jian lun zhongguo de zhanlue yanji de yiyi' [How to conduct Grand Strategy research: on the significance of the study of China's Grand Strategy], *Guoji Zhengzhi Yanjiu* [*Studies of International Politics*], 4: 33–45.

Men Honghua (2005) *Goujian zhongguo da zhanlue de kuangjia* [*Building a Framework for China's Grand Strategy*], Beijing: Peking University Press.

Men Honghua (2015) 'Kaiqu zhongguo quanmin shenhua gaige kaifang de xin shidai: jian lun weilai shinian zhongguo de da zhanlue zouxiang [Open China to deepen the new era of reform and opening up: on China's Grand Strategy in the next decade]', *Xuexi yu tansuo* [*Study and Exploration*], 8: 40–44.

Men Jing and Barton, B. (2011) 'Introduction: China and the EU in Africa: changing concepts and changing policies' in Jing Men and B. Barton (eds), *China in the European Union in Africa: Partners or Competitors?*, Farnham: Ashgate, pp 1–20.

Menegazzi, S. (2017) *Rethinking Think Tanks in Contemporary China*, Basingstoke: Palgrave.

Mertha, A. (2009) '"Fragmented authoritarianism 2.0": political pluralization in the Chinese policy process', *The China Quarterly*, 200: 995–1012.

Metzgar, E. (2015) 'Institutions of higher education as public diplomacy tools: China-based university programs for the 21st century', *Journal of Studies in International Education,* 20(3): 223–41.

Milhaupt, C. and Zheng Wentong (2015) 'Beyond ownership: state capitalism and the Chinese firm', *The Georgetown Law Journal*, 103(3): 665–722.

Miller, T. (2019) 'Great leap outward: China's ODI and the Belt and Road Initiative', in J. deLisle and A. Goldstein (eds), *To Get Rich is Glorious: Challenges Facing China's Economic Reform and Opening at Forty*, Washington, DC: Brookings, pp 233–60.

Minzner, C. (2019) 'Intelligentsia in the crosshairs: Xi Jinping's ideological rectification of higher education in China', *China Leadership Monitor*, 62, www.prcleader.org/carl-minzner

Miranda, J. (2018) 'How China did not transform into a market economy', in J. Nedumpara and Zhou Weihuan (eds), *Non-Market Economies in the Global Trading System: The Special Case of China*, Singapore: Springer, pp 65–97.

Miskimmon, A., O'Loughlin, B. and Rosselle, L. (2013) *Strategic Narratives: Communication Power and the New World Order*, New York: Routledge.

MOFCOM (1997) 'Price law of the People's Republic of China', Ministry of Commerce, 31 December, http://english.mofcom.gov.cn/article/policyrelease/Businessregulations/201303/20130300046121.shtml

MOFCOM (2018) 'MOFCOM Department of Outward Investment and Economic Cooperation comments on China's outward investment cooperation in 2017', Ministry of Commerce, 18 January, http://english.mofcom.gov.cn/article/newsrelease/policyreleasing/201801/20180102706193.shtml

MOFCOM (2019a) 'Zhongguo duiwith touzi fazhan baogao 2018 [China's foreign investment development report 2018]', Ministry of Commerce, January, http://images.mofcom.gov.cn/fec/201901/20190128155348158.pdf

MOFCOM (2019b) 'MOFCOM Department of Outward Investment and Economic Cooperation comments on China's outward investment and cooperation in 2018', Ministry of Commerce, 17 January, http://english.mofcom.gov.cn/article/newsrelease/policyreleasing/201901/20190102829745.shtml

Mori, K. (1988) 'The impact of Sino–Soviet détente', *The Pacific Review*, 1(3): 290–95.

Mussington, D. (2018) 'Countering "Made in China 2025": strategy for Western powers in a cybered world', *Military Cyber Affairs*, 3(2): 1–12.

Nathan, A. (2016) 'Domestic factors in the making of Chinese foreign policy', *China Report*, 52(3): 179–91.

Naughton, B. (2015) 'The transformation of the state sector: SASAC, the market economy, and the new national champions', in B. Naughton and K. Tsai (eds), *State Capitalism, Institutional Adaptation, and the Chinese Miracle*, Cambridge: Cambridge University Press, pp 46–72.

Naughton, B. and Tsai, K. (2015) 'Introduction: state capitalism and the Chinese economic miracle' in B. Naughton and K. Tsai (eds), *State Capitalism, Institutional Adaptation, and the Chinese Miracle*, Cambridge: Cambridge University Press, pp 1–24.

Navarro, P. and Autry, G. (2011) *Death by China: Confronting the Dragon – A Global Call to Action*, Upper Saddle River, NJ: Prentice Hall.

NDRC (2017) 'Zhongguo duiwai touzi baogao [China foreign investment report]', National Development and Reform Commission, November, www.ndrc.gov.cn/gzdt/201711/W020171130400470019984.pdf

Nelson, F. (2015) 'George Osborne's epic kowtow to China. The Dalai Lama is right: the UK's China policy is about 'money money' – where the sale comes first', *The Spectator*, 26 September, www.spectator.co.uk/2015/09/cameron-and-osbornes-epic-kowtow-to-china/

Ni Chen (2012) 'Branding national images: the 2008 Beijing summer Olympics, 2010 Shanghai World Expo, and 2010 Guangzhou Asian Games', *Public Relations Review*, 38: 731–45.

Nolke, A. (2014) 'Introduction: toward state capitalism 3.0' in A. Nolke (ed), *Multinational Corporations from Emerging Markets: Towards State Capitalism 3.0*, Basingstoke: Palgrave, pp 1–15.

Nordin, A. (2012) 'Space for the future: exhibiting China in the world at the Shanghai Expo', *China Information*, 26(2), 235–49.

Norris, W. (2016) *Chinese Economic Statecraft: Commercial Actors, Grand Strategy and State Control*, Ithaca, NY: Cornell University Press.

Norton, S. (2015) 'China's Grand Strategy', University of Sydney China Studies Centre, https://sydney.edu.au/china_studies_centre/images/content/ccpublications/policy_paper_series/2015/chinas-grand-strategy.pdf

Nye, J. (1990) *Bound to Lead: The Changing Nature of American Power*, New York: Basic Books.

Nye, J. (2000) *Paradox of American Power: Why the World's Only Superpower Can't Go It Alone*, New York: Oxford University Press.

Nye, J. (2004) *Soft Power: The Means to Success in World Politics*, New York: Public Affairs.

Nye, J. (2009) 'Get smart: combining hard and soft power', *Foreign Affairs*, 88(4): 160–63.

Obe, M. (2019) 'Asian neighbors lose confidence in Xi Jinping's policies: survey', *Nikkei Asia Review*, 6 December, https://asia.nikkei.com/Politics/International-relations/Asian-neighbors-lose-confidence-in-Xi-Jinping-s-policies-Survey

OLGBRI (2017) *Building the Belt and Road: Concept, Practice and China's Contribution*, Beijing: Foreign Languages Press for the Office of the Leading Group for the Belt and Road Initiative.

Olins, W. (2005) 'Making a national brand' in J. Melissen (ed), *The New Public Diplomacy: Soft Power in International Relations*, New York: Palgrave Macmillan, pp 169–79.

Oliveira, R.T., Menzies, J., Borgia, D. and Figueira, S. (2017) 'Outward foreign direct investment from emerging countries: theoretical extension and evidence from China', *The International Trade Journal*, 31(5): 402–28.

Oltermann, P. (2018) 'Germany's "China City": how Duisburg became Xi Jinping's gateway to Europe', *The Guardian*, 2 August, www.theguardian.com/cities/2018/aug/01/germanys-china-city-duisburg-became-xi-jinping-gateway-europe

ONS (2019) 'UK foreign direct investment, trends and analysis: July 2019', UK Office of National Statistics, 29 July, www.ons.gov.uk/economy/nationalaccounts/balanceofpayments/articles/ukforeigndirectinvestmenttrendsandanalysis/july2019

Osborne, G. and O'Neill, J. (2015) 'It's in Britain's interests to bond with China now: the future prosperity of this country depends on us strengthening our relationship with the world's next superpower', *The Guardian*, 19 September, www.theguardian.com/commentisfree/2015/sep/19/george-osborne-britain-should-bond-china-now

Overholt, W. (1993) *China: The Next Economic Superpower*, London: Weidenfeld and Nicolson.

Pan Chengxin (2012) *Knowledge, Desire and Power in Global Politics: Western Representations of China's Rise*, Cheltenham: Edward Elgar.

Pan, S.-Y. (2013) 'China's approach to the international market for higher education studies: strategies and implications', *Journal of Higher Education Policy and Management*, 35(3): 249–63.

Pan, S.-Y. and Lo, J. (2017) 'Re-conceptualizing China's rise as a global power: a neo-tributary perspective', *The Pacific Review*, 30(1): 1–25.

Pan Yue (2006) 'Humanity and nature need to exist in harmony', *China Daily*, 27 July, www.chinadaily.com.cn/opinion/2006-07/27/content_650584.htm

Panda, J. (2020) 'Five reasons why Xi's "Peking model" will struggle post-COVID-19', *Pacific Forum*, 7 April, https://pacforum.org/wp-content/uploads/2020/04/20200407_ PacNet_19-1.pdf

Pang Zhongying (2008) 'The Beijing Olympics and China's soft power', Brookings Institute, www.brookings.edu/opinions/the-beijing-olympics-and-chinas-soft-power/

Pang Zhongying (2018) 'Quanqiu zhili zhongguo fang'an de leixing yu shishi fanglue [The characteristic and implementation strategy of the China Solution for global governance]', *Xueshujie* [*Academics*], 1: 5–12.

Paradise, J. (2009) 'China and international harmony: the role of Confucius Institutes in bolstering Beijing's soft power,' *Asian Survey*, 49(4): 647–69.

Paris, R. (2001) 'Human security: paradigm shift or hot air?', *International Security*, 26(2): 87–102.

Pauls, R. and Gottwald, J.-C. (2018) 'Origins and dimensions of the Belt and Road Initiative experimental patch-work or Grand Strategy?' in R. Taylor and J. Jaussaud (eds), *China's Global Political Economy: Managerial Perspectives*, London: Routledge, pp 31–54.

Pauley, L. (2018) 'China takes the lead in UN peacekeeping', *The Diplomat*, 17 April, https://thediplomat.com/2018/04/china-takes-the-lead-in-un-peacekeeping/

PBOC (2011) *2010 nian zhongguo quyu jinrong yunxing baogao* [*Report on China's 2010 Regional Financial Development*], Beijing: People's Bank of China.

Pearson, M. (1999) 'China's integration into the international trade and investment regime', in E. Economy and M. Oksenberg (eds), *China Joins the World: Progress and Prospects*, New York: Council on Foreign Relations Press, pp 161–205.

Pei Minxin (2020) 'China's coming upheaval: competition, the coronavirus, and the weakness of Xi Jinping', *Foreign Affairs*, 3 April, www.foreignaffairs.com/articles/ united-states/2020-04-03/chinas-coming-upheaval

Pence, M. (2018) 'Remarks on the administration's policy towards China', Hudson Institute, 4 October, www.hudson.org/events/1610-vice-president-mike-pence-s-remarks-on-the-administration-s-policy-towards-china102018

People's Daily (2020a) 'China offers global help in combating COVID-19', *People's Daily Online*, 24 March, http://en.people.cn/n3/2020/0324/c90000-9671552.html

People's Daily (2020b) 'China's anti-coronavirus efforts, public health system proves effective: African think tank expert', *People's Daily Online*, 6 April, http://en.people. cn/n3/2020/0406/c90000-9676526.html

People's Daily (2020c) 'Kuoda Guo da neixu bixu wajue guonei shichang qianli [Expansion of domestic demand must tap domestic market potential]', *People's Daily*, Commentary, 12 April, http://paper.people.com.cn/rmrb/html/2020-04/ 12/nw.D110000renmrb_20200412_4-01.htm

Pew Research Center (2013) 'America's global image remains more positive than China's: but many see China becoming world's leading power', Pew Research Center, 18 July, www.pewresearch.org/global/2013/07/18/americas-global-image-remains-more-positive-than-chinas/

Peyrouse, S. (2016) 'Discussing China: Sinophilia and Sinophobia in central Asia', *Journal of Eurasian Studies*, 1: 14–23.

Pieke, F. (2013) 'Contemporary China studies in the Netherlands', in W. Idema (ed), *Chinese Studies in the Netherlands*, Amsterdam: Brill, pp 159–90.

Pollack, J. (1984) *China and the Global Strategic Balance*, Santa Monica, CA: Rand.

Pomfret, R. (2019) 'The Eurasian landbridge and China's Belt and Road Initiative: demand, supply of services and public policy', *The World Economy*, 42(6): 1642–53.

Pompeo, M. (2019) 'The United States imposes sanctions on Chinese companies for transporting Iranian oil', US Department of State, 25 September, www.state.gov/the-united-states-imposes-sanctions-on-chinese-companies-for-transporting-iranian-oil/

Pu Xiaoyu (2019) *Rebranding China: Contested Status Signaling in the Changing Global Order*, Stanford, CA: Stanford University Press.

Pu Xiaoyu and Wang Chengli (2018) 'Rethinking China's rise: Chinese scholars debate strategic overstretch', *International Affairs*, 94(5): 1019–35.

Putz, C. (2019) 'Which countries are for or against China's Xinjiang policies?', *The Diplomat*, 15 July, https://thediplomat.com/2019/07/which-countries-are-for-or-against-chinas-xinjiang-policies/

Qin Yaqing (2014) 'Continuity through change: background knowledge and China's international strategy', *Chinese Journal of International Politics*, 7(3): 285–314.

Qiu Jing (2019) 'Why is China Still a Developing Economy?', *Beijing Review*, 26 April, www.bjreview.com/Opinion/201904/t20190426_800166194.html

Qiushi (2020) 'Rang hezuo de yangguang qusan yiqing de yinmai [Let the sunshine of cooperation disperse the haze of the epidemic]' *Qiushi*, 8, 15 April, www.qstheory.cn/dukan/qs/2020-04/15/c_1125857304.htm

Quinn, A. (2011) 'Clinton warns against 'new colonialism' in Africa', *Reuters*, 11 June, www.reuters.com/article/us-clinton-africa/clinton-warns-against-new-colonialism-in-africa-idUSTRE75A0RI20110611

Rajah, R., Dayant, A. and Pryke, J. (2019) 'Ocean of debt? Belt and Road and debt diplomacy in the Pacific', Lowy Institute, 21 October, www.lowyinstitute.org/publications/ocean-debt-belt-and-road-and-debt-diplomacy-pacific

Ramamurti, R. and Hillemann, J. (2018) 'What is "Chinese" about Chinese multinationals?', *Journal of International Business Studies*, 49(1): 34–48.

Ramasamy, B., Yeung, M. and Laforet, S. (2012) 'China's outward foreign direct investment: location choice and firm ownership', *Journal of World Business*, 47(1), 17–25.

Ramo, J. (2004a) 'China has discovered its own economic consensus', *Financial Times*, 8 May.

Ramo, J. (2004b) *The Beijing Consensus: Notes on the New Physics of Chinese Power*, London: Foreign Policy Centre.

Rathbun, B. (2009) 'It takes all types: social psychology, trust, and the international relations paradigm in our minds', *International Theory*, 1(3): 345–80.

Rathbun, B. (2017) 'Trust in international relations', in E. Uslaner (ed), *The Oxford Handbook of Social and Political Trust*, Oxford: Oxford University Press, pp 687–706.

Ren, D. (2020) 'China boosts face mask production capacity by 450 per cent in a month, threatening a glut scenario', *South China Morning Post*, 16 March.

Reuters (2020) 'Finland's emergency supply agency head quits over face mask purchase', *New York Times*, 10 April, www.nytimes.com/reuters/2020/04/10/world/europe/10reuters-health-coronavirus-finland-facemasks.html

Rogers, J., Foxall, A., Henderson, M. and Armstrong, S. (2020) 'Breaking the China supply chain: how the 'five eyes' can decouple from strategic dependency', Henry Jackson Society, May, https://henryjacksonsociety.org/wp-content/uploads/2020/05/Breaking-the-China-Chain.pdf

Rolland, N. (2019) 'Beijing's response to the Belt and Road Initiative's "pushback": a story of assessment and adaptation', *Asian Affairs*, 50(2): 216–35.

Rolland, N. (2020) 'China's vision for a new world order', NBR Special Report 83, 27 January, www.nbr.org/wp-content/uploads/pdfs/publications/sr83_chinasvision_jan2020.pdf

Romanoff, L. (2019) 'Tiananmen Square: the failure of an American-instigated 1989 color revolution', *GlobalResearch*, 24 September, www.globalresearch.ca/tiananmen-square-the-failure-of-an-american-instigated-1989-color-revolution/5690061

Romanoff, L. (2020) 'COVID-19: further evidence that the virus originated in the US', *GlobalResearch*, 11 March, www.globalresearch.ca/covid-19-further-evidence-virus-originated-us/5706078

Rosen, D. and Hanemann, T. (2009) 'China's changing outbound foreign direct investment profile: drivers and policy implications', Petersen Institute for International Economics Policy Brief, PB09-14, www.iie.com/publications/pb/pb09-14.pdf

Ruan Zongze (2015) 'Guojian xinxing guoji guanxi: Chaoyue lishi yingde weilai [Building a new type of international relations: transcending history to win the future]', *Guoji Wenti Yanjiu* [*International Relations Research*], 2: 16–30.

Rudyak, M. (2018) 'Will China's new aid agency be effective?', *The Interpreter*, Lowy Institute, 20 April, www.lowyinstitute.org/the-interpreter/will-china-new-aid-agency-be-effective

Rühlig, T. (2020) 'Who controls Huawei? Implications for Europe', UI Paper No. 5/2020, May, www.ui.se/globalassets/butiken/ui-paper/2020/ui-paper-no.-5-2020.pdf

Saich, A. (2015) *Governance and Politics of China: Fourth Edition*, Basingstoke: Palgrave.

Sanderson, H. (2015) 'China measures set to boost aluminium supply', *Financial Times*, 9 April, www.ft.com/cms/s/0/54e19340-de9f-11e4-8a01-00144feab7de.html#axzz3j3uRvpH5

Sassen, S. (1999) 'Embedding the global in the national', in D. Smith, D. Solinger and S. Topik (eds), *States and Sovereignty in the Global Economy*, London: Routledge, pp 158–71.

Sautman, B. and Yan, Hairong (2006) 'East mountain tiger, west mountain tiger: China, the West, and "colonialism" in Africa,' *Maryland Series in Contemporary Asian Studies*, 3, https://digitalcommons.law.umaryland.edu/cgi/viewcontent.cgi?article=1185&context=mscas

Sauvant, K. and Nolan, M. (2015) 'China's outward foreign direct investment and international investment law', *Journal of International Economic Law*, 18(4): 893–934.

Scobell, A. (2003) *China's Use of Military Force: Beyond the Great Wall and the Long March*, Cambridge: Cambridge University Press.

Scobell, A. (2012) 'Learning to rise peacefully? China and the security dilemma', *Journal of Contemporary China*, 21(76): 713–21.

Sceats, S. (2015) 'China's cyber diplomacy: a taste of law to come', *The Diplomat*, 14 January, http://thediplomat.com/2015/01/chinas-cyber-diplomacy-a-taste-of-law-to-come/

Schirm, S. (2010) 'Leaders in need of followers: emerging powers in global governance', *European Journal of International Relations*, 16(2): 197–221.

SelectUSA (2019) 'Foreign direct investment (FDI): United States', US Department of Commerce, www.selectusa.gov/servlet/servlet.FileDownload?file=015t0000000LKSn

Shambaugh, D. (1996) 'Containment or engagement of China? Calculating Beijing's responses', *International Security*, 21(2): 180–209.

Shambaugh, D. (2005) 'Return to the Middle Kingdom: China and Asia in the early twenty-first century', in D. Shambaugh (ed), *Power Shift: China and Asia's New Dynamics*, Berkeley, CA: University of California Press, pp 1–20.

Shambaugh, D. (2011) 'Coping with a conflicted China', *The Washington Quarterly*, 34(1): 7–27.

Shambaugh, D. (2013) *China Goes Global: The Partial Power*, Oxford: Oxford University Press.

Shambaugh, D. (2015) 'China's soft power push: the search for respect', *Foreign Affairs*, June–July: 99–107.

Shapiro, D., Vecino, C. and Jing Li (2018) 'Exploring China's state-led FDI model: evidence from the extractive sectors in Latin America', *Asia Pacific Journal of Management*, 35(1): 1–27.

Shi Jianping (2017) '"Zhongguo fang'an" yu qiaowu gongzuo xin jiyu [The China Solution and new opportunities for overseas Chinese affairs]', *Wuyi Daxu Xuebao Shehui Kexue ban* [*Journal of Wuyi University Social Sciences Edition*], 19(3): 9–14.

Shi Yinhong (2002) *The Rising China: Essential Disposition, Secular Grand Strategy, and Current Prime Problems*, Sasakawa Peace Foundation USA, www.spf.org/publication/upload/178474a17de.pdf

Shi Yinhong (2015) 'China's complicated foreign policy', ECFR, 31 March, www.ecfr.eu/article/commentary_chinas_complicated_foreign_policy311562

Shi-Kupfer, K. and Ohlberg, M. (2017) 'The party does not yet rule over everything: assessing the state of online plurality in Xi Jinping's "new era"', Merics China Monitor, 29 November, https://merics.org/en/report/party-does-not-yet-rule-over-everything

Shirk, S. (2007) China: Fragile Superpower, New York: Oxford University Press.

Silove, N. (2018) 'Beyond the buzzword: the three meanings of "Grand Strategy"', Security Studies, 27(1): 27–57.

Singer, D., Bremer, S. and Stuckey, J. (1972) 'Capability distribution, uncertainty, and major power war, 1820–1965', in B. Russett (ed), Peace, War, and Numbers, Beverly Hills, CA: Sage, pp 19–48.

Song Zhanghai (2017) 'Tuijin xinxing quanqiuhua yu goujian renlei mingyun gongtongti [Entering a new type of globalization and building a community of shared future for mankind]', Liliun yu Xiandaihua [Theory and Modernization], 5: 10–13.

Sørensen, C. (2019) 'That is not intervention; that is interference with Chinese characteristics: new concepts, distinctions and approaches developing in the Chinese debate and foreign and security policy practice', The China Quarterly, 239: 594–613.

Spring, A. (2009) 'Chinese development aid and agribusiness entrepreneurs in Africa', in S. Sigué (ed), Repositioning African Business and Development for the 21st Century, Dar Es Salaam: International Academy of African Business and Development, pp 23–33, www.iaabd.org/pdf/IAABD2009Proceedings_Final.pdf

SSHRF (2017) 'Beijing declaration', Full text of Beijing Declaration adopted by the First South–South Human Rights Forum, Beijing, 10 December, http://p.china.org.cn/2017-12/10/content_50095729.htm

State Council (1991) 'Human Rights in China', www.china.org.cn/e-white/7/index.htm

State Council (2005) 'China's Peaceful Development Road', www.chinadaily.com.cn/english/doc/2005-12/22/content_505678.htm

State Council (2011a) 'China's Peaceful Development', http://english.www.gov.cn/archive/white_paper/2014/09/09/content_281474986284646.htm

State Council (2011b) 'White Paper on Foreign Aid', http://english.www.gov.cn/archive/white_paper/2014/09/09/content_281474986284620.htm

State Council (2014) 'China's Foreign Aid', http://english.www.gov.cn/archive/white_paper/2014/08/23/content_281474982986592.htm

State Council (2015) 'Zhongguo zhizao 2025 [Made in China 2025]', Guofa 28, 8 May, www.gov.cn/zhengce/content/2015-05/19/content_9784.htm

State Council (2017) 'Guanyu jinyibu yindao he guifan jingwai touzi fangxiang de zhidao yijian [Guiding opinions on further guiding and regulating the orientation of overseas investment]', 4 August, www.gov.cn/zhengce/content/2017-08/18/content_5218665.htm

State Council (2018) 'China's Ministry of Culture and Tourism inaugurated in Beijing', 8 April, http://english.www.gov.cn/state_council/ministries/2018/04/08/content_281476105453512.htm

State Council (2019) 'China and the World in the New Era', http://english.www.gov.cn/archive/whitepaper/201909/27/content_WS5d8d80f9c6d0bcf8c4c142ef.html

Strange, A., Dreher, A., Fuchs, A., Parks, B. and Tierney, M. (2017) 'Tracking underreported financial flows: China's development finance and the aid-conflict nexus revisited', *Journal of Conflict Resolution*, 61(5), 935–63.

Strange, S. (1996) *The Retreat of the State: The Diffusion of Power in the World Economy*, New York: Cambridge University Press.

Strange, S. (1998) *States and Markets*, London: Pinter.

Suettinger, R. (2004) 'The rise and descent of "peaceful rise"', *China Leadership Monitor* (12), http://media.hoover.org/sites/default/files/documents/clm12_rs.pdf

Sullivan, R. (1992), 'Discarding the China card', *Foreign Policy*, 86(3): 3–23.

Sun Daizhen and Li Jing (2017) 'Zhongguo fang'an de shengcheng luoji [The logical form of the China Solution]', *Guowai Lilun Dongtai* [*Theoretical Development in Foreign Relations*], 12: 10–16.

Sun, H. (2007) 'International political marketing: a case study of its application in China', *Journal of Public Affairs*, 7(4): 331–340.

Sun Keqin (2020) 'Pandemic may further drive Europe, US apart', *Global Times*, 23 March, www.globaltimes.cn/content/1183435.shtml

Sun Wanning (2015) 'Slow boat from China: public discourses about the "going out" policy', *International Journal of Cultural Policy*, 21(4): 400–18.

Sun Zehai (2018) 'Wenhua zixin yu renleimingyun gongtongti de goujian' [Cultural Confidence and the Construction of the Community of Shared Future for Mankind]', *Hebei Qingnian Guanli Ganbu Xueyuan Xuebao* [*Journal of Hebei You Administrative Cadres College*], 30(2): 105–10.

Sutherland, D., Ning Lutan and Wang Jing (2012) 'An exploration of pyramidal business groups in China', in Wang Liming (ed), *Rising China in the Changing World Economy*, London: Routledge, pp 138–62.

Sutter, K., Schwarzenberg, A. and Sutherland, S. (2020) 'Covid-19: China medical supply chains and broader trade issues', Congressional Research Service, No. R46304, 6 April, https://crsreports.congress.gov/product/pdf/R/R46304

Suzuki, T. (2019) 'China's united front work in the Xi Jinping era – institutional developments and activities', *Journal of Contemporary East Asia Studies*, 8(8): 83–98.

Swaine, M. (2000) 'Does China have a Grand Strategy?', *Current History*, 99(638): 274–9.

Swaine, M. (2010) 'China's assertive behavior, part one: on "core interests"', China Leadership Monitor, Carnegie Endowment for International Peace, https://carnegieendowment.org/2010/11/15/china-s-assertive-behavior-part-one-on-core-interests-pub-41937

Swaine, M. (2012) 'Chinese leadership and elite responses to the US pacific pivot', China Leadership Monitor 38, http://carnegieendowment.org/files/Swaine_CLM_38_Final_Draft_pdf.pdf

Swaine, M. (2015) 'Chinese views and commentary on the 'one belt, one road' initiative', China Leadership Monitor 47, www.hoover.org/sites/default/files/research/docs/clm47ms.pdf

Szamosszegi, A. and Kyle, C. (2011) 'An analysis of state-owned enterprises and state capitalism in China', US-China Economic Security Review Commission report, 26 October, www.uscc.gov/sites/default/files/Research/10_26_11_CapitalTradeSOEStudy.pdf

Taliaferro, J., Lobell, S. and Ripsman, N. (2009) Neoclassical Realism, the State and Foreign Policy, Cambridge: Cambridge University Press.

Tan Xiaomei (2013) 'China's overseas investment in the energy/resources sector: its scale, drivers, challenges and implications', Energy Economics, 36: 750–58.

Taylor, I. (2006) China and Africa: Engagement and Compromise, London: Routledge.

Taylor, I. (2019) 'In a fix: Africa's place in the Belt and Road Initiative and the reproduction of dependency', Paper presented at 'One Belt, One Road and the Globalization of China's Political Economy', National Chiao Tung University, Hsinchu, Taiwan, 3 October.

Terrill, R. (1977) 'China and the world: self-reliance or interdependence?', Foreign Affairs, 55(2): 295–305.

Thayer, C. (2011) 'Chinese assertiveness in the South China Sea and Southeast Asian responses', Journal of Current Southeast Asian Affairs, 30(2): 77–104.

Thompson, D. (2005) 'China's soft power in Africa: from the "Beijing Consensus" to health diplomacy', China Brief, 5(21), https://jamestown.org/program/chinas-soft-power-in-africa-from-the-beijing-consensus-to-health-diplomacy/

Thussu, D., de Burgh, H. and Shi Anbin (2017) 'Introduction', in D. Thussu, H. de Burgh and Shi Anbin (eds), China's Media Go Global, New York: Routledge, pp 1–15.

Tian Pengying (2018) 'Lishi weiwu zhuyi yu renlei mingyun gongtongti [Historical materialism and the community of shared future for mankind]', Makesi Zhuyi Yanjiu [Marxism Research], 1: 119–27.

Timothy, D. and Kim, S. (2015) 'Understanding the tourism relationships between South Korea and China: a review of influential factors', Current Issues in Tourism, 28(5): 412–32.

Tingley, D., Xu, C., Chilton, A. and Milner, H. (2015) 'The political economy of inward FDI: opposition to Chinese mergers and acquisitions', The Chinese Journal of International Politics, 8(1): 27–57.

Timperlake, E. and Triplett, W. (1999) Red Dragon Rising: Communist China's Military Threat to America, Washington, DC: Regnery.

Timperlake, E. and Triplett, W. (2000) Year of the Rat: How Bill Clinton and Al Gore Compromised U.S. Security for Chinese Cash, Washington, DC: Regnery.

Tobin, L. (2018) Xi's vision for transforming global governance: a strategic challenge for Washington and its allies', Texas National Security Review, 2(1): https://tnsr.org/2018/12/xis-vision-for-transforming-global-governance-a-strategic-challenge-for-washington-and-its-allies/

Torres, D. (2017) 'China's soft power offensive', *Politico*, 26 December, www.politico. eu/article/china-soft-power-offensive-confucius-institute-education/

Triplett, W. (2004) *Rogue State*, Washington, DC: Regnery.

Tsai Wen-Hsuan and Zhou Wang (2019) 'Integrated fragmentation and the role of leading small groups in Chinese politics', *The China Journal*, 82: 1–22.

Tsang, S. (2019) 'Party-state realism: a framework for understanding China's approach to foreign policy', *Journal of Contemporary China*, 29(122): 304–18.

Tse, T.S.M. (2013) 'Chinese outbound tourism as a form of diplomacy', *Tourism Planning and Development*, 10(2): 149–58.

Tugendhat, T. (2020) 'Beijing uses a toxic brew of lies and fear to maintain power', *Mail on Sunday*, 5 April, www.dailymail.co.uk/news/article-8188239/Tom-Tugendhat-Beijing-uses-toxic-brew-lies-fear-maintain-power.html

Tull, D. (2006) 'China's engagement in Africa: scope, significance and consequences', *Journal of Modern African Studies*, 44(3): 459–79.

Tunsjø, Ø. (2018) *The Return of Bipolarity in World Politics: China, the United States, and Geostructural Realism*, New York: Columbia University Press.

UN (2017a) 'Resolution 2344 (2017)', United Nations Assistance Mission in Afghanistan, 17 March, https://unama.unmissions.org/sites/default/files/resolution_2344_2017_english.pdf

UN (2017b) *United Nations Disarmament Yearbook: Volume 47 (Part 1)*, New York: United Nations.

UN (2018) 'Social dimensions of the new partnership for Africa's development', UN Economic and Social Council, 8 August, www.chinahumanrights.org/uploadfile/2018/0615/20180615085020358.pdf

UNCTAD (2019) 'Foreign direct investment to Africa defies global slump, rises 11%', 12 June, https://unctad.org/en/pages/newsdetails.aspx?OriginalVersionID=2109

UNTWO (2018) 'World tourism barometer and statistical analysis, March–April 2018', United Nations World Tourism Organization, www.e-unwto.org/doi/abs/10.18111/wtobarometereng.2018.16.1.2

US Congress (2018) 'John S. McCain national defense authorization act for fiscal year 2019', 115 Congress of the USA, 4 August, www.govinfo.gov/content/pkg/BILLS-115hr5515enr/pdf/BILLS-115hr5515enr.pdf

US Department of State (2020) 'Virtual forum on expanding Taiwan's participation on the global scale', Office of the Spokesperson, Media Note, 2 April, www.state.gov/virtual-forum-on-expanding-taiwans-participation-on-the-global-stage/

Utomi, P. (2008) 'China and Nigeria', in J. Cooke (ed), *U.S. and Chinese Engagement in Africa: Prospects for Improving U.S. China Africa Cooperation*, Washington, DC: Center for Strategic and International Studies, pp 39–48.

Vangeli, A. (2019) 'Diffusion of ideas in the era of the Belt and Road: insights from China–CEE think tank cooperation', *Asia-Europe Journal*, 17(4):421–36.

Varrall, M. (2016) 'Domestic actors and agendas in Chinese aid policy', *The Pacific Review*, 29(1): 21–44.

Vogel, E. (1979) *Japan as Number One: Lessons for America*, Cambridge, MA: Harvard University Press.

Vuksanovic, V. (2020) 'China has its eyes on Serbia', *Foreign Policy*, 8 April, https://foreignpolicy.com/2020/04/08/china-serbia-aleksander-vucic-xi-jinping-coronavirus/

Wacker, G. (2015) 'The irreversible rise: a new foreign policy for a stronger China', in A. Amighini and A. Berkofsky (eds), *Xi's Policy Gambles: The Bumpy Road Ahead*, Milan: ISPI, pp 65–77.

Walder, A. (2004) 'The transformation of contemporary China studies, 1977–2002', in D. Szanton (ed), *The Politics of Knowledge: Area Studies and the Disciplines*, Berkeley, CA: University of California Press, pp 314–40.

Walter, C. and Howie, F. (2012) *Red Capitalism: The Fragile Financial Foundation of China's Extraordinary Rise*, Singapore: John Wiley.

Wang Danping and Adamson, B. (2015) 'War and peace: perceptions of Confucius Institutes in China and USA', *The Asia–Pacific Education Researcher*, 24(1): 225–34.

Wang Hongying (2003) 'National image building and Chinese foreign policy', *China: An International Journal*, 1(1): 46–72.

Wang Hongying and Xue Yinghu (2017) 'The new Great Leap Forward: think tanks with Chinese characteristics', CIGI Papers 142, www.cigionline.org/sites/default/files/documents/Paper%20No.142.pdf

Wang Hui (2005) 'The historical origin of China's neo-liberalism', in Tian Yu Cao (ed), *The Chinese Model of Modern Development*, New York: Routledge, pp 61–87.

Wang Jianwei (2019) 'Xi Jinping's "major country diplomacy": a paradigm shift?', *Journal of Contemporary China*, 28(115): 15–30.

Wang Jisi (2011) 'China's search for a Grand Strategy: a rising power finds its way', *Foreign Affairs*, 90(2): 68–79.

Wang Qishan (2019) 'Upholding peace and cooperation and building a community with a shared future for mankind', address at Opening Ceremony of the Eighth World Peace Forum, 8 July, www.fmprc.gov.cn/mfa_eng/wjdt_665385/zyjh_665391/t1679950.shtml

Wang Qiuyi (2018) 'Quanqiu zhili zhong de zhongguo fang'an ji qi gongxian (The China Solution for global governance and its contribution)', *Dangdai Shijie (Contemporary World)*, 4: 54–7.

Wang Wen (2019) 'China not in a position to lead the world', *Global Times*, 26 November, www.globaltimes.cn/content/1171156.shtml

Wang Yi (2017a) 'Forge ahead under the guidance of general secretary Xi Jinping's thought on diplomacy', *Study Times*, 1 September, www.fmprc.gov.cn/mfa_eng/wjdt_665385/zyjh_665391/t1489143.shtml

Wang Yi (2017b) 'Toward peace and development for all', Speech at the General Debate of the 72nd Session of the United Nations General Assembly, 21 September, www.fmprc.gov.cn/mfa_eng/wjdt_665385/zyjh_665391/t1496244.shtml

Wang Yi (2017c) 'Advance the global human rights cause and build a community with a shared future for mankind', Speech at the opening ceremony of the first South–South human rights forum, Beijing, 7 December, www.fmprc.gov.cn/mfa_eng/wjdt_665385/zyjh_665391/P020171211565335323921.pdf

Wang Yi (2017d) 'Speech by Foreign Minister Wang Yi at the opening of symposium on international developments and China's diplomacy in 2017', 10 December, www.fmprc.gov.cn/mfa_eng/wjdt_665385/zyjh_665391/t1518130.shtml

Wang Yi (2018a) 'Join hands across the ocean for a new era', Remarks at opening ceremony of the second ministerial meeting of the China-CELAC forum, 23 January, www.fmprc.gov.cn/mfa_eng/wjdt_665385/zyjh_665391/t1528692.shtml

Wang Yi (2018b) 'Multilateralism, shared peace and development', General Debate of the 73rd Session of the United Nations General Assembly, 28 September, www.fmprc.gov.cn/mfa_eng/wjdt_665385/zyjh_665391/t1600861.shtml

Wang Yi (2018c) 'Speech by H.E. Wang Yi State Councillor and Minister of Foreign Affairs at the opening of symposium on the international situation and China's foreign relations in 2018', 11 December, www.fmprc.gov.cn/mfa_eng/wjdt_665385/zyjh_665391/t1621221.shtml

Wang Yi (2019a) 'Remarks at Ministry of Foreign Affairs 2019 New Year reception', 31 January, www.fmprc.gov.cn/mfa_eng/wjdt_665385/zyjh_665391/t1634534.shtml

Wang Yi (2019b) 'Speech at opening ceremony of the coordinators' meeting on the implementation of the follow-up actions of the Beijing Summit of the Forum on China-Africa Cooperation', 25 June, www.fmprc.gov.cn/mfa_eng/wjdt_665385/zyjh_665391/t1675596.shtml

Wang Yi (2019c) 'A joint response to climate change: a better environment for our planet', Remarks at UN Climate Action Summit, 23 September, www.fmprc.gov.cn/mfa_eng/wjb_663304/wjbz_663308/2461_663310/t1700987.shtml

Wang Yi (2019d) 'Toward a better future through development cooperation', Statement at UN High-Level Political Forum on Sustainable Development, 25 September, www.fmprc.gov.cn/ce/cenp/eng/zgwj/t1701246.htm

Wang Yi (2019e) 'China today: a proud member of the global community', Statement at the General Debate of the 74th Session of the UN General Assembly, 27 September, www.fmprc.gov.cn/mfa_eng/wjdt_665385/zyjh_665391/t1703219.shtml

Wang Yi (2019f) 'Puxie zhongguo tese daguo waijiao de shidai huazhang [The era of writing great power diplomacy with Chinese characteristics]', *Renmin Ribao* [*People's Daily*], 23 September, http://paper.people.com.cn/rmrb/html/2019-09/23/nw.D110000renmrb_20190923_1-07.htm

Wang Yiwei (2008) 'Public diplomacy and the rise of Chinese soft power', *The Annals of the American Academy of Political and Social Science*, 616(1); 257–73.

Wang Yong (2016) 'Offensive for defensive: the Belt and Road Initiative and China's new Grand Strategy', *The Pacific Review*, 29(3): 455–63.

Wang Yu (2018) 'The political economy of joining the AIIB', *The Chinese Journal of International Politics*, 11(2): 105–30.

Wang Yunxiang (1996) 'Zhongguo weixi lun xi [Analysing the China Threat theory]', *Guoji Guancha [International Survey]*, 3: 35–40.

Wang Zheng (2014) 'The Chinese dream: concept and context', *Journal of Chinese Political Science*, 19(1): 1–13.

Wank, D. (1998) *Commodifying Chinese Communism: Business, Trust, and Politics in a South Coast City*, Cambridge: Cambridge University Press.

Watkins, S. (2019) 'China and Iran flesh out strategic partnership', Petroleum Economist, 3 September, https://www.petroleum-economist.com/articles/politics-economics/middle-east/2019/china-and-iran-flesh-out-strategic-partnership

Weissmann, M. (2019) 'Understanding power (shift) in East Asia: the Sino-US narrative battle about leadership in the South China Sea', *Asian Perspective*, 43(2): 223–48.

Wendt, A. (1992) 'Anarchy is what states make of it: the social construction of power politics', *International Organization*, 46(2): 391–425.

Wheeler, N. (2018) *Trusting Enemies: Interpersonal Relationships in International Conflict*, Oxford: Oxford University Press.

White & Case (2017) 'China's rise in global M&A: here to stay', Rhodium Group/ White & Case, 24 March, http://rhg.com/wp-content/uploads/2017/03/chinas-rise-in-global-ma-here-to-stay.pdf

White House (2014) 'Fact sheet: U.S.–China joint announcement on climate change and clean energy cooperation', Office of the Press Secretary, 11 November, https://obamawhitehouse.archives.gov/the-press-office/2014/11/11/fact-sheet-us-china-joint-announcement-climate-change-and-clean-energy-c

White House (2020) 'United States strategic approach to the People's Republic of China', 20 May, www.whitehouse.gov/wp-content/uploads/2020/05/U.S.-Strategic-Approach-to-The-Peoples-Republic-of-China-Report-5.20.20.pdf

Whiting, S. (2004) 'The cadre evaluation system at the grass roots: the paradox of party rule', in B. Naughton and Dali Yang (eds), *Holding China Together: Diversity and National Integration in the Post-Deng Era*, Cambridge: Cambridge University Press, pp 101–19.

WHO (2020) 'Report of the WHO-China joint mission on coronavirus disease 2019 (COVID-19)', World Heal Organization, February, www.who.int/docs/default-source/coronaviruse/who-china-joint-mission-on-covid-19-final-report.pdf

Williams, R. (2019) 'Dolce & Gabbana is still paying for insulting Chinese women', *Bloomberg*, 7 March, www.bloomberg.com/news/articles/2019-03-07/dolce-gabbana-is-still-paying-for-insulting-chinese-women

Williamson, J. (2010) 'The impact of the financial crisis on development thinking', Max Fry Annual Lecture, University of Birmingham, 13 October 2010, www.iie.com/publications/papers/williamson20101013.pdf

Windybank, S. (2005) 'The China Syndrome', *Policy*, 21(2): 28–33.

Wintour, P. (2020) 'Dawn of Asian century puts pressure on EU to choose sides, says top diplomat', *The Guardian*, 25 May, www.theguardian.com/world/2020/may/25/asian-century-marks-end-of-us-led-global-system-warns-eu-chief

Womack, B. (2016) *Asymmetry and International Relationships*, New York: Cambridge University Press.

Wong, A. (2018) 'More than peripheral: how provinces influence China's foreign policy', *The China Quarterly*, 235: 735–57.

Wong, C. (2020) 'Too soon, too loud: Chinese foreign policy advisers tell 'Wolf Warrior' diplomats to tone it down', *South China Morning Post*, 14 May, www.scmp.com/news/china/diplomacy/article/3084274/too-soon-too-loud-chinese-foreign-policy-advisers-tell-wolf

Woo, W.T. (1999) 'The economics and politics of transition to an open market economy: China', OECD Development Centre Technical Paper 153, https://doi.org/10.1787/322178001745

Wu, F. (1981) 'From self-reliance to interdependence? Developmental strategy and foreign economic policy in post-Mao China', *Modern China*, 7(4): 445–82.

Wu, F. and Seach, A. (2008) 'Would China's sovereign wealth fund be a menace to the USA?', *China and World Economy*, 16(4): 33–47.

Wu Qianlan (2013) *Competition Laws, Globalization and Legal Pluralism: China's Experience*, Oxford: Hart.

Wu, W. and Xie, E. (2020) 'Coronavirus: China bans export of test kits, medical supplies by firms not licensed to sell them at home', *South China Morning Post*, 1 April, www.scmp.com/news/china/society/article/3077953/coronavirus-china-bans-export-test-kits-medical-supplies-firms

Wu You (2018) 'The rise of China with cultural soft power in the age of globalization', *Journal of Literature and Art Studies*, 8(5): 763–78.

Wu Yuanhua, Wu Yulin and Li Juan (2018) 'Xi Jinping guanyu quanqiu zhili de zhongguo fang'an [Xi Jinping on the China Solution for global governance]', *Quanzhou Shifan Xueyuan Xuebao [Journal of Quanzhou Normal College]*, 36(3): 1–8.

Wu Zhong, Karp, P. and Wang Yan (2010) 'China's International Poverty Reduction Center as a platform for South–South learning', *Development Outreach*, 12(2): 32–4.

Wübbeke, J., Meissner, M., Zenglein, M., Ives, J. and Conrad, B. (2016) 'Made in China 2025: the making of a high-tech superpower and consequences for industrial countries', Merics Papers on China 2, https://kritisches-netzwerk.de/sites/default/files/merics_-_made_in_china_2025_-_the_making_of_a_high-tech_superpower_and_consequences_for_industrial_countries_-_76_seiten_1.pdf

Wuthnow, J. (2008) 'The concept of soft power in China's strategic discourses', *Issues and Studies*, 44(2): 1–28.

Wuthnow, J. (2017) 'Chinese perspectives on the Belt and Road Initiative: strategic rationales, risks, and implications', Center for the Study of Chinese Military Affairs Institute for National Strategic Studies China Strategic Perspectives, No. 12, October, https://inss.ndu.edu/Portals/68/Documents/stratperspective/china/ChinaPerspectives-12.pdf

Xi Jinping (2012) 'Speech at "The Road to Rejuvenation"', 29 November, https://chinacopyrightandmedia.wordpress.com/2012/11/29/speech-at-the-road-to-rejuvenation/

Xi Jinping (2014) 'Xi Jinping zai deguo keerbo jijin hui de yanjiang' [Speech at the Körber Foundation]', 29 March, http://politics.people.com.cn/n/2014/0329/c1024-24772018.html

Xi Jinping (2015a) 'Bianzheng weiwu zhuyi shi zhongguo gongchandangren de shihjieguan he fangfalun [Dialectical materialism is the world outlook and methodology of Chinese communists]', Speech at 20th collective study group of the 18th Politburo, 23 January, www.qstheory.cn/dukan/qs/2018-12/31/c_1123923896.htm

Xi Jinping (2015b) 'Towards a community of common destiny and a new future for Asia', Keynote Speech at Bo'ao Forum for Asia, 28 March, www.xinhuanet.com//english/2015-03/29/c_134106145.htm

Xi Jinping (2015c) 'Working together to forge a new partnership of win-win cooperation and create a community of shared future for mankind', Speech at the General Assembly of the 70th Session of the UN General Assembly, 28 September, https://qz.com/512886/read-the-full-text-of-xi-jinpings-first-un-address/

Xi Jinping (2015d) 'Xieshou xiaochu pinkun cujin gongtong fazhan – zai 2015 nian jian pin yu fazhan gaoceng luntan shang de zhuyi yanjiang [Keynote speech at the 2015 poverty reduction and development high-level forum]', 16 October, www.xinhuanet.com//politics/2015-10/16/c_1116851045.htm

Xi Jinping (2015e) 'Zai quanguo zhengxie xinnian chahuiwei shang de jianghua [Speech at new year's tea party of the national committee of the Chinese People's Political Consultative Conference]', 31 December, www.cppcc.gov.cn/zxww/2016/01/01/ARTI1451626779071522.shtml

Xi Jinping (2015f) '2016 nian xin heci [2016 New Year Message]', www.xinhuanet.com/politics/2015-12/31/c_1117643074.htm

Xi Jinping (2016a) 'Zai zhexue shehui kexue gongzuo zuotan de jianghua [Speech at symposium on philosophy and social sciences]', 18 May, www.xinhuanet.com/politics/2016-05/18/c_1118891128.htm

Xi Jinping (2016b) 'Speech at a ceremony marking the 95 anniversary of the founding of the Communist Party of China', *Qiushi* (English Language Edition), 1 July, http://english.qstheory.cn/2016-12/20/c_1120042032.htm

Xi Jinping (2016c) *Xi Jinping's Speeches at the G20 Hangzhou Summit*, Beijing: China International Publishing Group/Foreign Languages Press.

Xi Jinping (2017a) 'Jointly shoulder responsibility of our times, promote global growth', Speech at World Economic Forum, Davos, 17 January, www.china.org.cn/node_7247529/content_40569136.htm

Xi Jinping (2017b) 'Work together to build a community of shared future for mankind', Speech at UN Office, Geneva, 18 January, http://iq.chineseembassy.org/eng/zygx/t1432869.htm

Xi Jinping (2017c) 'Work together to build the Silk Road Economic Belt and the 21st Century Maritime Silk Road', Speech at opening ceremony of the Belt and Road Forum for International Cooperation, 14 May, www.xinhuanet.com//english/2017-05/14/c_136282982.htm

Xi Jinping (2017d) 'Working together to usher in the second "golden decade" of BRICS cooperation', Speech at opening session of BRICS Business Forum, Xiamen, 3 September, www.xinhuanet.com//english/2017-09/03/c_129695215.htm

Xi Jinping (2017e) 'Secure a decisive victory in building a moderately prosperous society in all respects and strive for the great success of Socialism with Chinese Characteristics for a New Era', Speech delivered at the 19th National Congress of the Communist Party of China, 18 October, www.xinhuanet.com/english/download/Xi_Jinping's_report_at_19th_CPC_National_Congress.pdf

Xi Jinping (2018a) 'Openness for greater prosperity, innovation for a better future', Speech at the Bo'ao Forum for Asia, 10 April, www.uscnpm.org/blog/2018/04/11/transcript-president-xi-addresses-2018-boao-forum-asia-hainan/

Xi Jinping (2018b) 'Carrying forward the Shanghai Spirit to build a community with a shared future', Speech at 18th Shanghai Cooperation Summit, Qingdao, 10 June, www.xinhuanet.com/english/2018-06/10/c_137244587.htm

Xi Jinping (2018c) 'Keeping abreast of the trend of the times to achieve common development', Speech at the BRICS Business Forum in Johannesburg, 26 July, www.xinhuanet.com/english/2018-07/26/c_129920686.htm

Xi Jinping (2018d) 'Work together for common development and a shared future', Speech at Opening Ceremony of Beijing FOCAC Summit, 3 September, .xinhuanet.com/english/2018-09/03/c_129946189.htm

Xi Jinping (2018e) 'Work together for an open global economy that is innovative and inclusive', Keynote speech at opening of First China Import Expo, Shanghai, 5 November, www.xinhuanet.com/english/2018-11/05/c_137583815.htm

Xi Jinping (2019a) 'Working together to deliver a brighter future for Belt and Road cooperation', Keynote Speech at the Opening Ceremony of the Second Belt and Road Forum for International Cooperation, 26 April, www.fmprc.gov.cn/mfa_eng/zxxx_662805/t1658424.shtml

Xi Jinping (2019b) 'Promoting high-quality development of Belt and Road cooperation', Remarks at Leaders' Roundtable of The Second Belt and Road Forum for International Cooperation, 27 April, www.fmprc.gov.cn/mfa_eng/zxxx_662805/t1659454.shtml

Xi Jinping (2019c) 'Deepening exchanges and mutual learning among civilizations for an Asian community with a shared future', Keynote speech at the Opening Ceremony of The Conference on Dialogue of Asian Civilizations, 15 May, www.fmprc.gov.cn/mfa_eng/wjdt_665385/zyjh_665391/t1663857.shtml

Xi Jinping (2019d) 'Staying focused and taking solid actions for a brighter future of the Shanghai Cooperation Organisation', Remarks at 19 Meeting of the Council of Heads of State of The Shanghai Cooperation Organisation, 14 June, www.fmprc.gov.cn/mfa_eng/wjdt_665385/zyjh_665391/t1672362.shtml

Xi Jinping (2019e) 'Working together for new progress of security and development in Asia', Remarks at Fifth Summit of the Conference on Interaction and Confidence-Building Measures in Asia, 15 June, www.fmprc.gov.cn/mfa_eng/wjdt_665385/zyjh_665391/t1672539.shtml

Xi Jinping (2019f) 'Pushing China's development of an Ecological Civilization to a new stage', Qiushi (English Language Edition), 11(2), http://english.qstheory.cn/2019-09/17/c_1124932126.htm

Xi Jinping (2019g) 'Working together to build a high-quality world economy', Remarks at Osaka G20 Summit, 28 June, www.fmprc.gov.cn/mfa_eng/topics_665678/xjpcxesgjtfh/t1676619.shtml

Xi Jinping (2020) 'Fighting COVID-19 through solidarity and cooperation: building a global community of health for all', Statement at Virtual Opening of the 73rd World Health Assembly, 18 May, www.globaltimes.cn/content/1188716.shtml

Xiao Xinfa (2018) 'Zhongguo fang'an ji qi jiazhi gongshi [The China Solution and its value consensus]', Shehui Kexue Dongtai [Social Sciences Dynamics], 3: 24–30.

Xiao Yuefan (2013) 'The Politics of Crisis Management in China', unpublished PhD thesis, University of Warwick.

Xie Wenjuan and Zhang Qianyuan (2018) 'Lun goujian renlei mingyun gongtongti de siwei yiti [On the four in one and building a community of shared future for mankind]', Shehui Zhuyi Yanjiu [Socialism Studies], 2: 56–64.

Xinhua (2016) 'President Xi urges new media outlet to "tell China stories well"', Global Times, 31 December, https://www.globaltimes.cn/content/1026592.shtml

Xinhua (2019a) 'Interview: "China a threat to liberal international order" a losing argument', Xinhuanet, 3 June, www.xinhuanet.com/english/2019-06/03/c_138113631.htm

Xinhua (2019b) 'Xi Jinping: xuexi makesi zhuyi jiben lilun shi gongchandangren de bixiu ke [Xi Jinping: learning the basic theory of Marxism is a compulsory course for communists]', Qiushi republished by Xinhuanet, 15 November, www.xinhuanet.com/politics/leaders/2019-11/15/c_1125236929.htm

Xinhua (2020a) 'Chinese Embassy slams some British media over "groundless" coronavirus accusation', Xinhuanet, 1 April, www.xinhuanet.com/english/2020-04/01/c_138937074.htm

Xinhua (2020b) 'China publishes timeline on COVID-19 information sharing, int'l cooperation', Xinhuanet, 6 April, www.xinhuanet.com/english/2020-04/06/c_138951662.htm

Xu Jian (2014) 'Rethinking China's period of strategic opportunity', China International Studies, March/April: 51–70.

Xu Jin (2016) 'Debates in IR academia and China's policy adjustments', Chinese Journal of International Politics, 9(4): 459–85.

Xu Jin (2018) 'An examination of the concepts and principles of China's major-country diplomacy with its own characteristics for a new era', Contemporary International Relations, 28(4): 1–25.

Yahuda, M. (2013) 'China's new assertiveness in the South China Sea', *Journal of Contemporary China*, 22(81): 446–59.

Yan Shuhan (2018) 'Gagie kaifang de chenggong wei jiejue renlei wenti gongxianle zhongguo zhihui zhongguo fang'an [The success of reform and opening has contributed Chinese Wisdom to the China Solution to solve human problems]', *Wenhua Ruanshili* [*Cultural Soft Power*], 4: 18–25.

Yan Xiaojun and Huang Jie (2017) 'Navigating unknown waters: the Chinese Communist Party's new presence in the private sector', *China Review*, 17(2): 37–63.

Yan Xuetong (2018) 'Chinese values vs. liberalism: what ideology will shape the international normative order?', *The Chinese Journal of International Politics*, 11(1): 1–22.

Yan Xuetong (2019) *Leadership and the Rise of Great Powers*, Princeton, NJ: Princeton University Press.

Yang Guangbin (2016) 'Wei shehui zhidu tansuo tigong zhongguo fang'an [Providing a China Solution for the exploration of social systems]' *Renmin Ribao* [*People's Daily*], 5 December, http://theory.people.com.cn/n1/2016/1205/c40531-28924331.html

Yang Guisen and Li Zhonghe (2018) 'Renlei mingyun gongtongti shi zhongguo zhihui dui renlei wenming de xin gongxian [Community of shared destiny is the new contribution of Chinese Wisdom to human civilization]', *Guizhou Daxue Xuebao Zhehuikexue Ban* [*Journal of Guizhou University Social Sciences Edition*], 36(1): 1–5.

Yang Jiechi (2017) 'Study and implement General Secretary Xi Jinping's thought on diplomacy in a deep-going way and keep writing new chapters of major-country diplomacy with distinctive Chinese features', 17 July, www.xinhuanet.com/english/2017-07/19/c_136456009.htm

Yang Jiechi (2018a) 'Working together to build a world of lasting peace and universal security and a community with a shared future for mankind', Address at the Opening Ceremony of the Seventh World Peace Forum, Tsinghua University, Beijing, 14 July, www.fmprc.gov.cn/mfa_eng/zxxx_662805/t1577242.shtml

Yang Jiechi (2018b) 'Remarks by H.E. Yang Jiechi at the foreign policy session of the 2018 annual meeting of the Valdai Discussion Club', 18 October, www.fmprc.gov.cn/mfa_eng/wjdt_665385/zyjh_665391/t1605521.shtml

Yang Jiemian (2014) 'Zhan zai xin qidian de zhongguo waijiao zhanlue tiaozheng [Strategic adjustment of China's diplomacy at a new starting point]', *Guoji Zhanwang* [*Global Review*], 1: 1–13.

Yang Keming (2012) 'The dependency of private entrepreneurs on the Chinese state', *Strategic Change*, 21(3–4): 107–17.

Yang Li (2018) 'Zengqiang renlei mingyun gongtonti yishi tuidong goujian renlei mingyun gongtongti [Strengthening the community of human destiny and promoting the construction of a community of shared future for mankind]', *Sheke Zongheng* [*Social Science Review*], 33(4): 5–10.

Yang Xiangfeng (2017) 'The anachronism of a China socialized: why engagement is not all it's cracked up to be', *The Chinese Journal of International Politics*, 10(1): 67–94.

Yao Yang (2015) 'China's approach to economic diplomacy', in J. Ikenberry, Wang Jisi and Zhu Feng (eds), *America, China, and the Struggle for World Order: Ideas, Traditions, Historical Legacies, and Global Visions*, Basingstoke: Palgrave Macmillan, pp 161–86.

Ye Didi (2019) 'Rediscovering the transition in China's national interest: a neoclassical realist approach', *Journal of Current Chinese Affairs*, 48(1): 76–105.

Ye Min (2019) 'Fragmentation and mobilization: domestic politics of the Belt and Road in China', *Journal of Contemporary China*, 28(119): 696–711.

Ye Zicheng (2011) *Inside China's Grand Strategy: The Perspective from the People's Republic*, Louisville, KN: University of Kentucky Press.

Yeophantong, P. (2013) 'Governing the world: China's evolving conceptions of responsibility', *The Chinese Journal of International Politics*, 6(4): 329–64.

Yeung, H. and Liu Weidong (2008) 'Globalizing China: the rise of mainland firms in the global economy', *Eurasian Geography and Economics*, 49(1): 57–86.

Yin Jiwu (2019) 'Preference expression under political constraints: an analysis of debates about China's use of Force', in Huiyun Feng, Kai He and Yan Xuetong (eds), *Chinese Scholars and Foreign Policy*, London: Routledge, pp 127–52.

You Ji (2016) 'China's National Security Commission: theory, evolution and operations', *Journal of Contemporary China*, 25(98): 178–96.

Yu Chengwen (2017) 'Shehui zhidu zhongguo fang'an de tansuo shijian [Exploration and practice of the social system of the China Solution]', *Tansuo* [*Exploration*], 1: 5–10 and 21.

Yu Jie (2019) 'China's technological prowess: implications for global alliances', in A. Amighini (ed), *China's Race to Global Technology Leadership*, Milan: ISPI, pp 39–56.

Yu Zheng (2019) 'Foreign direct investment in China', in Ka Zeng (ed), *Handbook on the International Political Economy of China*, Cheltenham: Edward Elgar, pp 61–75.

Yu Zhengliang (2012) 'Guanyu zhongguo da zhanluede sikao [Reflections on China's Grand Strategy]', *Mao Zedong Deng Xiaoping Lilun Yanjiu* [*Research on Mao Zedong Deng Xiaoping Theory*], 5: 95–101.

Yuan Peng (2018) 'China's international strategic thought and layout for a new era', *Contemporary International Relations*, 28(1): 18–42.

Zakaria, F. (2020) 'The new China scare: why America shouldn't panic about its latest challenger', *Foreign Affairs*, 99(1): 52–69.

Zanardi, C. (2016) 'China's soft power with Chinese characteristics: the cases of Confucius Institutes and Chinese naval diplomacy', *Journal of Political Power*, 9(3): 431–47.

Zeng Fanhua, Huang, W.C. and Heung, J. (2016) 'On Chinese government's stock market rescue efforts in 2015', *Modern Economy*, 7(4): 411–18.

Zeng Jinghan, Xiao Yuefan and Breslin, S. (2015) 'Securing China's core interests: the state of the debate in China', *International Affairs*, 91(2): 245–66.

Zeng Ka and Li Xiaojun (2019) 'Geopolitics, nationalism, and foreign direct investment: perceptions of the China threat and American public attitudes toward Chinese FDI', *Chinese Journal of International Politics*, 12(4): 495–518.

Zha Daojiong (2015) 'China's economic diplomacy focusing on the Asia-Pacific region', *China Quarterly of International Strategic Studies*, 1(1): 85–104.

Zhang Biao (2019) 'The perils of hubris? A tragic reading of Thucydides' Trap and China-US relations', *Chinese Journal of Political Science*, 24(2): 129–44.

Zhang Denghua (2018) 'China's new aid agency', The Interpreter, Lowy Institute, 19 March, www.lowyinstitute.org/the-interpreter/china-s-new-aid-agency

Zhang Denghua and Smith, G. (2017) 'China's foreign aid system: structure, agencies, and identities', *Third World Quarterly*, 38(10): 2330–46.

Zhang Falin (2017) 'Holism failure: China's inconsistent stances and consistent interests in global financial governance', *Journal of Contemporary China*, 26(105): 369–84.

Zhang Feng (2012) 'Rethinking China's Grand Strategy: Beijing's evolving national interests and strategic ideas in the reform era', *International Politics*, 49(3): 18–345.

Zhang Feng (2013) 'Chinese exceptionalism in the intellectual world of China's foreign policy', in R. Foot (ed), *China Across the Divide: The Domestic and Global in Politics and Society*, Oxford: Oxford University Press, pp 44–65.

Zhang Feng (2015) 'Beijing's master plan for the South China Sea', *Foreign Policy*, 23 June, https://foreignpolicy.com/2015/06/23/south_china_sea_beijing_retreat_new_strategy/

Zhang Hui (2018) 'Xi Thought enshrined as supreme guidance to China's diplomacy', *Global Times*, 24 June, www.globaltimes.cn/content/1108181.shtml

Zhang Jun (2018) 'Promote and protect human rights in the process of development', *China Daily* online, 8 October, www.chinadaily.com.cn/a/201810/08/WS5bba980ea310eff303280ea6.html

Zhang Shuxiu (2016) *Chinese Economic Diplomacy*, London: Routledge.

Zhang Yanbing, Gu Jing and Chen Yunnan (2015) 'China's engagement in international development cooperation: the state of the debate', Rising Powers in International Development Evidence Report 116, Brighton: Institute of Development Studies.

Zhang Yu (2016) 'Wei renlei dui genghao shehui zhidu de tansuo tigong zhongguo fang'an – shehui zhuyi shichang jingji de shijie yiyi [Providing China's plan for human exploration of a better social system: the world significance of Socialist Market Economy]', *Guangming Ribao*, 30 November, avwww.szhgh.com/Article/news/comments/2016-12-10/126302.html

Zhao Kejin and Shi Yan (2018) 'Goujian xinxing guoji guanxi de lilun yu shijian [Theory and practice of constructing a new type of international relations]', *Meiguo Yanjiu [American Research]*, 3: 32–56.

Zhao Lijian (2020a) 'CDC was caught on the spot...', Tweet, 12 March, https://twitter.com/zlj517/status/1238111898828066823

Zhao Lijian (2020b) 'This article is very much important to each and every one of us...', Tweet, 13 March, https://twitter.com/zlj517/status/1238269193427906560

Zhao Lijian (2020c) 'It is immoral & irresponsible...', Tweet, 13 April, https://twitter.com/zlj517/status/1249685749777059846

Zhao Lijian (2020d) 'Soul-searching questions for Navarro…', Tweet, 6 July, https://twitter.com/zlj517/status/1280131459429232645

Zhao Minghao (2015) 'March Westwards and a new look on China's Grand Strategy', Chahar Institute, March, www.charhar.org.cn/newsinfo.aspx?newsid=9219

Zhao Minghao (2019) 'Is a new Cold War inevitable? Chinese perspectives on US–China strategic competition', *The Chinese Journal of International Politics*, 12(3): 371 94.

Zhao Suisheng (2010) 'Chinese foreign policy under Hu Jintao: the struggle between low-profile policy and diplomatic activism', *The Hague Journal of Diplomacy*, 5(4): 357–78.

Zhao Suisheng (2014) 'A neo-colonialist predator or development partner? China's engagement and rebalance in Africa', *Journal of Contemporary China*, 23(90): 1033–52.

Zhao Suisheng (2018) 'A revisionist stakeholder: China and the post-World War II world order', *Journal of Contemporary China*, 27(113): 643–58.

Zhao Xiaofeng (2018) 'Xi Jinping renleimingyun gonggongti sixiang yu rujia lunli' [Xi Jinping's community of shared future for mankind thinking and Confucian ethics]', *Fazhi yu Shehu [Law and Society]*, 2: 122–5.

Zhen Han and Paul, T.V. (2020) 'China's rise and balance of power politics', *Chinese Journal of International Politics*, 13(1): 1–26.

Zheng Yongnian and Tok, S.K. (2007) '"Harmonious Society" and "Harmonious World": China's policy discourse under Hu Jintao', University of Nottingham China Policy Institute Briefing Series Issue 26, www.nottingham.ac.uk/iaps/documents/cpi/briefings/briefing-26-harmonious-society-and-harmonious-world.pdf

Zhou Hu (2018) 'Zhongguo fang'an de jiben neihan, tichu yiju ji shijie xing yiyi [The basic connotation of the China Solution and its worldwide significance]', *Zhonggong Nanjing Shiwei Dangxia Xuebao [Journal of the Party School of Nanjing Municipality]*, 1: 12–17.

Zhu Chenghu (2011) 'Guanyu dangqian shijie zhanlue geju de ji dian sikao [Some reflections on the contemporary world strategic structure]', *Shijie Jingji yu Zhengzhi [World Economics and Politics]*, 2: 4–12.

Zhu Zhiqun (2013) *China's New Diplomacy: Rationale, Strategies, and Significance*, Farnham: Ashgate.

Zimmerman, E. (2019) 'The Foreign Investment Risk Review Modernization Act: how CFIUS became a tech office', *Berkeley Technology Law Journal*, https://papers.ssrn.com/sol3/papers.cfm?abstract_id=3368723

Zoellick, R. (2005) 'Whither China: from membership to responsibility?', Remarks to National Committee on U.S.–China Relations, New York, 21 September, https://2001-2009.state.gov/s/d/former/zoellick/rem/53682.htm

Index